RICHARD MAGNUS, LIM HUI MIN, MAY LUCIA MESENAS & VALERIE THEAN (eds.)

Joint publication by the Subordinate Courts &
Ministry of Community Development and Sports

REBUILDING LIVES, RESTORING RELATIONSHIPS

Juvenile Justice and the Community

EASTERN UNIVERSITIES PRESS

First published 2003
by Times Media Private Limited
(Academic Publishing) under the imprint
Eastern Universities Press.
Times Centre, 1 New Industrial Road,
Singapore 536196
Fax: (65) 6284 9772
E-mail: tap@tpl.com.sg
Online Book Store:
http://www.timesacademic.com

Printed by Vine Graphic Pte Ltd, Singapore

National Library Board (Singapore) Cataloguing in Publication Data
Rebuilding Lives, Restoring Relationships: Juvenile Justice and the Community /
Richard Magnus... [et al.] (eds.). – Singapore:
Eastern Universities Press, 2003.

p. cm.

"Joint publication by the Subordinate Courts
& Ministry of Community Development and Sports."

ISBN: 981-210-269-8
ISBN: 981-210-219-1 (pbk)

1. Juvenile delinquents – Rehabilitation – Singapore.
2. Problem youth – Rehabilitation – Singapore.
3. Juvenile delinquency – Singapore – Prevention.
4. Juvenile justice, Administration of – Singapore.
I. Magnus, Richard.
II. Singapore. Subordinate Courts.
III. Singapore. Ministry of Community Development and Sports.

HV9203
364.36095957 — dc21
SLS2003009910

London • New York • Beijing • Shanghai • Bangkok • Kuala Lumpur • Singapore

Contents

The following is a list of the contributors to the book:

Dr Joseph Paul Ozawa
Senior Director, Family and Juvenile Justice Centre

Ms May Lucia Mesenas
Magistrate

Ms Lim Hui Min
Magistrate

Mr Ong Chin Heng
Magistrate

Mr Mark Tay
District Judge

Dr Anthony Loh
Panel Adviser

Mr Loganswaran Ramoo
Volunteer

Associate Professor Ho Peng Kee
Senior Minister of State for Law and Home Affairs, and Chairman of the Inter-Ministry Committee on Youth Crime

Mr Abdul Halim Aliman
Director, Community Development, Yayasan Mendaki, and Panel Adviser of the Juvenile Court

ASP Marc E Kwan Szer
Community Involvement Division, Police Headquarters

Ms Ng Bee Leng
Deputy Executive Director, BEYOND Social Services, and Head, Bukit Ho Swee Family Service Centre

Mr Alfred Tan
Executive Director, Singapore Children's Society

Mrs Tan-Kek Lee Yong
Deputy Director, Psychological and Guidance Services, Ministry of Education

Mrs Yeo Chin Nam
Principal, Henderson Secondary School

Mrs Tan Ai-Lin
Head of Department (Discipline), Bedok North Secondary School

Ms Chomil Kamal
Chief Probation Officer, Ministry of Community Development and Sports

Mrs Corinne Koh
Deputy Director, Ministry of Community Development and Sports

Ms Ng Poh Leng
Deputy Director, Ministry of Community Development and Sports

Mr Teo Heok Khiang
Discipline Master, Damai Secondary School

Ms Bernadette Alexander
Assistant Director, Ministry of Community Development and Sports

Ms Dahlia Aris and Ms Goh Sok Hoon
Aftercare Supervision Officers, Prisons Department

Ms Carol Balhetchet
Director, Youth Development Centre, Singapore Children's Society

Ms Ngo Lee Yian
Senior Assistant Director, Ministry of Community Development and Sports

D J Carruthers
Chief District Court Judge, New Zealand

Dr Willie McCarney
Vice-President, International Association of Youth and Family Judges and Magistrates

Dr David M Altschuler
Principal Research Scientist, Institute of Policy Studies, John Hopkins University, USA

Editorial Committee

Richard Magnus
Senior District Judge, Subordinate Courts

Lim Hui Min
Magistrate and Deputy Registrar, Subordinate Courts

May Lucia Mesenas
Magistrate and Deputy Registrar, Subordinate Courts

Valerie Thean
District Judge, Subordinate Courts

The cover illustrations are by
Chang Mei Fen, Pearlyn
Primary 2, Fuhua Primary School

Ng Siew Ling, Jacqueline
Primary 6, Townsville Primary School

Illustrations within the book are by
Marvin Bay,
District Judge, Subordinate Courts

Foreword

This book is testimony to the close partnership of the various stakeholders in the area of juvenile justice and child protection in Singapore. In this regard, I am pleased that the Ministry of Community Development and Sports and the Juvenile Court have been working closely in the best interests of children and young persons.

In every society, there is always a small segment of children and youth who are at risk or have brushes with the law. My Ministry shares the principle of the Restorative Justice model adopted by the Subordinate Courts, which recognises the potential for positive change in young offenders. We believe that individuals and families are capable of overcoming their difficulties, becoming self-reliant and should be empowered to do so.

The well-being of children is the key to sustained development in a country and to peace and security in the world. The responsibility for meeting this essentially lies with the state, family and the community. It is the commitment and action from across the board: non-governmental organisations and entrepreneurs, religious leaders and journalists, parents and teachers, and children and adolescents themselves that transmit this into a reality. Kudos therefore to the team of people who developed the concept for this book, which puts in print the hard work and remarkable efforts that go behind the rebuilding of each child's life.

Dr Yaacob Ibrahim
Minister
Ministry of Community Development and Sports

Introduction

The Juvenile Court's primary role is that of an adjudicator of juvenile misdemeanours. When a child misbehaves, the Court is there to mete out punishment. However, we have long recognised that punishment for wrong-doing alone will not direct wayward children onto the right path. To achieve this broader purpose, the Court uses the Restorative Justice framework. Restorative Justice recognises the potential for change and reform in young offenders and delinquent youths. It seeks to balance the need for effective deterrence against the need for rehabilitation and restoration. Its ultimate goal is to re-integrate the offending juveniles or delinquent youths back into their families and community.

Juvenile justice is not only a matter for the Juvenile Court. This book is therefore written in collaboration with the Ministry of Community Development and Sports. It has several contributors, notably the Senior Minister of State for Law and Home Affairs, Associate Professor Ho Peng Kee. This delicate task of rebuilding lives is one in which the community plays a vital part. Effective family and community support and control can help to keep our juveniles out of crimes in the first place and equip them to lead a productive and law-abiding life. The book accordingly contains articles contributed by judges and psychologists of the Family and Juvenile Justice Centre, articles from the network of professional experts in juvenile justice, from both governmental and non-governmental organisations, from the international as well as the local community, as well as contributions from the children themselves — the very youth whom we hope to guide and educate, and in whom we place our hope for the future.

This book is divided into three parts. The first part of the book highlights the role of the Juvenile Court. It deals with the juvenile justice process, its legal procedures and principles, and the services provided by the Juvenile Court and the Family and Juvenile Justice Centre. There are also the personal perspectives of those working in the Juvenile Court, and those who have taken part in its programmes and activities. The second part of the book shows the work of the community. It deals with juvenile justice programmes and initiatives conducted and supported by the various governmental and non-governmental agencies in the community, as well as the schools. It also contains the personal testimonies of those working in the field of juvenile justice, as well as the voices of the juveniles themselves. The last part of the book contains the views and insights of eminent members of the international juvenile justice community. Cultures may differ, but the aspirations of parents for their children, of societies for their youth, are not dissimilar, even across continents.

Richard Magnus
Senior District Judge
Subordinate Courts of Singapore

PART **I**

RESTORATIVE JUSTICE

The Court's Perspective — Principles, Procedures and Programmes

CHAPTER 1

The Juvenile Court of Singapore[1]

MAGISTRATE MAY LUCIA MESENAS and
MAGISTRATE LIM HUI MIN

Jurisdiction

The Juvenile Court is presided by a Juvenile Court Magistrate appointed by the President of the Republic of Singapore.[2] The Juvenile Court is also assisted in its decision-making by a panel of lay advisers.[3] The primary piece of legislation that governs proceedings in the Juvenile Court is the Children and Young Persons Act (Cap. 38) (CYPA).

The Juvenile Court deals with three categories of cases, namely:

1) Criminal offences committed by juveniles below 16 years old (Juvenile Arrest Cases — JAC);[4]
2) Juveniles who are Beyond Parental Control[5] (BPC); and
3) Juveniles who are in need of Care and Protection Orders[6] (CPO).

A "juvenile" is a male or female person who is 7 years of age or above, and below the age of 16 years.[7]

In all cases, the Juvenile Court must ascertain the age of the child or young person each time he appears before the Juvenile Court, in order to assume jurisdiction correctly.

Juvenile Arrest Cases

As a general rule, the Juvenile Court tries criminal offences committed by children (*7 years of age and above but below 14 years old*) or young persons (*above 14 years old and below 16 years old*).[8]

Section 33(6) of the CYPA states that "a person who has attained the age of 16 years on the date of commencement of the hearing of the charge shall not be tried for any offence by a Juvenile Court." Hence, any child or young person must be ***below*** 16 years at the time he or she is charged or tried (i.e. whether he pleads guilty or claims trial).[9]

The **exceptions** to the general rule are where:[10]

- The child or young person is jointly charged with another person who is above 16 years of age, in which case the juvenile will be tried in the adult court together with that other person; or,
- The offence is triable only by the High Court. However, even offences triable only in the High Court can be tried in the Juvenile Court[11] if the following two conditions are satisfied:
  a) The Public Prosecutor applies to the Juvenile Court to try such an offence; and
  b) The "legal representative" of the child or young person concerned consents to the offence being tried in the Juvenile Court.

A "legal representative" includes any person assisting the child or young person in his defence to the charge, for example, his lawyer, parents or guardian.[12]

Once the upper age limit prescribed by the CYPA is reached, the Juvenile Court must relinquish jurisdiction, and transfer the case to the adult criminal courts.

Beyond Parental Control and Care and Protection Cases

The Court can assume jurisdiction over "children" and "young persons" for BPC and CPO cases as long as they are below the age of 16 years when they are first brought before it. However, for BPC cases, the juveniles brought before the Court would usually be 10 years old and above but below 16 years.

Philosophy: The Restorative Model of Juvenile Justice

The Juvenile Court embraces the Restorative Model of Juvenile Justice. This means that we seek to restore or re-integrate the wayward juvenile back into society, as a useful and productive member of the same. We seek to accomplish this by:

a) Holding the offender accountable for his behaviour and having him take responsibility for the consequences of his offending act — this may be by way of reparation to society in the form of community work, restitution, compensation or an apology to the victim, as well as by placing the offender on probation or in a corrective institution;
b) Allowing the victim, where appropriate, to confront the offender to make him aware of the harm caused by his offending act/behaviour; and
c) Requiring parents to take responsibility for their child's behaviour and empowering them to play a greater role in the rehabilitation of the offender.

By embracing the Restorative Model of Juvenile Justice, we recognise the potential for change in young offenders and delinquents, and the importance of rehabilitating them. However, at the same time, we must also be mindful of the need to protect society from the depredations of crime, as well as the rights of the victim to see justice done for the wrongs that they have suffered. The Juvenile Court discharges a primary obligation as a court of law. It is not a provider of social services. It therefore must uphold the principles of personal accountability and public protection. A delicate balance has to be struck between deterrence, retribution and rehabilitation.

Myriad factors have to be considered before the Juvenile Court can make the appropriate order in respect of the child or young person:

- rehabilitation and reformation (i.e. for the juvenile to make a positive change in his behaviour, as well as in his attitudes towards others and towards society at large);

- removal of the juvenile from undesirable surroundings;
- what is required for the education and training of the juvenile;
- what is required for the welfare of the juvenile;
- adequate family support (i.e. whether the juvenile has co-operative parents);
- compensation of the victim;
- protection of the public;
- the extent of the risk of further offending by the juvenile ; and
- punishment of the offender (i.e. to ensure that the juvenile gets his just deserts for the offence which he has committed).

Procedures and Powers

Special Rules for Juvenile Cases

The procedure for dealing with juvenile offenders in the Juvenile Court is largely similar to that used in the adult criminal courts, but there are special rules in place to avoid labelling the juvenile offender as a criminal or to expose him to adult offenders:

a) Words like "conviction" or "sentence"[13] are not used in the Juvenile Court. Instead, expressions like "finding of guilt" and "orders" are used.

b) The "findings of guilt" of the Juvenile Court are disregarded for the purposes of any Act under which any disqualification or disability is imposed on convicted persons.[14]

c) The proceedings in the Juvenile Court are shielded from the full glare of publicity in that attendance at hearings in the Juvenile Court is largely restricted to people directly concerned in the case and bona fide representatives of the media.[15] The media are prohibited from revealing the identity of any juveniles involved in the proceedings. This restriction can however be lifted with the permission of the Juvenile Court or the Minister of Community Development and Sports.[16]

d) As far as reasonably possible, the young person in the Juvenile Justice system is kept separate from other adult accused persons from the time of arrest to trial.[17] The Juvenile Court is in a separate building from the main criminal courts. Adult accused are never tried in the same courtroom as juveniles.[18] There are separate lock-ups for adult and juvenile offenders.

Special Role and Rights of Parents

a) The Juvenile Court may require the presence of the parents or guardian of the child or young person charged before it, unless it is satisfied that it would be unreasonable to require their attendance.[19] The Juvenile Court invariably requires parents to be present at all court hearings unless it is impractical to do so, for example if the parents' whereabouts are unknown. Even if the parents are incarcerated in prison, they are brought up from prison to attend court. When the parents or guardian attend, they must stand alongside their child in open court.

b) Where the offender does not have legal representation, the parents or guardian are entitled to assist the offender in the conduct of his defence.[20]

c) Where the child or young person admits the offence or the Juvenile Court is satisfied that the offence is proved, the parents or guardian can mitigate on behalf of their child.[21]

d) The child or young person's parent or guardian may lodge an appeal against the judgement or order of a Juvenile Court.[22]

Panel of Advisers

Unlike the adult criminal courts, the Juvenile Court is assisted in its decision-making by a Panel of Advisers nominated by the President of the Republic of Singapore. The fully constituted Juvenile Court consists of the presiding Magistrate and two advisers from this Panel of Advisers.[23] These advisers are lay volunteers and come from diverse professions, including school principals, psychologists, and leading figures of the business community. They bring a fresh perspective to the Court from their particular fields of expertise and from their working experiences. They also have strong community links, and are thus able to offer practical and useful help and suggestions on long-term plans of action to be made in respect of each juvenile.[24]

Juvenile Arrest Cases (JAC)

When determining the method of dealing with a juvenile (after making a finding that the juvenile is guilty of the crime with which he has been charged), the Juvenile Court normally calls for a written report (the Probation Report) on the juvenile's social background, family history, school record or other matters, which is done by an officer from the Ministry of Community Development and Sports (MCDS). In some instances, psychological and psychiatric reports may also be called for. The Juvenile Court, with the assistance of the MCDS officer (i.e. Probation Officer) and the Panel Advisers, will then assess the risk of the offender to society as well as identify the needs of the offender before making the appropriate order.

The **main factors** that the Court will consider in deciding the appropriate dispositional orders to make include:

a) the gravity of the offence;
b) the offender's educational and employment status;
c) the presence or lack of effective and responsible parents and guardians;
d) the character of the offender;
e) the extent of the risk of re-offending;[25]
f) the recommendations of the probation officer or any other person who has been asked to prepare a report on the offender.

Juvenile Offender Behaviour (JOB) Criteria

A pre-sentencing tool known as the Juvenile Offender Behaviour (JOB) Criteria has been developed for the Juvenile Court by the psychologists of the Family and Juvenile Justice Centre.[26] JOB Criteria is a method of evaluating a juvenile's potential for rehabilitation which harnesses principles of developmental psychology and criminology. Matters such as the gravity of the offence(s) committed and the offender's risk factors are considered in the JOB Criteria.

Three areas are analysed and weighted:

(a) *The severity of the offence.* The severity of the offence is given a weighting based on the maximum legal sentence for the offence;
(b) *Risk factors.* These include factors such as chronic use of alcohol and/or drugs by the juvenile's parents, their parenting style, whether the juvenile is or was a gang member, the age the juvenile first engaged in criminal behaviour, and the juvenile's past and present performance in school. Each of these factors is given a weighting. The factors and their weightings were derived from a thorough analysis of predictive factors of criminal recidivism from relevant psychological and criminological literature; factors were then cross-evaluated by both local experts (magistrates, police, probation officers, etc.) as well as feedback by international authorities such as Dr Willie McCarney;[27] and
(c) *Proximate risk, protective and determining factors.* These factors assess the juvenile's recent behaviour or circumstances. The factors include whether the juvenile has expressed remorse during remand, and the extent and sincerity of the remorse expressed; the desire and ability of the juvenile's parents to supervise him, outcomes of Family Conferences, the juvenile's courtroom behaviour etc.

The psychologist will read the Probation Report, and glean pertinent information from it. There is a whole list of factors that the psychologist will look out for (as set out above). An overall risk score and risk level are calculated from an analysis of these factors. Each individual is placed on a continuum from "*adolescence-limited*" to "*life-course-persistent*". Adolescence-limited offenders are those who can safely be taken to be merely passing through a developmental phase, and who will probably grow out of their rebelliousness and wayward behaviour in time. On the other hand, life-course persistent youths are those who show clear signs of chronic, persistent criminality which may lead them to be repeat offenders over time.

The actual numerical scores obtained through the JOB Criteria are released to the Juvenile Court Magistrate prior to the juvenile being dealt with. This is known as the JOB Criteria Risk Score. Using the JOB Criteria Risk Score for reference, the Magistrate will exercise his or her discretion to make the appropriate orders, and to create an individualised plan for rehabilitation, for each juvenile. The JOB Criteria Risk Scores merely serve as a guide for the Juvenile Court Magistrate in making the appropriate orders and are not binding on the Court.

Powers of the Juvenile Court

The Juvenile Court is empowered[28] to deal with a juvenile offender upon a finding of guilt in many different ways. Institutionalisation of the juvenile is the last resort. The various options are:

1. Discharge of the Offender

The offender may be granted an absolute or conditional discharge.[29] An absolute discharge is in practice, however, never made for juvenile offenders. This is because those juveniles who would merit an absolute discharge would have been diverted from the court system and warned by the police, and/or placed on the Guidance Programme,[30] and undergone counselling. Those juveniles who are charged in court would largely be those recalcitrant offenders whom the Court could not appropriately discharge from the system.

A conditional discharge is one where the offender is discharged on condition that he does not commit any offences within a prescribed period (maximum 12 months[31]). If the offender is of good behaviour for the prescribed period, then he will be considered not to have any criminal antecedents. If the offender breaches the bond, then he will be brought back to Court, and fresh orders can then be made in respect of the original offence that he committed.

2. Committal to the Care of a Relative or Other Fit Person

The Court may commit the offender to the care of a relative or fit person for a specified period of time.[32] (A fit person is anyone who is deemed by the Court to be suitable to care for the child, such as the superintendent of a children's home, or a foster parent registered with MCDS.)

3. The Offender's Parent or Guardian to Execute a Bond to Exercise Proper Care and Guardianship

This order[33] is usually made in conjunction with a Probation Order. Such an order is imposed to ensure the parents' or guardians' responsibility in relation to the offender's welfare, maintenance and rehabilitation. This is a financial bond. If the parents do not exercise proper care and guardianship of the offender, then the sum of money under the bond may be forfeited.

4. Probation Order

This is the usual order made by the Juvenile Court. A Probation Order places the offender under the supervision of a Probation Officer for a period of not less than six months and not more than three years.[34] This order[35] may be made singly or in addition to any one or more of the following orders:

- committal to the care of a fit person or relative;
- binding the offender's parents/guardians;
- performing community service (up to 240 hours);
- offender to be detained in a Place of Detention or an Approved Institution[36] over such weekends (up to 52 weekends) as the Court thinks fit;
- payment of a fine, costs or damages;

Further, a Probation Order can also be coupled with any one or more of the following orders:[37]

- offender to be detained in a Place of Detention (not more than three months);[38]
- payment of a fine, costs or damages

The Court may also attach conditions to the Probation Order that it thinks are necessary for securing the good conduct of the offender or preventing him from re-offending.[39] Such additional conditions can include curfews, residence in Approved Institutions or attending specific programmes to address the risks faced by, and the needs of, the offender, for example, the StreetWise Programme and the Smoking Cessation Programme which deal with gang involvement and smoking habits respectively. In order to stop the juvenile being involved with gangs (which invariably leads to the commission of offences like rioting, unlawful assembly, and gang robbery), conditions like restricting the juvenile's movements to certain areas (where gangs are prevalent) can also be imposed.[40]

With effect from January 2003, selected juvenile probationers (who have been recommended by their probation officers for this programme) have been placed on a *pilot* electronic monitoring (EM) programme initiated by the Probation Services Branch, MCDS. EM is a technological means of assuring curfew compliance by the juvenile offenders who are placed on probation. The offender is tagged with an electronic device that fits snugly around the ankle. This device sends a continuous signal to a Home Monitoring Unit (HMU) located in the offender's residence. The HMU is linked to a centralised control unit (to be monitored by a security company, (CISCO)) that registers the movement of the offender during the curfew period. In the event that the probationer is not at home during the time curfews, the HMU will be triggered, whereupon the details of the offender's non-compliance (i.e. the date and time he breaches the time curfew) will be noted by CISCO. The offender's Probation Officer will subsequently be notified of the curfew violations and will investigate the circumstances surrounding the violation and take appropriate breach action, where necessary. The maximum EM period under the pilot programme is four months. Probation Officers can recommend to the Court that the electronic tag be removed at the end of three months if the probationer's progress is satisfactory.

A juvenile probationer who is selected for the EM programme must be at least 15 years of age and must have at least one supportive parent/significant other who is willing to undertake the responsibility of supervising him.

The objectives of EM are fivefold: firstly, to provide alternatives to institutionalisation without compromising public safety; secondly, to prevent offenders from leaving their residence during stipulated curfew hours; thirdly, to restrict the offender from frequenting undesirable locations during curfew hours; fourthly, to ensure that the offender spends more time at home, to create an environment for developing greater rapport amongst members of the family, and finally, to improve the offender's chances of successfully completing the Probation Order and reintegrating into the community.

The standard EM agreement which is signed by the probationer and his parent or guardian states the responsibilities of the probationer and his family members during the EM period. The agreement also provides for the consequences of violation of the conditions under the EM programme including the need to pay for any damage to the EM equipment.

After the one-year pilot period is up, the EM programme will be evaluated by the MCDS, and modified, if necessary.

The additional requirement of residence in an Approved Institution is normally made for juveniles who have an unsatisfactory home environment but who otherwise satisfy the usual requirements for probation. The maximum duration of residence at an Approved Institution is 12 months.[41]

Probationers who are ordered to reside at an Approved Institution are permitted to work or pursue their education in schools outside the confines of the institution after an initial period of one month at the institution.

The Court may also make an order of residence in a non-gazetted home if the Probation Report shows that the institution is prepared to accept the offender and the programmes offered by the home are more suitable for the needs of the juvenile. The Hiding Place, Teen Challenge Youth Centre and the Singapore Boys' Town are voluntary institutions that commonly accept juveniles. The programme that the probationer has to undergo with such voluntary institutions usually lasts 18 months.

The risks and needs assessment of the probationer are carefully assessed during the investigations phase, before the Court makes orders in respect of the juvenile. Risks and needs assessment forms an integral part of the Probation Officer's recommendations. During the period of probation, the probationer will be consistently monitored by the Probation Officer from MCDS. Operationally, Probation Orders have been classified into three grades to cater for the varying intensity of the various risks and needs of individual probationers. These are Administrative Probation, Supervised Probation and Intensive Probation.[42]

In appropriate cases, the Probation Officer will make use of any statutory or voluntary agency which might contribute to the probationer's welfare, as well as take advantage of any available social, recreational, religious or educational facilities suited to the probationer's age, ability and temperament. For example, the Probation Officer may arrange tuition classes for a probationer at the Singapore Indian Development Association, or counselling sessions at a family service centre. Where appropriate, the Probation Officer will ensure that the probationer is in suitable and regular employment.

It must be remembered that the offender (if he is 14 years old and above) must consent to the Probation Order and all its attached conditions before probation can be granted.[43] If the offender does not consent to some or all of the conditions of probation, then the Court will have to impose an alternative order, which will probably be a more severe form of punishment than probation.[44] In practice, therefore, it is extremely rare for an offender to refuse to consent to any of the conditions attached to a Probation Order.

5. Community Service

The Juvenile Court can impose community service orders of up to 240 hours as a "stand alone"[45] order (i.e. an order on its own) or in addition to a Probation Order.[46]

For "stand alone" orders, community service must be completed within 12 months, and is monitored by Probation Services, MCDS. Community service orders imposed as part of the condition of probation will last as long as the Probation Order subsists. Community service which the juveniles may be assigned under the community service orders imposed include: feeding residents of old folks' homes, cleaning old folks' homes or children's homes, building maintenance work, library work, working with the disabled, weeding and general gardening.

6. Detention at a Place of Detention

Juveniles can be committed to a Place of Detention for a period not exceeding six months.[47] (This is different from the Approved School regime [see "***Approved School Order***" below], where the minimum period of residence is two years.) Juveniles who are committed to a Place of Detention are those who have pleaded guilty in Court, and of whom the Court has taken the view that they should be given a "short sharp shock". The two gazetted places of detention are the Singapore Boys' Home and the Toa Payoh Girls' Home. Juveniles sent to a Place of Detention without any other orders being made do not undergo any formal programme and are tasked to perform minor chores and undergo foot-drills. Sometimes they are given counselling. However, such stand alone orders are rarely imposed, because most juveniles would require a longer period of detention for successful rehabilitation.

Some juveniles are granted probation after they are placed in a Place of Detention for up to three months (see "***Probation Order***" above). Indeed, if a Probation Order is granted, the Court cannot order the juvenile to stay in the Place of Detention for more than three months.[48] Such orders are meant for the offenders to undergo the "short, sharp, shock" treatment before community-based rehabilitation can commence. This is targeted at juveniles who are suitable for probation but would benefit from exposure to a more structured and disciplined programme first. It is also meant for probationers who breach their Probation Orders and need to be disciplined without a revocation of their Probation Orders. It is hoped that the tougher programme in the institution would have a salutary effect on the offender and reduce the likelihood of his/her re-offending.[49]

Where the offender is found guilty of another offence by the Juvenile Court whilst he is still detained in the Place of Detention, the Court may extend the period of detention that is being served by the offender instead of making a fresh order.[50] The maximum age for which a person can be detained in a Place of Detention is 18 years.[51]

7. Weekend Detention

Offenders can be detained in a Place of Detention or an Approved Institution for up to 52 weekends as the Court thinks fit.[52] Such an order can be imposed singly or in combination with any one or more of the following orders:[53]

- committal to the care of a fit person or relative;
- binding the offender's parents/guardians;
- probation between six months and three years;
- perform community service (up to 240 hours);
- payment of fine, damages or costs

Weekend detention orders commence at 3 p.m. Saturday and end at 5 p.m. on the Sunday immediately following that Saturday.[54] The Court may make an order for the juvenile to be committed to a Place of Detention for up to six months, and then order weekend detention thereafter.[55] Currently, offenders are placed in either the Singapore Boys' Hostel or the Toa Payoh Girls' Home when such orders are imposed. One of the objectives of imposing such orders is to curb the offender's activities on weekends where there is a high risk of the offender mixing with negative peers and indulging in undesirable activities. It also allows a juvenile who has committed a fairly serious offence, but has a supportive family environment, to remain with the family and continue his education without disruption. Structured programmes are conducted in such institutions during the weekends for the juveniles on whom such orders are imposed.[56] Examples of such programmes are programmes to teach life-skills, social skills, and studying techniques. Sports and games will also be organised.

8. Approved School Order

For offenders who are assessed to be unsuitable for probation, the Juvenile Court may commit them to an Approved School.[57] This option is usually invoked for juveniles with a high risk of re-offending. Juveniles who commit serious offences, who exhibit a nonchalant attitude towards community-based supervision or have strong associations with highly undesirable peers are normally sent to an Approved School regime for a period of not less than two years, and not more than three years.[58] Although the juvenile may be under 16 years at the time that the Juvenile Court commits him for a term in the Approved School, he may be over 16 years by the time this period is over. However, the juvenile can be detained in the Approved School after the age of 16. The maximum age at which a person can be detained in an Approved School is 19 years and 6 months.[59]

The Approved School regime provides a structured and controlled environment to rehabilitate the offender. There are facilities in all Approved Schools to cater either "in-house" or outside the institution (depending on the offender's behaviour), to the offender's academic or vocational needs.[60] Depending on their behaviour and response to the rehabilitation programmes, residents in these institutions may be granted home leave during weekends and may be allowed to return to their schools and employment after an initial period of residence, which is usually about six months.

Of the five Approved Schools, three are presently run by voluntary welfare organisations (VWOs) which meet the specific rehabilitative needs of the offenders and they are open institutions, i.e.:

a) Salvation Army Gracehaven (for both non-Muslim boys and girls);

b) Muhammadiyah Welfare Home (for Muslim boys only); and
c) Pertapis Centre for Women and Girls (for Muslim girls only).

The remaining two Approved Schools run by the Ministry of Community Development and Sports (MCDS) are:

a) Singapore Boys' Home (SBH) (for boys of all religious faiths);
b) Toa Payoh Girls' Home (TPGH) (for girls of all religious faiths).

Juveniles who are sent to the SBH or TPGH exhibit a greater degree of delinquency and possess more risk factors as compared to those sent to Salvation Army Gracehaven or Muhammadiyah Welfare Home.[61]

Where the offender is found guilty of another offence by the Juvenile Court while he is still serving his order in an Approved School, the Court may also extend the period of his/her detention in that Approved School instead of making a fresh order.[62]

An Approved School order can be made <u>singly</u> or in addition to one or more of the following orders:

- binding the offender's parents/guardians;
- payment of fine, damages or costs

9. Payment of a Fine, Damages or Costs

Offenders may be ordered to make reparation to society by way of a fine, or to the victim by an award of damages.[63] This order is rarely made on its own but is normally coupled with a Probation Order. In the case of a child (7 years old and above but below 14 years old), the parents/guardians will be ordered to pay the fine or damages on behalf of the child, while in the case of a young person (14 years and above, but below 16 years), the parents/guardians may be so ordered. Such an order will not be made against the parents/guardians if the Court is satisfied that the parents/guardians cannot be found or that they have not conduced (i.e. caused or contributed) to the commission of the offence by neglecting to exercise due care over the child or young person.[64]

Where a charge against a child or young person is proved, the Juvenile Court can make an order for damages or costs to be paid by the parent or guardian or require him to give security for the good behaviour of the child or young person, *without recording a finding of guilt against a child or young person.*[65] This means that there will be no record at all that the juvenile had committed the offence.

For any sum imposed and ordered to be paid by the parent or guardian or forfeiture of any such security, such sums may be recovered from him in the manner provided by the Criminal Procedure Code (Cap. 68) as if the order had been made on the conviction of the parent or guardian of the offence with which the child or young person was charged.[66] This means that the Court can attach and sell the parent's property to recover the sums ordered, as if the parent himself had been convicted of the offence and had been bound by the bond in respect of it. Rarely, however, are these extreme measures necessary.

10. Reformative Training Centre

If the Juvenile Court is satisfied that it is expedient with a view to a juvenile's reformation that he should undergo a period of training in a reformative training centre, it may order him to be brought before a District Court[67] to be considered for reformative training.[68] However, the following conditions must be satisfied:

a) the offender must be at least 16 years old; or
b) the offender is above 14 years and previously been dealt with by a court in connection with another offence and had, in respect of that other offence, been ordered to be sent to an Approved School.

A juvenile offender is rarely transferred to the District Court for such a purpose at his first appearance in Juvenile Court. In any event, few juveniles turn 16 years of age just as they are to be sentenced. This order is usually made in cases where the Court feels that the offender's rehabilitation would be best served by him being sent to a very strict, regimented environment. This is when his behaviour is so unruly that he cannot be detained in an Approved School.[69]

Family Conference[70]

Initiated by the Juvenile Court in 1996 as a court programme, the Family Conference (FC)[71] is now enshrined in the CYPA. A child or young person who has been found guilty of committing an offence may be dealt with by ordering him to attend an FC, in addition to any of the dispositional orders already stated above. The FC may deal with the juvenile in one or more of the following ways:

a) reprimand the offender;
b) administer a formal caution to the offender against further committing any offence;
c) require the offender to pay compensation to the victim of the offence;
d) require the offender to perform community service (up to 240 hours);
e) require the offender to apologise to the victim; or
f) require the offender to do such act as the FC has recommended to be appropriate in the circumstances.

During the FC itself, the FC facilitator may require the juvenile to apologise to the victim. He may also caution the juvenile about his offending behaviour. The FC facilitator will generally be a psychologist or counsellor from the Family and Juvenile Justice Centre.

The persons attending the FC will include the juvenile, the parents of the juvenile and any other significant persons in the juvenile's life. Teachers from the juvenile's school, the juvenile's Probation Officer, and his counsellor (if any) may also be present. If there is a high likelihood that the juvenile will eventually be ordered by the Juvenile Court to reside in an Approved Home, Approved School or other institution, a representative from the relevant institution will be invited to attend the FC. The victim (and the victim's parents, if the victim is a child) of the juvenile's offence will also be invited to attend, but is not required to do so.

The prescribed procedure of the FC is stated in the Children and Young Persons (Family Conferencing) Regulations 2001.[72] The FC will begin by the facilitator explaining the FC procedures and the purpose of the FC to those present. The facilitator will then invite each person present to share their views on the juvenile's offending behaviour, and his general lifestyle. The juvenile himself will be invited to comment on these issues. When all the views invited have been given, the facilitator will deliberate on the issues raised and views given with the members of the FC (the victim, the juvenile and his family will be absent from this discussion). The FC will then come to a consensus on the recommended course of action for the Juvenile Court to take in relation to the juvenile. This is then communicated to the Juvenile Court Magistrate after the FC during a chambers discussion. The Juvenile Court Magistrate will take into account the views of the FC, but will not necessarily follow them.

In the event that the offender fails to attend the FC or comply with any requirement of the FC, the matter shall be reported to the Juvenile Court, after which the Juvenile Court can impose any of the dispositional orders under section 44 of the CYPA as highlighted above.[73]

In line with the Juvenile Court's philosophy of restorative justice, some common objectives of the FC include:

1. Confrontation

The offender is confronted by relevant parties such as his family members, the victim, and the victim's parents, regarding issues such as telling the truth, denial, taking responsibility, accountability, impact of the crime on the victim and others (especially the offender's family). In the course of this confrontation, the FC facilitator may reprimand the offender and caution him on his misbehaviour. Issues of compensation may also be discussed. This process is known as "re-integrative shaming"— it is a process to make the offender change for the better by realising the consequences of his misbehaviour and its impact on his family and on the victim.

2. Reconciliation

The offender is led towards apologising to the victim of the offence, to his family, and to any other relevant parties; expressing remorse for his misdeeds; and reconciling with all parties.

3. Assessment

The following issues will be assessed from the events taking place during the FC:

a) The resolution of any relationship problems between the child or young person and his parent or guardian.
b) Rehabilitation of the child or young person.
c) The assistance the parent or guardian of the child or young person requires in order to exercise control and discipline over the child or young person.

4. Evaluation and Recommendations

The FC can be an avenue to explore any issue the Magistrate deems appropriate when the court environment is not appropriate (due to the large number of cases involved, time constraints, etc.). Some examples of such issues are: the likely degree of the juvenile's and his family's co-operation or compliance with specific dispositional orders that the Juvenile Court could impose, an evaluation of the juvenile's level of remorse or potential for recidivism, determination of appropriate custody (care, etc.) arrangements for the juvenile, investigation of additional offences, and so on.

Mandatory Counselling

In addition to the dispositional orders that the Juvenile Court can impose, an additional order can be made by the Court for the child or young person **<u>and</u>** the parent or guardian to undergo counselling, psychotherapy or other programme for the following purposes:

- resolving any relationship problems between the child or young person and the parent or guardian;

- rehabilitating or assisting in the rehabilitation of the child or young person;[74]
- enabling the parent or guardian to manage the child or young person;
- enhancing, promoting, or protecting the physical, social and emotional well-being and safety of the child or young person.

Such provisions in the legislation as well as the other amendments in the CYPA, are intended to ensure parental responsibility and participation in the rehabilitation process. Parental responsibility is especially important, as parents must ultimately be the carers, nurturers and protectors of our children and young people. So they must take this responsibility seriously. The state should step in only as a last resort.[75]

The Court can also impose a bond to be entered into by the parent or guardian of the child or young person to comply with such an order. Failure to comply with the order would render the parent or guardian guilty of an offence and liable to a fine of up to $2,000.

Beyond Parental Control (BPC) Cases

The CYPA enables parents or guardians of a child or young person to lodge complaints against their children as being beyond their control.[76] The parent or guardian lays a complaint before the Juvenile Court Magistrate.[77] If the complaints are accepted by the Juvenile Court, the cases are referred to as "Beyond Parental Control" (BPC) cases.

The Juvenile Court only makes a BPC order if the parent can prove that:

- the child or young person is beyond his control;
- that he (i.e the parent) understands and **consents** to the making of the order; and
- the Court is satisfied that it is expedient so to deal with the child or young person.

Procedures

Before the BPC complaint is sworn, the parents are attended to by counsellors from the Singapore Children's Society, who will try and resolve the matter without Court intervention. The Court has also implemented the Pre-Complaint Counselling programme to divert borderline BPC cases out of the Juvenile Justice system. Under the Pre-Complaint Counselling programme, when parents come to the Juvenile Court to lodge a Beyond Parental Control complaint against their child, and the Court is of the view that the child's behaviour does not merit the intervention of the Court, the Court will then refer parties for counselling at the Singapore Children's Society Youth Development Centre, thus diverting them out of the Court system. The Court will review the matter in four weeks. If the counselling is successful, and the relationship between the child and his parents have improved, then the parents will apply to withdraw the complaint that they made. The family may still continue counselling with the Singapore Children's Society even after the withdrawal of the complaint. If the counselling is not successful, and the Singapore Children's Society counsellor recommends Court intervention, then the Court will proceed to deal with the complaint.

If the whereabouts of the child or young person are unknown or the parent or guardian is unable to get him to attend court, the Court may issue a Warrant of Arrest for the child or young person to be brought to the Juvenile Court. When the warrant is executed and the BPC child is brought to Court, the Juvenile Court Magistrate will confirm that the parent/guardian is proceeding with the complaint before calling for a Social Report (which is similar in nature to the Probation Report for Juvenile Arrest Cases) on the juvenile.[78]

Pending the preparation of the Social Report by MCDS, the Court may remand the juvenile at a remand home.[79] If the Court is of the opinion that the juvenile is amenable to his parents' or guardian's authority or control (at least for the interim period pending the Social Report, and that the juvenile's behaviour does not warrant a period of remand as yet), the Court will release him back to the custody of the parent or guardian pending the Social Report.

Powers

The Court will consider the Social Report and consult with the Panel of Advisers to consider the appropriate orders to make. In appropriate cases, the Court may also require parties to attend a Family Conference. The Juvenile Court is empowered to make the following orders[80] for BPC cases:

a) Placement for a specified period, not exceeding three years, under the supervision of an approved welfare officer or of some other person appointed for the purpose by the Court ("statutory supervision");[81] or
b) Residence in an Approved Home for not less than two and not more than three years.

If the BPC juvenile is assessed to be unsuitable for statutory supervision, he may be placed in the following Approved Homes:[82]

a) Salvation Army Gracehaven (for non-Muslim boys and girls)
b) Pertapis Children's Home (for Muslim boys)
c) Pertapis Centre for Women and Girls (for Muslim girls)
d) Muhammadiyah Welfare Home (for Muslim boys and girls)
e) Singapore Boys' Home (for boys of all religious faiths)
f) Toa Payoh Girls' Home (for girls of all religious faiths)

It should be noted that options e) and f) above are only used for those BPC cases where the juveniles are particularly difficult to manage and there is a high risk of them absconding from an open institution or from their own homes.

Mandatory Counselling

The Juvenile Court can also impose an additional order for the child or young person and the parent or guardian to undergo counselling, psychotherapy or other assessment or treatment for the rehabilitation of the child or young person.[83]

Variation or Discharge of Order

The BPC order may be varied or discharged if the Court is satisfied that it is in the best interest of the child or young person to do so. This can be made upon the application of the Director of Social Welfare (from MCDS, hereinafter referred to as the "Director") or a protector[84] or the parent or guardian of the child or young person.[85] This usually arises when the BPC order is about to expire and the child or young person is still in need of further assistance through rehabilitative or community intervention and the parent or guardian may not be in the position to exercise any form of control or supervision on the child or young person. In such cases the BPC order may be extended. The risk and needs of the child and young person have to be carefully assessed at that juncture.

Care and Protection Order (CPO) Cases

When is a child in need of care and protection?

A CPO can be imposed for a child (of <u>any</u> age) or young person in any one of the following situations:[86]

a) the child or young person has no parent or guardian;
b) the child or young person has been abandoned by his parent or guardian[87] and no other suitable person is willing to take care of him;
c) the parent or guardian is unfit/unable/has neglected to exercise proper supervision and control over the child or young person **<u>and</u>** the child or young person is falling into bad association/is in moral danger/is beyond control;
d) the child or young person has been, or is being at risk of being ill-treated;[88]
e) the child or young person needs to be examined/investigated/treated for the purpose of restoring/preserving his health/development and his parent or guardian refuses to do so;
f) the child or young person behaves in a manner that is or is likely to be harmful to himself or to any person;[89]

g) the child or young person suffers from emotional injury;[90]

h) the child or young person is a:
   - victim of a relevant offence[91] committed or believed to have been committed; or
   - member of the same household as another child or young person who is a victim of such an offence committed/ believed to have been committed **and** the perpetrator/ alleged perpetrator is the parent or guardian **or** the parent or guardian is unlikely/unwilling to protect the child or young person from such an offence;

i) the child or young person is found to be:
   - destitute or wandering without any settled place of abode and without visible means of subsistence;
   - begging or receiving alms or loitering for such purposes;
   - carrying out illegal lotteries, illegal hawking, gambling or other undesirable activities; or
   - using or inhaling any intoxicating substance for the purpose of inducing or causing in himself a state of intoxication.[92]

Procedures

The procedures for initiating a Care and Protection Order case are as follows:

For Urgent Cases

The following is applicable to those cases where the child must be immediately removed from his current environment.

Removal of Child and Committal to Place of Safety

The Director, a protector or a police officer not below the rank of sergeant is empowered to remove a child and commit him to a Place of Safety if there are reasonable grounds to do so.[93] The relevant authority can do this by entering any premises without warrant and with such assistance, and by such force as may be necessary, by night or by day, remove a child and commit him to a Place of Safety.[94] Such measures are necessary in order to prevent possible harm or further injury from occurring to the child. Such powers also include producing the child or young person before a registered medical practitioner or an approved welfare officer,[95] for an assessment or for any medical or other treatment necessary.

Within three working days of the removal of the child or young person by the Director, protector or police, the child has to be produced before the Juvenile Court so that Care and Protection Orders may be made.[96] In the event of non-compliance of this condition, the Director, protector or police must inform the Juvenile Court of the removal and the reason for which it was not possible to comply with this condition. Thereafter, the Juvenile Court can proceed to make interim Care and Protection Orders until such time as the child or young person may be brought before the Juvenile Court.[97] The interim orders would basically be for the child to be placed in a Place of Safety[98] pending the Social Report to be furnished on the child.

The Social Report is prepared by an approved welfare officer from MCDS, and will be furnished to the Court in order to assist the Court in deciding on the most appropriate orders to make in respect of the child. An order for the child or young person or his parent/guardian to undergo medical, psychological or other assessment as the Court thinks necessary, can also be made[99] to assist the Court in its decision-making process.

Other Cases

For other cases where the child is already in a safe environment, and the welfare officer is of the view that urgent interim Care and Protection Orders are not required, the officer will lay a complaint to the Court requesting for a Care and Protection Order for the child, on the basis that there has been some evidence that the child has been abused or neglected. Upon receipt of the complaint, the Court will order a Social Report on the child, and fix a hearing date four weeks later,[100] at which date the Social Report will be presented in Court. At that hearing, the Court will then make the appropriate orders after hearing the views of the child's parents or caregivers, as well as the welfare officer.

Powers

The Juvenile Court may impose any one of the following orders if the child or young person is in need of care and protection:[101]

a) requiring the parent or guardian to enter a bond to exercise proper care and guardianship of the child or young person;
b) committing the child or young person to the care of a fit person;
c) committing the child or young person to an Approved Home or Place of Safety; or
d) placing the child or young person under the supervision of a protector/an approved welfare officer or any other person appointed by the Court.[102]

In considering the appropriate order to be imposed, the welfare of the child or young person is of paramount consideration.[103]

Mandatory Counselling

The Court can also impose any conditions or directions as it thinks fit to ensure the safety and well-being of the child or young person. Orders for the child or young person or parent/guardian to undergo mandatory counselling, psychotherapy or other assessment and treatment can also be made for the purposes of the child or young person's rehabilitation.[104]

Staying the Course — Monitoring Cases after Orders Made

The Juvenile Court continues to closely monitor JAC, BPC and CPO cases even after dispositional orders have been made. These cases are reviewed in the following ways:

- For JAC only — by various constituted committees (the Juvenile Probation Case Committee (a sub-committee of the Probation Committee[105]) and the Advisory Board[106]).

- By the Juvenile Court, when it calls for a review of the case after a certain time frame.
- By the Juvenile Court when the Probation Officers or approved welfare officers provide information updates to the Court on the juvenile on their own initiative, if the need arises.

The purpose of the various reviews is not only to ensure that the rehabilitation plan is adhered to as closely as possible, but to allow variations in the orders made to be sought in view of changed circumstances. More information on each type of review is set out below.

By the Juvenile Probation Case Committee and Advisory Board

The Probation Committee is constituted by the Minister of the MCDS, who will appoint each member of the Committee.[107] The Committee meets annually to review the work of the Probation Officers and Volunteer Probation Officers. The Committee is divided into two Case Committees:[108] an Adult Probation Case Committee (APCC) and a Juvenile Probation Case Committee (JPCC). The Probation Case Committees receive and consider written and oral reports from Probation Officers and Volunteer Probation Officers on the progress of their probationers, and afford such help and advice to the Probation Officers in performing their duties as may be necessary. The JPCC is chaired by the Juvenile Court Magistrate and its members include two Panel Advisers, the Chief Probation Officer, representatives from the police, and two other offices from the Probation Services Branch (MCDS).

The JPCC[109] meets once every two months to review the cases which have undergone probation for the first six months.[110] In practice, this review is done in the probationer's absence, by studying the relevant reports prepared by Probation Officers, and also from discussions with those Probation Officers and case workers from the Approved Institutions or other institution attending the review. However, the Juvenile Court will list those cases where the probationer appears from the reports to be doing exceptionally well or exceptionally badly for court appearance for encouragement or reprimand from the Juvenile Court Magistrate himself or herself.

Advisory Board Review

Residents' progress in the Approved Schools and Approved Homes regime are assessed at monthly meetings of the Advisory Board, a body constituted by the Minister of the MCDS[111] to review such residents. Members of the Advisory Board are appointed by the Minister, and include social workers, educators, police officers, and medical doctors. The Juvenile Court Magistrate is a member of this Board. The Director of Social Welfare, on the advice of the Advisory Board, may release the residents on licence after they have completed 12 months in the Approved Schools/Approved Homes regime. This is notwithstanding any prior order made by the Juvenile Court.[112] Residents released on licence are liable to be recalled to serve the unexpired portion of the Approved School/Approved Home order if they fail to comply with any conditions under the licence. Advisory Board meetings are invariably done in the absence of the juvenile and his parents, through reading reports prepared by the case workers in the Approved Schools and Approved Homes, and through discussions with the case workers and superintendents of these institutions, who will also attend the reviews.

Court-Ordered Review

Over and above the six-monthly reviews, the Juvenile Court may decide to place "high-risk" or "unstable" probation or Approved School/Approved Home cases for review very shortly after making the relevant orders. The period could be one to three months after the order is first made. This is to ensure that such cases are very closely monitored, so that remedial action can be taken should the juvenile manifest any problems with the probation or Approved School/Approved Home orders.[113]

Information to Court by Probation Officer

The Juvenile Court has created a form used by the Probation Services Branch known as "Information to Court". This form will update the Court on the progress of the juvenile since he was placed on probation, with recommendations or requests for variations on the Probation Order made, for example, the lifting of certain time restrictions in the original Probation Order to enable the juvenile to go for an overnight camp organised by his school. This enables the Court to be apprised of contemporaneous relevant information about the probationer, and of the directions of the Court which are being sought by the Probation Officer.

The Schools-Probation-Courts (SPC) Link

This initiative links the Juvenile Court and the Probation Services Branch with 40 secondary schools. The aim is to enhance the supervision of probationers who are students by designating certain teachers in the participating schools as Operations Managers. The Operations Managers act as the schools' representatives for "pre-order investigation" and "post-order" management of juvenile probationers. When a probation report is ordered by the Court, the Operations Manager will obtain the relevant school reports on the juvenile for the Probation Officer, upon the Probation Officer's request. He may also give his own feedback on the juvenile's behaviour, if he has been involved in disciplining the juvenile previously. After the juvenile is placed on probation, the Operations Manager will monitor his progress. He will be the one giving reports on the juvenile's behaviour when the juvenile's case is reviewed.

Beyond Parental Control Cases

There is no statutory requirement for a review to be done in those cases where BPC orders have been made. However, the Court will call for a review of these cases where it is of the view that there is a high risk of the child breaching the BPC order made.

Care and Protection Order Cases

For Care and Protection Order cases, either the court will call for a review of the case three to six months after the Care and Protection Order is made; or the institution taking care of the child or the approved welfare officer from the MCDS will request the Court to review the case. At the review, the Court will decide whether the child can be re-integrated with his family, or whether the order for the child to stay on in the institution should be extended, or what other orders would be suitable for the care and protection of the child. The child and his parents will have to attend the review in court.

Breach of Orders — Powers to the Court

Where an offender contravenes any order or condition made by the Juvenile Court, the Court is empowered to make any of the following orders:[114]

- Fresh orders under Section 44(1) of the CYPA;[115]
- Variations to the original order or any condition in that order. (For example, the Court may have made a Probation Order with conditions requiring the juvenile to remain at home from 9 p.m. to 6 a.m. and also to perform 50 hours of community service. The varied order can include stricter conditions, such as requiring the juvenile to remain at home from 6 p.m. to 6 a.m., and to increase the number of hours of community service which he has to perform.)
- Directing the offender to comply with that part of the original order or any condition of that order which has not been complied with.

1. Breach of Conditions of Probation

In addition to the Court's powers under the CYPA (as set out above) in respect of a breach of its orders, a breach of a **Probation Order** is specifically governed by the Probation of Offenders Act.[116] Where the offender breaches the conditions of probation, the procedure is as follows:

a) The Probation Officer will make a complaint to the Magistrate setting out the nature of the breach.

b) Usually the probationer will be informed by the Probation Officer to be present. If the probationer is not present, the Court may issue a summons for his attendance.
c) If the breach is ***minor***, the Court may **warn** the probationer and release him with no further action taken.
d) However if it is ***more serious***, the Court will request for a **progress report** to be prepared by the Probation Officer. This report will focus on the conduct of the probationer during the probation period. The case is fixed before the fully constituted Juvenile Court for consideration. Pending the preparation of the progress report, the Court may remand the probationer in a Place of Detention or release him on bail.[117]
e) There are ***three options*** available to the Court when it decides to "breach" a probationer; namely:
    (i) to allow the present Probation Order to continue or to extend the period of probation up to a maximum of three years; or
    (ii) to fine the probationer for the breach itself up to a maximum of $500 but to continue with the present Probation Order; or
    (iii) to deal with the probationer as a fresh offender on the original charge for which he was placed on probation.[118]

2. Breach by the Commission of a Further Offence

In such cases, the Court will deal with the probationer as if he is a fresh offender on the original charge for which probation was imposed. The practice is to impose an Approved School Order if the juvenile re-offends whilst on probation, unless the subsequent offence is very minor (for example, littering). However, depending on the circumstances of some cases, the Probation Orders may be varied to include more stringent conditions.

It is sometimes the case that a juvenile who re-offends whilst on probation (or even whilst on an Approved School order) not only has a breach action taken against him, but is charged for this new offence as well. The position at law is that orders made pursuant to breach proceedings are not tantamount to, and thus do not constitute a "conviction" on a fresh charge. Thus, it is entirely possible for a juvenile to be both "breached" and subsequently charged for the offence(s) that amounted to the breach of probation conditions. This will not offend against the "double jeopardy rule" (*autrefois convict*[119]).

3. BPC Cases on Statutory Supervision

If and when the child or young person fails to comply with an order of statutory supervision, the social worker from Singapore Children's Society may institute a complaint in Court.[120] The juvenile and his parents are afforded an opportunity to explain and respond to these complaints. The Court may remand the juvenile pending a progress report.

The progress report will be considered by a fully constituted Juvenile Court, which may make one of the following orders:[121]

a) Make a fresh statutory supervision order or extend the existing order; or
b) Order the juvenile be sent to an Approved Home for a minimum of two years and a maximum of three years.

4. "Breaching" Residents in Approved Schools and Approved Homes

The manager of an Approved School or an Approved Home may initiate breach proceedings against a resident by making a representation to the Juvenile Court that the young person is of so unruly[122] a character that he cannot be detained at the place as ordered.[123] The reason for doing this is to prevent the unruly resident from "contaminating", or for the safety of, the rest of the residents. The representation will particularise the unruly acts of the resident as well as the dates, times and places of these acts. The resident is offered an opportunity to explain himself or engage a counsel to do so. The Juvenile Court, if satisfied that there is justification for the breach action will call for a progress report on the resident and fix the case for consideration before the fully constituted Juvenile Court.

If the Juvenile Court is satisfied that the young person is so unruly as to be unfit to reside at the present institution, it is empowered[124] to mete out the following orders:

a) Order the resident to be transferred to another Approved School which the Court considers more suitable and detain the resident there for the unexpired period of detention; for example, an unruly female resident may be transferred from the Salvation Army Gracehaven home to the Toa Payoh Girls' Home (which has a stricter regime than Salvation Army Gracehaven);
b) If a resident is 16 years of age, or if he is above 14 years, in certain situations,[125] he may be transferred to the District Court to be dealt with in accordance with the Reformative Training regime. (see Section 10 at page 19 above on Reformative Training)

However it is also open to the Court, if the case is appropriate, to give the young person a stern warning with respect to his behaviour and direct him to continue his present detention in the Approved School or extend the existing order.[126]

Programmes

Preventing juveniles from committing misdemeanours and moulding them into useful and productive citizens is a more efficient use of society's resources than rehabilitating offending or wayward juveniles. Towards this end, programmes have been designed by the Juvenile Court to educate young people on juvenile justice issues, to teach them peaceable methods of resolving their disputes, and to provide those who need it with a specialised programme of counselling, or a mentor family. Research is also carried out by the Juvenile Court on juvenile justice issues, in order to identify specific problems to be tackled, to measure the success of its current programmes, and to design more effective programmes for the future. The Juvenile Court programmes and research activities are all co-ordinated and carried out by the Family and Juvenile Justice Centre (FJJC). The FJJC consists of social workers, counsellors and psychologists employed by the Subordinate Courts, in order to enable a holistic and multi-disciplinary approach to be adopted to tackle issues of familial conflict and juvenile misbehaviour.[127]

ENDNOTES

1 For more information on juvenile justice issues, visit us at our website: www.juvenilecourtofsingapore.gov.sg

2 Section 32(1) of the Children and Young Persons Act (hereinafter CYPA), Singapore Statutes, 1994, revised edition, amended by 20 of 2001.

3 Section 32(3) of the CYPA; See page 7 below for more details on the Panel of Advisers.

4 Section 33 of the CYPA.

5 Section 50 of the CYPA.

6 Section 49 of the CYPA.

7 Section 2(1) of the CYPA.

8 Section 33 of the CYPA.

9 See pages 115-21 in Legal Principles below.

10 Sections 33(2) and (3) of the CYPA.

11 Section 33(2)(a) – (b) of the CYPA.

12 Section 42(5) of the CYPA — In the absence of a legal representative, the Juvenile Court can allow a juvenile's parents or guardian or in their absence, any relative or responsible person to assist him in conducting his defence.

13 Section 41 of the CYPA.

14 Section 36 of the CYPA; For example, under Section 33A of the Misuse of Drugs Act (Cap. 185), if a person is convicted twice of consumption of a specified drug under Section 8(b) of the Act, there is a minimum mandatory imprisonment term of five years, and a minimum penalty of not less than three strokes of the cane. If a juvenile is convicted of a drug offence under Section 8(b) and found guilty in the Juvenile Court, this antecedent will not amount to a "conviction" for the purposes of attracting the enhanced punishment under Section 33A of the Misuse of Drugs Act when the juvenile becomes an adult and is charged and convicted subsequently for the commission of another offence (i.e. second offence) under Section 8(b).

15 Section 34(2) of the CYPA. Under Section 34 of the CYPA, only certain persons are allowed to sit in the public gallery of the Juvenile Court — namely, members and officers of the Court, parties to the case before the Court, their counsel, witnesses and other related parties, bona fide representatives of news agencies, and such other people as the Court may specifically authorise to attend the court proceedings.

16 Section 35(2) of the CYPA, amended by Act 20/2001 wef 1 October 2001.

17 Section 29 of the CYPA.

18 The exception is when the juvenile offender is jointly charged with another person who is above 16 years old — see Section 33(3) of the CYPA.

19 Section 31 of the CYPA.

20 Section 42(4) of the CYPA.

21 Section 42(8) of the CYPA.

22 Section 48 of the CYPA.

23 Section 32 of the CYPA.

24 For the perspective of a Panel Adviser, see Section 4.2 at page 152.

25 See the section on Juvenile Offending Behaviour (JOB) Criteria at page 8.

26 See Chapter 2 for more information on the Family and Juvenile Justice Centre.

27 See Chapter 8 for Dr Willie McCarney's article "Restorative Justice: International Approaches".

28 Section 44 of the CYPA.

29 Section 44(1)(a) and (b) of the CYPA.

30 See page 216 for details on the Guidance Programme.

31 See Section 8(1) of the Probation of Offenders Act, Cap. 252, Singapore Statutes, 1994 revised edition.

32 Section 44(1)(c) of the CYPA.

33 Section 44(1)(d) of the CYPA.

34 Section 44(1)(e) of the CYPA.

35 Section 44(2)(a)(i) and 44(2)(a)(iii) of the CYPA.

36 See Appendix A for a list of Approved Institutions; only two places are designated as Places of Detention under the CYPA: the Singapore Boys' Home and the Toa Payoh Girls' Home; see Section 7, page 16 for more details on "Weekend Detention".

37 Section 44(2)(a)(ii) of the CYPA.

38 Section 44(3) of the CYPA.

39 Section 5(2) of the Probation of Offenders Act, Cap. 252.

40 Police and Probation Officers have worked out which areas where gangs are known to operate. Probation Officers will, in appropriate cases, recommend to the Court that an order be made, as a condition of probation, for the juvenile to stay away from certain designated areas which are known to be haunts for gang activities.

41 Section 5(3)(b) Probation of Offenders Act Cap. 252; Gazetted Approved Institutions are the Singapore Boys' Hostel and Bukit Batok Hostel.

42 See endnote 5 on page 146 for more details on Administrative, Supervised and Intensive Probation.

43 Section 5(4) of the Probation of Offenders Act, Cap. 252.

44 See Chapter 3, Part II, Section 3 at page 135 (Court's Discretion and Punishment Options).

45 Section 44(1)(f) and Section 44(2)(a) of the CYPA.

46 Section 44(2)(a)(i) of the CYPA.

47 Section 44(1)(g) of the CYPA.

48 Section 44(3) of the CYPA.

49 Parliamentary Report on the Second Reading of the Children and Young Persons (Amendment) Bill, Col. 1610, sitting date: 20 April 2001.

50 Section 44(6) of the CYPA.

51 Section 47(a) of the CYPA.

52 Section 44(1)(h) of the CYPA.

53 Section 44(2)(a)(iii) of the CYPA.

54 Section 44(4) of the CYPA.

55 Section 44(2)(b) of the CYPA.

56 Parliamentary Report on the Second Reading of the Children and Young Persons (Amendment) Bill, Col. 1610, sitting date: 20 April 2001.

57 Section 44(1)(i) of the CYPA.

58 See Chapter 3, Part II, Section 2 at page 131 (Court's Discretion and Punishment Options).

59 Sections 47(b) and 77(3) of the CYPA; A juvenile who is 16 years and 6 months old at the time that a fresh order is made for him to be sent to an Approved School/Approved Home for three years (this usually happens when the juvenile breaches his Probation Order, and institutionalisation is felt to be the most appropriate order in the circumstances), will be released from that institution once he reaches the age of **19 years**. If the same juvenile, however, absconds from the Approved School/Approved Home before the expiry of his three-year period of detention, and he is caught and returned to the Approved School/Home, then he will have to serve out that much of the unexpired portion of his period of detention plus the period for which he was at large, until he reaches the age of **19 years and 6 months.**

60 For examples of these programmes, see Chapter 5, Section 5.11 at page 220 on Residential Rehabilitation.

61 See endnote 58, supra.

62 Section 44(6) of the CYPA.

63 Section 44(1)(j) of the CYPA.

64 Section 39(1) of the CYPA.

65 Section 39(3) of the CYPA.

66 Section 39(5) of the CYPA, Section 361 of the Criminal Procedure Code, Singapore Statutes, 1994 revised edition, Cap. 68.

67 Section 44(1)(k) of the CYPA.

68 Section 13(4) of the Criminal Procedure Code, Cap. 68, and Section 44(1)(k) of the CYPA.

69 See Legal Issues at pages 140-45; Section 6.1.3 at page 245.

70 Also see Carruthers, D.J., Restorative Justice and Juvenile Justice—A Comparison of the Singapore and New Zealand Experience, at Chapter 7.

71 Section 45 of the CYPA. In 1996, another form of conferencing similar to Family Conferencing, termed "Family Care Conferencing" was implemented to target juveniles who are beyond parental control. Since the year 2000, Family Conferences are applicable to all three categories of cases, namely the Juvenile Arrest Cases, Beyond Parental Control cases and Care and Protection Order cases. See also pages 51-54.

72 Vide S477/2001 (Subsidiary Legislation).

73 Section 45(3) of the CYPA.

74 This can include resolving any relationship problems between the parents which are hindering effective parenting.

75 Parliamentary Report on the Second Reading of the Children and Young Persons (Amendment) Bill, Col. 1613, sitting date: 20 April 2001.

76 Section 50 of the CYPA.

77 Pursuant to Section 133(1) of the Criminal Procedure Code, Cap. 68.

78 This is prepared by the Child Welfare Officer of the Ministry of Development and Sports.

79 Section 2 of the CYPA. Currently the two gazetted remand homes are the Singapore Boys' Home and the Toa Payoh Girls' Home for males and females respectively.

80 Section 50(1)(i) and (ii) of the CYPA.

81 This function is currently undertaken by social workers from the Singapore Children's Society.

82 An Approved Home regime is the structured institution where BPC cases are committed.

83 Section 51 of the CYPA.

84 A "Protector" is the Director of Social Welfare and includes any public officer or other person who is appointed or authorised by the Director under Section 3(3) of the CYPA, to exercise the powers and perform the duties of a protector under the Act — Section 2 of the CYPA.

85 Section 50(3) of the CYPA.

86 Section 4 of the CYPA.

87 Efforts must be made by the Child Protection Officers to ascertain any other suitable person who is willing and able to exercise care or guardianship in respect of the child or young person. If not, a CPO can be applied for — section 4(b) of the CYPA.

88 i.e. Ill-treatment by the parent/guardian or any other person and the parent/guardian, being aware of the ill-treatment or risk, has not protected or is unlikely or unwilling to protect the child/young person from such ill-treatment — Section 4(d) (i) and (ii) of the CYPA.

89 Either one of two conditions must be satisfied: (i) the parent/guardian is unable or unwilling to take the necessary measures to remedy the situation or (ii) the remedial measures undertaken fail — Section 4(f) (i) and (ii) of the CYPA.

90 Emotional injury can be caused as a result of serious and persistent conflict between the child/young person and his parent/guardian or between his

parents or guardians such that family relationships are disrupted — Section 4(g) of the CYPA.

91 A relevant offence would be an offence which has been committed against the child, such as voluntarily causing hurt to the child, molest or rape of the child.

92 Section 4(*i*) of the CYPA.

93 Section 9(1) of the CYPA.

94 Section 9(1) (a) of the CYPA; Also see Appendix A, Part I at page 376 for a list of Places of Safety.

95 Such approved welfare officers include psychologists in the Psychological Services Unit (PSU) from MCDS.

96 Section 9(5) of the CYPA.

97 Section 9(6) of the CYPA.

98 Section 27 of the CYPA; also see Appendix A, Part I at page 380 for a list of all Places of Safety.

99 Section 49(6) of the CYPA.

100 The hearing date can sometimes be fixed in less than four weeks depending on the urgency of the case.

101 Section 49(1) of the CYPA.

102 Order under (d) above can be made in addition to either one of the orders under (a) – (c): Section 49(1)(d) of the CYPA. However, where a juvenile is ordered to reside in an Approved Home or Place of Safety under Section 49(1)(c) of the CYPA, very rarely would the Juvenile Court invoke Section 49(1)(d) in addition to that as the Superintendent or Manager of the Approved Homes or Places of Safety would be the ones responsible for the welfare of the juvenile under their care.

103 Section 49(5) of the CYPA.

104 Section 51 of the CYPA.

105 See Section 4 of the Probation of Offenders Act, Cap. 252.

106 Section 76(2) of the CYPA.

107 See endnote 105.

108 Rule 13 of the Probation of Offenders Rules, Cap. 252, R1 (1990 Edn).

109 Apart from reviewing cases, the JPCC is updated on the various programmes initiated by the Probation Services Branch (MCDS) together with the Family Service Centres as well as the many research studies conducted on probationers to monitor the effectiveness of various programmes. The JPCC also discusses policy issues/decisions made by the MCDS that affect probationers, and the views of the Committee are sought in these matters.

110 However, under the Probation of Offenders Act, they are only required to review those cases where an offender has been ordered to reside in an Approved Institution for more than six months, and he has already spent six months there. See Section 6(6) of the Probation of Offenders Act, Cap. 252.

111 Section 76(4) of the CYPA.

112 Sections 76(2) and 76(4) of the CYPA.

113 Examples of remedial action include stern warnings given by the Juvenile Court Magistrate for the Approved School/Approved Home cases followed by a further review thereafter for the juvenile to prove himself or herself, or more stringent conditions imposed under the Probation Order for probation cases.

114 Section 44(5) of the CYPA.

115 See pages 10-23 for information on all the orders which the Juvenile Court can make under Section 44(1) of the CYPA.

116 Section 7(2)(a) of the Probation of Offenders Act, Cap. 252.

117 Section 42(11)(c) of the CYPA.

118 See Section 44(5) of the CYPA as above.

119 For more information on the principle of "autrefois convict", see the Legal Issues section at page 138.

120 Section 52 of the CYPA.

121 Section 52 read with Section 50 of the CYPA.

122 See the section on Legal Issues for a definition of "unruly" at page 140.

123 Section 44(7) of the CYPA.

124 Section 44(7)(a)–(b) of the CYPA.

125 Where the offender has attained the age of 14 years but is below 16 years, and has previously been dealt with by a Court in connection with another offence and had in respect of that other offence been ordered to be sent to an Approved School (Singapore Boys' Home and Toa Payoh Girls' Home). The Juvenile Court must also be satisfied that it is expedient for the offender's reformation that he should undergo reformative training – Section 44(7)(b) of the CYPA.

126 Section 44(6) of the CYPA for JAC and Section 50(3) of the CYPA for BPC cases.

127 For more information on The Family and Juvenile Justice Centre, see the chapter so titled at page 45.

ANNEX: CASES DEALT WITH BY THE JUVENILE COURT FROM 2000 – 2002

A. Youths Charged in or Brought to the Juvenile Court

	Number	% of Total Cases[1]	Total No. of Residents in Singapore[2&3] 7– below16 Years OR below 16 years[4]	% of Total No. of Residents in Singapore[2&3] 7– below 16 Years OR below 16 years[4]
Juvenile Arrest, etc, Cases (JAC)[5]				
2000				
Juveniles dealt with[6]	715	76%	428,920	0.17%
2001				
Juveniles dealt with[6]	546	73%	438,940	0.12%
2002				
Juveniles dealt with[6]	848	77%	449,440	0.19%
Beyond Parental Control (BPC)				
2000				
Juveniles dealt with[6]	177	19%	743,060	0.02%
2001				
Juveniles dealt with[6]	158	23%	751,040	0.02%
2002				
Juveniles dealt with[6]	205	29%	758,000	0.03%
Child Protection Order (CPO)				
2000				
Children dealt with[6]	50	5%	743,060	0.01%
2001				
Children dealt with[6]	42	6%	751,040	0.01%
2002				
Children dealt with[6]	54	8%	758,000	0.01%

Notes:

1 This figure is obtained by dividing the number of juveniles or children dealt with for the particular category (i.e. JAC, BPC or CPO), with the total number of juveniles/children dealt with across all three categories (i.e. JAC, BPC and CPO).

2 Singapore residents refer to Singapore citizens and permanent residents who reside in Singapore.

3 Source: *Monthly Digest of Statistics*, Department of Statistics. Statistics for residents below 16 years are calculated based on proportional apportioning.

4 For JAC, the base residents include youths from 7 – below 16 years. For BPC and CPO cases, the base residents include children/youths below 16 years.

5 Juvenile Arrest, etc, Cases includes JAC, PS, SS & Tickets and others.

6 The term "Juveniles dealt with/Children dealt with" refers to the number of youths who were charged or brought to the Juvenile Court.

ANNEX (Cont'd)
B. Top Five Offences for Juveniles (Fresh JAC, PS, Summons & Tickets Cases Only) by Cases[1]

TOP 5 JUVENILE OFFENCES IN 2000[2]

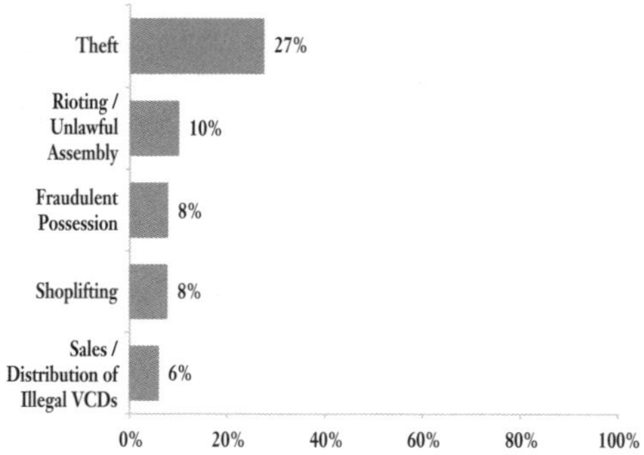

Total Offences Committed by Juveniles (By Case files) = 984

TOP 5 JUVENILE OFFENCES IN 2001[2]

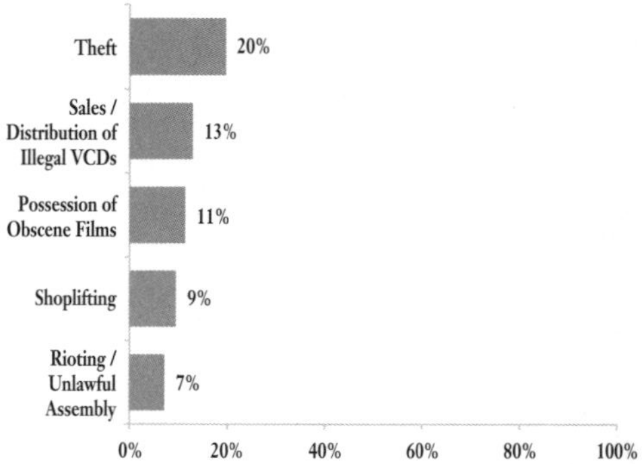

Total Offences Committed by Juveniles (By Case files) = 902

TOP 5 JUVENILE OFFENCES IN 2002

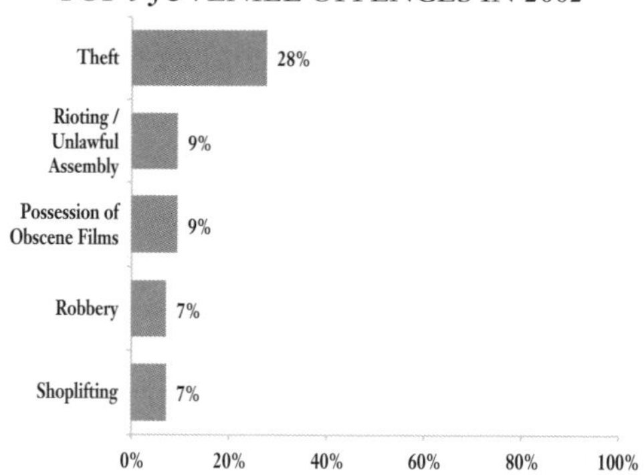

Total Offences Committed by Juveniles (By Case files) = 1,827

Notes:

1 The "Fresh cases" category consists of the actual case files received by the Juvenile Court. Each case can involve more than one juvenile, who can be charged with one or more charges.

2 The remaining percentage of Juvenile offences for each year consists of a variety of different offences, such as joy-riding, computer hacking, voluntarily causing hurt, and so on. The volume of these offences is, collectively, significant. However, when broken down into individual offences, the volume for each individual offence is not significant enough to merit separate categorisation on the bar chart for each year. For this reason, the percentages reflected in the bar charts will not add up to 100%.

CHAPTER 2

The Family and Juvenile Justice Centre

This section deals with the work of the Family and Juvenile Justice Centre (FJJC) in supporting the Juvenile Court in its mission to achieve restorative justice. The philosophy of the FJJC is explained, and the details of the various programmes designed and run by the FJJC are set out here.

The FJJC views the community in which the juvenile justice system operates as an ecological system in which the relationships within families, amongst individuals, and between organisations are the binding forces. Building and maintaining such relationships are the focus of FJJC's programmes.

A key concept which FJJC employs in its work is that of the "transformative opportunity" — that crucial moment where, caught in the crucible of circumstances from which he cannot escape, an individual (guided by an experienced counsellor or psychologist) experiences a transformation in his thinking, adopting a new, positive mindset and attitude. Activities such as Family Conferencing and Family Justice Team conferencing are intended to create "transformative opportunities" for juveniles and their families. Three illustrations of Family Conferencing are set out at the end of this section, to show the creation of such transformative opportunities, and their translation into transformative moments for the individuals and families involved.

2.1 The Family and Juvenile Justice Centre[1]

JOSEPH PAUL OZAWA

Ph.D., Senior Director and Senior Consultant Psychologist [2]

Restorative and Transformative Justice

As the Center for Court Innovation of the New York State Unified Court System has so appropriately stated, *"like it or not, courts are where the problems are..."*[3]. The Courts are indeed a focal point, a crucible of disputes and seemingly implacable conflicts and interpersonal traumas, where the unfortunate manifestations of dysfunctional relationships and family systems disorders are played out. Whether in respect of divorces, family violence, child protection, juvenile misdemeanour, drug offences or crimes of violence or sexual assault, the Courts serve not only as centres to adjudicate and punish, but also to facilitate the potential transformation, rehabilitation, and restoration of those who come before it. A reduced crime rate depends not only on deterrence — stopping people from committing crimes because they fear the consequences of being caught — but also on tackling the root disorders which fester, breed and give rise to violations of acceptable human norms of behaviour. In tackling such root disorders, the Courts are dealing with complex human relationships and attitudes — and seeking to transform, heal, and harmonise them.

The Family and Juvenile Justice Centre

In recognition of the fact that adjudicating and dealing with complex human interactions are vital to the functioning of a transformative and restorative judicial system, the Subordinate Courts of Singapore have enlisted the services of a group of counsellors, social workers and psychologists — a group now known as the Family and Juvenile Justice Centre (FJJC). The FJJC was formed in the year 2002 by the merging of two previously separate groups — the Family Conciliation and Resolution Centre (FAMCARE) and the Psychological Services Unit.

FAMCARE (formed in the year 1996) consisted of social workers and counsellers whose core business was to support the work of the Family Court by doing counselling and family violence work, writing court-ordered evaluation reports in respect of child custody and access disputes, and promoting public education in family justice issues. The

Psychological Services Unit (formed in the year 2000) supported the work of the Juvenile Court by conducting family conferences, doing work in offender profiling, research in criminal and juvenile justice issues, and promoting public education in juvenile justice issues. With the formation of the Psychological Services Unit, the Subordinate Courts of Singapore first began utilising professionally qualified psychologists "in-house" rather than as external, consultative professionals. Thus, psychologists became available to all the courts on a daily basis, and forensic psychology became one of the tools used by the Subordinate Courts in its mission to achieve transformative and restorative justice.

Members of the FJJC support the work of the Juvenile Court by designing and running its programmes, and also assisting the Juvenile Court Magistrate in her decision-making by doing offender profiling work and conducting family conferences. Details of the work done by FJJC is set out in the section on "Programmes" below.

Forensic Psychology in Juvenile Justice

Forensic psychology is broadly defined by many authorities as the "application of psychology to the law in general."[4] Connolly and McKellar[5] define forensic psychology as the application of psychology to the procedures of courts of law, whereas others such as Bartol and Bartol[6] consider forensic psychology to be research into behaviour related to the legal processes and the professional practice within the legal system. The most broadly accepted notion is as defined in a joint statement of the American Psychology-Law Society and Division 41 of the American Psychological Association, which defines forensic psychology as follows:

> "....all forms of professional psychological conduct when acting, with definable foreknowledge, as a psychological expert on explicitly psycholegal issues, in direct assistance to courts, parties to legal proceedings, correctional and forensic mental health facilities, and administrative, judicial, and legislative agencies acting in an adjudicative capacity."[7]

This definition of forensic psychology is reflected in the speech made by the Honourable The Chief Justice on 13 September 2000 at the International Youth Justice Conference 2000 in Singapore, where, in announcing the formation of the Psychological Services Unit, he stated that it should be:

> "part of the Subordinate Courts, and not (merely as an) adjunct (body)... This is to ensure that the juvenile system is sufficiently informed and guided by other relevant disciplinary professions in dealing with juveniles and their behaviours."

The Chief Justice went on to expound on the concept of restorative justice, by stating:

> "this is individualised justice. Personal and special attention is paid to each juvenile offender, his character, his family and environment for a holistic approach....Judicial disposition would need to be multi-systemic. At its core must be the specific needs and problems of the offender and his integration within his family who must play a critical role, and within his community and peer environment...there must be a continuum of graduated yet flexible sanctions that responds to the needs of each juvenile offender while providing for community safety...(therefore).. immediate and therapeutic intervention by the Juvenile Court Judge...or the Psychological Services of the Juvenile Justice Centre...is appropriate at the first sign of delinquent behaviour for a youth at risk or beyond parental control, or for breach of the law or judicial order or institutional discipline..."[8]

The mandate of the psychologists of FJJC is therefore to act as experts on the psychological issues which arise in the course of, and out of, court proceedings; and also to apply the principles of psychology in re-inventing and refining the juvenile justice system, in order to achieve the goal of restorative justice. Among other things, this involves expertise in: criminology, victimology, criminal recidivism, profiling or evaluation of offenders, and research into dysfunction, deviance, psychopathology, and criminal behaviour in individuals.

Towards a Family and Juvenile Court Ecology

In the year 2001, the Family Court and Juvenile Court (which had previously been housed in different buildings) came under one roof in the same building. Sharing common constituents, the two courts and divisions began a process of integration, tackling such issues as marital breakdown, neglect and abuse, and juvenile crime in a holistic and co-ordinated manner. Professor Barbara Babb of the University of Baltimore School of Law[9] has eloquently argued for a "family ecology" in the court context, where "courts must view neighbourhoods, religious organisations, and other associations or institutions within which family members participate as having the potential to influence the family's legal matters, and unified family courts must adopt a systematic approach to accommodate the complex factors affecting families' lives".[10] Looking beyond individual litigants, an ecological framework tackles juvenile and family justice issues on many levels and on many fronts. The focus of the system is on the building and maintaining of social and familial relationships. All the projects initiated and run by the FJJC are part of this ecological framework.

Transformative Moments

Another key concept which underlies the work of psychologists of the Subordinate Courts of Singapore is the notion of a "*transformative opportunity*."[11] In terms of human potential, every court case is an opportunity — a possibility for the positive transformation of individuals and their families: in their characters, their relationships to each other, and in their attitudes towards society. Sometimes a father or mother who has long been "missing" in the juvenile offender's life will show up due to a court summons. In other cases, an offender's court appearance will be accompanied by a retinue of family members who may otherwise never get together, even for special holidays! Given the sometimes intimidating court setting, the presence of police and lawyers, and the seeming finality of an impending dispositional order, sentence or decision regarding a settlement, this particular event becomes a critical incident, a moment of truth. Seizing this opportunity in the charged atmosphere of a Family Conference,[12] a trained forensic psychologist who is familiar both with the pertinent laws relating to the case and with psychological dynamics can facilitate change. He or she can, for example, confront a parent in denial, elicit hidden information, shame a wayward youth into reformation, or reconcile family members who are severely estranged. In this manner, transformative opportunities may facilitate restorative/therapeutic justice — by reconciling parties and repairing relationships. Beyond simply providing reparations or financial compensations for victims, such moments can facilitate the development of respectful and lawful relationships, repair emotional damage, and restore a sense of control and responsibility to parents, victims and the community.

Fundamentally, "*crime is a violation of a relationship among victims, offenders and the community.*"[13] When interests clash, desires differ, respect is absent, accepted standards of interpersonal relationships are breached, behaviours become inappropriate, pathological, deviant or dysfunctional, and a "wrongful" act is committed. It is not just the victim of the crime who is hurt by this wrongful act, but the whole community.[14]

In familiar settings such as a void deck, coffee shop, kitchen, bedroom, bank, apartment corridors, workplaces or storefronts, the conflict can even escalate, abetted by interested bystanders. The breach of relationship is magnified by the number of such interested, participating bystanders. However, as William Ury has argued so convincingly,[15] a third party can become a voice of transformation, "*...the voice that urges us to heal old grievances; it is the capacity to listen to the other side and show empathy; it is the impulse to respect the basic human needs of all*".[16] The court representatives thus become that critical "third party," their authority increasing with the formality of court proceedings, and their perceived level of expertise. The use of potential legal sanctions increases the likelihood of such a "third party" being taken seriously by all concerned. The possibilities for escaping the conflict, denying the issues or subterfuge decrease once the accused has to contend with the full weight of the court proceedings. By the time a family member who has bashed another family member appears before a judge who has the power to sentence him/her to ten years in prison, avoidance, denial, late settlements, excuses are often reduced to a simple statement, "Please have mercy on me, Judge!" This becomes the transformative opportunity.

Certainly there are parallels in psychotherapy or counselling. This is an induced moment, popularised by the late Dr. Fritz Perls of *Gestalt*[17] fame. Unlike conventional counselling which may take years of insight and cajoling to effect breakthroughs, the crucible of the Courts has the potential to instantaneously heat up the psyche to a boiling or flash point where, in a critical moment, personal or interpersonal revelation or change quickly emerges.

Programmes

The following section describes various services and programmes initiated and run by the FJJC, which support the concept of transformative and restorative justice. These services and programmes fall into three categories: intervention, research, and education. Intervention programmes seek to remedy the problems which have already developed, and are either discovered or are apparent, by the time the juvenile appears in Court. Education programmes aim to prevent such problems from arising in the first place. Research is done to identify the specific areas which would benefit from intervention or education, and to enable FJJC to design the most effective methods to do so.

I. Intervention

Family Conferences (FCs)

Family Conferences within the context of the Juvenile Court of Singapore are not just counselling sessions with families. Rather, FCs are a unique blend of judicial hearing, mediation and counselling.

The FCs are conducted in a meeting room adjoining the Juvenile Court and are attended by the juvenile, the juvenile's family, and the significant persons in the juvenile's life, including supervision officers from the Ministry of Community Development and Sports (MCDS) and/or other social service agencies. The victim (and the victim's parents, if the victim is a child) of the juvenile's offence will also be invited to come, but is not required to do so. The FC usually precedes the final dispositional order which takes place in open court.

As the juvenile and his family (save for the victim) are requested to participate by the Court and can be officially summoned if required, attendance is compulsory. Within this context, the FC is an excellent example of a "transformative opportunity".[18] The various participants in the FC would be placed together in the same room for the very first time, thus setting the scene for confessions, confrontations, admissions and apologies — which are the first step to reparation for the victim, the transformation of the juvenile and his family, and the restoration of the juvenile to the community.

Using this concept, FCs were used to lead offenders to accepting responsibility for an offence through a process of "re-integrative shaming", i.e. making the offenders feel guilty and ashamed of the misdemeanours that they had committed.[19] However this focus for FCs was found to be too limited in scope. It did not, by itself, restore the juvenile to more harmonious relationships with his family, or change his life-philosophy or attitudes towards society. Re-integrative shaming has been retained, but only as one option in a panoply of flexible and variable FC objectives.

At times, reprimands, compensatory requirements, cautions or formal undertakings are utilised in order to bring accountability and personal commitment into the lives of an offender and his/her families. At other times, victims and their families are brought in, in order to confront the perpetrator, to elicit apologies/compensation from the juvenile, or to allow the victims to ventilate their own feelings. This acts both as a way for restitution to be made to the victim as well as making the juvenile and his family aware of the impact of crime on victims, hopefully increasing their level of empathy towards other people.

Additionally, there can be reconciliation between family members, apologies, or the confrontation of the offender or his family members with issues of truth-telling, irresponsibility, shame, denial, injustice, rejection, and so on. FCs also act as a platform, a launching-off point for mandatory counselling, convincing an individual or family of the validity and importance of further therapy or family counselling by appropriate community or governmental agencies.

Finally, FCs can be a place where preliminary screening is done by court psychologists for various disorders in the juvenile. This will enable early and effective referrals to be made for mental disorders or disabilities in the juvenile. For example, some FCs have dealt with mentally retarded offenders, autism, Asperger's syndrome, self-mutilating behaviour, Munchausen syndrome by proxy,[20] pyromania (i.e. an obsession with fire), exhibitionism, paedophilia, voyeurism, severe conduct disorder, borderline personality disorders, or attention-deficit disorder with hyperactivity, and obsessive-compulsive disorder.

The path of rehabilitation, reparation and restoration is charted for each individual case during the FC, by the facilitator in consultation with the other members of the FC. The role and/or responsibility of each individual, his or her family and significant persons in the individual's life, including his supervision officers, will be carefully mapped out. The facilitator will also refer the cases for management by specialised agencies where necessary.

The wheels are thus set in motion for supervision officers from MCDS and/or other social agencies to follow-up and work with all parties to effect permanent change in these individuals and families outside the court setting — in the heart of the community. In this way, the collective influence and commitment of the community is harnessed to enhance and sustain the momentum of change arising from the induced transformative moment elicited during the FC. The continuity of court direction in these cases is further established through regular court reviews, fixed after the FCs, to monitor the progress of each case over time. These court reviews are presided by the Juvenile Court Magistrate. Additional FCs may also be called for by the Magistrate if he or she deems that they would be beneficial for the juvenile during his or her review of the case.

See pages 63-69 for an account of three FCs which brought the juvenile offender and his family to a transformative moment, along the path of restorative justice. Also see the Annex to this chapter the cases which have undergone Family Conferencing and the corresponding breach and re-offending rates thereafter. The figures have been encouraging.

The Juvenile Offender Behaviour (JOB) Criteria

One of the clearest applications of forensic and psychological profiling and analysis done in the court context is the Juvenile Offender Behaviour (JOB) Criteria, which was developed by the Court's psychologists. It is essentially an evaluation of the juvenile's likelihood of re-offending and his propensity to do so. It places juvenile offenders along a continuum from "developmental-limited" (i.e. a transition stage which will pass) to "life-course persistent" (i.e. exhibiting high-risk characteristics for re-offending). The JOB Criteria is not a fixed, immutable and deterministic score, but rather a broad set of predictors which can be used in a discretionary way by the Juvenile Court Magistrate, who would refer to it when deciding on the most appropriate orders to make.[21]

The factors making up the JOB Criteria were culled from a literature review of developmental psychologists, criminologists and jurists who have conceptualised "life-course persistent" versus "adolescence-limited" offenders based upon "taxonomies" of antisocial behaviour (Moffitt, 1993; Nagin, Farrington & Moffitt, 1995; Scott & Grisso, 1997; Motiuk, 2000).[22]

Project HEART (Healing and Reconciliation Therapeutic Programme)

Thousands of people are divorced each year. In the year 2000, for example, over 5,000 divorces were granted in Singapore.[23]

The ripple effect of marital breakdown is significant. Marital breakdown often leads to abuse, neglect, children running away from home, and juvenile delinquency. Divorce is usually a good predictor of subsequent criminal or deviant activity. In the USA, it was found that 70%[24] of juvenile criminals who were a threat to the public came from broken homes. In a separate study by the Bureau of Justice Statistics, 82%[25] of incarcerated juveniles came from broken homes. Further, it was shown that divorce posed the strongest correlation with robbery rates in American cities.[26]

For these reasons, Project HEART was initiated, with the intention of reducing the divorce rate in Singapore, and improving the quality of the relationship between couples experiencing tensions in their marriage. It is hoped that a positive impact on the level of juvenile delinquency will be brought about by ensuring that fewer children grow up in broken homes.

Under this programme, where couples have contacted selected lawyers for legal advice, but have not decided to commence divorce proceedings, the lawyers will refer the couples to the relevant agencies for assessments. In appropriate cases, the couples will be referred for counselling, and other marriage enrichment programmes, so as to work at their marital problems. The Eagles Mediation and Counselling Centre, selected lawyers, and counselling agencies in the community from different religious groups as well as non-religious groups are the Court's partners in this programme. The full list of organisations taking part in this programme are:

- Eagles Mediation and Counselling Centre (EMCC)
- Fei Yue Family Service Centre (FSC)
- Wesley Methodist Counselling Centre
- SINDA Family Service Centre
- Shan You Counselling Centre
- Family Life Society
- Action on Family Life and Marriage Enrichment (AFLAME)

Project SAVE (Substance Abuse and Violence Elimination)

Substance abuse and family violence are criminogenic. That is to say, they are factors which, if present, could potentially influence a person to adopt criminal behaviour, particularly if he is exposed to these factors from a young age. There are many reasons for this. One reason is because a person who witnesses substance abuse and family violence from a young age is more likely to model this behaviour. Another reason is because if a young person lives in a family where the caregivers are substance abusers and/or are violent, he is much less likely to have a stable and secure environment in which to grow up. This lack of structure affects the young person's education, discipline and value systems. He is thus much more vulnerable to negative influences.[27] The Subordinate Courts had done a study on the respondents in applications for family violence in December 2000.[28] In examining over 1,000 cases, it was found that in approximately 22% of the cases, alcohol played a major role in the alleged violent episodes.

Project SAVE was therefore set up, to provide counselling intervention for abusers who consume alcohol, in order to help them eliminate their alcohol addiction, in addition to tackling the issue of their use of family violence. At the intake counselling stage, an applicant for a personal protection order would be asked to fill in a questionnaire, designed to determine whether the respondent is an alcohol abuser. At the mentions stage, the respondent will be requested to fill in a more detailed questionnaire. The counsellor will then make recommendations to the Court, based on the contents of the questionnaire, on whether it would be appropriate to order the respondent to attend the Project SAVE programme. Those respondents who are ordered to go for this programme will attend mandatory counselling at the Community Addiction Management Programme (CAMP), in the Institute of Mental Health (IMH). These cases are channelled through and funded by the Ministry of Community Development and Sports. Under CAMP, specialised counselling for alcohol addiction will be provided in addition to counselling which addresses issues of the respondents' use of violence.

It is hoped that this will go some way towards eliminating alcohol abuse and violence in families, thus saving children from psychological, as well as physical, harm.

Youth Family Care (YFC) Programme

A large number of delinquent youths who come under the supervision of the Juvenile Court are from broken, dysfunctional, and indeed, often destructive, families. As crime, addiction, interpersonal disorders and the like are often inter-generational, the absence of good role models in the family leads to an endless chain of disorders passed on from one generation to the next. How can a child learn to be a healthy, wholesome parent when he or she has never witnessed a functional family?

To tackle this problem, the Court has initiated the YFC programme in which juveniles who lack family support, and are placed on probation or statutory supervision,[29] are matched with volunteer mentor families. The mentor families will befriend, support, and encourage these young people, by engaging them in family and social activities for as long as the probation or statutory supervision order subsists or until the Court otherwise orders. The mentor families serve as role models not only for the juveniles themselves, but also for the juvenile's parents, particularly in the Beyond Parental Control cases.[30]

The mentor families for this programme are drawn from community networks established by Touch Community Service, Pertapis Children's Home, MENDAKI and the Ramakrishna Mission. Thus a juvenile will have a good chance of having a matching family, no matter what his cultural, socio-economic and religious background.

Specialised training is conducted by the Singapore Children's Society to equip sponsor families with the professional skills required to work with these juveniles on probation or on statutory supervision.

Family Justice Team Programme

Research has shown that a significant proportion of juvenile delinquents or youths at risk come from divorced or dysfunctional families.[31] In order to address the underlying causes of offending behaviour in such cases, a holistic approach will be undertaken in respect of families facing multiple proceedings in the Juvenile and Family Courts simultaneously. Under the Family Justice Team programme, where there are both Juvenile and Family Court proceedings, each court will be kept informed of the progress of the other court's proceedings, and the necessary arrangements will be made to ensure that the orders made by one court will enhance the effectiveness of, rather than clash, with the other. In appropriate cases, the same judge will deal with both the Juvenile Court and the Family Court proceedings. A team of social workers and psychologists will be assigned to deal with the case, in order to provide counselling services for the whole family (these sessions are known as "Family Justice Team Conferences", and are intended to create "transformative opportunities" in the same way as Family Conferences do (see page 51 above for more details on Family Conferences)); and to ensure that all issues relevant to the juvenile and his family are tackled during the counselling sessions. Programmes for the whole family will also be recommended by the Family Justice Team which will address both the juvenile justice as well as the family issues.

II. Education

Peer Group Advisers Programme

In this programme, students in selected secondary schools are given a chance to sit in on court proceedings as well as take part in discussions with the Juvenile Court Magistrate in his Chambers before judgement is passed. In the year 2001, students in this programme role-played in a *Mock Teen Court*, reprising roles as prosecutor, defence counsel, the juvenile offender, parents and the panel of advisers to the Mock Teen Court. All these activities serve to educate teachers and students from secondary schools on the juvenile justice process. It also gives the Juvenile Court a contemporary peer group perspective of the offending criminal act.

The Subordinate Courts conducted surveys amongst the participating students in November 1997, December 1998 and November 1999 to evaluate the programme and the results have shown that the objectives were overwhelmingly achieved.[32] The programme has not only made the students more aware of, and sympathetic to the concept of restorative justice, it has also imparted students with the urge to support their peers who are in trouble, and to form groups and programmes to do so.

Peer Mediation Programme

In 1997, the Peer Mediation programme was introduced in selected secondary schools. The philosophy of peer mediation is to encourage effective conflict resolution without the use of violence and other forms of anti-social behaviour. Peer mediation aims not only to resolve the conflict, but to restore relationships, thereby reducing the need for school, police or court intervention in disputes between juveniles. This in turn will lead to a more harmonious climate within the school and the community, and will prepare students to live in a society which emphasises law and order and the peaceful resolution of conflict.

The aims of peer mediation are achieved by equipping students with interpersonal skills to manage and resolve conflict, to empower the students to assume responsibility for resolving conflicts in school, and to promote greater awareness and acceptance of mediation as a mode of conflict resolution. Students act as mediators between two or more of their peers who are caught in a conflict and who want to achieve a constructive resolution of it.

In 1998, peer mediation was extended to primary schools. Unlike the secondary schools' peer mediation programme which involves a proper sit-down discussion, the primary schools have a "Conflict Manager Programme" where pairs of conflict managers (i.e. appointed students) move around the school playground during recess to settle minor conflicts amongst their peers.

As at the end of 2001, a total of 261 teachers from 154 secondary schools have been trained in the Peer Mediation programme.

The Subordinate Courts have also forged links with various organisations in the community, e.g. the Community Development Councils (CDCs), the Community Mediation Centres, the Ministry of Law and the Ministry of Education, to involve the community in peer mediation in schools.

The first collaboration with Marine Parade CDC in 1999 saw 100 student mediators trained by volunteer mediators, such as lawyers, who had been trained in mediation techniques by professional mediators as well as by officers from the Ministry of Education. A district judge from the Subordinate Courts also attended the event and gave a talk on mediation. Marine Parade CDC funded and organised this event. This was followed by yet another joint collaboration with Sembawang-Hong Kah CDC in the subsequent two years for 2000 and 2001, training about 80 students on each occasion.

TeenQuest

The Justice Teen Quest was first launched by the Juvenile Justice Centre for the June 2000 school holidays. This programme is targeted at youths between 9 to 15 years old, and has been a yearly event since its inception. In its inaugural year, the event was organised in collaboration with the Ministry of Community Development and Sports and the Marine Parade CDC. Participants in the programme had to take part in a series of educational activities, such as quizzes, which were designed to teach societal and relationship values, to reinforce the need for respect for law and authority, and to raise public awareness of the juvenile justice process. The programme was extremely successful, with over 2,000 students taking part, and a great deal of positive feedback was received from the participants.

The theme of the Justice Teen Quest programme launched for the September 2001 holidays was that of a Family Challenge. The event was organised in collaboration with the Central Singapore CDC and Promise.works.[33] The programme saw 35 families working close together in a series of educational quizzes and games to win various prizes. The programme covered topics which included the juvenile justice process and family values.

For the year 2003, the programme was organised by the Family and Juvenile Justice Centre in collaboration with Singapore Children's Society (SCS) and South West CDC. Unlike the previous years' programmes which were quiz-based, the year 2003 programme focussed on offering youths a chance to be truly creative, tapping on their innate talents and not just academic knowledge. Youths were asked to represent pertinent issues related to families in crisis, juvenile delinquency and crime to educate their peers. They accomplished this via different modes of performance/presentation. Topics were chosen with the aid of youths from the SCS Youth Development Centre to ensure that they cater to the target audience. Participants had the choice of using multi-media (power-point presentations, video, slides etc.), print media (write-ups, charts, models etc.) and artistic channels (street art, drama, dance, rap, etc.) to make their presentations.

The aim of this programme, in addition to imparting knowledge and life-skills, is to also model healthy peer interaction for participants.

III. Research

Another key aspect of the work of the FJJC is providing research and conducting literature reviews for Court use, to assist in programme formulation, and to monitor the effectiveness of programmes. For example, both the JOB Criteria and Project SAVE were created as a result of empirical research showing the links between family background and recidivism, alcohol and family violence.[34] Publications of research done and literature reviews conducted by members of the FJJC include the following:[35]

- Baptist, K. (2000). Family Violence Counselling at the Family Justice Centre. *Families in Conflict: Theories and Approaches in Mediation and Counselling*. Singapore: Butterworths.
- Dawood, K. (2000). Divorce Counselling at the Family Justice Centre. *Families in Conflict: Theories and Approaches in Mediation and Counselling*. Singapore: Butterworths.
- Subordinate Courts. (Dec. 2000). Alcohol or Drug Abuse: Relationship to Family Violence. Research Bulletin Issue No. 25.
- Subordinate Courts. (Oct. 2000). Evaluation of KIDS Line Programme. Research Bulletin Issue No. 24.
- Ozawa, J. (Jul. 2001). Juvenile Offender Behaviour (JOB) Criteria: Assessing Risk of Recidivism in Juvenile Court. Singapore Law Gazette.
- Ozawa, J.P., Han, L.J. & Teong, E. (Aug. 2001). Addressing the Criminogenic Effects of Divorce: A Pre-Petition Divorce Intervention Programme. Singapore Law Gazette.

- Subordinate Courts. (Mar. 2001). Profile of Female Juvenile Offenders. Research Bulletin Issue No. 26.
- Subordinate Courts. (Dec. 2001). Study of the Effectiveness of Protection Orders. Research Bulletin Issue No. 28.
- Ozawa, J. P. (Apr. 2002). Transformative Justice: Psychological Services in the Criminal, Family and Juvenile Justice Centres of the Subordinate Courts of Singapore. *Applied Psychology: An International Review*, *51(2)*, 218-35.
- Ozawa, J.P. (2002). Juvenile Delinquency: An Asian Perspective. *Hedges and Edges*. Care Corner Singapore.

In the years to come, the FJJC intends to do research on areas such as bullying and its correlation with juvenile delinquency and chronic mental disorders; drug-involvement and recidivism; the motivations behind property-related offences; the type of family patterns which are particularly predictive of later Court appearances (e.g. divorce, acrimonious custody battles, family violence, sexual abuse, etc.); and the key factors in determining which couples are most at risk of divorce. It is hoped that the research done will enable FJJC to design the most effective programmes to rehabilitate juvenile delinquents, to prevent juvenile delinquency, and to strengthen and maintain harmonious family relationships.

Conclusion

The eco-system of the Courts includes the offenders, their families, their victims, their schools, the community and relevant governmental officers (police, probation officers, welfare officers, psychologists, social workers, school officials, and so on) — all of whom must act in a co-ordinated way to bring not just order, but a permanent and positive structure into the often chaotic and aimless lives of the juvenile offenders.

In a juvenile justice system like ours where transformation, rehabilitation and restoration of the juvenile to his family and to society are the objectives, the FJJC plays a critical role. Targeting those key, "transformative opportunities", when judicial authority or influence can affect an enduring change, and operating systemically in collaboration with community agencies, families, professionals, and other key constituences, those who work in the FJJC can be catalysts of rehabilitation. Whether predicting an individual's likelihood of being a criminal recidivist, delving into the criminogenic roots of society (such as divorce, abuse, domestic violence, inadequate parenting, etc.), assessing criminal disorders (such as voyeurism, paedophilia, pyromania, etc.), conducting research into court-related issues (such as bullying, the motivations for property crimes, the relationship of substance abuse and family violence, etc.), counselling troubled youths and their families, or facilitating a healing and reconciliation process (for example, facilitating the restitution or compensation of victims in FCs), the FJJC is an instrumental participant in assisting the Juvenile Court to become a centre of transformative and restorative justice.

2.2 Family Conferences — Three Illustrations[36]

Skeletons in the Family Closet Revealed

RIDZWAN, aged 13

Ridzwan was a 13-year-old boy who had sexually assaulted his half sister, half brother and cousins. Both of Ridzwan's parents lodged a Beyond Parental Control complaint against him in the Juvenile Court. Following this, a Social Report by the Ministry of Community Development and Sports on Ridzwan was called for by the Juvenile Court. A psychiatric report was also called for.

The psychiatric report from the Institute of Mental Health reported that Ridzwan's remorse level was minimal and his sexual urges very strong. However, there was no apparent explanation for his deviant sexual behaviour. The boy's parents were summoned into the Family Conference to discuss the situation and to explore possible options for a dispositional order given his sexual tendencies.

During the FC, issues surfaced in the Social Report such as possible incest due to Ridzwan's having been bathed by his maternal grandmother or his bathing with his siblings, but did not seem to reveal any new information. However, Ridzwan's mother admitted that the maternal grandmother had been sexually abused and raped by the maternal grandfather. The mother herself had also been raped and had run away (subsequently being placed in a hostel).

After interviewing each of the family members in turn regarding these issues, the wall of denial and secrecy began to break down. In the course of continued probing of Ridzwan's mother, it was revealed that Ridzwan had seen what was probably pornography during a time when he was with his elder sister and had seen sexually inappropriate behaviour between his elder sister and her boyfriend. Then, he admitted that he had seen violent and sexual uncensored CD Roms played by the elder sister (who was aged 21). It was further revealed that the elder sister in question was now in a Drug Rehabilitation Centre for stealing and drugs. The family was stricken with sadness when they realised the possible causes of Ridzwan's sexual misbehaviour, and when they reflected on all the painful truths which had been revealed in the course of the FC. They recognised that they were in need of professional help to deal with their family predicaments.

Unlike the reports from earlier psychiatric assessments in which Ridzwan showed no remorse for his misdeeds, after a confrontation with the members of his entire extended family, he broke down in tears. The impact of the court environment, and the gravity of the setting created a "transformative moment" for all parties.[37] His mother expressed great disappointment with his behaviour but said that she was prepared to forgive him. She reassured him that he was still loved by the family. The stepfather nodded in agreement. Ridzwan was very touched and he apologised to them for his perverse actions. He was in tears. He reached out to hold his parents' hands, performing the traditional Malay *salam* (a form of showing respect to an elder by kissing his hand), asking for their forgiveness. They readily accepted his apology. At this point, there was a great relief by his family, and a resolution on the family's part to participate in his future rehabilitation.

For purposes of protection for the public and to further his rehabilitation, and due to the severity of the offences committed by Ridzwan, he was sent to the Singapore Boys' Home (SBH) for three years. His treatment plan included PAST[38] (Positive Adolescent Sexuality Treatment programme — a group work programme run by MCDS psychologists for the rehabilitation of sexual offenders). The case worker at SBH was also tasked to work with the family to tackle issues. The family was recommended to go for psychological assessment and follow-up counselling to tackle the issues of coping with incest in the family, the parenting of Ridzwan's half siblings in the aftermath of the abuse they had suffered, and the future management of Ridzwan. This would help prepare the family for Ridzwan's integration back to the community after his stint in SBH.

It can be seen from this case study that the "new information" revealed during the FC was critical to Ridzwan's future restoration to his family and to the community. The reasons for his offences were revealed, and the ground was set for his rehabilitation and for counselling for the whole family.

Tackling Family Violence and Abuse

SIANG YAP, aged 14

Siang Yap was charged with participating in a gang assault at a shopping centre arcade. However, the FC was convened to deal with what seemed to be the very indifferent attitude of the boy's father towards his son, as well as apparent strains between the boy's mother and father, which might affect the question of whether Siang Yap could be returned for home-based probation.

As the FC began, Siang Yap's father appeared completely oblivious, even saying he had "no idea why he was in court" and "no idea that his son even had a problem." He even argued, "I don't even know what day today is." When pressed, the father finally admitted that he was a part-time lorry driver and had no excuse for his lack of involvement in his son's life.

Interviewed during the FC, without the father present, the boy and mother revealed a different version of life at home. Siang Yap said that he had often "run away" due to his father's violence. The boy said he had been hit by his father and when his mother tried to intervene, she had been hit as well. The mother wept throughout the FC and when confronted with the testimony of a counsellor, Ms Chu, from a local family service centre, she admitted that she had been concerned about issues such as maintenance, physical abuse, and even possible sexual abuse by her husband of Mei Li, her 13-year-old daughter. This was new information. The allegations of potential sexual abuse of the daughter were then explored. The mother suspected the father was "running his hands over the girl's body whilst she was asleep" and had said that she had "seen this in the dark." She was advised how to deal with future suspected molestation. She admitted that the father, in his rages, had hit all the children.

The counsellor, Ms Chu, and the court social worker were instructed to further assist Siang Yap's mother in the possible filing of a personal protection order (PPO) against Siang Yap's father. Siang Yap himself was placed on 18 months split probation with residence in the Singapore Boys' Hostel, an environment away from his abusive father where his chances of being rehabilitated could be maximised.

Subsequently, Ms Chu and the court social worker assisted Siang Yap's mother in filing a court PPO application. PPOs were eventually granted against the father in favour of the mother, Siang Yap, his sister, and youngest brother. It was subsequently reported by the court social worker to the Juvenile Court that the mother felt "empowered" and "no longer helpless" over her predicament and felt capable of protecting her children after obtaining the PPOs.

It can be seen that the FC not only pointed the Court towards the most appropriate order to make in respect of Siang Yap, but it also resulted in the empowerment of the mother and the protection of all of Siang Yap's siblings through related court processes. In this sense, the FC was a holistic process, covering the entire family. Of special note is that even Siang Yap's sister, who was not present at the FC, is now protected from future sexual abuse.

Mending a Fractured Family

GOPAL, aged 15

Gopal came to the Court's attention after his mother lodged a Beyond Parental Control (BPC) complaint. According to the mother, Gopal's primary problems were violence and unruly behaviour against authority figures, including herself, running away from home and associating with bad company.

However, during investigations, the mother became inconsistent in her account. She downplayed her son's misbehaviours and wanted to have him on Statutory Supervision at home. She appeared defensive and insecure about her son's relationship with her in relation to her estranged abusive husband. An FC was called by the Magistrate to get to the bottom of the matter and explore what would be the most appropriate placement for Gopal's rehabilitation.

The mother came into the FC ready to defend her son and she continued to maintain that her son had merely shoved her and not beaten her unlike what she had initially claimed in her BPC complaint. Gopal's father, who had been in contact with Gopal, was also present. Both parents were verbally abusive towards each other, blaming each other for the plight of their son. Each wanted to look good.

As the FC went on, it was revealed that a Personal Protection Order was issued for the mother against the father years ago. They had a tumultuous and abusive relationship. The father abused alcohol. The police were often involved in settling their disputes. The parents also revealed that they were divorced recently. A decree nisi had been granted but they were still in the process of contesting the ancillary matters (i.e. custody of the children, maintenance and matrimonial property). Interim custody of Gopal was granted to the mother with access to the father. They had a mediation session in the Family Court but failed to settle the ancillary matters proceedings.

All these were revealed when Gopal was sent out of the room to reflect on his behaviour. The parents had raised their voices at each other all this time. However they were promptly confronted by the

FC facilitator with the statement that they had been too pre-occupied with their own "adult" affairs at the expense of discussing Gopal's issues. They were reminded that the FC was not going to be another forum for them to continue their dispute. It was made clear that the FC was to discuss what would be in the best interest of their son and daughter. Their hostile behaviour in the Conference was given as a stark example of how selfish their pre-occupation with themselves was. They were asked to reflect on how their actions might have contributed to their current state of affairs. The parents then took a moment for this reflection. The mother broke into tears and the father softened his stand. Both apologised for their conduct. Both admitted that their continual conflict with each other and the anger/grief they each carried individually had been transferred to their children.

When Gopal was brought back into the room subsequently, they acknowledged their oversight to the FC and conveyed to the boy their regrets and their conviction to change to be better parents henceforth. They were also willing to put aside their differences for the sake of the children. They appeared highly affected by the divorce proceedings and wanted very much to settle their dispute over the ancillary matters in a manner that would not affect the children. They were willing to seek help separately to deal with their own emotions and issues so as to cope better. The boy was very emotional upon seeing his parents break down. He cried uncontrollably on the shoulder of his father. His mother gave him a huge hug and the re-assurance that she loved him very much. All their attitudes were completely transformed during the FC.

Gopal had been accustomed to using aggression to communicate and solve problems due to the circumstances in which he grew up. This was what he had learned from his parents' behaviour. His parents' admission of their own mistakes and their resolve to learn to become better people facilitated the rehabilitation process for Gopal. He accepted his parents' wish to have him stay in Boys' Town. Both parents felt it would be good to have him stay there while they took some time to settle their own issues. Gopal was recommended by the FC facilitator to be on 24 months statutory supervision in Boys' Town. As a result of the FC, both the juvenile and his parents had a new beginning in their relationship with each other, and found more constructive ways to resolve their issues with each other. The parents were ordered to go for counselling — the father, to treat his alcohol problem and tendency to use violence, and also to help him manage his anger; the mother to resolve any issues she might have arising from being a victim of spousal violence; and for both parties to resolve their relationship problems. Thus, in spite of the changed circumstances — the parents' divorce, Gopal's stay in Boys' Town — Gopal actually came to have a better relationship with his parents than before.

ENDNOTES

1 For more information on the Family and Juvenile Justice Centre, visit us at our websites: www.familycourtofsingapore.gov.sg and www.juvenilecourtofsingapore.gov.sg

2 I am indebted to the following members of the Family and Juvenile Justice Centre for assisting me in the research for this chapter: Annie Lee (Senior Assistant Director), Lynette Stephens (Senior Psychologist), Han Li June (Senior Psychologist), Ronald Lim (Senior Counsellor), Goh Soo Cheng (Social Worker), and Elaine Teong (Psychologist).

3 Feinblatt, J. & Berman, G. (1999). Informed Decisions: Technology in the Courtroom, Center for Court Innovation, New York State Unified Court System, p. 2.

4 Blackburn, R. (1993). *The Psychology of Criminal Conduct*, (p. 309). Chichester: John Wiley & Sons.

5 Connolly, K. & McKellar, P. (1963). Forensic Psychology. *Bulletin of the British Psychological Society*, *16*, 16-24.

6 Bartol, C.R. & Bartol, A.M. (1987). History of Forensic Psychology. In I.B. Weiner and A.K. Hess (eds.), *Handbook of Forensic Psychology*. New York: Wiley.

7 Committee on Ethnical Guidelines for Forensic Psychologists. (1991). Specialty Guidelines for Forensic Psychologists. *Law and Human Behavior*, *15*, 655-65.

8 Yong Pung How, Chief Justice of Singapore, International Youth Justice Conference 2000, 13 September 2000.

9 Babb, B.A. & Moran, J.D. (1999). Substance Abuse, Families, and Unified Family Courts: The Creation of a Caring Justice System, *Journal of Health Care Law and Policy*, *3(1)*, 1-43.

10 See *id.* at 14-15.

11 A term coined by the author, Dr. Joseph Paul Ozawa, to describe such moments of opportunity where the positive psychological transformation of individuals is made possible due to the sudden confluence of events brought about by Court appearances.

12 Family Conferences are described later in this chapter, but essentially are enshrined in the Children and Young Persons Act (CYPA) of Singapore. For more information on FCs, see Chapter 1 on The Juvenile Court of Singapore at pages 20-22.

13 Cooley, D. (1999). From Restorative Justice to Transformative Justice: Discussion Paper, Law Commission of Canada, Catalogue No. JL 2-6. Canada. Ron Classen of the Center for Peacemaking and Conflict Studies in Fresno (1996) has similarly stated that "Crime is primarily an offence against human relationships and secondarily a violation of a law (since laws are written to protect safety and fairness in human relationships)." (Claasen, 1996). Thus crime is a legal issue. However, that legal issue is rooted in jurisprudence designed to deal with human and relational offences.

14 The Center for Restorative Justice and Mediation in "Restorative Justice for Victims, Communities and Offenders," University of Minnesota, St. Paul, Minnesota, 1996, states, "Restorative justice emphasizes the ways in which crime hurts relationships between people who live in a community. Crime is seen as something done against a victim and the community and not simply as a violation against the state."

15 Ury, W.L. (1999). *The Third Side: Why We Fight and How We Can Stop*, New York: Penguin Books.

16 See endnote 15 above.

17 The "Gestalt" school of thought in psychology postulates that there are moments, when, as a result of sudden revelations, an individual comes to a sudden understanding about a situation. It is as if the pieces of a puzzle have come together for him, and he sees the big picture. Corey, G. (1996). *Theory and Practice of Counselling and Psychotherapy*. 5th ed. CA: Brooks and Cole.

18 See endnote 12.

19 Braithwaite. (1989). *Crime, Shame and Reintegration*, United Kingdom: Cambridge University Press.

20 Persons who have Munchausen syndrome deliberately exaggerate and/or fabricate and/or induce physical and/or psychological-behavioural problems in themselves. The primary purpose of this behaviour is to gain some form of internal gratification, such as attention, for themselves. Munchausen syndrome by proxy is the causing of physical or psychological illness in another person, generally a child, in order to gain attention.

21 For more information on JOB Criteria, see Chapter 1 on The Juvenile Court of Singapore at page 8.

22 Moffitt, T.E. (1993). Adolescence-limited and Life-course-persistent Antisocial Behaviour: A Developmental Taxonomy. *Psychological Review, 100 (4)*, 674–701.

Motiuk, L.L. (2000). Classification and Recidivism: Canadian Experience and Other Countries. Presented during the International Conference on Youth Justice 2000: Managing a New World in Transit, Singapore.

Nagin, D.S., Farrington, T.P. & Moffitt, T.E. (1995). Life-course Trajectories of Different Types of Offenders. *Criminology, 33 (1)*, 111–39.

Grisso, T. & Scott, E.S. (1997). Symposium on the Future of the Juvenile Court: The Evolution of Adolescence: A Developmental Perspective on Juvenile Justice Reform. *Journal of Law and Criminology*.

23 Singapore Department of Statistics. (September 2000). *Statistics on Marriages & Divorces, 1999.*

24 Clark, R., *Crime in America.*

25 Bureau of Justice Statistics, 1998, *L.A.Times.*

26 Sampson, R.J. (1987) *Crime in Cities.*

27 Blum, K., & Payne, J.E. (1991). *Alcohol and the Addictive Brain.* New York: Tree Press; Erickson, M.T. (1998). *Behaviour Disorders of Children and Adolescents.* 3rd ed. New Jersey: Prentice Hall; Kashani, J.H. & Allan, W.D. (1998). *The Impact of Family Violence on Children and Adolescents.* California: Sage Publications, Inc.

28 Subordinate Courts. (December 2000). Alcohol or Drug Abuse: Relationship to Domestic Violence. Research Bulletin Issue No. 25.

29 The YFC Programme may be expanded to include juveniles under Approved School/Home orders. For information on probation, statutory supervision, and Approved School/Home orders, see Chapter 1, The Juvenile Court of Singapore, pages 11, 25 and 17 respectively.

30 For information on Beyond Parental Control cases, see Chapter 1 The Juvenile Court of Singapore, page 23.

31 See endnotes 23-25 for details of the relevant research.

32 Subordinate Courts. (April 2001). Study of the Rippling Effects of the Peer Advisers Programme. Research Bulletin Issue No. 27.

33 A non-governmental organisation of young professionals doing youth outreach work.

34 See endnotes 27 and 28 for details of the relevant research.

35 Some of the publications listed here were published before the FJJC was formed, by members of the then Psychological Services Unit (formed in the year 2000) and Family Conciliation and Resolution Centre (formed in 1996). These two units were subsequently merged to form the FJJC in the year 2002.

36 The illustrations in this section are based upon the FC facilitators' notes and personal recollections from actual cases. However, the names, specific details and identifying characteristics of all parties in the illustrations have been changed or modified to protect the identities of the juveniles and their families. The key interactions, dialogues and accounts of the emotional dynamics of the FCs featured in these illustrations have, however, been retained.

37 See pages 49-51 for more details on what constitutes a "transformative moment" in court — it is a time when the gravity of the situation, the court environment, and the mandatory gathering of families often leads to emotionally charged, honest responses, which pave the way to a restoration of relationships between those present.

38 Refer Chapter 5, Section 5.11 at page 223, The Residential Rehabilitation Branch for more details on the PAST programme.

ANNEX
UPDATED STATISTICS ON FAMILY CONFERENCING

Family Conferencing	No. Conducted	No. of Juveniles Breached[1] (As at end-Dec 2002)	No. Re-offended[2] (As at end-Dec 2002)	% Breached	% Re-offended
Jul – Dec 1994	7	2	0	28.6%	0.0%
1995	47	7	3	14.9%	6.4%
1996	34	7	4	20.6%	11.8%
1997	30	2	1	6.7%	3.3%
1998	19	6	0	31.6%	0.0%
1999	7	3	1	42.9%	14.3%
2000	17	4	1	23.5%	5.9%
2001[3]	68	13	0	19.1%	0.0%
2002	69	2	1	2.9%	2.2%
Total (Jul 1994 – Dec 2002)	**298**	**46**	**11**	**15.4%**	**4.0%**

Notes:

1 "No. of juveniles breached" refers to the juveniles for Juvenile Arrest Cases (JAC) and Beyond Parental Control (BPC) cases who breached the conditions stated in the given orders.

2 "No. of juveniles re-offended" refers to the juveniles who have been charged as a Juvenile Arrest Case (JAC) and who committed a further offence before the expiry of the order.

3 Figures revised as at January 2003.

CHAPTER 3

Case Law and Case Studies

3.1 Offences Committed by Juveniles

The offences committed by juveniles are many and varied. Drug possession and consumption, assault, molest, theft, shoplifting, joy-riding, and even computer hacking, are some of the offences committed by juveniles which are set out in this section.

The following case studies provide an insight into the considerations taken into account by the Court before an order is made. Information and input from many sources are sought — from schools, employers, parents, relatives, court psychologists and probation officers. The whole life of the juvenile is thoroughly examined and analysed. His family circumstances are scrutinised. All these factors play a part in the Court's decision on what orders to make in respect of the juvenile.

The case studies also illustrate how, through the creative use of sentencing options, the Court strives to ensure that the juvenile is given the best opportunity for rehabilitation and restoration into society.

Offences Committed by Juveniles

DISTRICT JUDGE MARK TAY and
MAGISTRATE MAY LUCIA MESENAS

What Happens When a Juvenile is Charged and Found Guilty

In every case, after the juvenile is charged in Court with the offence that he is accused of committing, and he is found guilty, the juvenile's parents will be asked to mitigate on his behalf. The juvenile himself will be asked if he has anything to say about the offence, in order for the Court to gauge his level of remorse. The Court will ask the juvenile's parents questions to determine the relationship between the juvenile and his parents, and their level of supervision of the juvenile's activities.

The case will then be adjourned for a Probation Report which is prepared by the Probation Services Branch of the Ministry of Community Development and Sports (MCDS). The Probation Officer will interview the juvenile's parents and the significant persons in his life. He will get reports from the juvenile's schools, and interview his teachers and his discipline master, and other relevant personnel. He will also interview counsellors, social workers and any other relevant people who may have been in contact with the juvenile in the past. The Probation Officer will detail the juvenile's past behaviour, educational achievements, activities and family background in the report. The report will also give details on the juvenile's friends, gang memberships, and any negative habits such as drinking, smoking, late nights, etc. The juvenile's behaviour and relationship with his family since he was charged in Court will also be closely examined. The Psychological Services Unit of the MCDS will sometimes be requested by the Probation Officer to make a psychological assessment of the juvenile. This will usually be done in cases where the juvenile appears to have mental problems, is very aggressive, or has committed sexual offences. After the Probation Report is prepared, a copy will be sent to the Family and Juvenile Justice Centre (FJJC) which will then prepare the JOB Criteria Risk Score[1] for the case.

The Juvenile Court Magistrate will then deliberate on the case in chambers together with the Panel of Advisers, the officer of the Family and Juvenile Justice Centre who prepared the JOB Criteria Risk Score, and the Probation Officer who prepared the report. Occasionally, a representative from the juvenile's school will attend the chamber discussion. The purpose of the chamber discussion is to decide on the most appropriate orders to make for the rehabilitation of the juvenile, and to decide what plan of action would be in the juvenile's best interests. The needs of the juvenile's family will also be discussed and addressed, if necessary.

After the chamber discussion, the Juvenile Court Magistrate will then go into open court. The juvenile and his parents or caregiver will be asked if they have any comments on the Probation Report, and in particular, the views they have regarding its recommendations. Once the Magistrate has heard from the juvenile and his parents or caregiver, he or she will then make the appropriate orders.

Psychiatric reports from the Child Guidance Clinic are sometimes ordered by the Court for particularly serious sexual offences, or where the juvenile appears to have marked psychiatric problems.

Case Studies

The following are case studies of juveniles who have been charged with offences in the Juvenile Court, been found guilty, and had orders made against them. The cases are divided according to the type of offences committed.

Assault

Voluntarily causing hurt to a public servant in the discharge of her duty — Section 332 of the Penal Code (Cap. 224)

PP v. M (JAC 528/98)

Facts:

The juvenile, *M*, was a 15-year-old secondary school student. The victim was his female form teacher. Sometime in April 1998, *M* was asked by his teacher, *J*, to hand in his assignment, whereupon he tossed his book on the latter's table. His teacher told him to take his book back and hand it up in a more disciplined manner. The juvenile again tossed it on the table which resulted in the teacher referring him to the principal who suspended him. In anger, *M* returned to the classroom to retrieve his belongings and to confront his teacher. In the course of the confrontation, *M* swung his bag at *J* but the latter managed to block it with her left forearm. However, *M* managed to slap his teacher with his left hand on her right cheek. All these events unfolded in the full view of *M*'s classmates.

The matter was referred to the principal and a police report was made. The boy was subsequently expelled and charged in the Juvenile Court for an offence of voluntarily causing hurt to a public servant (the teacher) who was performing her duty, an offence under Section 332 of the Penal Code. The juvenile pleaded guilty to the charge.

Background of juvenile:

The juvenile is the only child of two working parents. The father was noted to be little involved in his son's life, although concerned about his son's education. His mother was assessed by the Probation Officer to have a permissive parenting style.

Education:

The reports from the juvenile's primary school revealed a boy who was average in his studies and regular in attendance. The juvenile was originally in the Express stream of his secondary school but was subsequently channelled to the Normal stream before his expulsion following the assault on his teacher.

Conduct:

The juvenile was noted by the Probation Officer to be hot-tempered, disruptive and rude. He had a long and varied list of misbehaviour which encompassed truancy, cigarette possession, smoking, consumption of alcohol, and aggressive behaviour towards fellow students and teachers. Among the more noteable instances of his aggressive behaviour included assaulting a classmate, throwing a chair on the ground in front of his form teacher, and challenging his principal to expel him.

Psychological assessment:

The psychological assessment done by MCDS opined that the juvenile did not appear to show real empathy for his victim. Although he was aware of the consequences of his behaviour, he tended to rationalise his actions by finding excuses. It was recommended that the juvenile be placed in a highly structured environment which could provide him with adequate supervision and monitoring. He would also be required to undergo anger management courses in order to learn the appropriate coping skills to counter his aggressive traits.

Recommendation by Probation Services Branch:
Probation was not recommended in view of poor parental supervision, unsatisfactory conduct in his secondary school, his previously unregulated lifestyle and the lack of remorse on the part of the juvenile.

DPP's address on Court disposition:
The Prosecution urged the Court to take a very serious view of the offence and highlighted the following factors:

1) The assault was committed wholly without provocation from the victim;
2) There were two distinct acts of assault, i.e. swinging the bag at the victim and slapping the victim;
3) The juvenile had by his actions severely undermined the authority of the victim as a teacher entrusted with the responsibility of educating her students. There was a strong public interest to ensure that such acts of defiance and violence by students against their teachers would not be condoned by the justice system;
4) Such defiance and aggression levelled at a teacher in full view of the other students during a lesson, undermined the authority reposed in the victim teacher who had to return to the classroom to educate the students after the offence.

The Prosecution submitted that the juvenile was unsuitable for community-based rehabilitation, i.e. probation, and that it would be more appropriate for the juvenile to be committed to a closely-supervised institution where a strict regime is enforced.

Order of Court:
After considering all the factors set out above, the Juvenile Court made an order for the juvenile to reside in an Approved School, the Singapore Boys' Home, for 30 months.

Causing Hurt

Causing Grievous Hurt — Section 324 of the Penal Code (Cap. 224)

PP v. O (JAC 1269-70/2000)

Facts:
This case had captivated the media and public attention for almost six months because of the horrifying acts of depraved torture meted out by a group of teenagers, the youngest being 11 years old (the juvenile featured in this case study) and the oldest being 18 years old, against a 14-year-old female victim. For about 17 days, the schoolgirl victim was held captive in an apartment and tortured repeatedly by seven teenagers. They tortured her by punching, kicking and hitting her repeatedly with an iron rod, wooden stick and books, and scalding her with boiling water. There were also several atrocious acts by the teenagers of forcing the victim to perform an obscene act on a dog as well as forcing her to insert objects into her private parts. The 11-year-old juvenile pleaded guilty to two charges of hitting the victim with books and poles. The victim was hospitalised for 34 days after her ordeal and was badly scarred, both physically and emotionally.

Background of juvenile:
The juvenile came from a dysfunctional family where there was little parental supervision. The father, an odd-job worker, had several brushes with the law which resulted in his incarceration at various penal institutions, including the 17 days where the young victim was confined and tortured. He was almost completely uninvolved as a caregiver for his children. There was evidence that the father took the juvenile with him when he was peddling illegal VCDs. He claimed that this was

necessary as there was no one at home to look after her. The mother was at the material time a waitress at a karaoke lounge and had to work from 6 p.m. to 3 a.m. This resulted in a total absence of any supervision at home. The juvenile had three older sisters aged 15, 17 and 18 at the time of the offence. These siblings were also involved in the torture of the teen victim and received prison sentences ranging from two to six years. The family seldom spent any time together.

Education:
The juvenile was a Primary 5 student at the time of the offence. She was actually reported to have a positive attitude towards school and at one stage put in a lot of effort to become the top pupil in her class. There had been no disciplinary actions taken against the juvenile in the past and she was well-liked by her teachers.

Psychological assessment:
The psychologist from MCDS opined that the juvenile's violent tendencies as manifested in the current offences could stem from the anti-social socialisation that she received from her family. The family was assessed to be highly dysfunctional and was characterised by a chronic history of criminal conduct, parental violence and neglect. There was also a total lack of appropriate parental supervision and control. As the juvenile was cared for by her older siblings who in turn possessed anti-social traits and kept bad company, the situation was aggravated, resulting in the juvenile possibly modelling her sisters' aggressive and violent tendencies. The absence of positive socialisation from her caregivers resulted in the juvenile's acceptance of delinquent mores and the normalisation of such violent acts.

In view of the poor parenting practices and the highly dysfunctional parental background, the psychologist recommended that the juvenile be placed in a structured and secure environment where she could be closely supervised. She should also undergo individual therapy for her violent behaviour, to teach her empathy and moral reasoning. Family therapy which would address the juvenile's parents' anti-social behaviour and parenting practices was also recommended.

Recommendation by Probation Services Branch:
This was a highly dysfunctional family where the father had minimal involvement in caregiving functions. His negative background also made him an extremely poor role model. The mother, being saddled with the onerous caregiving responsibility for four children, exacerbated the problem by adopting a lax and passive attitude towards the company kept by her children and the activities they indulged in. This was most clearly demonstrated during the 17 days of the victim's confinement and torture.

In view of this, probation was not recommended.

Special considerations:
The nature of the offences was extremely disturbing as was the highly dysfunctional family and the high risk of negative exposure in the household. The mother's glaring passivity and apparent acquiescence of the entire episode of torture was of pivotal concern. The total abdication of parental authority and the highly dysfunctional family background appeared to be the underlying causes of the juvenile and her sisters' offences.

Order of Court:
The Court made an order for the juvenile to undergo rehabilitation in an Approved School regime, the Toa Payoh Girls' Home, for the maximum period of three years. The Court urged the juvenile's parents to attend family therapy sessions, as recommended by the MCDS psychologist, which would be co-ordinated by the juvenile's assigned case worker from the Toa Payoh Girls' Home.

Voluntarily causing hurt to maid — Outraging modesty of maid — Section 323, Section 354 read with Section 73 of the Penal Code (Cap. 224)

PP v. L (JAC 1489-95/2000)

Facts:
Sometime in September 1999, a 15-year-old teenager assaulted his maid with a belt, chair, drumstick and his fist, on her shoulder, nose and ear. He also molested the maid by biting her breast on one occasion. He pleaded guilty to three charges and consented to the remaining four charges being taken into consideration. Most of the assaults were committed when he was 13 years old and precipitated by seemingly minor incidents wherein the maid was perceived by him as not doing her duties properly. In the molest incident, the juvenile bit the maid's breast after pouncing on her while she lay sleeping in the flat's storeroom. After the molest incident, he returned to his room and resumed playing his computer games.

Background of juvenile:
The juvenile is the youngest in the family of three brothers. The parents were divorced and all the children resided with their working mother. There was no contact with the father. The juvenile shared a close personal relationship with his mother. He did not share a close relationship with his brothers as they always teased and bullied him. The juvenile and his brothers spent most of their leisure time playing computer games. The juvenile usually spent three to four hours per day playing these games, some of which had violent content.

The mother employed the maid as she was very busy with her work and often worked extended hours. According to the mother, the maid was often unable to perform her chores satisfactorily. She felt that the maid agency was responsible for this state of affairs as the maid, by reason of her very young age, could not competently perform her duties, and had to pester the juvenile for help. The mother believed that the offences were committed by the juvenile in retaliation for being pestered by the maid.

The Probation Officer found the juvenile's relationship with the maid victim difficult to comprehend. On the one hand, he claimed that he treated her as a younger sister as he sympathised with her background. He taught her simple English, simple cooking and how to operate electrical appliances. On the other hand, he found her to be intrusive and irritating, with poor personal hygiene. He described how he found her irritating in several instances such as when she walked into his room when he was playing computer games, tapped his shoulders when she wanted to communicate and left his schoolbag in the storeroom. He commented that he would rather play computer games than talk to her.

The juvenile admitted that he had a problem with anger management. He attributed this to being a victim of bullying at school and at home (by his second brother). He viewed the maid as a weak person and saw her as an avenue to vent his frustrations. His mother was shocked that her son was capable of the aggressive behaviour detailed in the charges as she considered all her children "good boys" who spent most of their time at home.

Education:

The juvenile was a Secondary 2 student in the Normal (Academic) stream. He had been retained previously. Feedback from the primary school revealed that his overall conduct was good though he was noted to be disinterested in his studies. In secondary school for the current year, he was absent for 35 days without valid reason. He was also involved in two cases of fighting. His conduct was rated as fair. He was assessed to be a mischievous teenager who lacked supervision and guidance at home. However, his form teacher did not feel that he was rebellious or malicious. His academic performance was poor. The mother was assessed to be co-operative and concerned but was not in a position to exert effective control. This was partly due to her long working hours. The juvenile and his brothers were often left unsupervised at home.

Psychological assessment:

The juvenile was assessed to be a socially and emotionally immature boy who appeared to lack insight and remorse for his offending behaviour. In his largely unsupervised home environment, he started indulging in computer games at a very early age. This was his main after-school activity. The juvenile appeared to have social interaction difficulties. It was noted that some of the assault incidents appeared to be the consequences of frustration and intolerance at being interrupted from his computer gaming. On other occasions, he appeared to have no clear motives for assaulting the maid. One plausible reason for his aggressive behaviour could stem from his derogatory perception of the maid. Other contributing factors could include his underlying anger at being bullied in school and by his second brother at home. The mother appeared to be a largely absent parent who provided little supervision of the juvenile when she did return home.

The psychologist recommended that the juvenile would benefit from residing in a structured and supervised environment. He should also be involved in activities that would improve his social interaction skills. He should play fewer computer games and attend counselling, to learn emotional management skills and empathy. The mother should be taught stress management and more effective parenting skills.

Recommendation by Probation Services Branch:
The Probation Officer also noted that the juvenile came from a family where there was little supervision and attention given to him. His mother worked long hours in fulfilling the role of sole breadwinner. His older brothers led independent lives and had little time to act as positive role models for the juvenile. There was a need to strengthen the family relationship. The mother appeared ready to make concerted efforts to play an active part in providing encouragement and guidance. There was little motivation for the juvenile to perform academically as he always felt out-classed by his brothers, and this difficulty was compounded by his addiction to computer games. This led to the undesirable but inevitable consequence of his being manifestly under-socialised.

The key areas which needed to be addressed in the juvenile's rehabilitation plan included: the need to inculcate moral feelings of empathy and sympathy for others in him, to stop him from indulging in self-pity, to raise his self-esteem, to help him manage his anger, and to strengthen his family relationships.

In the circumstances, a Probation Order coupled with a stay in a hostel setting was considered to be beneficial for the juvenile, and enable him to pick up the proper social and moral values. This would also enable the family to work on issues of discipline and care.

Special considerations:
During the court proceedings, the juvenile attributed his offences to the violent computer games that he indulged in. Although this cannot be scientifically proved or disproved, the juvenile did appear to be dwelling within his own cyberworld, where he escaped from reality. Each time he assaulted the maid, he would resume his computer games as though nothing had happened.

Order of Court:
The Juvenile Court made a split probation order for 36 months, of which the first 12 months was intensive probation, followed by 24 months of supervised probation. The additional conditions of the split probation included the following:

1) to abide by a time restriction from 10 p.m. to 6 a.m.;
2) to reside in an Approved Institution, the Singapore Boys' Hostel, for a period of 12 months;
3) to perform 240 hours of community service in accordance with the proposed community programme;
4) to attend a prison visit arranged by the Court;
5) to continue psychological treatment with the Psychological Services Unit of the Ministry of Community Development (as it then was);
6) for the mother to be bonded for $10,000 to exercise proper care and guardianship of the juvenile;
7) for the mother to attend 80 hours of counselling for a period of 12 months;
8) for the mother to contribute $200 monthly for the juvenile's upkeep during his stay at the Singapore Boys' Hostel;
9) quarterly case reviews.

In the implementation of the Probation Order, the plan of action proposed by the Probation Officer was adopted. This included the following:

1) to attend group therapy to learn anger management, social and therapy skills;
2) to arrange for the mother to attend counselling courses to learn effective child and adolescent management skills;
3) to closely monitor the juvenile's stay in the hostel environment;
4) to assign him to appropriate agencies to perform his community services;
5) to attach a male Volunteer Probation Officer to him upon his discharge from the hostel.

Computer Hacking

Offences under the Computer Misuse Act (Cap. 50A)

PP v. K (JAC 207-16/2000)

Facts:
Sometime in September 1999, a 15-year-old teenager hacked into the intranet server of Sparksmedia Pte. Ltd., and a Pacific Internet server. Using internet tools, which he downloaded from the Internet, he made a list of directories and file names he found in the Pacific Internet server, and created an account for himself in the Sparksmedia's system. The juvenile pleaded guilty to three charges under the Computer Misuse Act (Cap. 50A) and consented for seven similar charges to be taken into consideration.

Background of juvenile:
The juvenile comes from a complete and closely knit family. Both parents were concerned about their children and rarely left them alone without adult supervision. The family members had meals and spent time together in the evenings. The juvenile was respectful and obedient and had never given his parents cause for worry in his conduct

or in education matters. He was mild-mannered, very accommodating and helpful to family and friends alike. He had designed a website for his father's company. He did not indulge in any undesirable activities nor keep any late nights.

Education:
The juvenile was an exemplary student in both his primary and secondary schools. His excellent grades in the PSLE exams resulted in him being channelled to a top secondary school. At the time of the offence, he was in Secondary 4 and sitting for his GCE "O" levels. He had no disciplinary problems and was noted to have a keen interest in computer and basketball. He built his own computers and designed web pages. According to the school reports, he was regarded as a motivated student leader who often helped others in their schoolwork. He was a member of the school team which emerged victorious in a recent computer competition.

Recommendation by Probation Services Branch:
The juvenile's family and school feedback attested to his exemplary conduct and excellent academic record. The offences appeared to have been committed as a result of impulsive curiosity rather than premeditation.

Since becoming aware of the offences, the juvenile's parents limited his access to the computer and checked on him regularly when he was on-line. They had lengthy discussions with the juvenile to express their disappointment over his commission of the offences with a view to making him appreciate the full ramifications of his actions. They also emphasised to him the need to steer away from all sorts of wrongdoing and had been very supportive in helping to steer him through this difficult period.

With his permission, the juvenile's classmates were informed that he was the one found guilty of the hacking offences which had been highlighted in media reports. This was his way of facing up to the consequences of the offence and to allow himself to be used as an example to deter others from following a similar course. His classmates had rallied around him with positive moral support.

The arrest and court proceedings left a deep impact on the juvenile and his family which resulted in him being determined to steer away from future wrongdoings and to make amends for his offences. His public confession to his classmates was a manifestation of his sincere repentance.

In view of this very positive attitude and determination, sterling parental support and guidance, positive school affiliation and his undoubted adeptness in handling computers, it was considered that the juvenile could be steered towards channelling his remarkable abilities to constructive causes which could benefit the entire community.

Special considerations:
In passing an order for probation with community service, the Juvenile Court distinguished this case from the precedent set by the Honourable Chief Justice Yong Pung How in ***Public Prosecutor v. Muhammad Nuzaihin bin Kamal Luddin*** *[2000] 1 SLR 34*. In that case, the Chief Justice ruled that probation was inappropriate for hacking offences as keeping the offender indoors did not ensure that such offences would not be repeated. Furthermore, the seriousness of cyber-crimes warranted a period of imprisonment to deter would-be offenders.

In meting out a Probation Order with 200 hours of community service, the Juvenile Court distinguished the instant case from the earlier precedent as it was premised on the rehabilitation and restoration of the juvenile. In the earlier case, the defendant was an adult. Different sentencing principles applied. Rehabilitation and restoration are the guiding principles in making the appropriate orders for a juvenile offender, but not in sentencing an adult offender.

The Court noted that the juvenile's conduct in school had been exemplary and his post-offence conduct, especially that of channelling his talents to constructive outcomes, were commendable. The Court emphasised that the Probation Order should not be perceived by the offender, the victim and the members of the public as a "let-off" for his offences as the imposition of a Probation Order was an individualised measure with rehabilitation as a paramount objective. The juvenile would also be closely monitored through quarterly reviews during the tenure of the comprehensive split Probation Order. In the event of any breach of the terms of probation or if his progress became unsatisfactory, the Probation Order could be varied or probation could be revoked altogether, and he could be ordered to undergo a stricter regime in an Approved School like the Singapore Boys' Home.

Order of Court:
The Juvenile Court made a split probation order for 18 months, of which the first three months was intensive probation, followed by 15 months of supervised probation. The additional conditions of the split probation included the following:

1) to abide by a time restriction from 10 p.m. to 6 a.m.;
2) to perform 200 hours of community service in accordance with the proposed community programme;
3) to attend a prison visit arranged by the Court;
4) for his parents to be bonded for $5,000 to exercise proper care and guardianship of the juvenile;
5) for a case review in three months.

In the implementation of the Probation Order, the plan of action proposed by the probation officer was adopted. This included the following:

1) to engage him in developing programmes to aid continuous learning by the elderly and people with disabilities;
2) to develop web-pages for parents of other probationers to raise awareness of ways to supervise youths so as to prevent them from committing cyber-crimes;
3) to conduct sharing sessions with probationers on IT uses and abuses and the consequences of "hacking".

Driving Offences

Driving without a licence — Section 62(5) Road Traffic Act, Cap. 276); Driving without insurance coverage — Section 3(1) Motor Vehicle Third Party Risk and Compensation Act, Cap. 189); and Careless driving — Rule 29 Road Traffic Rules.

PP v. A (TP 336/98)

Facts:
Sometime in April 1998, the 15-year-old juvenile managed to obtain the keys to a motor van when his work colleague left it on a coffee-shop table whilst going to the restroom. On the instigation of a friend, he drove the motor van without thinking about the consequences. He claimed that he wanted to experience the joy of driving. Whilst driving, he collided into another parked car. No one was injured although there was substantial damage to the vehicles. The juvenile pleaded guilty to three charges, namely, driving whilst under 16 years of age (Section 62(5) Road Traffic Act, Cap. 276), driving without insurance coverage (Section 3(1) Motor Vehicle Third Party Risk and Compensation Act, Cap. 189) and careless driving (Rule 29 Road Traffic Rules).

Background of juvenile:
The juvenile comes from a very unfortunate background. The father was in his late 50s and unemployed. His mother left the family sometime in 1994 and did not maintain contact with her children. Like his three other siblings, the juvenile was educationally sub-normal. His father was depressive and unable to offer any care to the children. Voluntary welfare organisations provided financial and other assistance to this family.

Education:
The juvenile attended a special school since 1992 as he was found to be functioning slower than those in his age group. He often played truant to join the neighbourhood youths in loitering at the void decks, often getting into trouble.

Employment:
At the time of the offence, the juvenile worked for a supplier of roasted meat who offered him the job after taking pity on him. Not only did his employer offer him a job at the roasted meat factory but also provided him accommodation at the factory premises. The employer even ensured that the juvenile went home weekly to visit his father and set aside a portion of his salary for the father.

Psychological assessment:
The psychologist noted that there was minimal and ineffective supervision from the single parent. The family was observed to have a history of mental deficiency. This factor would increase the juvenile's susceptibility to negative influences. The employer's provision of employment, accommodation and supervision to the juvenile were assessed to be positive factors in his rehabilitation. It was recommended that the juvenile's working and living arrangements be maintained as he responded positively to his boss.

Recommendation by Probation Services Branch:
Probation was not recommended. However the Court was urged to consider alternative options to the institutionalisation of the juvenile, because of certain special considerations (see below).

Special considerations:
The employer shared a close relationship with the juvenile. He was present during the juvenile's Court hearings and several interviews, before the Court made its final orders, at the Ministry of Community Development (as it then was). For all intents and purposes, the employer provided the juvenile with constructive employment and foster care. The employer was commended by the judge for having taken such a keen interest in the boy's welfare and upbringing despite the absence of any blood ties. It appeared to the Court that his employer could be counted upon to supervise the juvenile responsibly.

Order of Court:
The Court made an order granting the juvenile a Conditional Discharge for nine months.

Drugs

Possession and Consumption — Sections 8(a) and (b) of the Misuse of Drugs Act (Cap. 185)

PP v. W (JAC 1520-1526/2001)

Facts:
Sometime in November 2001, the 15-year-old juvenile was arrested at the void deck of a HDB flat where she was spotted by police and found with blood-shot eyes and a runny nose. Suspecting that the juvenile may have consumed drugs, the police arrested her and subjected her to a urine test which was subsequently found to be positive for drugs.

The juvenile pleaded guilty to four counts of drug-related offences (possession as well as consumption of drugs) including consumption and possession of controlled drugs, namely, Ketamine. The remaining three charges for drug-related offences and shoplifting were taken into consideration for the purposes of sentencing.

Background of juvenile:
The juvenile claimed that she started consuming Ketamine in May 2000 for fun and was first arrested in June 2000 for doing this. Despite the initial arrest, she continued to consume drugs as she was troubled by her family problems. Furthermore her peers were also consuming drugs and they would consume the drugs together. The juvenile was repeatedly arrested by the police for drug-related offences. Her history of drug abuse included the consumption of Ecstasy, followed by glue-sniffing before progressing to consuming Ketamine. In 1999, the juvenile had been arrested and given a stern warning by the police for theft of chocolates from a supermarket.

The juvenile is the only child in the family. Her parents were separated following the father's bankruptcy due to debts owed to creditors. As a result, her father sold their flat and moved to Indonesia to work. Both the juvenile and her mother had been living in rented flats ever since. In October 2001, the mother's boyfriend moved in to stay with the juvenile and her mother. Her relationship with her mother deteriorated since then as she could not get along with her mother's boyfriend.

Her mother had not been able to effectively supervise the juvenile. Caning, pinching and throwing things at the juvenile had not been effective means of disciplining her. Her father on the other hand doted on her and had never laid a hand on her.

Education:
Reports from her school revealed that she played truant and was not interested in her studies.

Employment:
The juvenile worked for a few months in 2001 as a games controller in East Coast Park but stopped since the company no longer required her services.

Conduct:
The juvenile kept late nights and only came back home at midnight. Or else, she would stay overnight at McDonald's, void decks or at friends' houses where she would be with her friends, chatting or playing cards. At the time of the interview for the Probation Report, the juvenile claimed that she had lost contact with her friends from a secret society. The Probation Officer could not establish whether this was true or not. However, two weeks prior to the juvenile's appearance in court, she stayed away from home after her mother's boyfriend chased her out of the house. Her mother was unaware of her whereabouts. She stayed with a friend during this period of time and managed to survive on only $50. It seemed unlikely that she would not have contacted her gang friends during this time.

She had been smoking (ten sticks per day) since she was 14 years old and claimed that she was influenced by her friends to do so. The juvenile found it difficult to quit and her mother accepted her smoking habit as well.

Her abuse of drugs started when she was 12 or 13 years old and started with Ecstasy followed by Ketamine. She also tried glue-sniffing subsequently on a regular basis with her friends but stopped when she started consuming Ketamine. Her mother allowed her to consume drugs at home as she was afraid that the juvenile would consume them outside. Strangely enough, although the juvenile stated that she did not get on with her mother's boyfriend, she had consumed drugs with him, and he had helped to settle her drug debts before.

The juvenile also stole her mother's jewellery once and pawned it, after which she spent the money on food and clothes. Her mother did not take any action on the matter as she found it pointless to scold her.

As the juvenile's father was not living in Singapore, he was unaware of the juvenile's problems in school or at home. He was under the impression that she was doing well in school as her mother did not update him on her behaviour in school or at home. Her mother refused to do so as she did not want to worry the father.

Her mother was, however, not confident in supervising her, and she felt that institutionalisation would keep the juvenile away from her negative peers. In any event, the mother indicated that she was going back to Hong Kong (she was a citizen of Hong Kong) and was in fact staying in a hotel at the time the probation report was prepared.

Recommendation by the Probation Services Branch:
The Probation Officer assessed the juvenile to have many high risk factors of re-offending, which included her drug-taking activities, poor family support (the mother being lax and permissive and her father being stationed in Indonesia), smoking, stealing habits, previous gang involvement, moral danger (her sexual involvement with her boyfriends), late nights. It was opined that she would require a structured and closed environment to provide her with discipline as well as to keep her away from her undesirable peers and activities.

Order of Court:
Considering all the circumstances of the case, and given the serious nature of the offences, the Juvenile Court made an order for her to reside in an Approved School (Toa Payoh Girls' Home) for 27 months.

Extortion

Extortion — Section 385 of the Penal Code (Cap. 224)

PP v T (JAC 318/99)

Facts:
The 13-year-old juvenile claimed trial to the charge of extorting between $20,000 to $30,000 from his 14-year-old schoolmate by threatening the latter that a headman from the "Gi Hai Kim" (a secret society) would beat him up. After a three-day hearing, the juvenile was found guilty of a charge of attempted use of threat to injure in order to commit extortion, an offence under Section 385 of the Penal Code (Cap. 224). During the hearing, evidence was adduced that sometime in February 1999, the juvenile, *T*, told the victim that the gang leader, "Ah Boon" needed the money to set up an altar and the victim would be beaten up if he did not hand over between $20,000 to $30,000. In consequence of this threat, the victim, a 14-year-old student stole a large sum of money from his grandmother and from this sum, handed two $10,000 notes ($20,000) to the juvenile. The juvenile and "Ah Boon" were caught sometime in March 1999 in an ambush when the victim handed over a further $1,000.

Background of juvenile:
The juvenile came from an intact family. He had an older sibling who was in secondary school. His parents ran a food stall in a hawker centre. The father was uninvolved in supervising the child, citing his busy work commitments. The mother was the primary caregiver and was assessed by the probation officer to be lax, permissive and indulgent.

Education:
The juvenile was, prior to his expulsion, a secondary one student in the Technical stream. He was expelled as a result of this offence. He had also failed in his Secondary 1 examinations.

Conduct:
The primary school reported that the juvenile was bad tempered and aggressive and had scant respect for authority. He was assessed to be disruptive and defiant in class. His parents were observed to have little control over him as they did not seem to be able to curb the juvenile's misbehaviour despite the school alerting them to the situation on numerous occasions. The school also reported that he had been seen shouting at his parents.

The secondary school reported a long and varied list of disciplinary problems from the juvenile which included 19 offences in the first three months of the year before he was expelled. These offences included smoking, vandalism, threatening his class monitor with violence, assaulting students, possessing a dangerous weapon in school, using vulgarities on teachers, and challenging a teacher to a fight.

One notable aspect of his notoriety was that his classmates rallied together to present a petition to the school principal to remove him from the class as they could no longer tolerate his bullying. An excerpt from the petition reads as follows:

> "We, the students ... would like to ask that *T* (i.e. the juvenile) be out of our class because we cannot stand his nonsense any more. He likes to spit and beat our classmates...
>
> We are happy and our class is quiet since the day he is suspended but now he is back to disturb us. We have spoken to our parents who may want to report to MOE. Please give us peace and take *T* out of our class because the end-of-year final exams are near and we need to study."

Psychological assessment:

The psychologist noted that the juvenile's aggressive behaviour and conduct problems could stem from maternal overprotection and neglectful paternal parenting. The juvenile was unable to accept responsibility for his actions as he tended to downplay the seriousness of his actions and divert blame onto others or on unfortunate circumstances. His mother was observed to consistently minimise the juvenile's misbehaviour by claiming that he had been framed.

It was recommended that the juvenile be placed in a structured environment with strict supervision. He would benefit from individual counselling which would focus on his aggressive tendencies. His mother was recommended to receive help in providing proper guidance and supervision of the boy, with special emphasis on realising the significance of her son's offences and misbehaviour.

Pre-Sentence recommendation by Probation Services Branch:

Probation was not recommended. It was assessed that the juvenile's behavioural problems could only be addressed within a structured environment with a strict regime.

Considerations of the Juvenile Court:

The mother, being undoubtedly concerned for her son's welfare, had gone to the extreme by playing down the seriousness of his misbehaviour. The father was conspicuously absent throughout all 14 court appearances, contending that he was busy tending to his hawker stall. His parents attempted to rationalise the juvenile's misbehaviour as youthful pranks, and also the result of being framed by undesirable peers. Despite being found guilty by the Juvenile Court after trial, the mother maintained that her son was framed but declined to file an appeal against the finding of guilt. The mother was admonished by the Juvenile Court for being overly protective and feigning ignorance of her son's misdeeds. She claimed, for example, that she was not aware of the petition by her son's classmates to have him removed and that she never received any letter informing her of the juvenile's expulsion. There was overwhelming evidence to the contrary that she had been so informed. The Juvenile Court also chided the mother for viewing her son as "slightly naughty" and his numerous disciplinary problems as "childish pranks".

Order of Court:
The Juvenile Court made an order committing the juvenile to an Approved School, the Singapore Boys' Home, for 36 months — the maximum period permitted by the Children and Young Persons Act. To reinforce parental obligations, the Court also made a Contribution Order against the parents to make monthly payments of $100 to the Singapore Boys' Home during the tenure of the order.

Molest

Outraging Modesty in Aggravated Circumstances — Section 354A(1) of the Penal Code (Cap. 224)

PP v. O (JAC 940-1/99; JAC969/99 and JAC 973/99)

Facts:
The 15-year-old juvenile pleaded guilty to molesting four women separately and assaulting three of them between April and May 1999. Five of the nine charges were taken into consideration. All the offences occurred in or near HDB lift landings in the Eunos and Ubi area. All his female victims were in their 20s and stayed in the vicinity of the crime scenes. At the time when the dispositional order was imposed, the juvenile was 16 years and 1 month old.

On 21 April 1999, the 24-year-old victim was molested by the juvenile in the lift when she was returning home around midnight. As the lift was ascending, he tore her blouse with both hands and scratched her breast. She struggled and punched him on the face. He pushed her to the floor but she managed to kick his groin. When the lift door opened, he managed to escape via the staircase despite a concerted effort by the victim to detain him. In the process of effecting his escape, the juvenile hit the victim on her neck.

On 15 May 1999, he molested his 25-year-old victim in the lift and tried to remove her T-shirt and bermudas. He was unsuccessful as the victim put up a violent struggle. When the lift door opened, the juvenile attempted to escape but the victim caught hold of him. During the struggle, he kicked the back of her legs and she fell backwards. He then laid on top of the victim and molested her by pulling up her T-shirt and tearing off her bra. Before escaping, he told her to *"have a nice day"*. In her police report, the victim stated that she was nearly raped by the juvenile.

On 22 May 1999 at about 12:10 a.m., he followed a 28-year-old woman to a lift and pulled up her T-shirt. Despite her struggle, the juvenile managed to molest the victim by pressing her left breast with his right hand. He also assaulted her by hitting her shoulders with his hands until the lift door opened whereupon he made good his escape via the staircase. When the police were informed, the victim reported she was nearly raped.

On 30 May 1999 at about 1 a.m., he molested a 27-year-old woman in the lift by pulling up her singlet and placing his hands within to grab her left breast. The victim screamed and put up a struggle. The juvenile managed to escape when the lift door opened.

The juvenile was eventually arrested on 4 June 1999 at about 11:20 p.m. at the void deck of a HDB block in the Ubi area during an ambush operation mounted by the police.

Background of juvenile:

The juvenile is the only child of rather elderly parents. They resided in a two-room rental flat and were waiting to move into bigger premises. His mother was the primary caregiver and was very close to him, keeping very close tabs on his education and activities. The father maintained a cordial relationship with his son but left the management of the household and his son to his wife. His parents informed the Probation Officer that their son was very well-behaved and had never given them any cause to discipline him.

Education:
At the time of offence, the juvenile was a secondary 4 (Express/Special) student from a top secondary school in Singapore. At his primary school, he performed exceptionally well in the PSLE examinations. There were no disciplinary problems in the primary or secondary school. Despite being aware of the offences, the school remained supportive of the juvenile. His schoolmates treated him normally. The school appealed for him to be allowed to return to his studies and to take the GCE "O" levels at the end of the year. In the event that the juvenile was committed to an institution, the school was willing to provide support to enable him to take his exams there. The juvenile's 31 classmates tendered a joint petition to the authorities to give him a second chance by not committing him to an institution. An excerpt of the petition read as follows:

> "... to err is human. We understand the severity of his action but would like to appeal to you to be more lenient during the sentencing and allow [the juvenile] to spend the last few months of his Secondary 4 life with us. After all, many of us feel that sending him to a Boys' Home might not necessarily be the best option for him as he might plunge into despair and lose all willpower as well as his enthusiasm for his studies. This will probably also shatter his self-confidence. It would certainly be a waste for allowing someone like [the juvenile], who has the potential to excel academically. By allowing him to remain in school, we are confident that we, as a class, can cause him to turn over a new leaf with our continued support and encouragement."

Psychological assessment:
The Court had ordered the juvenile to undergo a psychiatric assessment. The psychiatrist concluded that intensive psychotherapy was necessary to counter the juvenile's strong sexual urges. The juvenile was assessed to have little personal space and scant opportunity to cope with sexuality issues in view of the highly controlled environment at home. His mother was assessed to be very protective,

strict and controlling. The psychiatrist recommended a period of residence in a hostel together with a programme at the Child Guidance Clinic to work on the juvenile's issues of anger, sexual impulses as well as the parenting style of his parents.

Recommendation by Probation Services Branch:
These offences were disturbing as they involved the use of serious acts of aggression and violence over a considerable period of time to gratify the juvenile's sexual impulses. There is also evidence to suggest that with each offence, the juvenile was becoming increasingly bolder as the lapse between offences became progressively shorter. The offences were clearly premeditated and committed at times and places where his victims were at their most vulnerable.

The Probation Officer did not support the psychiatrist's recommendation for a probation period with hostel stay and intensive psychotherapy as it was felt that his risk of re-offending under a community-based rehabilitation programme like probation was high. This would imperil the public. It was recommended that for intervention efforts to be sustained, the risks and needs issues would be best addressed in a very closed environment, like the Singapore Boys' Home.

Prosecution's address on Disposal Orders:
The prosecution urged the Juvenile Court not to place the juvenile on probation as he had committed a series of very serious and premeditated offences by waylaying his victims and hurting them when they resisted his advances.

Special considerations:
The juvenile was a few days short of 16 years old when he pleaded guilty to the four charges. The Juvenile Court then adjourned the matter for a Probation Report incorporating psychological and psychiatric evaluations of the juvenile. At the adjourned date for the Court to consider appropriate orders, the juvenile was 16 years and

1 month. Under the law (Children and Young Persons Act (Cap. 49) and the Criminal Procedure Code (Cap. 68)), the Juvenile Court is empowered to order the juvenile to be brought before a District Court for him to be considered for committal to a Reformative Training Centre (RTC).[2] When a youth is sentenced to undergo reformative training at the RTC, it is because the District Judge is of the opinion that he is suitable for rehabilitation, albeit in a very strict institution, after taking into account his age, character, previous conduct and circumstances of the offence. There is a minimum stay of 18 months in the institution and a maximum of 18-24 months for the aftercare programme. The RTC, unlike the Singapore Boys' Home, is administered by the Prisons Department. The Singapore Boys' Home comes under the auspices of the Ministry of Community Development and Sports.

In declining to place the juvenile on probation or in an Approved School regime, the Juvenile Court focused on the seriousness of the offences. Despite the scholastic achievements of the boy, the series of offences, and in particular, the violent manner of commission revealed a deep-seated criminal aggression which required serious correction. The Court was satisfied that the boy required reformative training to do this.

Order of Court:
The juvenile was remanded at a remand centre[3] pending a suitability report for reformative training. At the adjourned hearing date, a District Court was satisfied that reformative training was required and made the order accordingly.

Smoking

Possession of cigarettes whilst under 18 years old — Section 11(1) of the Smoking (Control of Advertisements and Sale of Tobacco) Act, (Cap. 309)

PP v A (MOH 80/2000)

Facts:

The 13-year-old juvenile pleaded guilty to one charge of possession of cigarettes in March 2000 whilst being under the age of 18 years. This was the fourth time since the accused had been caught for committing smoking-related offences under Section 11(1) of the Smoking (Control of Advertisements and Sale of Tobacco) Act, Cap. 309. He had on three previous occasions been dealt with administratively for the offence and had paid composition fines ranging from $15 to $40.

Background of juvenile:

The juvenile's father was strict and concerned but was unable to control his son. The father frequently went for short overseas business trips, averaging three to four times per month. The juvenile's mother committed suicide in 1990 due to depression.

Despite his young age, the juvenile was violent and aggressive towards his caregivers, particularly the stepmother and grandmother. It was revealed that he had on one occasion soiled his stepmother's towel with urine. He also demanded money from his stepmother and accused her of being a "free-loader" on his father. He would use force on his stepmother if she tried to mete out corporal punishment to discipline him. He would even beat the maid with his fist and use a badminton racquet to hit his grandmother. He consistently lied and failed to inform his parents of his whereabouts. He would go to the extent of adjusting the clock such that he could go out earlier and duplicated the house keys without permission.

The stepmother was concerned for the juvenile's welfare but was also overwhelmed by his bad conduct. The juvenile had been largely cared for by his paternal grandmother who had been described by the parents to the probation officer as "doting" and who had "spoilt" the juvenile. The grandmother passed away in 1995. However, the stepmother reported that a year before her death, the grandmother had expressed to her that she could not control the boy, and suggested that he be sent to an institution. When she was alive, the grandmother often recorded the misdeeds of the juvenile so that the father could deal with him when he came home. The father would try to counsel the juvenile, but usually had to resort to caning him. The stepmother expressed fear in handling the juvenile when his father was away.

Education:
The juvenile was a Secondary 2 (Normal Academic) student at the time of the offence. He had a record of misbehaviour and open defiance in school since primary school. He was not academically inclined and exhibited poor conduct in school. His form teacher in the primary school reported that he was disruptive in class. In secondary school, he committed many offences, primarily smoking, playing pranks on classmates and being rude to teachers during lessons. There were also reports of fighting, vandalism and theft. He also did not show remorse or repentance after being punished in school and often continued in his misconduct. The stepmother revealed that she received complaints from his primary school and their neighbourhood almost every week since he was in Primary 2. She recalled that the juvenile was involved in the bullying and extortion of Primary 1 boys.

Psychological assessment:
The psychologist opined that due to the professed inability of the family to exercise effective control over the juvenile's behaviour, the home environment was unsuitable for his rehabilitation. It was recommended that the juvenile be placed in a structured and secure environment where he could be closely supervised and monitored. It was also recommended that the juvenile be referred for counselling to enhance his skills in the appropriate expression and management of negative emotions. Family sessions were also recommended to increase positive communication patterns.

Recommendation by Probation Services Branch:
The juvenile's defiant and aggressive tendencies merited deep concern. The probation officer recommended a stringent and structured environment to curb his worrisome behaviour and to facilitate positive changes in his general attitude.

Special considerations:
In considering the paramount concern of the Juvenile Court to reform and rehabilitate the juvenile, the Court felt that despite the relative non-severity of the offence, imposing the maximum fine of $50 was highly inappropriate. The Court contemplated the possibility of probation or probation with residence at an Approved Institution. The latter was also not feasible in view of his defiant attitude toward authority figures. This would make his rehabilitation in an open hostel environment difficult. A Probation Order was also unsuitable in view of the inadequacy of parental supervision. Similarly, a short-term detention in a Place of Detention was inappropriate as it did not offer programmes to rehabilitate the juvenile. The Juvenile Court was of the opinion that the juvenile needed the more rigid and highly structured programme of an Approved School regime to help rehabilitate him.

Order of Court:
An Approved School Order (Singapore Boys' Home) for the minimum period of two years was made. The Court also decided to make a Contribution Order against the father of the juvenile to the Singapore Boys' Home, having regard to the means of the father. The father was ordered to pay $500 monthly to the Singapore Boys' Home, to which payment he consented.

On appeal to the High Court by the juvenile, through his father, the Chief Justice affirmed the decision of the Juvenile Court but the amount of monthly contribution was reduced to $300. The father of the juvenile was ticked off by the Chief Justice for not being able to control his son.

Theft

Theft of a motor vehicle — Section 379A Penal Code (Cap. 224)

PP v. A (JAC 12/2002 and JAC 46/2002)

Facts:
Sometime in December 2001, at about 11 p.m., a 15-year-old juvenile and his accomplices, *A* and *B*, met at a void deck. One of them suggested to the juvenile and *A* to steal a motorcycle. The juvenile and *A* proceeded to the carpark to pick a motorcycle to steal while *B* acted as a lookout. Using a house key and after several attempts, *A* was able to start the ignition, after which he started riding the motorcycle together with the juvenile and *B*. The motorcycle was later abandoned by *B* and subsequently recovered four days later. The juvenile pleaded guilty to one charge of stealing a motorcycle together with *A* and *B* under Section 379A of the Penal Code Cap. 224. Another similar offence committed earlier was taken into consideration for the purposes of sentencing.

Background of juvenile:
The juvenile comes from a big family of six children, including himself. Due to his parents' financial difficulties, the juvenile and siblings were unable to continue schooling. As the father was the sole breadwinner, and his mother was in ill-health (she suffered from high blood pressure), the juvenile stopped school to work in order to help contribute to the household expenses.

The juvenile was described as quiet at home and would help around the house if he was asked. However his peers here left much to be desired. He had been associating with members of a secret society gang for almost four years on a daily basis. He smoked and kept late nights as well. After the theft offences were committed, he attended counselling at a family service centre for one session prior to being charged in Court.

Education:
The juvenile only studied till Primary 6 and his academic performance was poor. Furthermore, his attendance in school was also irregular. There were disciplinary problems like fights that took place between the juvenile and his schoolmates in school. As the juvenile was not academically inclined, the parents allowed him to stop school and to

work in order to help contribute to the household expenses. However, he did not contribute to the household expenses in the long term (see Employment, below).

Employment:
After he left school, he worked in fast-food restaurants like KFC and Taco Bell for a few months, but subsequently quit as he found the job either too tiring or he was not paid his salary as he was not going to work regularly. In this manner, he worked sporadically for about a year and a half. After working for four weeks in his last job, he decided to spend more time with his friends instead, and never got another job. So he was unemployed for at least one and a half to two years prior to his being charged in Court.

Recommendation by Probation Services Branch:
The juvenile's risk factors were his negative peers who were gang-related and with whom he had been associating with for the past four years. He committed theft-related offences (for which he was charged) within five days of each other, evincing his impulsiveness and risk-taking nature. Leaving school prematurely may have also increased his risk of re-offending. His parents were lax and permissive in their supervision of the juvenile, especially when they allowed him to leave school. His other delinquent traits included smoking and keeping late nights, which marked an undisciplined lifestyle. There was clearly a need of some structure to ensure the juvenile stayed on the right path.

Order of Court:
The Juvenile Court made an order for the juvenile to be placed in a Place of Detention for two months following which probation would commence upon his discharge, for 24 months, with the following conditions:

1) to reside for 12 months in Bukit Batok Hostel;
2) to abide by a time restriction from 9 p.m. to 6 a.m.;

3) to perform community service for 100 hours;
4) to attend a prison visit arranged by the Court;
5) to attend any relevant rehabilitative programmes.

Other conditions of probation included a bond by the parents of the juvenile for the sum of $2,000 to exercise proper care and guardianship of the juvenile, and for them to attend counselling as ordered by the Court. Such counselling would include parenting sessions relevant to the rehabilitative needs of the juvenile. Failure on the part of the parents to attend the counselling would entail a bond of $1,000 to be forfeited by the Court.

Theft from a vehicle — Section 379 of the Penal Code (Cap. 224)

PP v. F (JAC 1046-1047/2001, JAC 1065-1078/2001 and JAC 1102-1103/2001)

Facts:

The 15-year-old juvenile was found guilty on six counts of theft from vehicles and one count of housebreaking. The remaining 11 charges, consisting of theft-related offences, consumption of controlled drugs and possession of an obscene VCD, were taken into consideration for the purposes of sentencing. The juvenile had suggested to his accomplices to break into the vehicles with a key he had found. Thereafter they proceeded to break into a series of cars and stole items (in particular cash cards) found in the respective cars.

Since 1999 till July 2001, the juvenile had admitted that he and his friends had broken into more than 100 cars. They would usually do so when they were short of money. Even while he was arrested and placed on police bail, he continued to steal from vehicles. Within one week after his arrest for such offences, he committed the housebreaking offence with his friends as one of them intended to steal cigarettes from a coffee-shop.

Background of juvenile:

The juvenile's father was currently serving a 20-year imprisonment term, whilst the mother had previously been placed on probation for three years for drug trafficking. As the father was imprisoned several times, he was rarely at home to supervise his four children, including the juvenile. After his parents divorced, the mother had custody of two children including the juvenile. As relatives were unable to take care of them while the mother was at work, the juvenile resided in Pertapis Children's Home for two years at the age of nine. Subsequently, the mother remarried and they all lived with the stepfather.

Education:

The juvenile's attendance in school was irregular. Even when he was present, he would misbehave himself (throwing stones at his classmates or disrupting classes by disturbing others) and steal things. Attempts were made by the mother to get the juvenile to go for counselling, but they failed. Following his continued misbehaviour in school, his mother withdrew him from school.

Employment:

The juvenile worked in three fast-food restaurants for not more than three months in each restaurant. He worked at his most recent job in a fourth fast-food restaurant for a year, but was terminated when he failed to turn up for work for a week. For his previous jobs, he either left or was terminated as a result of quarrels with management.

Conduct:

The juvenile became increasingly defiant and argumentative ever since he left school and started mixing with negative peers who were from a secret society gang. He would go out with his friends to discotheques (where the gang hung out) till the wee hours of the morning or he would stay away from home for a few days to a month, without informing his parents of his whereabouts. Despite his parents locking him in his room to prevent him from going out, he would climb out of his window and scale 14 stories to the ground floor below. He had been smoking since 12 and smoked up to ten cigarettes a day. Coupled with an active sex life, he would also indulge in alcohol, and experiment with drugs like heroin, and glue-sniff. As the headman of a gang who had about 18 younger members under him, the juvenile imposed a $50 membership fee per month on each gang member. He and his gang friends would go to a particular discotheque to hang out. He also claimed that he had previously slashed a male with a knife for touching his girlfriend's bottom.

Recommendation by Probation Services Branch:
The mother's supervision of the juvenile was lax and ineffective. Despite the stepfather, who tried all means to discipline him, the juvenile refused to heed anyone's advice to change his ways. Clearly the parents were unable to exert any control or supervision if probation were to be imposed.

The juvenile's lack of remorse and his nonchalant attitude, as well as his strong affiliation to a gang, were just some of the high-risk factors of his re-offending. The juvenile would thus require a strict and disciplined environment to instill in him a sense of responsibility as well as to keep him away from his negative peers.

Order of Court:
At the time the dispositional order was imposed, when the Juvenile Court was considering the various sanctions available, the juvenile turned 16 years old. Given the circumstances highlighted above, the Juvenile Court was of the view that it would be expedient for the juvenile's rehabilitation that he should undergo some form of reformative training. The matter was thus transferred to the District Court for sentencing. A Reformative Training report (to assess the juvenile's suitability for Reformative Training) was obtained and the District Court sent him to a Reformative Training Centre for three years.

Rioting and Theft in a Dwelling — Section 147 and Section 380 of the Penal Code (Cap. 224)

PP v. L (JAC 1317-8/2000 and JAC 1321/2000)

Facts:
The 14-year-old juvenile admitted to two counts of shoplifting a hat, lighter and a belt in Orchard Road in June 2000. He was also involved in a rioting case in May 2000 when the juvenile, together with ten other accomplices attended a "settlement talk" in Toa Payoh. This arose out of some disparaging remarks made by members of the rival group. It resulted in the eventual assault of two victims who sustained superficial injuries.

Background of juvenile:
The juvenile comes from an upper middle class background and is the elder of two children. His father was a pediatrician who operated a private clinic. The mother was a part-time nurse. The parents were strict disciplinarians who imposed strict parameters for the juvenile. He shared a very close relationship with his paternal grandparents.

His parents imposed a curfew of 6 p.m. on him. However, since the beginning of 2000, he would return home after 10 p.m., sometimes as late as 2 a.m. His parents would always wait up for him to rebuke him. Sometimes, his father would lodge a "missing persons" report at the nearby Neighbourhood Police Post (NPP) or threaten to bring him to see the police officers. Since late 1999 to late July 2000, the juvenile started to behave defiantly towards his father. Their arguments were often so heated and loud that police officers from the NPP were activated to intervene. During this rebellious period, he refused to disclose his activities and the identities of his friends. The parents even sought the services of a private investigator to track him. They also enlisted the help of teachers, social workers and a psychiatrist to change their son but these efforts yielded little progress.

In February 2000, the juvenile joined a secret society which operated at Far East Plaza. He was motivated by a sense of loyalty to his friends. He thought it would be fun and wanted to belong to a group in which his friends were also members. For several months, he loitered around the vicinity of Far East Plaza with his fellow gang members and was involved in attending "settlement talks", funeral wakes and gang fights. After the rioting incident, his father brought him to the Secret Societies Branch of CID. He claimed that as a result of this, he left the gang in that same month. Prior to this, his father had also actively sought out other gang members to request them to leave his son alone. After leaving the gang, the juvenile tattooed himself with a dragon from his right chest to right arm for $80. This infuriated and saddened his parents. Initially, he refused to have the tattoo removed. Eventually, he heeded their advice and underwent seven sessions of laser treatment to have it removed at a total cost of $5,800.

Education:
The juvenile was currently repeating Secondary 2 in the Express stream of a neighbourhood school. He had previously been a student in two well-known schools but disciplinary problems in these resulted in suspensions and eventual expulsion. All his offences were committed when he was in the former schools.

He performed well in his primary school and was in the EM1 stream.[4] Whilst at his first secondary school, the teachers reported that he had a string of serious misconduct since Secondary 1. He was openly defiant to the teachers as he used vulgar language on them and walked out of the classroom without permission. He often played "pranks" on his classmates by "stealing" their belongings. He was also caned for bullying, fighting and using vulgarities on a teacher. He was assessed to be suffering from Attention Deficit Hyperactivity Disorder and his parents were advised to seek medical help. On academic abilities, the juvenile was assessed to be an intelligent boy who needed to focus his energy on meaningful pursuits. After a spate of disciplinary offences that spanned 16 months, he was suspended and eventually transferred to the second secondary school. The last incident was when he picked up a classmate and threw him on the concrete floor.

The juvenile was only in the second secondary school for three weeks before he was expelled. He reported for school on the first day with long dyed hair. During the next two weeks, he was rude and defiant to the teachers. He was expelled as a result of his shoplifting offences which occurred during an occasion when he and some classmates played truant. During the three weeks' stint, he was noted to be weak in many subjects.

Psychological assessment:
The juvenile was referred by his present secondary school to seek counselling at the Child Guidance Clinic. The consultant psychiatrist assessed that he had a strained relationship with his parents. He was also heavily influenced by his undesirable peers. In the months following the arrest, the juvenile had made vast improvements in his relationship with his parents and showed a keen desire to return to his studies. The psychiatrist recommended a period of probation coupled with a stern warning that the juvenile would be incarcerated in a structured and secure environment should he re-offend.

Recommendation by Probation Services Branch:
The juvenile's problematic behaviour stemmed from his strong and indiscriminate attachment with his undesirable peers. This was exacerbated by his rebellion against his parents' authoritative control. His parents' efforts at sourcing community resources to steer him back to the correct path had proved futile. It was only with his arrest and subsequent remand at the Singapore Boys' Home (pending police investigations) that he gradually made efforts to improve himself and mend relations with his parents. The four days remand gave him the opportunity to reflect and he began to appreciate his parents' concerns and efforts in standing by him despite the disappointment and misery he had brought upon the family. He appeared remorseful and determined to effect positive changes in his life. His conduct and communications with his parents improved tremendously. He was less resentful of his parents' supervision. His grandfather, a retired educator, even accompanied him on some of his activities and

encouraged him to spend more time at home to concentrate on his studies. He was also returning home earlier than the 6 p.m. curfew. The family had also changed to adopt a softer approach on him, resulting in him becoming more receptive to their requests and advice. His parents felt more confident that he was more amenable to change. Accordingly, they were very willing to be supportive in any rehabilitation plans.

The Probation Officer recommended a period of probation at home with a review of the situation after three months.

Special considerations:
The offences committed by the juvenile and his indiscriminate association with undesirable peers appeared to be an extreme reaction/ rebellion towards his parents' authority and a manifestation of the poor communication between them. Investigations by the probation officer turned up a poem entitled "A Fateful Day", which the juvenile had penned at the height of his depression.

A Fateful Day

The rain fell in ferocious sheets, my heart masked infinite sorrow.

The sky was bleak, and my heart was clouded with despair.

The waters were wild with fury, but my heart was numb.

The sun hung in the sky, the grasses swaying in the wind.

The lake lapped at its bank, the flowers blossomed throwing off its wafts of fragrant scent.

The sky that was bleak mirrored my thoughts.

The waters that were wild were tantamount to the rage that churned within my very soul.

The regret I felt was walled by none.

Relieve my sorrow, Oh Great One.

For the sorrow that churns within me

Churns like no other. The sadness knows no limit, no bounds and leaps within me.

One of the juvenile's school teachers praised the juvenile's compassion and noted that his conduct had improved markedly in the past few months prior to the court order. She also remarked upon his above average writing skills and his intelligence.

Order of Court:
The Court ordered 24 months split probation (of which six months were intensive and the remaining 18 months supervised[5]) with the following conditions:

1) to abide by a time restriction from 9 p.m. to 6 a.m.;
2) to perform 120 hours of community service;
3) to attend an anti-secret society talk;
4) to attend a prison visit arranged by the Court;
5) to attend any relevant rehabilitative programmes recommended by the probation officer.

The juvenile's parents were also ordered to execute a bond of $5,000 to exercise proper care and guardianship.

3.2 Legal Issues Arising in Juvenile Cases

This section sets out various legal issues concerning juvenile cases which have arisen over the years in the areas of jurisdiction, sentencing and punishment, breach proceedings, and so on. The legal issues are illustrated by setting out the salient facts of the particular cases in which these issues arose, and analysing the decisions made in them, with reference, where applicable, to the relevant legislation.

The main piece of legislation governing juvenile cases is the Children and Young Persons Act (Cap. 38) (CYPA). Hence, all of the cases in this section would involve the application or interpretation of various sections of the CYPA, in addition to acts such as the Probation of Offenders Act (Cap. 252) and the Criminal Procedure Code (Cap. 68). The CYPA underwent major amendments in the years 1993 and 2001.

All the cases highlighted in this section represent the bulk of major cases involving juveniles over the last decade or so. They comprise cases which have gone on appeal from the Juvenile Court to the High Court, as well as cases which have been dealt with by the High Court at first instance. This section also illustrates the effect of some of the legislative amendments, by setting out the pre-amendment position and post-amendment position on various issues. Some of these cases are actually illustrative of the pre-amendment positions. By discussing these cases in conjunction with the changing legislative landscape, it is hoped that the various developments in the legal principles and jurisprudence applicable to juvenile justice issues can be more comprehensively studied and traced through the years.

3.2 Legal Issues Arising in Juvenile Cases

MAGISTRATE ONG CHIN HENG

I. Jurisdiction

The first broad area of issues relates to the jurisdiction of the Juvenile Court. In summary, the jurisdiction of the Juvenile Court is specified in Section 33 of the CYPA. However, the operation of certain particular provisions within this section would be interesting to highlight, including the parts touching on the age threshold for juveniles, and restrictions on the jurisdiction of the Juvenile Court in certain situations. These issues are individually discussed in greater detail under their respective headings.

1. Relevant Date for Determining When an Accused Person can be Tried in the Juvenile Court

This issue concerns when an accused person can properly be said to be a "juvenile" over whom the Juvenile Court has jurisdiction. This is a particularly important issue in cases where the accused person is approaching or has reached his 16th birthday. Essentially, the current position is found in Section 33(6) of the CYPA, which provides that a person must be below the age of 16 on the "date of commencement of the hearing of the charge". The commencement of the hearing of a charge is taken to refer to the time at which the accused person gives his plea. It follows therefore, that for a person to be dealt with by the Juvenile Court, he must be brought before the Court, charged, and his plea taken before his 16th birthday. Failing this, the Juvenile Court will not have jurisdiction over the accused person, and he will have to be charged and tried in an adult criminal court instead. The discussion under this heading looks at the legislative and case history on this important aspect of the Juvenile Court's jurisdiction, leading up to the present position.

Pre-1993 position:

HBT v. PP
(MA 78/1991/01) High Court [1992] 1 SLR 756
Karthigesu J
24 July 1991

The appellant was born on 21 June 1972. He was charged with an offence under Section 326 of the Penal Code (Cap. 224) which was alleged to have been committed on 6 November 1987, when he was only 15 years 5 months old. He was charged in the Juvenile Court on 8 December 1987, when he was still below 15 years 6 months of age. However, by the time his case came up for trial in October 1988, the appellant was over 16 years old. The presiding magistrate in the Juvenile Court ruled that the Juvenile Court did not have jurisdiction to try the case and transferred it to the District Court, where the case came up for hearing in June 1989. It was, however, then transferred back to the Juvenile Court as the district judge ruled that the Juvenile Court did have jurisdiction over the case. By the time the case came back before the Juvenile Court in March 1991, the appellant was already over 18 years old. The presiding Juvenile Court magistrate (not the same one as before), again ruled that the Juvenile Court did not have the jurisdiction to try the case and accordingly ordered that it be heard by another court. The appellant appealed against this order.

The High Court, in allowing the appeal, held that the intent of Section 48 (now Section 33) of the CYPA was that a charge against a young person should be heard and finally disposed of in a Juvenile Court.

The only date which could be determined with any certainty was the date on which the offence was committed. The legislature could not have intended that the jurisdiction of the Juvenile Court was to be founded on the determination of the offender's age by reference to some indeterminate date such as the date of apprehension, or the date when he was charged with the offence, or the date when the hearing of the charge commenced in Court, or the date when the hearing was concluded and the accused convicted and sentenced. Thus in order to determine the jurisdiction of the Juvenile Court, the one and only relevant factor to be considered was the age of the offender at the time of the commission of the offence.

The order of the magistrate was therefore set aside and the case directed to be tried in the Juvenile Court. The judge further noted that this case was not without its difficulties, whichever of the views expressed either by the appellant or by the Public Prosecutor were accepted as being correct, anomalous situations could arise in some extreme cases in either of the two views.

Analysis and post-1993 developments:

It must be noted that the section dealing with the jurisdiction of the Juvenile Court at the time that this case was dealt with was Section 48 of the CYPA (pre-1993 version). The old provision reads as follows:

48. - (1) Subject as hereinafter provided, no charge against a child or young person shall be heard by a Court of summary jurisdiction which is not a Juvenile Court:

Provided that -

(a) where a child or young person is charged with an offence or offences triable only by the High Court, he shall be tried by the High Court;

(b) a charge made jointly against a child or young person and a person who has attained the age of 16 years shall be heard by a court of appropriate jurisdiction other than a Juvenile Court; or

(c) where in the course of any proceedings before any court of appropriate jurisdiction other than a Juvenile Court, it appears that the person to whom the proceedings relate is a child or young person, nothing in this section shall be construed as preventing the Court, if it thinks fit to do so, from proceeding with the hearing and determination of the proceedings.

(2) A Juvenile Court shall have jurisdiction to try all offences which, but for subsection (1), would be triable only by a Magistrate's Court or a District Court.

However, there have been two further amendments since then, which make the above position obsolete.

In 1993, there was an amendment to the CYPA, which included an amendment to the section dealing with jurisdiction (see portion in bold below):

Jurisdiction of Juvenile Court

33. - (1) No child or young person shall be charged with or tried for any offence by a Court of summary jurisdiction which is not a Juvenile Court except that —

(a) where a child or young person is charged with any offence triable only by the High Court, he shall be tried by the High Court;

(b) a charge made jointly against a child or young person and a person who has attained the age of 16 years shall be heard by a Court of appropriate jurisdiction other than a Juvenile Court; or

(c) where, in the course of any proceedings before any Court of appropriate jurisdiction other than a Juvenile Court, it appears that the person to whom the proceedings relate is a child or young person, nothing in this section shall be construed as preventing the Court, if it thinks fit to do so, from proceeding with the hearing and determination of the proceedings.

(2) A Juvenile Court shall have jurisdiction to try all offences which, but for subsection (1), would be triable only by a Magistrate's Court or a District Court.

(3) ***A person who has attained the age of 16 years on the date of commencement of the hearing of the charge shall not be tried for any offence by a Juvenile Court*** but where in the course of any trial before a Juvenile Court the child or young person to whom the trial relates attains the age of 16 years, nothing in this subsection shall prevent the Court from proceeding, if it thinks fit, with the trial. (emphasis added)

(4) Where on 21st March 1993, a trial relating to a person who has attained the age of 16 years has commenced before a Juvenile Court, the Court may proceed, if it thinks fit, with the trial.

In particular, the new Section 33(3) effectively legislatively overruled the position taken in *HBT*, making the **date of commencement of hearing of the charge** the relevant date in determining the Juvenile Court's jurisdiction.

However, what this refers to is still apt to be vague. This may either refer to the date that the accused is merely charged in court, or it may require that a plea be taken, before it can be said that a "hearing" has commenced. There is currently no case law on this point, but in the writer's view, the correct position is that a hearing should be taken to have "commenced" only when the accused either pleads guilty or claims trial to the charge. It is submitted that hearings are distinguishable from mentions, and as such, a mere mention of the case in court will not qualify sufficiently as a "commencement" of a hearing. A hearing can only be properly said to have started upon the accused claiming trial, in which case a trial commences, or upon the accused pleading guilty, in which case a hearing of the statement of facts, antecedents and mitigation ensues.

In October 2001, there were further amendments to Section 33. Section 33(3) was re-phrased and re-numbered into the new Sections 33(6) and (7). The most current version reads:

Jurisdiction of Juvenile Court

33. - (1) Subject to the provisions of this section, no child or young person shall be charged with or tried for any offence by a Court of summary jurisdiction except a Juvenile Court.

(2) Where a child or young person is charged with any offence triable only by the High Court, he shall be tried by the High Court unless —

(a) the Public Prosecutor applies to the Juvenile Court to try such offence; and

(b) the legal representative of the child or young person concerned consents to the offence being tried by the Juvenile Court.

(3) Where a charge is made jointly against a child or young person and a person who has attained the age of 16 years, the charge shall be heard by a Court of appropriate jurisdiction other than a Juvenile Court.

(4) Where, in the course of any proceedings before any Court of appropriate jurisdiction other than a Juvenile Court, it appears that the person to whom the proceedings relate is a child or young person, the Court may, notwithstanding subsection (1), proceed with the hearing and determination of the proceedings if it thinks fit.

(5) A Juvenile Court shall have jurisdiction to try all offences which, but for subsections (1) and (2), would be triable only by a Magistrate's Court, a District Court or the High Court.

(6) ***A person who has attained the age of 16 years on the date of commencement of the hearing of the charge shall not be tried for any offence by a Juvenile Court.*** (emphasis added)

(7) ***Where in the course of any trial before a Juvenile Court the child or young person to whom the trial relates attains the age of 16 years, nothing in this subsection shall prevent the Juvenile Court, if it thinks fit, from proceeding with***

the trial and dealing with the child or young person in accordance with the provisions of this Act. (emphasis added)

(8) In this section, "legal representative", in relation to a child or young person who is charged with an offence, includes any person assisting the child or young person in his defence to the charge.

It should be noted that this re-phrasing and re-numbering does not change the position with regards to **the date of commencement of hearing** as the relevant date to be considered in determining if an accused can be tried by the Juvenile Court (see the portion in bold above). In summary, the joint effect of the current Sections 33(6) and (7), is to require that a person must be below the age of 16 at the start of his hearing, but if he should turn 16 in the course of the trial, the Juvenile Court has the discretion to carry on dealing with him, provided it thinks fit. This is basically similar to the position after the 1993 amendments.

The substantive impact of the 2001 amendments was more with regards to Sections 33(2) and (8) which essentially now allow the Juvenile Court to deal with offences which hitherto were triable only by the High Court, provided that both the Public Prosecutor and the juvenile's legal representative desired this. See the next section for fuller discussion on this point.

2. Offences Triable only in the High Court

This issue revolves around situations where a juvenile accused is charged with an offence that is only triable by the High Court. These would be offences with prescribed penalties of more than ten years' imprisonment (i.e., being beyond the District Court's jurisdiction), including capital offences. The current position is that for such cases, the starting point is that the juvenile must be tried by the High Court. However, the Juvenile Court will have the jurisdiction to deal with the matter if the Public Prosecutor applies to the Juvenile Court to try the juvenile accused, and the juvenile's legal representative (e.g., parent or legal guardian) consents to this. This is significantly different from the position before the legislative amendments in 2001. Previously, the Juvenile Court had absolutely no scope for dealing with juvenile offenders once the offences they were charged with were triable only by the High Court. The discussion under this heading will deal briefly with the legislative and case history leading up to the present position.

Pre-2001 position — case illustration:

PP v. (1)FSJ; (2)LWF; (3)AWK and (4)TBL

(CC 24/1996) High Court (unreported)
Sinnathuray J
26 August 1996

The four accused persons pleaded guilty to a charge of culpable homicide not amounting to murder punishable under Section 304(a) read with Section 149 of the Penal Code (Cap. 224). The first three accused were juveniles, but the offence was triable only in the High Court. As such they were dealt with in the High Court.

All four accused were members of the "Ang Soon Tong" triad society, and the death occurred during an altercation with members of the rival "Sio Kun Tong" secret society.

Investigations revealed that the common object of all the gang members present (which included the four accused) was to cause hurt to the deceased. Investigations further revealed that it was the intention of the gang members, together with the four accused who were present during the attack, to cause bodily injuries which were likely to cause death. The deceased Ng Ban Sen was struck in pursuance of the common object to cause hurt. He was subsequently conveyed to the National University Hospital, where he subsequently died without regaining consciousness.

A medical report from the hospital at the time of his admission detailed his having suffered a skull fracture, and an emergency scan showed a left-sided extradural haematoma as well as some bruising and swelling with intracerebral bleeding on the right side of the brain.

The judge called for probation reports and reformative training centre (RTC) reports. After considering the reports made on the four accused, he made the following orders:

(i) The first accused was placed on probation for three years with the usual conditions and a further condition that he remained indoors from 9 p.m. to 6 a.m.
(ii) The second and third accused were ordered to be sent to the Singapore Boys' Home for three years.
(iii) The fourth accused was sentenced to five years' imprisonment to be detained at such place as the Minister determined. The judge had been prepared to accept the RTC report and order the fourth accused to undergo reformative training. However, he did not want to undergo reformative training. So the judge sentenced him to five years' imprisonment instead.

Analysis and post-2001 developments:

As mentioned above, it should be noted that the position has since changed. Since October 2001, it has been possible for a juvenile to have his case tried in a Juvenile Court provided that the Public Prosecutor applies to the Juvenile Court to try that offence; and additionally, the legal representative of the juvenile concerned consents to the offence being tried by the Juvenile Court. The section defines "legal representative", in relation to a child or young person who is charged with an offence, to also include any person assisting the child or young person in his defence to the charge, which would include the juvenile's parents or guardian, for example.

The current Section 33 CYPA is reproduced below with the relevant portions in bold:

Jurisdiction of Juvenile Court

33. - (1) Subject to the provisions of this section, no child or young person shall be charged with or tried for any offence by a Court of summary jurisdiction except a Juvenile Court.

(2) Where a child or young person is charged with any offence triable only by the High Court, he shall be tried by the High Court unless -

(a) the Public Prosecutor applies to the Juvenile Court to try such offence; and

(b) ***the legal representative of the child or young person concerned consents to the offence being tried by the Juvenile Court.*** (emphasis added)

(3) Where a charge is made jointly against a child or young person and a person who has attained the age of 16 years, the charge shall be heard by a Court of appropriate jurisdiction other than a Juvenile Court.

(4) Where, in the course of any proceedings before any Court of appropriate jurisdiction other than a Juvenile Court, it appears that the person to whom the proceedings relate is a child or young person, the Court may, notwithstanding subsection (1), proceed with the hearing and determination of the proceedings if it thinks fit.

(5) A Juvenile Court shall have jurisdiction to try all offences which, but for subsections (1) and (2), would be triable only by a Magistrate's Court, a District Court or the High Court.

(6) A person who has attained the age of 16 years on the date of commencement of the hearing of the charge shall not be tried for any offence by a Juvenile Court.

(7) Where in the course of any trial before a Juvenile Court the child or young person to whom the trial relates attains the age of 16 years, nothing in this subsection shall prevent the Juvenile Court, if it thinks fit, from proceeding with the trial and dealing with the child or young person in accordance with the provisions of this Act.

(8) ***In this section, "legal representative", in relation to a child or young person who is charged with an offence, includes any person assisting the child or young person in his defence to the charge.*** (emphasis added)

3. Limitation of Juvenile Court's Jurisdiction in Cases where a Juvenile is Jointly Charged with Adults

This section relates to the situations in which a juvenile is jointly charged with adults (i.e., accused persons who are at least 16 years old). In short, the position under Section 33(3) CYPA makes it clear that in such cases, the Juvenile Court must relinquish jurisdiction in favour of the other court which will then hear the case against all the accused persons jointly. A case illustration of this is given under this heading.

Case illustration:

PP v. (1)STP, (2)LAG, (3)NTW; (4)LHC and (5)TSM
(CC 52/1997) High Court (unreported)
MPH Rubin J
24 November 1997

The five accused persons pleaded guilty to a charge of causing grievous hurt, in the prosecution of the common object of their unlawful assembly, under Section 325 read with Section 149 of the Penal Code (Cap. 224). The High Court dealt with the matter. The first four accused were 16 years old and above, while the fifth accused was below 16 years of age, but was also dealt with by the High Court, having been jointly charged with the other four accused. All five accused were members of a secret society known as "Ang Meng Tong". On 25 May 1997, at the Bedok Central Branch of McDonalds, they, together with their headman "Ah John", being members of an unlawful assembly and in prosecution of their common object, caused grievous hurt to a member of "Gi Leng Kiat", which was a rival secret society. "Ah John" went on to inflict fatal blows upon the victim, causing his death. The five accused were then arrested, but their headman "Ah John" remained at large. They admitted to the Statement of Facts without qualification and were convicted accordingly.

After hearing pleas in mitigation by counsel, the judge called for pre-sentence reports. Having then reviewed the reports and all the factors pleaded in mitigation, he was of the view that the manner in which the offence was committed, the planning involved, and the harm inflicted, did not indicate the offence to be an act of sudden impulse or momentary outburst by foolish and confused youths, but rather by secret society members blindly loyal to their society. This warranted a sentence that would bring home the message that corrosive, anti-social behaviour would not be tolerated. The accused persons had shown utter contempt of law and order.

The judge then imposed on each of the accused, a sentence of three years' imprisonment (including the fifth accused who was a juvenile). But as regards the fifth accused, as he was only 15 years and 7 months at the time, he was ordered to serve his sentence in such place and under such conditions as the Minister determined as provided under Section 38 of the CYPA.[6]

This case illustrates the operation of Section 33(3) of the CYPA, which states that *"where a charge is made jointly against a child or young person and a person who has attained the age of 16 years, the charge shall be heard by a Court of appropriate jurisdiction other than a Juvenile Court."* Notwithstanding this, it must be noted that where punishment of the juvenile is concerned, the Court will be empowered to mete out any of the sanctions that the Juvenile Court could have meted out to the juvenile under Section 44(1) of the CYPA.[7]

II. Court's Discretion and Punishment Options

The next general area of issues relates to the sentencing or punishment of juvenile offenders. It is appropriate to note that there are many more punishment options that the Juvenile Court may choose from when dealing with juveniles. This is due to Section 44 of the CYPA which lists the powers that the Juvenile Court may exercise once an offence has been proved or admitted to by a juvenile offender. The available punishments include ordering the offender to undergo probation, perform community service, be detained in a place of detention, be sent to an approved school, or be brought before a District Court to be placed in a reformative training centre. Section 37 of the CYPA also specifically restricts an order of imprisonment from being made against a child absolutely, and against a young person unless the Court certifies that he is of so unruly a character that he cannot be detained in a place of detention or an approved school. Section 37(3) further provides that corporal punishment cannot be imposed on a juvenile by any court other than the High Court. These and other matters regarding sentencing and punishment are discussed below.

1. Discretion of Court under Section 235 of the Criminal Procedure Code (Cap. 68) to Exercise Usual Sentencing Powers to Impose Imprisonment and/or Fines

This issue relates to situations when a criminal court other than the Juvenile Court deals with a juvenile. Section 235 of the Criminal Procedure Code (Cap. 68) (CPC) also contains a provision relating to youthful offenders. In the CPC, "youthful offenders" are defined as persons between the ages of 7 and 16. Therefore, while the terminology is different, substantively, all "youthful offenders" under the CPC would also necessarily be "juveniles" under the CYPA. The interesting effect of Section 235 CPC is that if any criminal court convicts a youthful offender, that court may either imprison or fine the youthful offender in accordance with the penalty prescribed by the offence, or it may deal with the youthful offender under the punishment provisions in the CYPA. Yet, as mentioned above, Section 37(1) absolutely does not permit a child (i.e., below 14 years) to be imprisoned, while even against a young person (i.e., at least 14 but below 16 years), Section 37(2) requires the Court to be satisfied of his exceedingly unruly character before ordering imprisonment. This parallel regime has resulted in an apparent conflict between Section 37 CYPA and Section 235 CPC. There is case authority discussing this issue in particular, and the court's reasoning is provided in the following digest.

PP v. (1)OLX and (2)YKH

(CC 50/2000) High Court (unreported)
Amarjeet JC
24 July 2000

This was a case involving the wrongful confinement of, and the commission of various acts of torture and depravity on, a girl over a period of about 17 days in an Ang Mo Kio apartment. This digest will only make reference to the first accused. (For a write-up regarding one of the other accused who was 11 years old at the time of the offence, refer to pages 78-80 above.)

The first accused, who was 14 years old at the time of the offence and 15 at the time of sentencing, pleaded guilty to a total of seven offences. Some of the offences were committed together with the second accused and others in furtherance of their common intention. These other individuals were dealt with in the Subordinate Courts.

The charges on which the first accused was convicted, were:

(i) First charge — under Section 377 of the Penal Code (Cap. 224) — abetting by instigating the victim with threats to commit an unnatural offence with a dog, i.e., by sucking the penis of the said animal.
(ii) Sixth charge — under Section 147 of the Penal Code — being a member of an unlawful assembly with others, with the common object to cause hurt to the victim by slapping, punching and kicking the victim, thereby committing rioting.
(iii) Ninth charge — under Section 324 of the Penal Code — causing hurt to the victim by hitting her with a weapon, i.e., a stick.
(iv) Tenth charge — under Section 509 of the Penal Code — intruding upon the privacy of the victim and forcing her to strip naked and have her insert a marker and a Barbie doll's broken leg into her vagina.
(v) Twelfth charge — under Section 342 of the Penal Code — tying up and thereby wrongfully confining the victim.
(vi) Fourteenth charge — under Section 326 of the Penal Code — pouring hot water, i.e., a heated substance, on the body of the victim, thereby causing grievous hurt to her.
(vii) Fifteenth charge — under Section 342 of the Penal Code — tying the victim up with raffia and thereby wrongfully confining her.

In addition, the accused consented to six other charges being taken into consideration, including the 7th charge (rioting under Section 147 of the Penal Code), the 8th charge (causing grievous hurt under Section 326 of the Penal Code), the 11th charge (pouring hot water on the victim thereby causing grievous hurt under Section

326 of the Penal Code), the 13th charge (causing hurt under Section 323 of the Penal Code), the 16th charge (using criminal force by cutting the victim's hair under Section 352 of the Penal Code) and the 17th charge (pouring hot water on the victim thereby causing grievous hurt under Section 326 of the Penal Code). Many of the charges were similar in nature, each of them relating to separate and specific incidents over the entire 17-day period during which the victim was confined in the apartment.

The accused, being about 14 years old at the time of the offence and 15 at the time of sentence, fell within the definition of a "youthful offender", i.e., a person between the ages of 7 to 16, under Section 2 of the CPC. Under Section 235 of the CPC, when any youthful offender is convicted before any criminal court of an offence punishable by fine or imprisonment or both, the Court may either imprison or fine the youthful offender, or it may, in its discretion, sentence such an accused person under the punishment provisions of the CYPA. The punishment provisions under the CYPA are mainly set out in Sections 37, 38 and 44, and they generally constitute less severe punishments such as probation and community service orders, save for a provision for imprisonment contained in Section 37 which, however, can only be imposed if the Court certifies that the young person is of so unruly a character that such person cannot be detained in a place of detention or an approved school. Section 38 of the CYPA provides for detention for such specified period as a Court may determine, where certain grave offences have been committed by the young person, namely murder, culpable homicide not amounting to murder, attempted murder or voluntarily causing grievous hurt, but again, only if the Court is of the opinion that none of the other methods, such as probation or community service orders, by which the case may be legally dealt with is suitable.

The judge was of the opinion that in this case, the Court should exercise its power to punish the accused under its usual sentencing powers sitting as a criminal court as stated in Section 235 of the CPC, rather than dealing with the accused under the provisions of the CYPA. The judge then stated that in the exercise of such usual sentencing power, it would then be unnecessary for the Court to determine whether a youthful offender was "of an unruly character" or not, since that would only be necessary if the Court was invoking the CYPA to deal with the accused.

The vicious offences committed by the accused on the victim called for a punitive and deterrent sentence of imprisonment. There was no real provocation or aggression by the victim, other than the accused's allegations that the victim had failed to meet her at a scheduled place and time, and allegations that the victim had stolen the accused's pet hamster. The judge held that young offenders who engage in violence and cause serious injuries to others without provocation can and should expect to be imprisoned, and not expect to be handled with kid gloves by the Court. Nor should a minor provocation be made an excuse to inflict mindless violence on a person.

In the circumstances, and taking into consideration the six other charges consented to by the accused, the High Court sentenced her as follows:

First charge	— Section 377 (unnatural offence) — 2 years' imprisonment
Sixth charge	— Section 147 (rioting) — 18 months' imprisonment
Ninth charge	— Section 324 (hurt with weapon – a stick) — 2 years' imprisonment
Tenth charge	— Section 509 (intruding on sexual privacy) — 6 months' imprisonment
Twelfth charge	— Section 342 (wrongful confinement) — 6 months' imprisonment
Fourteenth charge	— Section 326 (pouring hot water) — 3 years' imprisonment
Fifteenth charge	— Section 342 (wrongful confinement) — 6 months' imprisonment

In concluding, the judge considered the 1st, 10th and 14th charges to be the most serious in the circumstances. As such, the sentences of two years, six months and three years respectively thereunder, were ordered to run consecutively. The sentences in respect of the other charges were to run concurrently. In sentencing the accused, the judge also took into account the totality principle by moderating the sentence. The total sentence of imprisonment was therefore 5 years 6 months.

As seen in the precedents set by the High Court in this and other cases, it is clear that any criminal court dealing with a youthful offender has the option of invoking its usual sentencing powers.

However, where the Juvenile Court is concerned, it is suggested that this option is not available. In the writer's view, this is because, whilst the Juvenile Court exercises jurisdiction of a criminal flavour, it cannot be rightly said to be a "criminal court" *per se*. It is submitted that the "criminal court" referred to in Section 235 of the CPC must be read in light of the framework set out in Section 6 of the CPC which states that the Courts for the administration of criminal justice in Singapore shall be the High Court, District Courts and Magistrate's Courts. It makes no mention of the Juvenile Court. As such it is ventured that the Juvenile Court is not a "criminal court" within the contemplation of the CPC.

Rather, it must be noted that the Juvenile Court is essentially a *sui generis* court created by the CYPA, being neither really a District Court nor a Magistrate's Court. Therefore it should follow that the procedures and powers of the Juvenile Court are circumscribed primarily by the CYPA, with the CPC provisions only serving to plug gaps. Since Section 37 of the CYPA specifically prohibits the imprisonment of children, and allows imprisonment of young persons only if they are of extremely "unruly character", the Juvenile Court's powers of punishment are to be accordingly limited. The Juvenile Court thus ought not to have the parallel option of invoking Section 235 of the CPC, in the light of the CYPA.

2. Factors to Consider in Choosing the Appropriate Approved School for Juvenile Offender to be Admitted to

This discussion deals with the choice of appropriate approved schools for juvenile offenders to be sent to. The case authority under this heading is an illustration of the various factors and considerations for the Juvenile Court to take into account when deciding where a juvenile offender should be sent to.

MY v. PP

(MA 157/2001) Juvenile Court
Magistrate Ong Chin Heng, Mr Ong Cher Keong (Panel of Advisers) and Dr Anthony Loh (Panel of Advisers)
29 May 2001

The accused pleaded guilty to a charge of simple rioting under Section 147 of the Penal Code (Cap. 224). Five other co-accused were dealt with by the Juvenile Court in respect of the same incident. The victim in this case suffered from a stab wound on his back. He was hypotensive and required a blood transfusion, and was warded in hospital for two days. The facts revealed that the accused had had an earlier altercation with the victim sometime in January 2001 over some staring incidents. He then went back to his gang, known as "010", to complain to them about the victim. The headman of the gang then decided to "teach the victim a lesson". So on 25 March 2001, a whole group of eight youths, including the accused, went in search of their victim, carrying along with them an assortment of knives and chains. When they found him alone, they confronted him and the accused kicked him from behind. Thereafter a scuffle ensued and the victim ended up being stabbed once, whereupon the accused and his accomplices fled the scene. The accused and five other co-accused were arrested and charged in the Juvenile Court, while the rest, being above 16 years old, were dealt with separately in a District Court.

The accused was a first-time offender, who asked for probation to be granted. On his behalf, the accused's mother urged the Court to impose a lighter sentence and stated that the accused would listen to her from now on. His stepfather also asked the Court to be lenient.

The Probation Officer, in the Pre-sentence Report, assessed that the accused was not suitable for probation, having considered the following risk factors:

(a) The ineffective supervision rendered by the accused's parents due to their being away from home for the major part of the day;
(b) The accused's lack of positive response to his mother's stepping-up of control and imposition of disciplinary measures;
(c) The accused's need for a stricter, more regimented environment, and possible ancillary need for religious guidance;
(d) The accused's past conduct and behaviour in school and at home which was poor, and which displayed his propensity to defy authority;
(e) The accused's association with negative peers and participation in gang activities; and
(f) The accused's apparent lack of appreciation of the seriousness of his offence in his conduct pending sentence.

The Court agreed with the Probation Officer's assessment that the accused was unsuitable for probation. However, the Court disagreed with the Probation Officer on another aspect of his recommendations — that of *which* Approved School the accused ought to be admitted to. Whilst the Probation Officer had recommended that the accused be admitted to the Muhammadiyah Welfare Home (MWH), the Court finally ordered the accused to be admitted to the Singapore Boys' Home (SBH) instead.

Although both the accused and another co-accused (who was dealt with by the Court on the same day) were assessed to be unsuitable for probation and were to be admitted to Approved Schools, as *between* these two juveniles, it was clearly necessary to impose different punishments.

This was essentially because of a clear difference in their culpability levels. The accused had been largely responsible for precipitating the offence in the first place, due to his complaint to the gang about his earlier altercations with the victim. Had it not been for the accused's festering grievance against the victim, the rioting incident would not have happened. The co-accused, on the other hand, was a blind follower in this instance. Although that did not make his actions any less criminal, at least he was not responsible for starting the chain of events leading to the commission of the offence.

Thus, in order to maintain a measure of parity, the accused had to be punished more severely than his co-accused. This could have been achieved either by sending the accused to an Approved School with a stricter regime, or by lengthening the accused's period of residence, or both. On a balance, the best option was to order the minimum period of residence, but in an Approved School with a stricter regime, for three reasons.

The first reason was that the minimum period of 24 months (the minimum period is specified in Section 44(1)(i) of the CYPA) was preferable to a longer period of residence. It was an important consideration to allow the accused to complete his punishment as quickly as possible and get on with his life thereafter, especially when a difference of a just few months could be a long time from a young person's point of view.

The second reason was that a more intensive regime in the SBH would be preferable to a more lenient one in the MWH. This would be more effective in rehabilitating the accused and instilling respect for authority, by delivering a short sharp shock as a wake-up call. SBH is a high-security institution, whereas MWH is an open institution with no security features to ensure that its residents do not abscond. SBH has a stricter regime — punishments for misbehaviour are more severe. Corporal punishment is used very sparingly in MWH, but it is a more common disciplinary measure in SBH. SBH has a more regimented lifestyle than MWH. The residents are monitored more closely, and have much less freedom to come and go around the compound as they please. In SBH, the residents are made to do foot drills and hard physical activities in addition to their sports programmes. MWH has sports on its curriculum, but no foot drills. Thus, juveniles who, in the Court's view, need a highly disciplined, closely controlled, and structured environment, would be sent to SBH rather than to a more open institution such as MWH.

The third reason was a practical one. It was desirable to keep the accused separate from his old gang member (the co-accused, who had been admitted to the MWH), lest they be tempted to jointly create more mischief, or influence the rest of the residents in the MWH.

In the circumstances, the Juvenile Court finally ordered the accused to reside in the SBH for a period of two years.

The accused appealed against this order, but subsequently, on the day of the hearing of the appeal, sought leave to withdraw the appeal. The High Court granted leave to the accused to withdraw his appeal.

3. Section 5(4) of the Probation of Offenders Act (Cap. 252) — Consent of Offenders to the Conditions of Probation is Required before Probation can be Granted

The case authority under this heading takes a closer look at the Probation of Offenders Act (Cap. 252), which governs the probation regime. In particular, it highlights the requirement for an offender to consent to the conditions of the proposed Probation Order, before the Court can proceed to make the Probation Order.

MF v. PP
(MA 352/1996) High Court [1997] 3 SLR 345
Yong Pung How CJ
14 July 1997

The appellant, a 14-year-old boy, was charged under Section 379 of the Penal Code (Cap. 224) with the theft of a wallet at a department store. He was found guilty after trial. With respect to the punishment to be imposed on the appellant, the Probation Officer had recommended that the appellant be placed on probation for 18 months with residence in Bukit Batok Hostel for a period of one year. This was the initial order of the magistrate in the Juvenile Court but, as the appellant did not consent to the conditions imposed on the probation, the order was then amended to a two-year stay at the Singapore Boys' Home (SBH).

The appellant then appealed against the finding of guilt on various grounds, which are not relevant for the purposes of this digest. Although there was no appeal against the magistrate's order of the two-year stay at the SBH, at the hearing of the appeal, the appellant's counsel invited the High Court to vary the order to one of probation instead, in view of the fact that the appellant's mother's chronic asthma made her dependent on the appellant.

On this issue, the High Court stated that it was obliged to follow the guidelines laid down in the Probation of Offenders Act where it is provided under Section 5(4) that, in the case of an offender who is not less than 14 years of age, **the Court shall not make an order of probation unless he expresses his willingness to comply with the requirements attached.** This the appellant had refused to agree to. Under such circumstances, the magistrate had no alternative but to order the appellant to be sent to the SBH for a mandatory minimum of two years, as set out in Section 44(1)(g) of the CYPA.

In the circumstances, there were clearly no grounds for varying the order in any way, nor was there any merit in the appellant's case to justify a setting aside of the magistrate's ruling. Accordingly, the High Court dismissed the appeal.

4. Factors to Consider in Determining Suitability of Granting Probation

This case examines the factors that the Juvenile Court takes into account before it decides if community intervention in the form of probation is suitable for the juvenile's rehabilitation.

PDE v. PP

(MA 59/2001) Juvenile Court
Magistrate May Lucia Mesenas, Mr Lee Tiong Peng (Panel of Advisers) and Mr Philip Leong (Panel of Advisers)
21 February 2001

The accused pleaded guilty to a charge of consuming a Class A controlled drug (Ecstasy) under Section 8(b) and punishable under Section 33 of the Misuse of Drugs Act (Cap. 185).

The accused was a first-time offender, who claimed that she was prepared to change and that she wanted to go back to school. On her behalf, the accused's mother urged the Court to give her one last chance and that she would exert stricter control over her daughter. She also assured that the accused would have to report to her everyday upon returning from school. Further, she added that she was separated from her husband and was therefore the sole breadwinner of the family.

However, in the Probation Report, the probation officer assessed that the accused was not suitable for probation, having considered the various risk factors as well as the accused's needs. In particular, the following were stated to be risk factors:

(a) There was ineffective supervision rendered by the accused's parents and an unacceptably tolerant attitude taken by them towards the accused's bad behaviour. In fact, the accused's parents gave contradictory accounts in their interviews with the probation officer, which indicated that they were lying in order to cover up for their daughter. Clearly, the accused's parents gave her a lot of freedom and allowed her to do whatever she liked. Lastly, her father was himself involved in drug-related charges. Thus, it was rather doubtful as to how much effective supervision they would be able to enforce if probation was granted.

(b) The accused's conduct and behaviour in school had deteriorated since 1998. The Probation Report also disclosed the accused's disciplinary record in secondary school to be less than impressive, with truancy being the main problem, having been present in school for only 78 out of 176 school days, thus reflecting a poor attitude and disobedience to school authority. Despite counselling, the accused also refused to participate in co-curricular activities as she refused to go to school on Saturdays.

(c) The deterioration of her behaviour was consistent with her mixing around with negative peers, especially at the point in time when she committed the present offence. In fact, she had been arrested, together with her friends, by the police at 5 a.m. in the morning. It was therefore doubtful if she would be able to dissociate herself from these negative peers when she had grown accustomed to such activities with them.

(d) The accused's own alarmingly lackadaisical attitude in her conduct pending sentence was of the biggest concern. Notably, she had, without excuse, missed two appointments with the Probation Officer prior to the Probation Report being put up.

On these occasions, the accused had claimed to be ill and unable to attend, but when house checks were conducted, she was found to have gone out to Orchard Road. More worryingly, the accused's mother appeared to be covering this up on behalf of her daughter. The accused failed to abide by the trial time restrictions imposed by the probation officer, and also failed to call the probation officer at 7 p.m. every day as instructed.

As such, the Juvenile Court ordered the accused to reside in the Toa Payoh Girls' Home for a period of two years.

The accused appealed against this order, but it was subsequently dismissed by the High Court.

III. Breach Proceedings

This last general area of issues covers breach proceedings. Breach proceedings may be commenced if an offender, without reasonable excuse, contravenes any of the conditions of his punishment order. Such proceedings are usually instituted by Probation Officers or superintendents of Approved Schools and Homes. Upon breach proceedings being brought against an offender, the Court has the power under Section 44(5) of the CYPA to make further orders, to vary the original order(s), or to direct the offender to comply with the original order(s).

1. Whether an Order Made Pursuant to Breach Proceedings Constitutes a Conviction on an Offence Concerning Substantially Similar Facts

This issue arises when an offender re-offends, and his re-offending conduct is also partly or entirely the basis of the breach proceedings. The question is whether, by not only charging the offender with a fresh offence, but also instituting breach proceedings against him, this would amount to an *autrefois convict* resulting in double jeopardy, or whether it would be otherwise oppressive against the offender. This is discussed in the following case digest.

GSG v. PP
(Crim Rev 13/2000) High Court (unreported)
Yong Pung How CJ
19 July 2000

The juvenile in this case was found guilty of certain property offences in May 1998 and was ordered to reside in the Salvation Army Gracehaven (Gracehaven) for 24 months (the "first order"). On 25 November 1999, the superintendent of Gracehaven instituted breach proceedings under Section 44(2)(a) of the CYPA (the "breach proceedings") against the juvenile. The Juvenile Court called for a progress report. In the report, presented on 14 December 1999, the superintendent stated that the juvenile often absconded from the home. Whilst at large, he had mixed with undesirable peers, smoked and loitered in the streets, and also engaged in sex with a female resident of the home. The Juvenile Court transferred the juvenile to the Singapore Boys' Home (SBH) for the unexpired period of the first order (i.e., approximately five months). Subsequently, on 27 January 2000, the juvenile was charged with and found guilty of three counts of carnal connection with a girl under 16 years, which were offences under Section 140(1)(i) of the Women's Charter (Cap. 353) — the juvenile had committed these offences on the occasions when he had absconded from the home. The juvenile was then sent to the SBH for 24 months (the "second order") with immediate effect.

The juvenile petitioned the High Court, asking that it exercise its power of revision to quash the finding of guilt made in respect of the carnal connection charges or to alter the second order by reducing the period of residence in SBH, on the grounds of *autrefois convict*[8] as well as an abuse of process.

The High Court held that the claim of *autrefois convict* failed because the breach proceedings did not concern facts or offences that were even substantially similar to those relating to the carnal connection proceedings on 27 January 2000. Furthermore, the breach proceedings did not involve the trial of a *specific* charge but rather were meant to assess the continued suitability of the juvenile remaining at the home, based on representations made by the manager of the home. The order sending the juvenile to SBH for the unexpired period of the first order was thus merely a transfer order and **did not amount to a conviction**. The second order imposed on the juvenile therefore could not be said to be a second conviction on substantially the same facts or offence.

With respect to the claim that the second set of proceedings amounted to an *abuse of process*, the High Court held that in order for the Court to quash the juvenile's conviction on the carnal connection charges, the juvenile had to show that the bringing of these proceedings against him was **oppressive** and thus an abuse of process. This the juvenile tried to do unsuccessfully, by asserting procedural irregularity. The juvenile cited the case of *Ng Kwok Fai [1996] 1 SLR 568* to support his position. However, *Ng Kwok Fai* dealt with the sentencing principles involved in imposing an order for reformative training — specifically, what kind of punishments can be imposed at the same time that a Reformative Training Order is made. This case was therefore wholly unrelated to the point the juvenile was trying to make. The juvenile therefore failed to prove that he suffered any prejudice as a result of the orders made pursuant to the breach proceedings, as well as the orders made in respect of the carnal connection charges.

The High Court accordingly dismissed the juvenile's petition.

2. Section 44 of the Children and Young Persons Act (Cap. 38) — Definition of "So Unruly a Character" in Breach Proceedings

This issue concerns when an offender can be said to be of "so unruly a character", such that the provisions in Section 44(7) of the CYPA can be invoked, for him to be transferred from a place of detention or approved school or home, to a reformative training centre. The definition of "so unruly a character" is discussed under this heading.

TC v. PP

(MA 180 & 201/2000) High Court (unreported)
Yong Pung How CJ
30 November 2000

The juvenile in this case had an established history of delinquency and had previously been expelled from his secondary schools for continual misconduct. In February 1998, at the age of 14 years, the juvenile was convicted for a series of theft offences. He was ordered by the Juvenile Court to reside in the Singapore Boys' Home (SBH) for a period of 30 months. While at the SBH, the juvenile continued with his errant ways and committed many misdemeanours. This included absconding from lawful custody and unlawfully disposing of a pair of handcuffs that he had been wearing when he escaped. The juvenile was later arrested and taken back to the SBH. However, he remained defiant and continued to misbehave even after his return. As such, breach proceedings were instituted against him. On 29 May 2000, the Superintendent of the SBH submitted a report to the Juvenile Court under Section 44(2) *[NB: now re-numbered Section 44(7) — see below]* of the CYPA. It enumerated all the misdeeds committed by the juvenile in the SBH and stated that he was of "so unruly a character" that he could no longer be detained in the SBH.

The Court was satisfied that the juvenile was of so unruly a character that he was unsuitable for detention in the SBH and a sentence of reformative training was more appropriate since the juvenile was already 17 years old. Thus, the Juvenile Court invoked its powers under Section 44(2)(e) CYPA to refer the juvenile to a District Court to be dealt with under Section 13 of the Criminal Procedure Code (Cap. 68). The matter was heard by a district judge who ordered the juvenile to continue his sentence in a reformative training centre.

The juvenile faced another two fresh charges for escaping from the SBH and for unlawfully disposing of the handcuffs he was wearing at the time of his escape. These proceedings were heard by a different district judge who also held that the juvenile should be sentenced to reformative training. As a sentence of reformative training had already been imposed earlier, the second sentence was ordered to run concurrently with the earlier term. The juvenile appealed against both sentences of reformative training.

On appeal, the High Court noted that there was no relevant case authority which had previously interpreted the phrase "of so unruly a character" (in the context of the CYPA) or even just the word "unruly". Therefore, the appropriate approach was to adopt the plain and literal meaning of the term and phrase. For this, the Court stated that it would be useful to refer to some of the definitions of the word "unruly" as stated in various dictionaries: in West's Legal Thesaurus/Dictionary, the word "unruly" was defined as "difficult to manage or control; hyperactive"; in The New Shorter Oxford English Dictionary, the same word was defined to mean "not easily controlled or disciplined; ungovernable; disorderly"; and in the Longman Dictionary of the English Language, the meaning stated was "difficult to discipline or manage" and "not submissive to control". In the present case, it was clear from the facts that the juvenile was of so "unruly" a character that he could not continue to be detained in the SBH. The Juvenile Court was thus entitled to exercise its powers under Section 44(2)(e) of the CYPA, to order the juvenile to be brought before a District Court with a view to being ordered to undergo reformative training.

As the juvenile was still young and had an unfortunate family background, the High Court agreed that he could be afforded another chance at rehabilitation. A custodial sentence of imprisonment was deemed unsuitable for him. A sentence of reformative training was thus the most appropriate since the juvenile clearly needed a more severe and regimented environment than that provided by the SBH. It further held that the order for concurrent sentences of reformative training was correct since a custodial sentence should not be ordered in respect of the two fresh charges, when a sentence of reformative training had already been imposed earlier for the breach action. In the circumstances, the appeal was dismissed.

Analysis:
This case referred to Section 44(2) of the pre-2001 version of the CYPA. This subsection has been re-numbered to Section 44(7). The differences between the old section and the new section are highlighted in bold below:

Old Provision (pre-2001 version) —
Powers of Juvenile Courts on Proof of Offence

44. - *(2)* Where a Juvenile Court is satisfied, on the representations of the manager of a place of detention, an approved school or an approved home, that a person ordered to be detained in the place of detention, approved school or approved home is of so unruly a character that he cannot be so detained, the Court may —

(a) order the person to be transferred to and detained in an approved school or in another approved school, as the case may be, which the Court considers more suitable for him and to be detained there for the whole or any part of the unexpired period of detention;

(b) where the person is a young person, order the person to be transferred to and detained in a Young Offenders Section for a period not exceeding six months;

(c) on completion of the period of detention in a Young Offenders Section ordered under paragraph (b), and on receipt of a satisfactory report of the person's conduct from the Director of Prisons, order the person to be sent back to the place of detention, approved school or approved home, from which he had been transferred, to complete the unexpired period for which he had originally been sent to the place of detention, approved school or approved home;

(d) on completion of the period of detention in a Young Offenders Section ordered under paragraph (b), order the person to be detained for a further period not exceeding six months if the Director of Prisons reports that his conduct, during the period of his detention, has been unsatisfactory; or

(e) where the person is a male and has attained the age of 16 years and the Court is satisfied that it is expedient with a view to his reformation that he should undergo a period of training in a reformative training centre, the Court may order him to be brought before a District Court to be dealt with under Section 13 of the Criminal Procedure Code. (emphasis added)

Amended Provision (with effect from October 2001) — Powers of Juvenile Courts on Proof of Offence

44. - *(7)* Where a Juvenile Court is satisfied, on the representations of the manager of a place of detention, an approved school or an approved home, that a person ordered to be detained in the place of detention, approved school or approved home is of so unruly a character that he cannot be so detained, the Court may —

(a) order the person to be transferred to and detained in an approved school or in another approved school, as the case may be, which the Court considers more suitable for him and to be detained there for the whole or any part of the unexpired period of detention; or

(b) order the person to be brought before a District Court to be dealt with under Section 13 of the Criminal Procedure Code (Cap. 68) if the person —

(i) has attained the age of 16 years; or

(ii) having attained the age of 14 years but being below the age of 16 years, has previously been dealt with by a Court in connection with another offence and had, in respect of that other offence, been ordered under subsection (1) (i) to be sent to an approved school, and the Juvenile Court is satisfied that it is expedient with a view to his reformation that he should undergo a period of training in a reformative training centre. (emphasis added)

Both the old and the new provisions deal with the situation where the juvenile offender has been institutionalised, i.e., sent to an Approved School, Approved Home or Place of Detention, and has been found to be of so unruly a character that he cannot be detained by that institution.

Under the old provision, the Court could transfer him to the Young Offenders Section of a prison for a maximum of six months. Upon completion of this six-month period, he could be transferred back to the Approved School or Approved Home or Place of Detention from which he had originally been transferred to complete the unexpired period of the original detention order — assuming that he received a favourable report from the Director of Prisons. If the report was not favourable, the Court could order him to be further detained in the Young Offenders Section for six months. Under these old provisions, only males who had turned 16 could be sent to the Reformative Training Centre (RTC) as a further punishment option.

Under the new provisions, the Court may now send a boy or a girl who is 14 years and above to an RTC for reformative training. However, if the offender is below 16 years of age, then the Court can only send him or her for reformative training, if he or she had been found guilty of a previous offence, and as a consequence, had been sent to an Approved School. The net effect of the amended provisions has been to lower the age threshold for a young person to be eligible for reformative training (albeit only in restricted circumstances as stated above), as well as to remove the gender distinction, such that girls are also now eligible for reformative training, when they previously were not. The scope of reformative training has thus been significantly broadened. As a consequence of this amendment, the regime for detaining juvenile offenders in Young Offenders Sections of prisons has accordingly been removed.

Henceforth, all juvenile offenders of at least 14 years of age, who are currently institutionalised, and are found to be of so unruly a character that they cannot be detained by that institution, can be sent to RTC, with the added requirement that for offenders below 16, the precondition is that they must already be in an Approved School in connection with a previous offence. This refined RTC regime is intended to replace the Young Offenders Section regime which used to exist under the pre-2001 CYPA provisions.

ENDNOTES

1 For more information on the JOB Criteria, see Chapter 1, The Juvenile Court of Singapore at page 8; see also Chapter 2, The Family and Juvenile Justice Centre at page 54.

2 At the time that the order in this case was made, only males aged between 16 and 21 years of age could be sent to a Reformative Training Centre.

However, since 1 October 2001, amendments were made to the Children and Young Persons Act (Cap. 38), which empowered the Juvenile Court to transfer juvenile offenders to the District Court for Reformative Training Orders to be imposed for boys and girls above the age of 14. However, for those boys and girls aged above 14 and below 16, they must have previously been found guilty of another offence for which they were ordered to reside in the Singapore Boys' Home or the Toa Payoh Girls' Home (Approved Schools) before a Reformative Training Order can be made in respect of them. See Sections 44(1)(k)(ii) of the Children and Young Persons Act (Cap. 38).

3 The male and female offenders are remanded in Queenstown Remand Prison (QRP) or Changi Womens' Prison (CWP) respectively for the purposes of assessing their suitability for reformative training.

4 Students who possess academic potential and who are able to learn at a faster pace, are placed in such classes.

5 There are three grades of probation, namely intensive, supervised, and administrative. Intensive probation means that contact with the probation officer is on a daily basis; face-to-face contact is at least three times a week. Supervised probation is when the probation officer sees a probationer at least once a week. Under the administrative probation scheme, contact would only be once a fortnight initially and progressively to once a month. For all grades of probation, the physical contacts are supplemented with phone contacts depending on the needs of each case.

6 Sections 38(1) and (2) of the Children and Young Persons Act (Cap. 38) state:

Punishment of certain grave crimes

38. —(1) Where a child or young person is convicted of murder, or of culpable homicide not amounting to murder, or of attempted murder, or of voluntarily causing grievous hurt, and the Court is of opinion that none of the other methods by which the case may legally be dealt with is suitable, the Court may sentence the offender to be detained for such period as may be specified in the sentence. Such places where the juvenile may be detained include prisons.

(2) Where a sentence has been passed under subsection (1), the child or young person shall, during that period, notwithstanding anything in the other provisions of this Act, be liable to be detained in such place and on such conditions as the Minister may direct.

7 Section 85 of the Children and Young Persons Act (Cap. 38) states:

Powers of Juvenile Court conferred on other courts

85. Except as otherwise provided, nothing in this Act shall affect the powers of a Magistrate's Court, a District Court or the High Court, and all the powers which may be exercised under this Act by a Juvenile Court may, in like manner, be exercised by a Magistrate's Court, a District Court or the High Court.

8 The term *autrefois convict* refers to a situation where a person is convicted and punished twice for the same offence.

CHAPTER 4

Voices from the Court

In this section, we share the thoughts of some of those people who work in the Juvenile Court and/or take part in its programmes and activities — a Panel Adviser, children who have taken part in a poetry competition organised by the Court, children from the Peer Group Advisers programme, and a volunteer family from our Youth Family Care programme.

4.1 Thoughts of a Juvenile Court Magistrate

MAGISTRATE MAY LUCIA MESENAS

To be a Juvenile Court Magistrate, you need to have a good grasp of human psychology. This is because you have to understand people in order to help them. In juvenile justice, the aim is not just to do justice in the case that is before me. It is to do right by the life of the child who has been brought to the Court.

To do right, I need to give that child a chance for a meaningful future. To do that, I need to make sense of his past. This will help me to decide what would be the best arrangements to make for him in the present.

Thus, matters which may seem quite peripheral to the actual crime the juvenile has committed — indeed, he may not actually have committed a crime, but merely be Beyond Parental Control or in need of a Child Protection Order[1] — are of great interest to the Court. Before any orders are made in respect of a juvenile, his entire life history and psychological profile will be placed before me. In this regard, an interest in people is a very helpful quality in a Juvenile Court Magistrate — as the focus is always on the personality, background and lifestyle of the juvenile.

Officers from the Ministry of Community Development and Sports will interview the juvenile's family members, and obtain reports from his school teachers, his counsellors, his discipline master. His grades, his hobbies, his weekend activities, his drinking and smoking habits, the type of friends he has, his conduct in school, his attitudes towards his classmates and teachers, his relationships with his siblings and with his parents, and the background of his family members, will all be painstakingly reported. In addition to these reports, I am sometimes also given reports from psychiatrists,[2] the JOB Criteria Risk Score,[3] as well as the input of the Family Conference facilitator, if a Family Conference[4] has been ordered for that case. After reading all this, I usually end up knowing the juvenile's life and personality better than his own parents!

Armed with this information, I then have to decide on the appropriate orders to make. Two juveniles who committed the same crime may be treated quite differently. One may be granted probation with community service, and get to stay in his own home, on condition that he obeys the nightly curfew imposed by the Court. The other may be ordered to reside in an Approved Home for two years. Similarly for the children who are reported to be Beyond Parental Control. Some may be placed on statutory supervision, ordered to attend some counselling sessions, and sent home. Others may be ordered to reside in an Approved Home for two years. Why does this happen? Because we are looking to find the arrangements which best fit the *offender* — not the offence. Or, in the case of children in need of care and protection, we are looking to find the arrangements which offer these children a better start in life than they have had thus far.

Clearly, a child from a stable family background, for example, who has had no disciplinary problems in school, is an average student, and does not have any gang connections, has an environment and lifestyle which is more conducive to an order for probation with a home-stay than a child who regularly truants from school, is a secret society member, and has very little parental supervision at home.

I do not make my decisions in a vacuum. I am aided by the advice and opinions of the Panel of Advisers,[5] the psychologists of the Family and Juvenile Justice Centre, probation officers, and sometimes, by representatives from the juvenile's school and his counsellors (if any). All of us will have the same information and the same goal: the rehabilitation of the juvenile and his restoration to society. But we may have different views on what are the best orders to make in order to do this. Discussions can become quite heated. The people involved are from a wide variety of backgrounds — the law, social work, education, psychology. We each bring our own perspectives to our solutions. An educator, for example, may focus on ensuring that the juvenile's education is not disrupted, and propose solutions which would allow him to continue attending school. A social worker may focus on solutions to ensure that the juvenile's family is given sufficient help to cope with unemployment, poverty, illness or whatever other challenges may be facing them. A psychologist may focus on the juvenile's state of mind — how remorseful he is, how willing he is to change.

The Juvenile Court Magistrate has to listen to all these views, testing their strengths and weaknesses with relevant questions and comments. The Magistrate needs to analyse those areas where a consensus can be achieved, and to guide those present at the discussion towards it. To do this kind of work means that you have to be a good listener. You must respect the opinions of others, but be able to analyse them critically. You must know how to lead a group discussion, and focus it.

At the end of the day, you need to have the confidence to decide between conflicting points of view if you cannot, through discussion, obtain a consensus. The responsibility for making the final order lies with the Juvenile Court Magistrate. But the journey towards that decision is one made with many companions — the Panel Advisers, the MCDS officers, the FJJC psychologists, etc. — in this regard, the Juvenile Court Magistrate must know how to be a team player as well as a team leader. This is so that all the different views and information do not confuse, but rather, serve to illuminate the destination.

When the child stands before me in the Juvenile Court, my aim is fourfold. I want him to understand why he has ended up in the Juvenile Court. What aspects of his lifestyle and behaviour have led him to commit the crime or acts which have led to his appearance in Juvenile Court? He must understand this, otherwise he will never change for the better. Then, I want him to understand that he has a choice. He has a choice to change his lifestyle and behaviour, and choose the path to redemption. There is no order that I make in the Juvenile Court that is not intended to offer the juvenile some hope of rehabilitation. I want him to see that. Thirdly, I want him to understand that he must choose, *now*. That if he misses this chance to make this choice, he may never get a second chance. Lastly, I want him to make what I would consider to be the right choice — towards a meaningful future, with a decent education, opportunities for employment, good relationships with those he cares about, and the chance to realise whatever goals he may wish for himself in life.

In order to fulfil these aims, and to make the court appearance an effective event in the juvenile's rehabilitation, I need to have an empathy for the juvenile — what motivates him, what saddens him, what touches his heart. Some juveniles have been so hardened by years of being physically abused by their fathers, for example, that the harshest words are like water off a duck's back to them. But the sight of someone they care about — perhaps a loving grandmother in tears over their behaviour, will cut them to the quick like nothing else would, and make them resolve never to do anything to make that person cry again. Other juveniles weep at a drop of a hat in an attempt to gain the Court's sympathy. These need a few sharp, well-chosen words to make them realise that their attempt to invoke pity has not impressed — and that an improvement in behaviour is the only acceptable demonstration of remorse for their misdeeds.

Thus, my understanding of the juvenile influences how I conduct the court session and what I say to the juvenile, as well as his parents. Like the juveniles, the parents require individualised approaches. If I am of the view that the parents are hardworking, well-meaning people who are just unable to control their headstrong child because they are too mild and gentle in personality, then I will try to strengthen their position by making it very clear to the juvenile that he should respect his parents and obey them. I will also emphasise to the parents the importance of being firm in disciplining their child, and encourage them to do so. If I am of the view that the parents are not really interested in the juvenile, and they are too focused on their own needs and their own lives to supervise or care for him, then I will remind the parents, in the strongest possible terms, of their responsibilities as parents.

Unsurprisingly, the Juvenile Court is the scene of many emotional moments. Tears, recriminations, angry words...People have shouted in court, wept, pleaded, cursed, knelt on the floor, threatened to harm themselves...and even fainted. I have to be sensitive to the emotional dynamics playing out in front of me in order to remain in full control of court proceedings at all times, and to maximise the value of all that happens. I personally have to remain calm, emotionally detached, and dispassionate at all times. Pity, annoyance, frustration, sorrow... are all emotions that I have to put aside, no matter how heart-wrenching the case, no matter how insolent the parents, or unremorseful the juvenile. The value of the Court to the people that come before it lies in its dignity and authority. This is what the Juvenile Court Magistrate must strive to uphold at all times, even in the most trying circumstances.

On a lighter note, the Juvenile Court Magistrate has a great deal of contact with the community. Thus, as a Juvenile Court Magistrate, it is important to enjoy meeting people, discussing ideas with them, and taking part in social events. We have many court volunteers working with us, and we also run many court programmes with the help and involvement of various community groups. Many community groups and organisations also seek the support of the Court for their youth programmes and outreach work. I have been invited to many events, such as Family Day in the Toa Payoh Girls' Home, "thank you" functions for volunteer probation officers, and ceremonies for Honorary Voluntary Special Constabulary in schools. I have also attended the "graduation ceremonies" for the Beyond Parental Control children on Statutory Supervision who have successfully completed their term. It is particularly heartening to see young people who were once in trouble perform plays, create artwork and poetry, and put up musical concerts. I also have regular meetings with our external stakeholders such as the Inter-Ministry Committee for Youth Crime, the police, the Ministry of Community Development and Sports, and the Singapore Children's Society. The exchange of ideas and information is vital in ensuring a co-ordinated national response to juvenile justice, and provides me with valuable insights on developments in this area.

The task is not an easy one. But it is all worth it when a youth who used to be the despair of his parents and teachers learns to stay out of trouble, passes his exams, and makes plans for his future. Or when parents who have abused and neglected their children, such that their children had to be taken away from them to live in an Approved School or an Approved Home, manage to learn how to provide a loving and stable environment for them to grow up in, and the whole family can be re-united under the same roof.

The work of the Juvenile Court will only stop on the day when all parents in Singapore become loving, responsible and mature, and when all children are law-abiding, disciplined and honest.

Sounds like an impossible goal? We at the Juvenile Court will never stop striving to reach it.

4.2 Reflections of a Panel Adviser

DR ANTHONY V H LOH
Principal
Bukit Merah Secondary School

Panel Advisers come from all walks of life. We are principals, psychologists, social workers, and leading figures in the business community. We bring a fresh perspective to the Court. When a case comes before the Juvenile Court, we consider it in the light of the experiences from our working lives and training. Principals, for example, would be familiar with the school system. We can suggest educational road maps for a juvenile, give information on educational courses, and so on. Psychologists would be able to contribute their insights on human behaviour. Social workers can share their perspectives on how to resolve the problems of the juvenile in the context of his entire family — as social workers are trained to deal with a person's problems in a holistic fashion, and to take a long-term view of any treatment that he receives. Panel Advisers have good community links. We can help to arrange for juveniles to be enrolled in schools, or to obtain jobs in organisations. In this manner, we assist the Court to make a decision which takes into account all the aspects of the juvenile's life, and help the Court to explore all possible options for his future.

Time spent as a Panel Adviser to the Juvenile Court can be very enriching and enlightening, even though at times it can be emotionally exhausting. Since January 1994 when the Ministry of Law first appointed me, I have been on duty every Tuesday for two months out of the year for Juvenile Arrest Cases (JAC) and every Friday for two months out of the year for Beyond Parental Control (BPC) cases — that makes 16 sessions for each year. The case reports, numbering between 10 to 15 each day, are sent to me a couple of days earlier for my study before the court session, which generally starts at 9.00 a.m. and seldom finishes before 1.00 p.m.

In the past nine years, I have come across a vast variety of JAC and BPC cases. Some are strange and puzzling. I have always wondered how a 12-year-old boy could intimidate his elderly grandmother during a funeral wake to such an extent that it became a police case, which was one of the cases that came before me. The boy wanted to go home whereas the grandmother wanted to stay on at the wake, so he got angry with her. How does a young boy come to treat his grandmother this way? What has gone wrong with the family dynamics? Likewise, I find it hard to understand how normally well-behaved teenagers from highly-educated families, studying in well-known established mission schools, could go about vandalising notice-boards in MRT stations at 2.00 a.m. Just a way to release tension after the final examinations?

When parents and the juveniles appear in Court together, the scene is usually very enlightening, sometimes amusing. Most parents feel terribly embarrassed standing in front of the judge and the Panel Advisers and often blame themselves for their children's past misdeeds. Sometimes, some parents are in prison and come to Court handcuffed and under escort to be with their children. Such appearances are always emotionally draining for everyone in the Court especially if the parents and juveniles have not seen each other for a long time. Occasionally, there are parents who attempt to negotiate for an outcome which best suits their own needs, while disregarding the needs of the child, or who unabashedly ask permission for their children to go for an overseas holiday before serving their order in the Home. The Magistrate is generally not amused by such a request.

One particular case of a 16-year-old Chinese girl whose mother lodged a Beyond Parental Control (BPC) complaint[6] against her has remained in my mind since February 1998 when I was on duty. Mary (not her real name), was the oldest of six children; the youngest was a 3-year-old girl. Another sibling, a 12-year-old girl, was hearing impaired and attended school at the Singapore Association for the Hearing Impaired. The three boys of the family, aged 13, 10 and 7, were in different primary schools. To support this large family, the father had to work long hours at a market collecting card boxes for recycling. Sometimes, the mother helped out if she could find the time. What shocked me most was that this family of eight was living in an old abandoned bus in Jurong! Was this possible? In affluent and modern Singapore? In the year 1998? And not far from the many HDB flats? Yet, despite their poverty and hardships, the parents had so much self-pride and did not want to ask for any financial assistance but just preferred privacy about their residence and means of livelihood.

In school, Mary was not a well-behaved girl. Not really unexpected if you knew her family circumstances. She was often absent — sometimes she worked late at night and did not return to her "bus". Other times, the parents did not even know where she was. Occasionally, she turned up in school in the company of what her school termed "undesirable" outsiders — unkempt youngsters who had dropped out of school, and, in a group, were likely to create trouble. Eventually, she was considered a "bad influence" for the other pupils and was asked to leave the school in July 1997 after failing her Secondary 3 Normal Technical mid-year exam. The school thought that she needed "a change of environment" and asked the parents to look for another school for her.

In court, Mary's illiterate mother pleaded for her daughter to be given another chance for an education. She mentioned that she had approached all the secondary schools she knew in Jurong but without any success. As a principal myself, I immediately felt the urge to help her. That same afternoon, I contacted the principal of Mary's former school, explained to her the extenuating circumstances of this case and appealed on her behalf — but in vain. So I decided that my own school — the Bukit Merah Secondary School, should take Mary in.

The very next day, Bukit Merah Secondary School opened its doors to Mary. The teachers were marvellous and, upon learning of her plight, they spontaneously wanted to help her in every way possible to ensure that she would lead a life like any ordinary teenaged girl. They were very sympathetic to her. Some even marvelled at her resilience. Which 16-year-old girl in Singapore could face her friends in school if she knew that they knew she was living in an abandoned bus? Which 16-year-old girl could attend school regularly if she had to work part-time in the evening and take care of her younger siblings early in the morning before leaving for school?

Mary is now 20 years old, having stayed out of trouble for the past few years. I am certain that the teachers in Bukit Merah Secondary School found great satisfaction in having helped her grow up to be a responsible citizen. Financially, the school provided her with the necessary books, stationery and uniforms, waived all fees as well as paid for her GCE "N" level exam fees. More importantly, the teachers gave her the necessary emotional support and understanding that any 16-year-old girl would need. In return, through helping her and others like her, my teachers and I have learned that we should treasure opportunities to help other juveniles without a school, so that they are given another chance for an education and for the future that they deserve to have in our society. It is never easy for such juveniles to return to society as healthy adults even with the help of dedicated and caring teachers. But, without such people in our schools, how will our juveniles be helped? The thought alone is terrifying. Fortunately, there are still teachers who are in the profession because they value the children under their care and treasure the opportunities to help those who have gone astray.

I certainly treasure the time spent going through the case reports and value the discussion sessions in chambers. They enrich my knowledge and appreciation of the difficulties faced by teenagers growing up in our modern society. Often I sympathise with those parents who have lost control of their teenagers or who are at their wit's end trying to bring their children back to the right path. Sometimes, all of us involved in the chamber discussion also find ourselves having great difficulties looking for an acceptable solution and ultimately having to accept one which is, at most, the least unsatisfactory. Some cases which remain long in my memory and trouble me considerably involve juveniles with low IQ. This is because we have limited facilities in this country to deal with such juveniles. If they are put into an open institution, which has no security features to ensure that its residents do not abscond, these juveniles are likely to abscond. However, if they are put into a high-security home, they will be in the company of juveniles who have committed more serious offences, and would therefore be vulnerable to bullying and negative peer influences. Thus, although a high-security home is not the ideal solution for them, we are not able to put them anywhere else which is more suitable — there is no high-security home specially catering for educationally sub-normal children. At least in the ordinary high-security home, they can be contained, monitored and given help.

In every case, we always want to rehabilitate the offending juvenile without, however, making light of his offence. To achieve this goal, it is necessary to have support from the family, effective supervision by the probation officers from MCDS or social workers from other voluntary agencies, the close co-operation of the school and the determination of the juvenile himself to turn over a new leaf. It is always the ardent hope of everyone working in the Juvenile Court to see our offending juveniles become law-abiding and useful citizens of tomorrow.

4.3 Volunteering as a Youth Family Care Parent

Story narrated by MR LOGANSWARAN RAMOO (aged 32) to MS CAROL BALHETCHET, Director, Youth Development, Singapore Children's Society

My name is Logan. I am a happily married man with a very supportive homemaker wife, Agnes, and two healthy young children, a boy, aged

11 years and a daughter, 10 years old. I worked hard to get to where I am today. I am an entrepreneur, in the business of logistics supply.

Life wasn't at all rosy for me some 10 or 20 years back. I remember when I was a teenager; there was no problem big enough that I would not get into trouble with. You name it and I probably tried it out — drugs, drinks, and even gang involvement, which usually led to bitter problems for my family. It reached a stage when my family decided that the only way they could deal with my behaviour was to ignore me. Finally, the streets became my home. One day, it hit me that I didn't want to live such a life any more. But by then, it was too late and there was no one around to help me. It was lonely and difficult to try to get people to trust and accept me. I learnt the hard way that the good life would not be given to me on a platter. I was constantly judged and had a difficult time struggling to prove myself. But this is all in the past now.

In November 2001, the Touch Community Service recruited me for a programme in which "normal" families are matched to support juvenile delinquents and their families, through the help of the Juvenile Court — the Youth Family Care (YFC) programme. This provided me with the opportunity to help teenagers in trouble. My thought was that maybe I could give them the chance that I never had.

The Singapore Children's Society arranged for us to attend a 2-day workshop to equip us with the necessary tools to handle youths at risk. It was interesting to be able to share some of my past stories with the other volunteer families. From this I learnt that our teenage years, though they may be turbulent, are the years that mould our character. The youths who have been put on the YFC programme have been given another opportunity to "get back on the straight and narrow". The chance to experience a "normal" environment, in the form of contact with a loving and intact family, even though their own home environment is not stable, is an important component of their rehabilitation.

When I first met Jaycee, the youth whom my family were supposed to mentor under the YFC programme, my head was filled with the overwhelming fear of possible problems. He was a tough-looking boy with tattoos and an attitude that would even challenge the attitude that I had in my younger days. Jaycee was charged with theft and breaking into cars. He was brought to the Juvenile Court and put on probation. "What have I got myself into?" I asked myself. But throughout the period that both my wife and I mentored Jaycee and his mother (who was a single parent), I never caved in to giving up on him. We have had our "ups and downs" but Jaycee sensed that we would always be there for him.

We would visit Jaycee at the Singapore Boys' Hostel (where the Court had ordered him to reside) every Friday, to provide him with moral support and encouragement. We would speak to the Hostel warden to find out how he was progressing. Initially Jaycee just used to talk to us about gangs and girlfriends. But it was heartening to find, as the weeks progressed, that he started to talk to us about more personal matters, such as his relationship with his natural mother, and about serious matters such as his education and his future. We would play the role of listener and advisor to him. I think he appreciated the fact that other people were interested in his life and his thoughts, and cared about him and his future. When he went on home leave, during the weekends, he would telephone us to let us know what he had spent his time doing. Our weekly calls were filled with stories from myself, my wife and Jaycee. We would also call Jaycee's mother once a week to find out how she was, and provide her with a friendly listening ear. Eventually, when we settled into a routine, I felt that his mother had also turned to us for a shoulder to cry on.

It is a year since I first met Jaycee and his family in a Family Conference in Court. He seems more approachable and less "frustrated" now. I hope that Jaycee may one day share his story with other juvenile delinquents and the lesson that he has learnt — i.e. that one should keep on the straight and narrow path — is one that can be learnt with much less "trauma" than what he went through.

I have also grown personally from this experience of being a YFC parent and am now ready to mentor another youth in trouble.

4.4 Perspectives through Poetry

These poems were written by students who had taken part in a poetry competition organised by the Subordinate Courts in the year 2001.

The aim was to provide teenagers with an opportunity to share their experiences and thoughts on the issues of family violence, separation, and family relationships through poetry. The last poem was written by a group of Peer Group Advisers for the Peer Group Advisers' programme conducted by the Juvenile Court in the year 2002. Participants in the programme were required, as one of the activities on the programme, to present their thoughts on juvenile justice issues in the form of poetry, dance, drama or music.

For Mum

I know I love her,
So does she.
But why are we drifting apart?
Am I not doing my part?
Or is it destined to be that way?

Recalling my younger days,
How happy life was with her by my side.
She cared for me,
She doted on me.
She never let me suffer.

Life has been changing.
Absorbed in my teenage life,
I seem to move further away from her.
It hurts her, as it does me.
Hopefully
A bridge can be built between us.

Gan Chea Ling, Jurong Junior College, aged 17

Shattered

Being thrown in the air as a child
Confident that you would be caught
Secure in the knowledge that you are safe
And that your parents will protect you as one

Little did you know that in the coming months
That feeling would be shattered
Like a fragile glass
That was put under pressure

Then finally the day came
When it all came to an end
We're going to the courts they said
We want to get a divorce

Cassandra Lai Shimin, Singapore Chinese Girls' School, aged 14

The Missing Childhood

I have been searching all around
Wandering everywhere
Looking for the one thing in my life
That was never really there

I walk along the streets at night
Reminiscing about my past
About the sad and frightened days I had
and the many painful scars

The days I had were lonely and dark
No one even said "Hi"
I remember clearly the nights I spent
Sleepless, wondering why

I never had any balloons
Or dolls with curly hair
The people around me thought me funny
And gave me long stares

I would like to ask you a question
I do not mean to sound rude
But please could you tell me
Have you seen my childhood?

Geraldine Richard, Crescent Girls' School, 14 years

Poetic Justice

I am the wrong, the guilty one,
The caught up, locked up, failure of a son.
The deviant individual, severed from the rest,
A fumbling shadow, until arrest.

[He lied to the gang. We wanted revenge.
This craving to stake, this thirst to quench.
Red mists of anger blurred my vision.
Clouded my mind, changed my decision.]

Plaster cracks, a picture torn,
Society's blame, a family's scorn.
The price to pay for a small mistake,
Wish from this hell-like place to wake.

[Past conscience, past sanity, past reason,
Scheming to bring him down for treason.
So one fine day we found him alone,
Beat him up, ignoring his moans.]

A darkened tunnel, no light at the end.
Broken dreams, a wayward friend.
Retribution for contributions of sin,
Fight a battle that you have to win.

[We left him for dead, taught him a lesson,
But justice prevailed and soon court was in session.]

White washed walls of tarnished souls,
Nightmares unravel, fears untold.
Hollow hallways, empty cells,
Secret horrors that no one tells.

[I prayed all night that I could go free,
That I could be released from this misery.]

Could there still be some future here?
Leave your troubles, shed your tears.

This is where you live once more,
Forgetting what you did before.

[The day was bright, the air was clear.
I had nothing more to fear.]

What I thought could only be the end of me,
Pollute my dreams, discard my fantasies.
Felt singed by hells' fires only to be rekindled,
The hateful memories of before now dwindle.

Once my prison, now my home,
New fates to face, but not alone.
Wounds are cleansed and scars are mended,
A chapter of my life has ended.

The law is harsh, but justice kind,
The guilt has vanished from my mind.
The blemished convict is no more,
Cleansed out newly from the core.

Fong Wei Teng Samantha, Na Yun Nicole, Loh Ji Nin, Chang Chooi Ping Claudia, Fu Jiaming Carolyn, Nanyang Girls' High School, all aged between 14-15 years old

ENDNOTES

1 See Chapter 1, The Juvenile Court of Singapore at pages 23-29 for more information on Beyond Parental Control and Child Protection cases.

2 Reports from psychiatrists would usually be ordered if the juvenile exhibits unusual behaviour (for example, highly sexualised or explosively violent behaviour) which leads the Court or the MCDS officer who prepares the report on the juvenile to feel that an evaluation of the juvenile's mental state is necessary.

3 See Chapter 1, The Juvenile Court of Singapore at page 8 for more information on the JOB Criteria.

4 See Chapter 1, The Juvenile Court of Singapore at pages 20-23 for more information on Family Conferencing.

5 See Chapter 1, The Juvenile Court of Singapore at page 7 for more information on the Panel of Advisers.

6 See Chapter 1, The Juvenile Court of Singapore at pages 23-26 for more information on the Beyond Parental Control regime.

PART II

REBUILDING LIVES

The Community's Perspective — Embracing Troubled Youths and Restoring Them to the Community

CHAPTER 5

Community Initiatives and Programmes — Early Intervention, Prevention and Rehabilitation

In this section, we see how the community reaches out to young people who are either in trouble, or who seem to be heading towards trouble. The Inter-Ministry Committee on Youth Crime is an organisation which co-ordinates these efforts and brings together all the various governmental and non-governmental organisations involved in this area.

Programmes are run by these organisations to prevent those on the verge of becoming juvenile delinquents from entering the court system, to help those who are already juvenile delinquents to mend their ways, to nurture those children from impoverished or disadvantaged backgrounds, and to educate young people in life skills, communication skills, sexuality, and the dangers of drug abuse.

In this way, the community works together to guide its vulnerable, tame its recalcitrant, and welcome its repentant, youth.

5.1 The National Response to Youth Crime

ASSOCIATE PROFESSOR HO PENG KEE
Senior Minister of State for Law and Home Affairs, and
Chairman of the Inter-Ministry Committee on Youth Crime

Formation of Inter-Ministry Committee on Youth Crime

In his 1994 National Day Rally Speech, the Prime Minister spoke about the formation of an Inter-Ministry Committee (IMC) on

Dysfunctional Families, Drug Abuse and Juvenile Delinquency. The number of juveniles arrested had risen from 1,205 in 1990 to 2,102 in 1994.[1] Although the absolute numbers were comparatively small, the rate of increase caught public attention, as it contrasted with the trend of falling general crime rates. In 1995, the IMC formed the Inter-Ministry Committee on Juvenile Delinquency (IMJD) to set directions and steer programmes for an integrated national response to tackling juvenile delinquency.

The IMJD was subsequently re-named The Inter-Ministry Committee on Youth Crime. It plays a pivotal role in combating juvenile delinquency and youth crime. Its success depends on the co-operation of various community agencies, as well as on the adoption of an innovative and holistic approach to tackling the problem of juvenile delinquency. In addition to working with the juvenile delinquents themselves, the IMYC also emphasises early intervention, research and the training of youth workers.

A Co-ordinated Community Response to Youth Crime

Juvenile delinquency and youth crime being a multi-faceted phenomenon, IMYC recognised early on that various agencies, both governmental and non-governmental, have to network closely to tackle it. Hence, IMYC member agencies such as the Ministry of Community Development and Sports (MCDS), Ministry of Education (MOE), Ministry of Home Affairs (MHA), National Council of Social Service (NCSS), National Youth Council (NYC), Singapore Police Force (SPF), Prisons Department and the Subordinate Courts meet to co-ordinate their policies and programmes.

Partnering Local Organisations

Besides co-ordination at a national level, the IMYC also actively works at the local level with Community Development Councils (CDCs), schools, voluntary welfare organisations (VWOs) and civic organisations (such as parent support groups). It organises networking conferences where government and non-government agencies come together to share expertise and discuss the phenomenon of juvenile delinquency in Singapore. Working at the local level also means strengthening families in IMYC programmes and involving youths to help other youths through mentoring and peer support programmes.

Youth Research

Youth research is strongly emphasised within the IMYC. The IMYC funds research on trends such as cyber-crime, shoplifting, and alcoholism. Data on youth crime is analysed and discussed at IMYC meetings. Through research, the IMYC is able to spot trends and service gaps. Counter-measures can then be quickly instituted to nip problems in the bud before they become more serious. Examples of youth research funded by the IMYC include: "Female Teenagers Coming Together: Group or Gang" (a 1998 study on the factors that influence female adolescents to be involved with gangs, by Ler Sze Yuan from the Department of Social Work and Psychology, National University of Singapore); "A Study on the Juvenile Shoplifting Phenomenon" (a year 2000 study by Esther Koh Hwee Cheng and Peace Wong of the Students Care Service), and "A Study on Cyberporn and Censorship" (a year 2000 study by students from the Nanyang Technological University, to investigate teenagers' access and exposure to pornographic materials online and parents' awareness of the problem, and what coping strategies they have adopted). Most recently, in 2001, the Department of Social Work and Psychology of the National University of Singapore was commissioned to conduct a study to understand the dynamics and patterns of drinking amongst Singapore youths. A total of 2,483 respondents between the ages of 13-33 were surveyed in the period of July 2001 to February 2002. 85% of the respondents were students from secondary schools, junior colleges, ITEs, and polytechnics and the remaining 15% of the respondents were youths from the Toa Payoh Girls' Home, Singapore Boys' Home, Kaki Bukit Prison School, Changi Women's Prison, Reformative Training Centre and Moon Crescent Prison.[2]

Innovative Programmes

The IMYC adopts a comprehensive range of measures to tackle juvenile crime — from prevention to enforcement to rehabilitation. Some of these innovative programmes include Project CRUSH (Cyberspace Risk and Where You Can Seek Help) which addresses the emerging issue of cyber addiction and other deviant Internet-related behaviour. Project CRUSH is a series of Internet Safety Roadshows and e-mentoring workshops for secondary schools that was conceptualised by Touch Community Services and supported by the Parent's Advisory Group for Internet (PAGi).

The roadshows are conducted during school assemblies, and they use skits and interactive quizzes to raise awareness of the risks in being part of the cyberspace community and to highlight various precautions that can be taken against these risks. The e-mentoring workshops are held over six weeks to train a select group of student mentors in helping to spread the message of Internet safety to their peers.

Since its launch on 11 September 2001, 36 schools and 25,301 students have participated in Project CRUSH and 104 e-mentors have been trained.

The IMYC also funds the Streetwise Programme (SWP)[3] to look specifically into the problem of street corner gangs. The SWP is a rehabilitative programme that is run by four VWOs (Beyond Social Services, Lakeside Family Centre, Teen Challenge and Youth Guidance Outreach Services) to help youths break away from their gangs and provide them with a second chance. The NYC co-ordinates the SWP among the four VWOs and two referral agencies, MCDS and the Criminal Investigation Department.

The SWP was launched on 1 November 1997. This six-month programme consists of 360 hours of counselling, group work, family conferencing, life-skills training, physical activities as well as academic and vocational training.

The Peer Mediation Programme[4] is another initiative by two IMYC partners, the Subordinate Courts and the MOE. Peer Mediation aims to curb disciplinary problems in schools by imparting practical skills to students to manage and resolve their conflicts before these escalate into deviant behaviours that require intervention by the schools, police or the Courts. As at the end of 2001, a total of 261 teachers from 154 secondary schools have been trained in this programme.

To further augment efforts against juvenile delinquency, the Honorary Volunteer Special Constabulary (VSC) (School) Scheme was introduced in 1997. The scheme, developed by SPF with the support of MOE, aims to help schools better manage school discipline and extend a symbol of police authority in schools. Eligible Discipline Masters, Discipline Teachers and Operations Managers of secondary schools and vocational training centres are trained and appointed as Hon VSC (School) Officers to serve as "teacher-cops". The scheme is a preventive measure to deter youth crime and gang activities among students. To date, 138 secondary schools and Vocational Training Centres are participating in the Hon VSC (School) Scheme.

The CDCs are also active partners in IMYC initiatives. For instance, North West CDC and South East CDC provide funds to set up two centres, Project Bridge and Project 180°, to reach out to out-of-school youths. Managed by YMCA Singapore and Fei Yue Family Service Centre respectively, the centres provide counselling, tutoring, mentoring, information and referrals to alternative learning opportunities. The centres seek to develop out-of-school youths in social, vocational, academic, life and recreational skills, thus creating a positive and lasting impact on their lives.

MCDS, MOE, NCSS, SPF and two VWOs (Students' Care Service and Singapore Children's Society) started the Guidance Programme, a six-month youth development programme that provides counselling to first-time juvenile offenders who have committed petty crimes with mitigating factors.[5] The involvement of such a broad spectrum of community organisations, both governmental and non-governmental, is a fine illustration of the co-ordinated and holistic nature of the national response to youth crime. The programme has expanded to involve ten VWOs currently.

Training Youth Workers

Besides supporting youth-at-risk programmes and youth research, the IMYC also supports the training of youth workers by organising training workshops, focus groups, international conferences and overseas attachment programmes.

For example, on 1 July 2002, the NYC and the Singapore Training and Development Association (STADA) organised a five-day training workshop in Adventure Counselling. Partly funded by the National Council against Drug Abuse (NCDA) and supported by MCDS, about 160 social workers and youth workers participated in the workshop conducted by Dr Michael Gass, a professor from the Department of Kinesiology at the University of New Hempshire. Participants of the workshop learnt the necessary skills needed to employ adventure-based techniques as an alternative prevention and intervention approach in working with youths.

NYC also provides IMYC funding to NCSS for courses for social workers keen to work with youths. For example, from 29 October 2002 to 1 November 2002, a four-day training course by NCSS was held to help youth and community workers acquire the basic skills in working with youths. Mr Mike Garland, a lecturer from the School of Social Policy at Massey University in New Zealand and Mr Darryl Gardiner, a youth worker of 17 years from New Zealand, conducted the course which was designed to equip youth workers with an understanding of the various emotional, relationship and life issues facing young people, and to explore the various methods of working with them.

One notable overseas training programme is the annual Singapore-Hong Kong Youth Workers Attachment Programme. The programme is a collaboration between the Hong Kong Federation of Youth Groups (HKFYG) and NYC and its objective is to promote a mutual understanding and the sharing of youth social work experiences between Hong Kong and Singapore social workers. Since 1996, NYC has been sending four youth/social workers to Hong Kong every year. The workers are attached to various agencies for two weeks. In turn, HKFYG sends two of its social workers to Singapore annually to be attached to a VWO for two weeks.

The Road Ahead

As long as there is juvenile crime in society, the battle cry for the IMYC will remain a resolute "Every youth convicted is one too many". The fight against juvenile delinquency is a dynamic and fluid one, given the ever-changing landscape of trends and influences on our youths. Youths must be made resilient against negative peer influences and the temptations to commit offences. This is achieved through the IMYC secretariat, NYC, which is the national agency for youth and youth sector development in Singapore. The NYC looks into "upstream" development of youths by cultivating youth interests, community-mindedness and leadership. The IMYC will continue to co-ordinate the national response to youth crime in the years ahead, confident in the belief that the care given by the community to its children will, in the years to come, bring care *for* the community into the hearts of its children.

5.2 Rebuilding Lives and Restoring Troubled Youths to the Community — The Malay/ Muslim Community's Response

ABDUL HALIM ALIMAN

Director, Community Development, Yayasan Mendaki, and
Panel Adviser of the Juvenile Court

Introduction

"The youths of today are the leaders of tomorrow" is an often said and heard phrase when we talk about the younger generation. In most societies, much hope and expectations are pinned on their youth, as they are the ones who would lead their respective societies into the future. Singapore is no exception. The Malay/Muslim youths of today are no exception too.

The youths of today are generally IT-savvy, educated, confident and knowledgeable. However, there is a segment of our youths which has fallen by the wayside — at-risk youths, out-of-school youths and juvenile delinquents. As every individual is important and Singapore believes in investing in its youths, these "troubled" youths can be and should be helped and given a second chance for their eventual re-integration into society as socially responsible and law-abiding citizens.

This section provides a brief outline of the Singapore Malay/ Muslim community's response in dealing with the issues affecting its youths in the areas of: the prevention of juvenile delinquency; the development of the potential of young people; and remediation for those who have run afoul of the law or who have exhibited behavioural problems.

National Initiatives and the Malay/Muslim Community's Response

The formation of the Inter-Ministry Committee on Youth Crime (IMYC) in 1995 has led to the adoption of a multi-prong approach in combating youth crime.[6] This approach calls for tackling the problem of juvenile delinquency on many fronts. The IMYC strategises and co-ordinates the efforts of different agencies in Singapore, putting in place a broad range of preventive, rehabilitative and enforcement measures to tackle the issue of juvenile delinquency and youth crime head-on. It draws resources from youth mentors, youth befrienders and volunteers, parent groups, youth organisations, self-help groups (i.e. the Chinese Development Assistance Council, Mendaki, Singapore Indian Development Associaton, Eurasian Association), voluntary welfare organisations (VWOs), religious institutions, government ministries such as the Ministry of Education, the Ministry of Community Development and Sports, the Ministry of Home Affairs (Singapore Police Force, Prisons Department), the judiciary, the National Youth Council (NYC), family service centres and so on. The Singapore Malay/Muslim community, being part of the larger Singapore society, has been and will continue to be an active participant in this national effort to tackle the issue of juvenile delinquency and youth crime.

Singapore Malay/Muslim Community's Initiatives

Various groups within the Malay/Muslim community such as Malay/Muslim organisations, mosques, family service centres, the self-help group (Mendaki) have risen to the occasion to play their part in helping to address the social concern of youths at risk. Some of the initiatives undertaken by these organisations (the full list of all the organisations is shown in Annex A to this chapter) is set out below:

Prevention and Development

As the saying goes, "Prevention is better than cure". Many of the Malay/Muslim organisations and mosques have organised various preventive programmes to reach out to youths at risk so as to enable them to be "crime- and drug-free". Some of these initiatives do not just target the youths but also their parents, so as to equip the parents with effective parenting skills, and enable them to supervise and guide their children more effectively. The mosques, for instance, have organised youth camps so as to provide religious guidance to these youths and to involve them in socially constructive mosque-based activities. The mosques also organise marriage preparation and guidance for young couples.[7]

Life skills and enrichment programmes for youths and students have also been organised by organisations such as Mendaki, AMP, 4PM, Darul Arqam, Taman Bacaan, PERDAUS, PERTAPIS, Muhammadiyah Association, YWMA, JAMIYAH and the three Mendaki-Affiliated family service centres.[7]

Examples of such preventive intervention programmes include those initiated by YWMA-Mendaki FSC through its POWER (**P**erseverance "Can Do", **O**ther Centred "Service by Doing", **W**illing to Learn "Walk the Talk", **E**mpowered "Dare to Dream", **R**esourceful "Never Say Die") programme or its HOME (**H**elp **O**utreach **M**otivate **E**ducate) programme. The POWER programme is a six-month-long programme for youths who have been placed on the Guidance Programme.[8] Youths who are placed on the POWER programme are required to work for the National Youth Achievement Award which is sponsored by the NYC. In order to win this award, the youths must do community work such as working with the handicapped or socially disadvantaged. They are thus given a goal to aim for and socially beneficial activities to occupy them. If they succeed in winning the National Youth Achievement Award, their achievement will strengthen their position when they apply for employment or admission to educational institutions in the future. The HOME programme is a programme for low-income families whose children receive payments from the School Pocket Money Fund run by the Straits Times newspaper. In order to receive the payments, the parents and children are required to attend various courses. For the children, there are courses in life-skills, self-motivation, adventure camps, anti-drug talks, literacy in information technology, and so on. The parents are required to attend parenting workshops. This ensures that these children from socially disadvantaged backgrounds receive the training and encouragement necessary to enable them to receive a proper education, rather than just financial assistance alone.

AMP has a preventive strategy programme for probationers serving National Service. This programme is run in collaboration with the Singapore Civil Defence Force. The probationers are required to go for various workshops in life-skills, parenting, and so on, in order to prepare them for life after national service and to make them more employable. AMP also runs an "Extreme Camp" for secondary students in the Normal stream. This is a three-day team-building adventure-learning camp to teach students how to work effectively with others, and also to strengthen their confidence and self-esteem. 4PM-MENDAKI FSC too reaches out to youths through its Youth VIBES (**V**ibrant, **I**lluminating, **B**eneficial, **E**nriching, **S**timulating) programme and its "Helping Children by Strengthening Families" programme and "Staying On Top" workshops for secondary school students. The "Helping Children by Strengthening Families" programme is similar to the HOME programme mentioned earlier — but each programme serves a different geographical area. The "Staying on Top" workshops are targeted at those students with behavioural problems. These students are required to attend weekly sessions where they are taught social and life skills. The VIBES programme is a sub-programme of the "Staying on Top" programme. The "Staying on Top" students consist of members of the "VIBES" programme after they have completed their "Staying on Top" workshops. In the VIBES programme, they will be taught leadership skills, and will be required to do community work, such as cleaning old folks' homes and working with the disabled. One example of a VIBES project is the socio-drama "Sesal" (meaning "Regret", in Malay). VIBES members wrote the script for this play, which featured teenage pregnancy and its consequences. It was also produced and performed by VIBES members to an audience of students, in order to provoke discussion and reflection on issues of teenage sexuality, marriage, and family values. Plans are now underway to perform this play to probationers, and to follow up with a workshop to discuss the issues arising in the play.

Other preventive programmes include 4PM's "BITE", an intensive programme with ITE students, to increase their awareness of information technology, and to teach them skills such as preparing a curriculum vitae, or how to conduct themselves in a job interview. It also teaches them to set career goals for themselves, and how to make a plan to achieve them. YWMA-Mendaki FSC-ROMM holds "Sexuality Seminars" for parents and children on issues of pre-marital sex and marriage. Yayasan Mendaki has an intensive programme for premature school leavers. When a student drops out of school or truants frequently, he is referred to Yayasan Mendaki by the school. Yayasan Mendaki then gets in touch with the student and counsels him to persuade him to go back to school. Those students who insist on not going back to school will be provided with pamphlets and information on alternative education. All the students will be invited to attend adventure camps and youth outreach programmes, including the "Chrysalis workshop", which is a two-day camp to teach those attending teamwork skills, to give them lessons in empathy, and to help build their self-esteem. Their parents will be invited to attend parenting workshops. Yayasan Mendaki also provides services for those children whose parents are in prison. Information on the children of prisoners will be given by the prison to the caregivers of the children.

Yayasan Mendaki will then contact the children to see if there is anything that needs to be done in terms of providing counselling for the children, or for their educational needs. The children will also be invited to join any workshops, programmes, and outings organised by Yayasan Mendaki or its affiliates.

The Young Muslim Secretariat of MUIS also reaches out to youths through its annual "Hijrah" walk in collaboration with PERDAUS and with the support of the NYC. The "Hijrah" commemorates the time when the Prophet Muhammad migrated from Mecca to Medina. Young people are encouraged to go on the "Hijrah" walk, where they have to walk from the evening, all through the night, until the next morning. This walk is then followed by a workshop on spiritual issues, which discuss the spiritual significance of the walk, and how it represents a migration to a better state of mind, a better way of conducting one's life. Finally, the YWMA Family Support Centre, As-Salaam, also provides support programmes for children and adolescents from single-parent families and facilitates a support group for single custodial mothers through its MAWAR (a term in Malay meaning to uphold the responsibilities of women, children and family) programme. The children and adolescents attend ten group sessions to help them deal with the grief they may feel at their parents' separation, and to enable them to move on to the next stage of their lives. The mothers have bi-monthly group sessions to provide mutual support and to discuss issues such as the challenges which face single parents, how to deal with their children's grief at their parents' separation, and so on. They are also invited to attend enrichment workshops to build their self-esteem.

Remedial and Rehabilitative Programmes

In the areas of remediation and rehabilitation Malay/Muslim organisations have also responded to the government's call for community groups to come forward to help in this effort. Organisations like PERTAPIS, JAMIYAH and the Muhammadiyah Association have responded positively by establishing and managing residential homes for those troubled children and youths who are either juvenile offenders, or children who require protection or youths who are beyond parental control. The YWMA-Mendaki and 4PM-Mendaki FSCs have also responded by being involved in the MCDS Guidance Programme and other initiatives.

Conclusion

The battle to tackle the issue of juvenile delinquency and youth crime continues. The strategy adopted by relevant government ministries to tap on the Malay/Muslim community's strengths to lend additional support to aid the rehabilitation of these young offenders is a good move. The combined efforts of all the various Malay/Muslim organisations and mosques to steer disadvantaged and wayward youths back to mainstream society and to encourage them to be involved with life-long learning initiatives will hopefully enable them to engage in meaningful activities and become law-abiding citizens.

The next step is for the Singapore Malay/Muslim community to develop a Masterplan to tackle various social issues facing the community with a view to identifying service gaps and to encourage and persuade more organisations and volunteers to come forward and to lend their helping hands in a more co-ordinated and effective manner. The battle will continue. The Singapore Malay/Muslim community can never afford to rest on its laurels. It must continually strive towards, and stand united in its quest for, excellence.

5.3 Reducing Juvenile Delinquency through Community Involvement: Community Partnerships with the Singapore Police Force

ASP MARC E KWAN SZER

Operations Officer, Community Involvement Division,

Operations Department, Police Headquarters

Introduction

Amidst a backdrop of increasing juvenile[9] delinquency in the early 1990s, the Singapore Police Force (SPF) commissioned several studies in 1994 to explain the causes of the phenomena.[10] In addition, the Inter-Ministry Committee on Youth Crime (IMYC)[11] initiated several measures to tackle the problem. As the causes of juvenile delinquency are multi-dimensional, the SPF has leveraged on key partnerships at the inter-ministry, grassroots, schools and VWO (voluntary welfare organisation) levels in order to tackle juvenile delinquency in a holistic manner.

Juvenile Crime between 1990 to 2000[12]

As shown in the graph below, between the years 1990 and 1995, the numbers of juveniles arrested reflected a steady upward trend followed by a levelling off between 1996 and 1998. The number of juveniles arrested then started to decline after the year 1998.

The period from January to October in the year 2001 saw a decline in juveniles arrested compared to the same period in the year 2000. A total of 1,109 juveniles[13] were arrested in comparison to 1,431 juveniles, respectively — a decline of 322 juvenile offenders or a percentage drop of 22.5%.

FIGURE 5.3.1: NUMBER OF JUVENILES ARRESTED FROM 1990 TO 2000

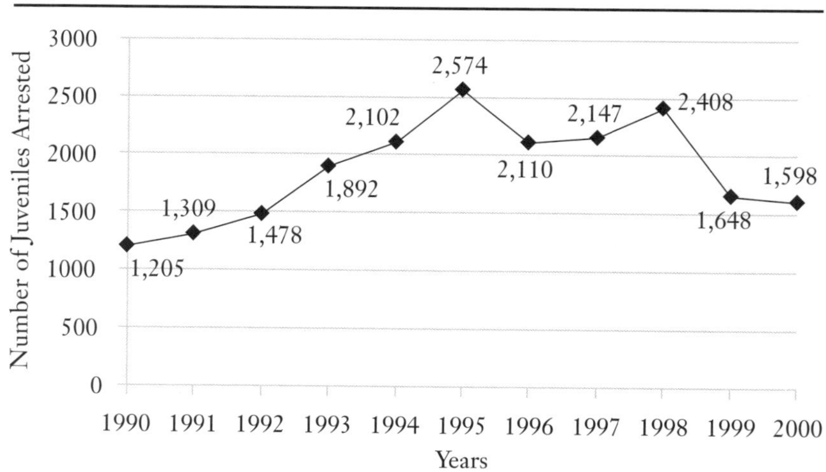

Community Involvement: Strategic Partnerships between the SPF and "Youth" Stakeholders

Juvenile delinquency is a serious problem with adverse societal ramifications if left unchecked. Since no one agency can single-handedly manage juvenile delinquency, it is important that the SPF co-ordinates efforts and shares expertise with other stakeholders in the juvenile justice process. The co-ordination of efforts and sharing of expertise is done through the work of the IMYC,[14] which co-ordinates the efforts of multiple agencies, thus rendering these efforts more effective in the battle against juvenile delinquency. The SPF is one of the members of the IMYC.

Through the IMYC and its community network, the SPF tackles juvenile delinquency from two main angles: "the preventive" and "the investigative". The "preventive" angle focuses on activities aimed at detecting and preventing juveniles from being involved in crime and gang activities while the "investigative" angle centres on post-arrest activities such as the cautioning and counselling of offenders.

Preventive Measures

Existing preventive measures in dealing with crimes committed by juveniles include:

(a) Formalised police-school liaison system

Police liaison officers (PLOs) are appointed for each school within the jurisdiction of each Neighbourhood Police Centre (NPC). The PLO will work closely with the school authorities — particularly the Discipline Master, the Operations Manager and those teachers who are appointed as Honorary Volunteer Special Constabulary (School) Senior Officers — and give advice on police-related matters. He will provide the school authorities with updates on youth crime trends, especially those that are of concern to the school, and will advise the school on the crime prevention measures it can take. The PLO will also conduct talks at school assemblies, or to groups of "at-risk" students identified by the schools. The talks will cover issues such as secret societies and the negative consequences of committing crimes. The PLO will also work together with the school to craft the Community Safety and Security Programme (CSSP) to implement solutions to address school-based safety and security concerns. (See below for more information on the CSSP.) In certain cases, upon the school's request, the PLO will "keep an eye" on certain students who are behaving badly, by observing their movements, or having an informal talk with them. If the type of delinquent behaviour exhibited by the student requires more specialised police monitoring, the PLO may refer the matter to a specialised unit such as the Secret Society Branch of the Criminal Investigation Department.

(b) Honorary Volunteer Special Constabulary (School) Scheme

School Discipline Masters/Mistresses, Disciplinary Teachers and Operations Managers from secondary schools may be appointed as Honorary VSC (School) Senior Officers under the Honorary Volunteer Special Constabulary (School) Scheme. This scheme enhances the role of school disciplinarians and projects the police presence and authority in schools.

The duties of the Hon VSC officers are to advise the school management on crime and police matters, counsel and mentor delinquent students, network with parents, grassroots leaders, VWOs and other youth development organisations, and, if necessary (and only as a last resort), enforce the law.

Hon VSC officers attend a two-week non-residential basic training course at the Police Academy. They are trained in Criminal Law, various police procedures and guidelines, self-defence tactics and the use of the revolver (although they are not issued with one subsequently). Visits to Neighbourhood Police Centres, the Criminal Investigation Department, the Singapore Boys' Home and the Juvenile Court are also arranged. Upon graduation, Hon VSC officers are issued with a police uniform and police warrant card. They are vested with police powers (for example, to arrest students who have committed seizable offences), but they are advised to exercise these powers as a last resort within the school compound and also during school-related activities outside of school which involve students and their safety or conduct.

Currently, eight out of ten secondary schools in Singapore have serving Hon VSC officers. (Note that only Discipline Masters/Mistresses, Discipline Teachers and Operations Managers of secondary schools under the Ministry of Education are eligible to be appointed as Hon VSC officers.) The Hon VSC (School) Scheme is open to all secondary schools under the Ministry of Education. The discretion is left to the individual school principal to nominate his/her staff to the scheme.

Investigative Measures

Current investigative measures in dealing with crimes committed by juveniles include:

(a) Guidance Programme (GP)[15]

Juvenile offenders who have been arrested by police for petty crimes may be placed under a six-month supervision and counselling programme with the consent and co-operation of their parents. Upon successful completion of the programme, police may caution these juvenile offenders in lieu of prosecution. This programme is a joint effort between the SPF and the Ministry of Community Development and Sports (MCDS) and its affiliate Social Service Agencies.

(b) StreetWise Programme (SWP)

The "StreetWise Programme" was jointly implemented by the National Youth Council (NYC) and the SPF. This is a six-month programme designed to discourage youths aged 13 to 18 years old from getting entangled in gang activities. The police through the Secret Society Branch (SSB) of the Criminal Investigation Department makes referrals of youths who are on the verge of joining gangs to the StreetWise Programme. These youths are "profiled" and identified through spot-checks on congregations of youths loitering in public areas by police patrols.

FIGURE 5.3.2: STREETWISE PROGRAMME

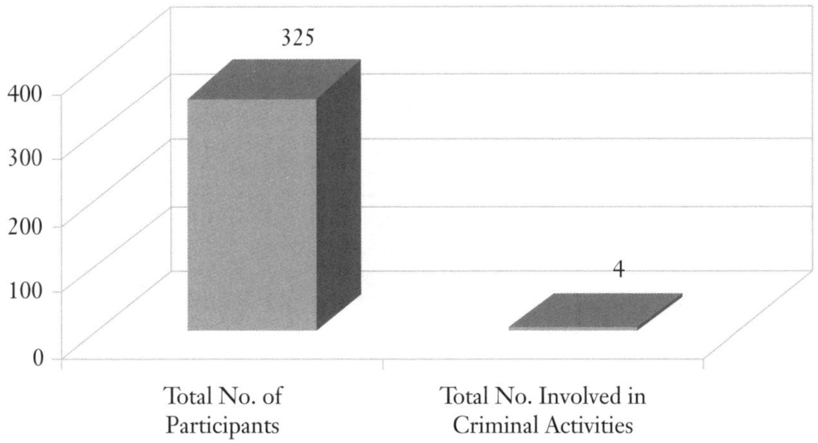

Under the StreetWise programme, the SSB officers will advise youths against involvement in gang activity by giving talks to emphasise its negative consequences, organising visits to prisons and monitoring the youths' adherence to voluntary curfews. Youths placed under the programme are also referred to the relevant VWOs for counselling and developmental training to inculcate life skills, and to provide them with academic and recreational support. Parents of these youths play an active role in the programme by ensuring adherence to the voluntary curfew and accompanying their child to the counselling sessions.

Since its inauguration in November 1997 till January 2001, the StreetWise programme has proven to be an effective means of combating juvenile crime. Out of a total of 325 youths who have undergone this programme in the time period set out above, only four have been involved in criminal activities during this time period.[16] (see figure 5.3.2 above.)

The Community Safety and Security Programme

The SPF has pioneered the introduction of the Community Safety and Security Programme (CSSP) to schools since April 2000. The purpose of the CSSP is to encourage the community to look after its own safety and security matters through self-help and mutual support. This enables the fostering of greater community cohesion amongst the various community organisations such as the police, schools and family service centres.

Schools are an integral part of the community. Common problems encountered in the school include the presence of gangs, bullying, fighting, vandalism, petty theft and truancy. The CSSP is a platform on which schools, through joint planning and action with Home Team[17] and community partners can address school-based safety and security concerns. In the CSSP, a programme or series of programmes which are designed to increase school safety and security by combating juvenile delinquency, are planned and created with the input of various organisations, which each have a role to play in the carrying out of the programme. In this manner, school CSSPs create a safer and more secure school community. They also engender greater civic consciousness amongst the various participants. As of November 2001, some 64 primary and secondary schools, vocational training centres and tertiary institutions are involved in crafting and implementing CSSPs.

An example of a CSSP is the "Triple-A Programme", which is a CSSP involving a Neighbourhood Police Centre (Choa Chu Kang Neighbourhood Police Centre), a family service centre (Fei Yue Family Service Centre), a secondary school (Regent Secondary School) and the parents of 33 students who were identified by the school for participation in this programme.

Using the concept of "Early Detection, Right Intervention", this CSSP is targeted at students between the ages of 13 and 15 years. This CSSP fills the gap between the Guidance Programme and the StreetWise programme in that it focuses on students who are not yet involved in crime or gangs but who have poor academic grades and/ or discipline problems and are therefore considered to be at risk of committing criminal activity in the future. The students identified for this programme were required to go for counselling sessions (provided by the family service centre), talks to raise their awareness on the consequences of being involved in criminal activity (by the police), and also to take part in meaningful activities organised by the school, such as community work. The parents of the students were also encouraged to go for parenting workshops and talks on youth issues provided by the family service centre. The Triple-A Programme was conducted between April and September 2001. At the completion of this programme, 21 of the 33 participants were awarded the National Youth Achievement Award (Bronze), which is an award given out by the National Youth Council for those young people who have devoted a certain amount of their time to community and social work.

Another example of a CSSP is the "STAR" (Safety Through Awareness and Responsibility) Project, which is a joint initiative by Jurong West and Bukit Batok Neighbourhood Police Centres, the Association of Women for Action and Research, and Theatreworks. The target audience for the project was school-going youths aged between 12 and 16 years old. The programme consists of a performance skit entitled "Making the Right Decision". The skit deals with numerous issues that students face at home, in school and in society at large. The key topics dealt with in the skit are: joining a gang, family violence, the dangers of internet meetings and sexual harassment. The STAR project was piloted from July 2001 to October 2001 in a number of secondary schools in the Bukit Batok and Jurong West areas, such as Swiss Cottage Secondary School, Hillgrove Secondary School, and Westwood Secondary School. From watching the skit, students learn positive ways of tackling difficult situations. In this way, the skit helps to inculcate an internal moral compass in the students, which will hopefully help them to navigate their way through life, always managing to stay on the straight and narrow path.

A final example of a CSSP comes from Woodlands Ring Secondary School. The school formed a CSSP working committee with grassroots leaders and the police with the objectives of achieving a safe neighbourhood, and promoting active citizenship not only in the students, but also in those residing in the Woodlands Ring neighbourhood. The committee has organised numerous talks and programmes towards this end. One example of a programme that they have organised is the Befrienders' Patrol. In this programme, representatives from the school, the Residents' Committees and the police conduct regular joint "patrols" around the neighbourhood to monitor both student and youth activities after school hours. During these walkabouts, students and youths loitering at the HDB void-decks and nearby shopping centres are reminded not to do so. For the students who are caught loitering, follow-up action such as counselling will be taken by the school. Those young people who are not students, but who are young enough to be, are invited to take part in social activities organised by the Residents' Committees. Suspicious-looking characters are checked, and warned by the police if they appear to be engaging in — or appear to be about to engage in — rowdy, intimidating or criminal behaviour.

Conclusion

The SPF will continue in its mission of protecting the community from juvenile crime through its strategy of building and leveraging on community partnerships. In this manner we hope to realise our vision of having a safe environment for our families to live in, for our enterprises to flourish, and for our children to grow up in.

5.4 Preventing Juvenile Delinquency in Children at Risk

NG BEE LENG

Deputy Executive Director, BEYOND Social Services,

Head, Bukit Ho Swee Family Service Centre

Rosie, female, age 11[18] — Scabies were all over her body and lice were infesting her hair when Rosie presented herself before the Juvenile Court judge to face a charge of theft in a dwelling. It was worrying what other diseases she might have contracted for she had been living on the streets for the past few months and had been sexually active with other street kids.

For Rosie, it all started with an innocuous absence from school for a day. Then the days turned into weeks and the weeks into months. In the end, Rosie chose to drop out from school and her parents could do nothing about it. They were too caught up with their own problems.

Rosie stayed away from home most of the time, returning only for a change of clothes and occasional pocket money from her parents. Out on the streets, she might have an occasional meal and a place to sleep with some families who were sympathetic to runaways. Other times, she slept on five-foot ways or on the street soccer court. She was never lonely, though. She always had other street kids for company. Life was "carefree" with no adults to control her and no school to guide her. Like the others, she could do whatever she liked, whenever she liked — life was often full of activities late into the nights. It was not long before she started shoplifting, smoking, glue sniffing and experimenting sexually.

Why did Rosie, a sweet adorable girl, end up in the Toa Payoh Girls' Home? As a baby, she never had a regular caregiver and her home environment was far from stimulating. At Primary 1, she was already showing signs of not coping with school. She did not have any pre-school education and was understandably behind her peers in her academic work. She was never able to catch up. On the contrary, this learning disparity grew wider as she progressed year by year through the school system. Rosie was disadvantaged from a very young age. With so many risk factors, was it not possible then to predict that she could end up a juvenile delinquent?

Children at Risk

A dysfunctional family is a significant predictor of juvenile delinquency. While it is true that juvenile delinquency cuts across all social classes, children of dysfunctional families from low-income backgrounds are at even greater risk. Studies have indicated that poor quality childcare (which is especially common in dysfunctional families), premature school-leaving, parental criminality, inconsistent parenting practices, family violence and living in neighbourhoods characterised by social disorganisation are significant risk factors for juvenile delinquency.[19] Such risk factors are highly prevalent in low-income dysfunctional families. The child in the case example above, Rosie, is typical of many other such children living in pockets of low-income communities in Singapore. Singapore has done well in providing the infrastructure and opportunities for upward social mobility but many such families are still trapped in the cycle of poverty and delinquency. What more can the State and the community do to prevent children born into disadvantaged dysfunctional families from being destined to a life of crime and poverty? It makes sense to invest in preventive work in the early stages. This is our philosophy at Beyond Social Services. We feel that to minimise and prevent juvenile delinquency, we have to start with preventive efforts with "at-risk" children from a young age. These children need to be nurtured, educated, and nourished, in order to give them as decent a chance to succeed in life as their peers from more privileged and stable backgrounds.

Preventing Juvenile Delinquency

At Beyond Social Services, our preventive efforts are two-pronged — targeting two groups of young at-risk children from different age ranges.

Kids United

First, we have *Kids United*, an after-school care and guidance programme, for at-risk children aged from 7 to 12.

Kids United is targeted at high-risk low-income children, especially the street-hardened ones whose parents are not able to provide adequately for their care and supervision. Left to their own devices on the streets, these children learn from a very tender age to shoplift, con or hustle passers-by for food and money. They also acquire gang-like behaviour like intimidation, bullying and smoking to survive on the streets. They have to act tough and "cool" in order to survive. Their parents often have delinquent lifestyles of their own, or are too caught up with their own personal and family problems to provide consistent care and stability for the children. These at-risk children were identified for our programme mostly through our outreach activities such as the street soccer games that we organise for the neighbourhood children. Others were identified through their families who were referred to our Centre for help for their financial difficulties which were brought about by chronic unemployment or drug/alcohol addiction problems.

Kids United provides care, concern, structure and stability, while teaching these children responsibility, fair play, teamwork, commitment to follow-through a task, and mutual and self-respect. These offer alternatives to the street culture of "big fish eats small fish", aggression, hustling, immediate gratification and crime.

By providing alternative supervision, care and guidance until 10 p.m. for these children, *Kids United* helps to reduce truancy, premature school leaving and delinquency. We hope to give these marginalised kids a better chance at breaking out of the cycle of poverty and delinquency that their families have been caught in for several generations.

At *Kids United*, the children receive daily meals, have supervised homework time, attend programmes that attend to and teach them personal hygiene, and engage in organised play activities. These basic needs for food, shelter and care, so often taken for granted in an affluent society like ours, are often not met adequately and consistently by the care-givers of these children. In addition to receiving basic care and supervision, these children learn perseverance, fair play, teamwork and self-discipline through weekly sports activities such as soccer and swimming. Every Wednesday during "*United Time*", children address issues such as aggression, tolerance and respect for differences regardless of colour, creed and religion, and learn emotional skills such as how to manage their anger, feelings of rejection, and so on, with the help of our social workers, who conduct group discussions and activities in these areas.

Healthy Start and Level Up

We network with grassroots organisations, other voluntary welfare organisations, childcare centres, and pre-school providers in the neighbourhood, as well as our own social workers, for referrals for our Healthy Start and Level Up programmes. In the year 2001, we also conducted a survey at a housing estate where many low-income families reside, from which we managed to identify more at-risk pre-schoolers for our programmes. The children attending our programmes will usually be the children of teenage parents, or whose parents have drug or alcohol addiction problems, or who are unemployed and in severe financial difficulties.

Identified children are first channelled to our Healthy Start programme, which is essentially a case management programme that includes child assessment, linking clients to appropriate services/ support and parental education. The Healthy Start social workers will assess the child's development, in order to see if he is ready, both socially and academically, to attend ordinary child-care and kindergarten classes. If so, the child will be referred to suitable child-care centres and kindergartens in the neighbourhood. If not, the child will be referred to our *Level Up* programme for pre-school education. In either case, the social worker will, if necessary, visit the child's home regularly, in order to teach the child's parents basic childcare skills and matters relating to health and hygiene. The parents will also be invited to attend parenting classes and groups organised by our Centre, to enhance their parenting skills.

Started in April 2001, *Level Up* is a programme targeted at young children aged two to six years old from low-income at-risk families. It is a foundational learning programme that aims to increase the readiness of such disadvantaged children for school-life when they enter Primary One, with the hope of increasing their chances of success in school.

Unlike mainstream parents who are eager to provide a learning headstart for their young children, parents of these children from low-income at-risk families may place a low priority on their children's education. Some do not even register their children for Primary One, let alone for pre-school education. Our recent survey of a low-income estate reveals that about one-third of the pre-school children are not receiving kindergarten or any other form of pre-school education.[20] Even if parents register their children for kindergarten, they may not be able to ensure that their pre-schoolers attend school regularly. This is supported by the evidence that a further 36.4% of those purportedly in school are found to be lagging behind in their mental development and growth, compared to others in their age group. In all, 67.3% of these children may not be adequately prepared for entering Primary One, thereby diminishing their chances of being successful in school.[21]

These children and their families need a lot of encouragement and support to ensure that they attend the *Level Up* programme consistently in order to develop socially and cognitively. Besides charging only a nominal fee and providing support and follow-up for the families, the curriculum and the pace of learning have to be appropriately pitched to the individual developmental stage of each child. Often, these children experience a chaotic home-life, which distracts and inhibits them from learning. Social workers and volunteers observe and assess every child's developmental needs as well as learning style. For example, an active child who is not able to sit still for an activity would be taught to learn about shapes, colours, and sizes by moving around the room searching for objects with the appropriate description. Also, the teacher-student ratio is kept at 1:4 so that each child can be given very close attention. An individualised curriculum is one that most mainstream kindergartens cannot provide and hence, these children cannot immediately benefit from the educational infrastructure already existing in the community. However, where possible and when a child is ready, we will integrate the child with the larger community by emplacing him in established childcare or pre-school programmes in the neighbourhood, through our Healthy Start programme.

Level Up is a three-hour daily programme. Children are divided into age-appropriate classes with the younger group learning more through play and exploration while the older age groups focus on language and mathematical skills to prepare them for school in Primary 1. The latter are run in collaboration with the Franciscan Missionary of Mary which has many years of experience in kindergarten education.

Results

Kids United is in its fourth year of running since its inception in 1998. The cumulative outcome based on our annual evaluation of the programme has been very encouraging. Children from *Kids United* have shown a significant reduction in truancy and many are still in school, a performance quite exceeding the trend in their families. Many have also taken a greater interest in school although they are still struggling to keep up with the school curriculum. There is a marked reduction in delinquent behaviours such as shoplifting, extortion, smoking and glue-sniffing. Besides learning socially desirable behaviours such as co-operation, delayed gratification, perseverance etc., many have learnt to believe more in themselves and not to be afraid to try to succeed. Compared to their gang-like behaviour three to four years ago and to street kids like Rosie who have not been through a similar programme, these children in *Kids United* have made tremendous progress. These findings are based on anecdotal evidence gleaned from observations by our social workers on the progress made by the 22 children who have and are still benefiting from the *Kids United* programme. We keep a file on every child in the *Kids United* programme as well as the *Level Up* programme. Regular discussions, both formal and informal, are held between the social workers about each child, and if necessary, meetings will be arranged with the child's parents to update them on their child's progress, and to raise any concerns with them.

From anecdotal evidence, it seems that the pre-schoolers in our *Level Up* programme for the two to six year olds have also made good progress. Enjoying going to school and attending our classes regularly are good achievements, considering the family backgrounds they are from. For the four to six year olds, the teachers reported that most of the children have shown good progress in their learning, with the exception of a couple of six year olds who need further help for school readiness next year. Two of the children have shown such good progress that they are ready for integration into the mainstream kindergartens next year. For the younger children where the programme has run for only ten months at the time of writing, the staff reported that the children have become more competent in their spoken English and are also more confident socially.

Future Plans

Believing in the positive impact of early intervention and encouraged by the outcome of our efforts so far, our Centre will seek to identify and work with more young children from at-risk families. If resources permit, we would like to extend our programmes to at-risk infants and toddlers aged 0 to 2 years old. This will enable us to carry out our mission to give each child who comes to our attention the best possible start in life, at the earliest possible time.

5.5 Being There for the Children

ALFRED TAN
Executive Director, Singapore Children's Society

Introduction

The Singapore Children's Society has come a very long way since its beginnings in 1952 in its mission to reach out to youths at risk. In its earlier years, our team of social workers had started conducting outreach activities for youths around the Toa Payoh area of Singapore. Later, we pioneered the "before and after school" concept for latchkey children. That was more than 20 years ago. We organised all kinds of activities that such latchkey children could take part in before and after school.

Today, the Singapore Children's Society runs programmes all around the island for disadvantaged children as well as youths at risk. Some of our major programmes are set out below:

Beyond Parental Control Statutory Supervision

In 1990, we started our pilot project on "Beyond Parental Control (BPC) Statutory Supervision", in collaboration with the Juvenile Court and the Ministry of Community Development and Sports. This programme has now been running successfully for over a decade.

When a juvenile is brought to Court because his parents have lodged a "Beyond Parental Control" complaint against him, the Court may then order the juvenile to be placed under the supervision of an approved welfare officer for a period of up to three years. This is known as "Statutory Supervision". The Singapore Children's Society provides the supervision officers for this regime.

The BPC Statutory Supervision regime involves close supervision and counselling for the youths referred to us through the Juvenile Court. The usual period of Statutory Supervision ordered by the Court is 12 to 18 months. These youths are assigned to trained social workers and counsellors. The social workers and counsellors will monitor their progress, counsel them, and supervise their activities. They will also do family therapy for the juvenile and his family, and conduct group therapy for the juveniles. These youths will learn social skills through this group therapy. The activities organised for the juveniles include outdoor activities such as adventure games which are intended to encourage parent-child bonding. The ultimate success of this programme is when the juveniles can form good ties with their families, especially with their parents.

For the past two years, when the juveniles have successfully completed their term of Statutory Supervision, the Singapore Children's Society have organised a graduation ceremony for them. The "graduates" perform songs, dances, skits, which they create themselves, under the supervision and guidance of the supervision officers, to an audience of their families, Panel Advisers, and supervision officers. The theme of the graduation ceremony is "Metamorphosis" — indicating a positive change in the lives of these young people. We plan to make this an annual event.

Project Cabin

The trouble that youths get into with their parents and the authorities often starts when they are in their pre-teenage years. The Singapore Children's Society has therefore introduced new programmes to reach out to some of the youths in primary or lower secondary schools. One of these programmes is Project CABIN. Basically, it is a school-based youth outreach project that provides an alternative "hang-out" place for children in a form of a fully equipped air-conditioned container Cabin. A Cabin is put into a school compound. Although it is located inside the school, for the children, it is a world of their own. It is where they can listen to music, watch television shows and get cold drinks from a fridge. There are books, comfortable chairs, board games, musical instruments. There is also companionship — both from their peers and from the social workers, parents and volunteers who man the Cabins. Cabins have been installed in 12 secondary schools. The Singapore Children's Society provides the container, the air-conditioning and a social worker to man the Cabin, while the school provides the furnishings and the furniture.

Roundbox

Project Roundbox hopes to capture the untapped creativity and energy of youths-at-risk by engaging them in a holistic and non-intrusive manner — through drama, music, craftwork, street dance and arts. This is done through the setting up of the Drop-in Centre, a place where young people can visit and sign up for lots of different artistic and creative activities, such as playing in pop music bands, learning face-painting, and modern dance.

Student Care Centre

The Singapore Children's Society runs a place called the Henderson Student Care Centre, which caters largely to low-income families living in the neighbourhood of the Centre. Children can go to the Centre after school, and take part in a variety of programmes, as well as receive tuition from volunteers. The programmes include the Step Thinker (to help slow learners cope with their schoolwork), ROOTS (a language enhancement activity conducted by volunteers from the Ministry of Education), and Rainbow (to teach the children of single parents how to cope with their parents' separation).

Tinkle Friend

Tinkle Friend is a telephone helpline service for young children, with the target group between 7 and 12 years of age. Many of the children who call come from single-parent households or dysfunctional homes. This helpline provides a listening ear for children who are left alone without adult supervision, who are bored, lonely or stressed, and helps them to cope with their problems.

Project Seeds

This is a pilot programme providing early intervention for children who are at risk of abuse. Children at risk of abuse are identified by their primary schools to the Singapore Children's Society. The Society then counsels the parents or caregivers of these children, conducts group therapy sessions and a support group for them. At the time of writing, three schools have agreed to take part in this programme.

Conclusion

We have other programmes to reach out to families and youths-at-risk. Years of working with many of these youths and their families have made us realise that the issues confronting them are multi-faceted, and compounded by the often stormy complexities that adolescence brings. There is no doubt these youths need help quickly, or their problems will snowball into adulthood.

Like the environment, changes amongst the youths in this new millennium are rapid and difficult to track. We hope to keep up with these changes through our new projects in the years ahead. We know it is an uphill task, but working closely with the government agencies and the community at large will, I hope, ensure our success in rebuilding lives and restoring the self-worth of all disadvantaged children in Singapore.

5.6 Addressing Discipline in the School System

MRS TAN-KEK LEE YONG
Deputy Director, Psychological and Guidance Services,
Ministry of Education

Introduction

Good discipline is a fundamental pre-requisite for learning. To learn, the pupil needs the discipline to focus his mind on the material to be learnt. No learning can take place in an ill-disciplined environment or amongst ill-disciplined pupils. Thus, schools must devote much effort to developing and maintaining good discipline.

The main goal in school discipline is to create an environment that is conducive to learning. Effective school discipline seeks to encourage responsible behaviour and discourage irresponsible, disruptive behaviour among pupils. To achieve this goal, schools need to tackle the matter from within the school as well as without. Discipline strategies need to be both preventative and remediative in nature. In addition, all school personnel, pupils, parents and relevant agencies in the community (e.g. the police, the Juvenile Court, the Ministry of Community Development and Sports) need to be involved in the discipline efforts of the school.

Discipline in the Home and the School

Parents are responsible for nurturing, guiding and protecting their children. During school hours, school personnel are also responsible for nurturing, guiding and protecting them. Principles that apply to developing good discipline in children at home apply equally in school.

Research into parenting styles has shown that the most effective[22] style is one where there is a balance between love and limits.[23] Key qualities of this style are that the child is loved, accepted and respected as an equal, integrated part of the family, co-operates with other family members and does his share in helping the family. He is accepted for who he is. He is given reasonable progressive challenges and permitted to develop at his own pace. Parents establish basic guidelines for behaviour in the family, clarify and give reasons for the limits set. These limits are firmly and consistently applied over time and to all children in the family without exception. Learning to take responsibility and develop self-discipline is a high priority. The child is given lots of practice in making choices, guided to see the consequences of those choices and encouraged to correct and learn from his mistakes. This parenting style is practised by both parents, who each model the responsible behaviour desired of their children.

The same qualities are echoed in research on school discipline. Orderly schools balance clearly established and communicated rules with a climate of care for pupils as individuals.[24] All school personnel communicate caring and respect for pupils. Pupils are taught emotional and social skills, in order to learn how to manage their emotions and relate appropriately to others. Programmes and activities are put in place to increase the pupils' social involvement and attachment to the school. Low achievers are helped to increase their chances of academic success. Discipline systems and policies are clearly set out, and distinguished between categories of offences, according to their seriousness, through the consequences for committing them. Rules are enforced in a fair and consistent manner.

Schools in Singapore aim to create a disciplined, stable and caring environment for their students. This is done through teaching the students vital life skills, as well as monitoring their behaviour closely, and paying close attention to their welfare. Close links with the community are forged and utilised in order to achieve this.

I now set out the programmes undertaken by various schools in Singapore, in this regard, under the supervision of the Ministry of Education (MOE).

Counselling, Careers, and Emotional Skills

In Singapore, the culture of care is promoted through the practice of pastoral care in school. Structures and referral systems for discipline and counselling are set up, with teachers as front-line caregivers, supported by a team of key personnel with further training in discipline and counselling. These include Heads of Pupil Welfare, Discipline Masters/Mistresses, Teacher Counsellors and Pastoral Care Co-ordinators. Counselling is extended to pupils with problems resulting in disciplinary misdemeanours, to help them correct their mistakes and make responsible choices, and to pupils with emotional and/or relationship problems, to help them resolve their problems effectively without having to resort to misbehaviour.

Pupils are taught emotional and social skills through lifeskills and sexuality education programmes in school. Schools use a combination of regular classroom lessons and enrichment activities, such as talks on boy-girl relationships, leadership training and adventure camps. Some schools have also implemented the Peer Mediation programme (for secondary schools) and the Conflict Manager programme[25] (for primary schools). Through these programmes, the message of peace-making is spread in schools as selected pupils, equipped with the skills to mediate conflicts, help their peers in conflict to resolve their disputes amicably before the conflict escalates into a misdemeanour.

Pupils are provided with career guidance. Through career guidance lessons and activities such as career talks and visits to institutions of further education, pupils are helped to explore educational and career options and develop plans for their future. A common characteristic of pupils with disciplinary problems is their lack of thought about the future and their inability to plan for it. The career guidance programme in school helps pupils to relate their current experiences in school to the demands of the real world. The hope and focus on the future generated by the career guidance programmes make learning more personally meaningful for pupils and decrease their desire to engage in disruptive behaviour in school.

The Community Network

It is well-recognised that the nurturing and development of a child cannot be the effort of one party alone. Therefore, MOE has developed a framework for the tripartite collaboration of the school, parents and community to achieve the aims of education. Hence, parents and the community are invited as key partners in the shaping of attitudes and behaviour of children. In managing a child's misbehaviour, schools seek the co-operation of parents.

School policies, including policies on discipline, programmes and activities are communicated to parents through parent meetings and newsletters. Parent Support Groups are set up to increase opportunities for parental involvement in school and dialogue between parents and school personnel. Regular teacher-parent conferences are held to discuss each pupil's progress in school. Teachers contact parents as soon as a pupil's academic performance and behaviour shows cause for concern. Parents are also advised on how they can support their child academically and how to enable their child to learn responsible behaviour at home. Where necessary, pupils and parents are referred to specialists from the MOE, the Child Guidance Clinic at the Ministry of Health, and family service centres for further assistance.

The MOE collaborates with the police in the Honorary Volunteer Special Constabulary (Hon VSC) School Scheme. Under this scheme, key school discipline personnel are appointed as "teacher-cops" who act as liaison officers in networking with the police. These teachers are trained by the police before appointment as Honorary Volunteer Constabulary (Hon VSC). The programme aims to enhance the effectiveness of discipline personnel by projecting a police presence in school through their Hon VSC status. The Hon VSCs maintain a close link with the police to keep juvenile delinquency problems and the youth-gang influence away from schools.

The MOE also works closely with the Central Narcotics Bureau, the Singapore Anti-Narcotics Association, and the National Council Against Drug Abuse to provide preventive drug education in school. Information sessions about the dangers of drug abuse are conducted, with visits for at-risk pupils to the Drug Rehabilitation Centres. These visits, organised with the help of the Prisons Department, confront pupils with the reality of the harsh consequences of drug abuse.

The MOE collaborates with the Subordinate Courts in the Peer Group Advisers Programme.[26] Through this programme, selected pupils are provided with the opportunity to participate in the juvenile justice system. This experience increases pupils' awareness of the juvenile justice system and criminal law in general, and helps to spread respect for law and order amongst them.

MOE networks with the Ministry of Manpower, the Economic Development Board and a variety of business organisations and institutions of higher learning. This is to provide schools with current information on education and career opportunities, and contacts for career talks, visits and work-shadowing/attachment programmes for pupils.

Conclusion

Our schools believe in the value of discipline and willingly expend effort to develop and maintain good discipline in school, because we want our children to grow into responsible, competent adults who will enjoy, and contribute to, the continued peace, prosperity, and security of our nation.

> "The message you give your children when you discipline with love is 'I care too much about you to let you misbehave. I care enough about you that I'm willing to spend time and effort to help you learn what is appropriate.' All children need the security and stability of food, shelter, love, and protection, but unless they also receive effective and appropriate discipline, they won't feel secure."
> **– Stephanie Marston, The Divorced Parent: Success Strategies for Raising your Children after Separation.**
> **Parent Educator and Author, 1994.**

5.7 Coming to School to Succeed

MRS YEO CHIN NAM
Principal
Henderson Secondary School

I am the principal of a neighbourhood school, Henderson Secondary School. We have over a thousand students, many of whom are from low-income families. I always tell the students — and this is the philosophy around which the whole school operates — that they come to school to be *successful*. They do not come to school to be drop-outs, juvenile delinquents or to waste their lives away. They come to receive a decent education, to develop themselves as people, to build good and caring relationships with others, and to plan for a meaningful future. They come to school to *succeed*. This is the mindset that we want to inculcate in our students, and this is what the school as a whole, together with our community partners, aims to do.

Programmes for Success

Towards this end, we have instituted numerous programmes and activities to help our students succeed. In our pastoral care and moral education lessons, we try to imbue the students with a sense of responsibility — to themselves, their families, their friends, their school, their community and their country. We do this in a practical and engaging way through analysing case studies, role-playing, games and so on. We also hold talks during assemblies, about the school's basic expectations of the students, and about the school's values — moral integrity, care and concern for others, teamwork, innovation, an appreciation for beauty, and a love for our country. On a practical level, there are talks to teach them about health matters, how to manage stress, how to manage their time, and motivational talks to inspire them to set targets for themselves, and to strive towards them. We organise talks by the police, by the Central Narcotics Bureau, and other organisations, to warn students about the negative consequences of taking drugs and engaging in criminal activity. Workshops are regularly conducted in subjects such as smoking, sexuality, and anger management. To develop a forward-looking mindset amongst the students, we provide them with career guidance in the form of general talks on what people in various professions do, and individual sessions with teachers which are focused on discussing the student's plans for his future. All students are required to participate in at least one co-curricular activity, such as a sport, a uniformed group, or an interest group such as the school band, in order to ensure that they grow up to be well-rounded individuals, and are not just "book-smart".

Nipping Juvenile Delinquency in the Bud at School

Of course, in addition to all these programmes, the school also has a comprehensive framework to identify and help students who are in trouble or in need. It is of course a great blessing for us to have strong committed partners like the Subordinate Courts and the Ministry of Community Development and Sports (MCDS) in this mission. The Subordinate Courts and the MCDS offer us fresh solutions and new hope when every measure that can be taken by the school fails, and the youth is beyond parental control, or has become a juvenile delinquent. Amongst other things, the MCDS offers a third-party professional perspective and a third-party home, whilst the Juvenile Court has the undisputed authority to rein in negligent or criminal individuals, both young and old. In fact, the existence of the Court is in itself an effective deterrent against potential misdemeanours.

However, even though many youths have been brought back onto the right path through the synergistic efforts of MCDS, the Juvenile Court, and the schools, my view is that parents and schools, being the main custodians of the majority of our youth, must work more closely together to ensure that they stay on the right path, or mend their errant ways before they get the compulsory attention of the Juvenile Court and the MCDS. The journey to rehabilitation is an arduous one and the danger of losing a youth in trouble permanently once he has entered the court system is certainly greater than if parents and schools are to detect his problems early on, and take the necessary measures to address them. Schools are in a good position to assess and help the children under their charge. After all, for five days a week, the young person is in a fairly confined area and a fairly disciplined environment for about six hours a day, being observed and related to by six to nine teachers and many other students. Any personal problems that the young person is facing are bound to show within this time.

Identifying and Helping Those in Need

The first step, of course, is for the school to know its students — not just their names, but their personalities. Not just their academic performance, but their hobbies. Not just their disciplinary and attendance records, but their family background. Only when you know a person intimately can you help him effectively.

Next, a school needs to have a way to identify students in trouble. The warning signals of a youth in trouble may be very subtle. Or they may be disguised as misbehaviour. Aggression and non-compliance with authority, for example could be the result of worry, caused by familial conflict. Constant tardiness could be due to an unhealthy sleep pattern at home, caused by a noisy environment and depression or distress, rather than laziness. What appears as an indifference to school and unwillingness to do homework could stem from poor eye-sight and an inability to read the whiteboard, resulting from the student having no money to buy a pair of spectacles. A school must learn to be sensitive to these warning signs, and how to interpret them.

In Henderson Secondary School, we have a system where there is a "Pupil Profile File" for every single student. This file contains information on the student's family background (for example, whether his parents are divorced, what their professions are, whether they have previously been incarcerated in a Drug Rehabilitation Centre, etc.). The student's academic performance and disciplinary record from his primary school will be noted. His interests and hobbies will also be recorded. This file is updated regularly — at least once a term — should fresh information come to the form teacher's attention. In addition, any relevant documents such as medical certificates, doctor's reports, disciplinary reports and so on are placed into the file. At least once a year (we are intending to make this twice a year in the near future) the teacher will have a private interview with the student, in order to ensure that the information in the Pupil Profile File is current. In this way, the school is able to keep vital information on every student — and to use that information to help him.

Those who are academically poor will be referred to reading and other learning support programmes. We also run a mentoring scheme, sponsored by Tanjong Pagar Community Development Council, where volunteer students from the National University of Singapore give tuition to and befriend our academically weaker students, giving them encouragement and moral support. Those who are financially poor will be given assistance — in the form of pocket money, money for uniforms, text-books, and even spectacles. We will also arrange for them to receive financial assistance from external sources such as the Ministry of Education, in the form of scholarships, bursaries, and subsidies for computer equipment. Students with special needs, such as those who have Attention Deficit Disorder and those with mild autism will be referred to the Ministry of Health for treatment. The school will work with the student's parents and the Ministry of Health in order to ensure that the student is able to cope with the school regime, and that he receives not just suitable treatment for his condition — but understanding from the people around him about it.

Students who have been transferred "downstream" (i.e. from an academically more rigorous stream to a less rigorous one, such as from the Express to the Normal stream) or those who have been forced to repeat a year because they have failed their examinations, will be counselled, and their academic performance monitored. Students in this position will suffer from low self-esteem and low morale. They may be taunted by other students for being stupid, for instance, and lash out in anger. Their relationships with their parents may suffer because their parents may be ashamed of them because of their poor academic performance, and say hurtful things to them. We give these students counselling, in order to teach them strategies to cope with all these situations. We try to make them understand that, at any moment in time, *they* have a choice on which path their life is going to take. Through such understanding, we hope to re-build their self-esteem and to inspire them to work hard to achieve their goals.

Success through Discipline

The regime that our school has implemented to deal with "problem" students builds on the philosophy and the programmes which I have discussed thus far. The key strategy behind this regime is to help the student — no matter how aggressive, insecure or problematic he is — to share this vision: *that he is in school to succeed.* Our goal as teachers is to lead the student to this realisation, and to show him how it can be achieved. But it is up to the student himself to make it into reality — *his* reality.

Students with disciplinary problems are categorised into five categories, depending on the offences they have committed, and on who refers the student for disciplinary action. Somewhat different protocols apply, depending on which category the student falls into. However, a student may fall into more than one category — and for our part, we try to preserve flexibility in the procedures for dealing with students. All discipline matters are managed by a specialist team of teachers, headed by the school Operations Manager[27] ("the discipline committee"). The five categories are as follows:

Category A: Students Involved in Serious Disciplinary Offences

Serious offences are those such as fights, smoking, theft, defiance and rudeness to teachers, assault, bullying, extortion, and cheating in tests and examinations.

In these cases, the student is required to write a Pupil Statement, giving his version of events. The teacher who observed the disciplinary offence will also write his version of events down in a Disciplinary Report form (the Blue form), which will be placed into the student's Pupil Profile file. An investigative interview will then be conducted with the student by the Operations Manager or one of the discipline team teachers, and any others involved in the incident, in order to get to the root of the matter. If the student has been at fault, he will receive punishment. Caning is used only as a last resort, and only after the student has been properly briefed on the reasons why he is being caned. The school may also suspend or expel students — but these are actions that will not be taken if we see any hope of rehabilitation for the student within the school context.

The student's parents will be informed about the matter, and a conference will be held with the parents and the school representatives, at which the student himself will be present. This is to ensure that the student's parents are aware of what the student has been doing in school, to find out more about how the parents are disciplining the student at home, and to ensure that both the school and the parents build on, rather than undermine, each others' efforts to guide and discipline the student.

The student himself will be required to reflect, with the help of a counsellor (either from the school or an external counsellor) on why he is in school. He will be asked to outline his targets, ambitions and dreams. He will be asked to think about what was wrong about what he did, and why. He will be urged to think of the school's values, and what he can do to act in line with these values in different situations.

The student's behaviour will be monitored by the discipline committee for a certain period, and regular written reports on his progress will be made by obtaining the feedback of all the teachers involved in teaching him. If his behaviour does not improve, his parents will be asked to attend conferences in school, if necessary. Even if the student's behaviour improves, he will continue to be monitored for at least a year, to ensure that he does not slip back to his old ways.

Category B: Students Referred or Identified by Teachers

The students in this category are not involved in criminal activity — yet — but are observed by the teachers to have problems, such as not doing their homework assignments, not bringing their books to class, absenteeism, late-coming, disruptive behaviour in class, and engaging in inappropriate boy-girl relationships.

The teacher will fill in a Blue form to surface the issue to the discipline committee. The committee will then arrange for the "Yellow form" to be filled in. This form profiles the student in several areas: his relationship with his teachers, his interaction with his peers, his general behaviour, his participation in class discussions, the regularity with which he submits his assignments, the quality of his work, and any other special issues that the person filling in the form sees fit to raise, for example, whether the student appears depressed or insecure. Every single teacher who teaches the student, and also the teacher in charge of the student's co-curricular activity, will fill in the form. Thus, the completed form contains feedback on the student from about nine to ten officers. This enables the reader of the Yellow form to get a very full and balanced picture of the student.

After the Yellow form is completed, the school will then arrange for a conference with the student and his parents, together with representatives from the school. The Yellow form will be shown to the student and his parents, analysed and discussed. Strategies will be mapped out on how the student can improve his behaviour, and programmes will be recommended for him, if necessary. Further counselling for the student will be arranged, and the student's behaviour will be monitored and his case reviewed at regular intervals.

Category C:
Students Referred by Parents

If a parent is unable to control his child, he may sometimes turn to the school for help. The students referred to the school by parents are those who are beyond their parents' control, often absent from home, or who are engaged in inappropriate boy-girl relationships.

A student who is referred to the school by his parent will be interviewed, to obtain his version of events. The Yellow form will be called for, and he will then be counselled by his form teacher. A conference with the form teacher, the counsellor, the student, the student's parents and a representative of the discipline committee will be held, in order to thrash out the various issues between parent and child, and to formulate a plan to improve the parent-child relationship and the student's behaviour at home. Further counselling may be provided for the student either in school or with an external counsellor. The situation will be monitored by the school. If there is no improvement in the student's behaviour at home, the school will refer the matter to MCDS (if the student appears to be in need of care and protection) or recommend the parent to file a Beyond Parental Control complaint against the student in the Juvenile Court.

Category D:
Students Surfaced by the Police, MCDS etc.

Category D students are usually those involved in criminal offences such as shoplifting, rioting, gang activities and smoking, who have been caught and arrested by the police.

When the school is notified of this by the relevant organisation, the student involved will be asked to write out his version of events in a Pupil Statement. He will be interviewed, and the Yellow form will be called for. Reports on his school performance and behaviour will be prepared. The Operations Manager will liaise with the police to give them all the relevant documentation, as well as the Yellow form itself. A conference will be held with the student, the student's parents and representatives of the school, in order to determine what help the school can give to the student at this stage, and to determine the student's educational future in the school, in the circumstances. The police will let the school know the outcome of any prosecution against the student, by liaising with the Operations Manager.

Category E: Students with Discipline Offences Related to Learning Disorders/Psychological Conditions, etc.

A student with Attention Deficit Disorder or mild autism or some such other psychological condition or learning disorder may often behave badly. For example, a boy with autism may react very badly to being teased, as he may not understand that the person teasing him means no harm. He may then react violently, and try to beat up the person teasing him. Such students are placed under this category.

Once a student is identified to be a Category E student, the Yellow form is called for, and the parents are called to attend a conference with representatives from the school. This is to ensure that the parents understand the nature of the student's disorder, and that they will work with the school in helping the student. Counselling sessions (usually by external counsellors who are trained to handle the particular disorder suffered by the student) will be arranged for the student. Teachers, and even the student's classmates will also be trained to assist the student in class as well as out of class. He will be monitored and his case reviewed at regular intervals.

Continuing the Vital Task

If a school has a framework and structure for grooming its students for success, for identifying students in trouble, for counselling and helping them, and monitoring their progress, the chances of keeping or turning these students away from the path of trouble are good. The work is not easy, however. Most of us in the school work a "12-hour shift", from 7 a.m. to 7 p.m. on weekdays! Students who have been in trouble may need two to three years of intensive monitoring, attention and care before they can be trusted to stay out of trouble permanently. In most cases, the work not only has to be done with the student alone, but with the student's parents also, whose poor parenting styles, or whose conflict, are often the root cause of the student's problems. The school therefore has to work hard to establish a relationship of trust not only with the student, but with his family. It is work that brings its own rewards, and is often the source of much hope and joy. But it is also work that requires much time, patience, skill and delicacy.

It is vital that each school takes up the task of reaching out to its youths in need and their families. This is because school is where the problems often first surface. School is where these problems can be nipped in the bud, before the troubled youth and his parents end up walking through the doors of the Juvenile Court, flanked by officers from the MCDS. School is where all youths can learn the life, social, and academic skills necessary to succeed. School is where they can learn — no matter how unfortunate their family circumstances, no matter how humble their background — to believe in themselves and in their future.

5.8 Working with Students in the Peer Mediation Programme — The Bedok North Experience

MRS TAN AI-LIN
Head of Department (Discipline)
Bedok North Secondary School

The Peer Mediation Programme is an initiative of the Subordinate Courts of Singapore which is supported by the Ministry of Education and the Court Mediation Centre (now renamed Primary Dispute Resolution Centre — PDRC). The objective of the Peer Mediation Programme is to reduce the number of juvenile arrests and to create a peaceful, non-violent environment in the school. Bedok North Secondary School was privileged to be selected as one of the four schools to pilot the programme in 1997 and the programme has continued in the school to this day.

Fighting and assaults do sometimes occur in the school and these usually result from misunderstanding and playfulness. Bedok North Secondary School finds Peer Mediation to be a proactive and viable alternative to simply caning the wrong-doers or finding other ways to punish them. The programme provides a positive force for personal growth, both for those conducting the mediation as well as for those attending it. It prevents disputes from developing into fights. In adopting this programme, the school is putting into action its belief that we can build a society that seeks to resolve all disputes in peaceful, non-violent ways.

The school selects a few Secondary Two students to be trained as mediators. They will then continue to serve as mediators until they graduate. Mediators are selected based on their personal abilities, which include communication skills, respect for their peers, self-confidence, empathy and leadership potential. The students learn to listen effectively, learn how to paraphrase the statements of others, and also hone their questioning skills. They develop brainstorming skills and learn to tackle difficult situations. Graduating mediators are also awarded CCA (Co-Curricular Activities) bonus points for their contributions in the field of peer mediation.

Students who need help in resolving their conflicts go directly to the teachers or mediators. The case will then be referred to the co-ordinator of the programme (a teacher in the school) who will make the necessary arrangements for mediators on duty to mediate. Mediation is always conducted by two Peer Mediators at one time — a senior and a junior mediator. Mediation is conducted after school in the Pupil Activity Centre (PAC), usually within two days of the reported conflict, so that conflicts will be resolved as soon as possible.

Follow-up discussions with the disputants and mediators by the co-ordinator of the programme are held after each mediation session. Disputants and mediators are also required to fill in a feedback form. Fortnightly feedback sessions between Peer Mediators and teacher advisers are also conducted, where Senior Mediators will provide feedback to their Junior mediation partners on their performance. In this manner, the skills of the mediators are developed. Feedback from students and staff on the Peer Mediation programme is obtained through surveys conducted at the end of each semester. This is used to make improvements to the programme.

Much was done to encourage students to refer themselves for mediation. This included getting disputants and mediators to speak to the student body during morning assemblies about their experiences. Banners were put up and each class had posters and the names and classes of the mediators. Since the year 2000, all Secondary 2 students have had to undergo a ten-lesson module on Conflict Resolution and Peer Mediation as part of their Pastoral Care syllabus. This has helped to increase the number of self-referrals for mediation from one or two each year in previous years to 16 in the year 2001.

A survey to evaluate the programme was conducted in 1998 by the PCCG (Pastoral Care and Career Guidance, now renamed Psychological and Guidance Services) Branch of the Ministry of Education. The survey[28] affirmed the school's belief in the benefits of the programme. Both mediators and disputants felt that they gained valuable life-skills that raised their self-esteem, and that they had also developed their problem-solving skills. They learned conflict resolution through the analysis of problems and the working out of solutions. They developed communications skills like listening, paraphrasing, and appreciating others' viewpoints. Pupils in the school felt that the Peer Mediation Programme taught them that conflicts could be resolved peacefully.

The programme benefits the school as a whole also. It is student-centred and so develops thinking, responsible and mature students. The reduction in the number of fights in school speaks volumes of the success of the programme. Our internal records show that in 2001, there were 21 fights, out of which 19 were in the first half of the year. In the year 2002, there were only 10 for the first half of the year. In a more disciplined climate, teachers have more time to focus on academic work rather than solving discipline problems.

The school also believes in helping to promote the skills of peer mediation beyond the school boundaries. Thus, the school collaborated with Marine Parade CDC, the Community Mediation Centre, the Primary Dispute Resolution Centre and the Subordinate Courts, in the training of peer mediators, in 1999 and 2000. In addition, teachers and peer mediators of the school trained the prefects of a nearby primary school in conflict management skills, in November 2001.

Bedok North Secondary School believes that Peer Mediation is a programme worth investing time in. Exposure to mediation concepts and the teaching of skills for the peaceful resolution of conflicts will not only continue to reduce the number of juvenile arrest cases in schools, it will also make the students into more caring, more peaceable citizens, able to resolve their conflicts in a non-violent and constructive manner. In recognition of the success of the peer mediation programme in the school, Bedok North Secondary School was awarded the Subordinate Courts Peer Mediation Excellence Award in April 2001.

5.9 Operation NightWatch — Watching over Juvenile Offenders in the Community

CHOMIL KAMAL
Chief Probation Officer
Probation Services Branch, Ministry of Community Development and Sports

Operation NightWatch (ONW) was piloted by the Ministry of Community Development and Sports (MCDS) in August 2002 to leverage on the keen interest and enthusiasm of experienced volunteer probation officers (VPOs) and to thereby facilitate curfew compliance by probationers. Through their friendly but firm enforcement, these mature and seasoned VPOs help probationers to exercise self-control, and observe the time restrictions set for them by the Court; thereby increasing the likelihood of them successfully completing their probation terms.

According to the records of the Probation Services Branch, 97% of all probation cases have time restrictions as a condition of probation. Physical checks are required for all these cases — telephone checks have limitations as teenagers have been known to divert their home telephone numbers to their mobile numbers. While there are ways to check if a call has been diverted or a probationer is claiming to be home when he is in fact outdoors, the verification process entails costs and requires the careful selection as well as training of those persons doing the checks.

Prior to the launch of ONW, full-time probation officers (POs) would conduct random checks on probationers to ascertain if they had kept to the time curfews imposed by the Courts. They were supported by about ten VPOs. Resource constraints had resulted in a less than desired level of curfew checks on those probationers who were not in the high-risk group.

Under ONW, 40 VPOs are involved in conducting these checks on probationers, with POs playing a supportive role. The VPOs are people from all walks of life — housewives, lecturers, doctors, academics and professionals — whose ages range from 30-60 years old.

The objectives of ONW are to:

1) enhance the active engagement of the community in strengthening the supervision of juvenile offenders living in the community;
2) provide greater scope in volunteer work, with POs playing only a supportive and facilitative role;
3) effectively and efficiently enhance surveillance of probationers, for their effective rehabilitation.

With the community playing an active role in the enforcement of probation orders through ONW, the number of physical checks on probationers has increased threefold, from over 100 (before ONW was launched) to the present rate of more than 400 cases checked each month. The higher frequency of checks signals a clear message to these probationers: they cannot get away with flouting curfew orders easily.

Since the launch of ONW, VPOs have been spending nights doing more than 400 curfew checks a month, and roaming all over Singapore in the course of doing so. Headed by the ONW Manager (also a volunteer), the 40 volunteers are split into groups to cover five different geographical areas in Singapore. The five group leaders then assign each group member to check on those probationers who live near them. Some walk, some take the bus, some drive. Each person has an assigned list of about 30 juvenile cases to check at any one time. Some need to be checked twice a month, others need to be checked once a month and yet others need only be given one check every two months. The frequency of the checks depends on the practice guidelines for each grade of probation[29] and the probationer's needs as assessed by the PO.

The curfew checking process is as follows: When the VPO arrives at the home of the juvenile he has been assigned to check, he will ask to see the juvenile. When the juvenile appears, he will then check the juvenile's identification card to ensure that he is the right person. The VPO will then fill in the curfew check form provided by the Probation Services Branch. If the juvenile is absent, the VPO will fill in the information accordingly, in the curfew check form.

As juveniles have a tendency to go out with their friends till late at night on weekends, some of the curfew checks are deliberately done on Saturdays and Sundays. The VPOs also undertake, as part of the ONW programme, curfew checks on those offenders who are given the "curfew compliance test" by the investigating PO at the pre-order stage.[30] The aim is to gauge if an offender can be counted on to adhere to the rules, if probation were to be granted by the Court.

Checks and balances are in place for VPOs to accurately identify the probationers being checked, to ensure curfew checks are done according to best practices, and to give timely feedback on the outcome of each check.

The VPOs' responsibilities include:

1) conducting checks on probationers according to the frequency specified by the probation officers and the practice guidelines set by the Probation Services Branch;
2) promptly returning the completed curfew check forms to the ONW Manager;
3) providing feedback to the ONW Manager on whether the probationers have complied with their curfew orders and noting down comments for probation officers to take follow-up action — for example, if the juvenile is observed to be smoking or consuming alcohol at home or keeping company with negative peers at home.

To ensure satisfactory service delivery by the VPOs, the ONW cluster leaders and Manager conduct random audits of their performance through surveys on probationers and their parents regarding the conduct and enforcement of the curfew checks. This ensures accountability by the VPOs for their performance and conduct, and safeguards the probationers against any impropriety in behaviour by the VPOs.

ONW is a one-year pilot programme. It will be reviewed after six months and at the end of the year-long period to assess its effectiveness in the enforcement of curfew orders. According to anecdotal evidence, however, the programme is already showing good results. POs and VPOs have reported that since the implementation of ONW, the probationers and their parents are making a serious effort to keep to their curfew hours. In some cases, the frequent checks by the VPOs have provided the POs with useful and regular information on probationers and their family situations, thus facilitating timely intervention in appropriate cases. One example of this is a curfew check which was carried out on a pair of siblings who were both placed on probation, which shed light on the reasons for their sudden poor progress in school and at home. The VPO discovered, in the course of his curfew check, that the siblings' mother (a single mother) was cohabiting with her new boyfriend, and that the siblings did not get along with him. On being informed of this by the VPO, the PO was able to undertake a reassessment and case planning exercise to identify the siblings' risks and needs in the light of their mother's new relationship and their adverse reaction to the new addition to the family. In this case, timely intervention in the form of a Family Conference in the Juvenile Court enabled the single mother and her children to air out their grievances and work towards a solution which both sides were reasonably satisfied with. The PO in turn, focused on helping the siblings to enhance their communication and conflict resolution skills through arranging counselling sessions for them.

Parents of juveniles on probation have welcomed the stepped-up enforcement of curfew checks. Some have really needed the help from an external source of authority (at least initially) to impose limits and boundaries on their children.

In line with the MCDS' philosophy of rehabilitating youth offenders through the "strengthen families, engage community" framework and the Juvenile Court's communitarian justice model, ONW gives the people in the community, through the ONW volunteers, greater autonomy, ownership and accountability in the rehabilitation of juvenile offenders in the community.

5.10 The Guidance Programme

CORINNE KOH
Deputy Director, Family and Child Protection and Welfare Branch,
Rehabilitation and Protection Division,
Ministry of Community Development and Sports

Background

The Guidance Programme (GP) was developed in response to a recommendation by the Inter-Ministry Committee on Dysfunctional Families, Juvenile Delinquency and Drug Abuse (IMC) which was set up in 1994 and chaired by Mr Abdullah Tarmugi, then Minister for Community Development. The IMC noted that the number of youths who took to crime doubled between 1980 and 1990. The IMC also noted that nearly one in three of the young offenders who were let off with a stern warning by the police returned to crime within two years.[31]

The IMC was of the view that the police warning system should be strengthened and proposed that:

(a) the police could recommend to the Attorney-General's Chambers (AGC) that the prosecution of the case be deferred until after the youth has been given a chance to attend a counselling programme; and
(b) the young offender's parents/guardians should be encouraged to attend these counselling programmes with their child/ward.

Following the IMC's proposals, in October 1997, the GP was put in place to provide a counselling and rehabilitative programme for juvenile offenders of petty offences. The GP enables juvenile offenders who complete the programme successfully to be let off with a stern warning in lieu of court prosecution. This diverts juvenile offenders from the court system, whilst giving them the opportunity to learn the skills necessary for their rehabilitation, and provides them with the emotional support and structure they require to do so.

Objectives of GP

The GP is a government-funded programme under the purview of the Ministry of Community Development and Sports (MCDS). It involves the police, schools and social service agencies appointed by MCDS to take part in this programme.

After the juvenile is arrested by the police for an alleged offence, and he has admitted to committing the offence, the police will recommend to the Attorney-General's Chambers that the juvenile be given a stern warning and placed on the GP, instead of being charged in Court. The police will only offer this option to juveniles who are first-time offenders and who have committed petty offences such as shoplifting of goods of low value, theft of small items, littering, and so on. To be eligible for the programme, the juvenile and his parents must agree to him being placed on the GP. Social workers from the social service agencies appointed by the MCDS to conduct this programme will be assigned to monitor the progress of the juvenile, guide his activities, and counsel him. The parents or guardians of the juvenile are also encouraged to attend the programme with their children or wards and to provide their full support to the social worker assigned to the juvenile during the period of the GP.

The usual requirement is for the juvenile to undergo a six-month programme in the first instance. After this period, the programme may be extended for another six months if deemed necessary, subject to the concurrence of the juvenile, his parents/guardians and the AGC.

The objectives of the GP are:

1) to help the juvenile recognise the offence he committed as a criminal act and to avoid committing further offences;

2) to help the juvenile acquire life-skills in self-control and in the handling of peer pressure; and
3) to allow the parents of the juvenile to acquire knowledge and skills in effective parenting and supervision.

The six-month programme encompasses:

(a) individual and family counselling;
(b) group work and support services; and
(c) review and termination work with the juvenile and his parents/ guardians.

The social worker assigned to do the individual and family counselling sessions with the juvenile and his family will monitor the progress of the juvenile and lay down certain rules the juvenile must obey, for example, a nightly curfew, and taking part in all the activities organised for him by the social worker.

Core activities include parents' support group sessions, group work for the juvenile and weekend family camps or functions. Besides these core activities, the social worker may, at his discretion, consider other programmes to enhance the work with the juvenile and his family, namely, tuition, interest group activities and community service. These activities are intended to enable the juvenile to practise life-skills, and to learn and experience enriching forms of "fun" by acquiring hobbies and taking part in wholesome activities. Visits to prisons and drug rehabilitation centres, to impress upon the juvenile the seriousness of the consequences of committing crimes and abusing drugs, will also be organised.

The final stage is the termination/review stage. This stage allows the juvenile and his family to review the impact of the programme on their lives and to prepare them for the future. The juvenile and his family members are also asked to consider, and will be advised on, whether they will continue to require the services of the social service agency or other agencies.

Upon the recommendation of the social worker, the juvenile may be taken off the GP if he makes good progress before the expiry of the six-month programme, with the concurrence of the police and the AGC.

Success Factors

Some 1,200 juveniles were placed on GP since its inception. There were 1,081 cases closed for the period 1998 to 2000. 87% of the juveniles completed GP successfully. A programme evaluation on the GP was conducted by the Family and Child Protection and Welfare Branch of MCDS, which was completed in January 2001. In addition, the Policy and Development Branch of MCDS embarked on a study of the recidivism rate of GP participants who were discharged from 1998 to June 1999.[32] From the programme evaluation, it was observed that the following factors were important in the rehabilitation of juveniles:

1) Parental Involvement in the juvenile's rehabilitation, which impressed upon the juveniles the seriousness of their offending behaviour or actions. Parents also benefited from the counselling and parenting programmes.
2) Structured Programme — Social workers exposed the juveniles to healthy activities which imparted them with both social skills and life skills. The experience of being arrested by the police and having to go for visits to the Prison or Drug Rehabilitation Centre (DRC) were effective deterrents to re-offending.
3) Sense of Discipline — The curfew imposed made it a habit for juveniles to return home early.
4) Commitment of social workers and families helped in the juveniles' rehabilitation.
5) Inter-agency networking — A strong collaboration among agencies was crucial. The social workers were able to seek assistance from the police if the juvenile is not responding well to GP. Feedback from schools helped to monitor the progress of the juvenile.

5.11 The Residential Rehabilitation Branch

NG POH LENG
Deputy Director
Residential and Rehabilitation Branch, Rehabilitation and Protection Division,
Ministry of Community Development and Sports

The Residential Rehabilitation Branch (RRB) at MCDS is responsible for the rehabilitation of youths who have been committed to juvenile corrective institutions by the Juvenile Court. These are youths who are deemed by the Juvenile Court to be in need of institutionalisation. The juvenile corrective institutions which are run by the RRB are:

1) Singapore Boys' Home (gazetted as an Approved School, an Approved Home, and a Place of Detention under the Children and Young Persons Act (Cap. 38));
2) Toa Payoh Girls' Home (gazetted as an Approved School, an Approved Home, and a Place of Detention under the Children and Young Persons Act (Cap. 38))

("the Homes")

3) Singapore Boys' Hostel (gazetted as an Approved Institution under the Probation of Offenders' Act (Cap. 252))

("the Hostel")

The RRB works with schools as well as employers in the community in order to achieve its goal of rehabilitating young offenders. It also runs a number of individual and group rehabilitative programmes within the Homes and the Hostel. Some of these programmes have been designed by the psychologists of the Psychological Services Unit (PSU). Psychologists have been employed in the Ministry since the early 1970s. However, it was not until October 1998 that the PSU was formally established as a unit within the Rehabilitation and Protection Division (RPD). With the mission of becoming a "clinical-forensic centre providing comprehensive psychological services to children, youths and families", PSU provides specialist services to the branches within RPD, including the RRB and the Homes and the Hostel under its charge.

The following are various programmes and services provided in the Homes and the Hostel for their residents:

Individual Care Plan

The Individual Care Plan is a road map for every resident who enters one of the Homes or the Hostel. The case worker assigned to each resident would assess the resident's needs and goals and map out an individual care plan to aid his rehabilitation and arrange for the plan to be put into action. For example, if the resident has a problem with controlling his anger, the case worker would arrange for him to attend an anger management programme. If he does not have basic literacy skills, the case worker will arrange for him to attend a reading programme.

If the resident of one of the Homes behaves well, he will be allowed to go home for weekends, and he will be allowed to leave the Home during the day to attend school, or to work. The ultimate goal is for the resident to be released on licence. The minimum time period that a resident has to remain in the Home before being released on licence is at least one year.[33] Being released on licence means that the resident is allowed to go home permanently, subject to his continued good behaviour. He will be monitored by an aftercare officer until the expiry of the court order mandating him to stay for a certain period of time in the Home.

The Individual Care Plan will set out the various targets that the resident should aim for during his stay in the Home, towards the ultimate goal of being released on licence.

For residents of the Hostel, the Individual Care Plan will set out the various activities which the resident should take part in during his stay in the Hostel, such as outdoor camps, sports, and tuition (which is conducted by volunteer students from the National University of Singapore).

Teaching Educational and Vocational Skills

BEST (Basic Education for Skills Training) and WISE (Worker Improvement Through Secondary Education)[34] classes are arranged for residents of the Homes and the Hostel in order to help them keep abreast of their peers who are still in the education system. For those who are more technically inclined, the Home provides MOST (Modular Skills Training) classes. These classes place residents, who are not able to return to school, in a better position to seek employment in the labour market by teaching them skills in areas such as electrical wiring and mechanical technology. The Basic Life Skills classes (BLISS) teach residents the various skills required for independent living. Residents learn to cook simple meals, keep their surroundings clean and upkeep their homes. In addition, personal grooming and social grace classes are held to train residents on how to present themselves at work and during interviews.

The Day Release Scheme (DRS)

The Day Release Scheme is a programme that allows residents of the Homes who have made good progress during their stay in the Home to be reinstated in the schools or be placed in employment. If the residents behave well, they will be allowed to attend schools or work in the community during the day. After work or school they will have to report back to the Home, where they stay at night.

Therapeutic Programmes

Therapeutic programmes address various areas of a person's development, which has been mapped out in the individual care plan.

These programmes include: the Anger Management Groupwork Programme; the Pre-DRS programme that deals with how to handle stressors and temptations; Positive Adolescent Sexuality Treatment (PAST) programme that caters for those who have committed sexual offences; and Special Needs for Adolescents Programme (SNAP) that caters to residents who are classified to be educationally subnormal.

Individual counselling is also conducted by the case workers in the Homes and the Aftercare Officers in the community. Cases that require more specialised counselling, such as trauma work with victims of abuse, and those cases where clinical disorders are present, would be referred to the MCDS psychologists.

Positive Adolescent Sexuality Treatment (PAST) Programme

The PAST programme is the first systematic group programme for adolescent sex offenders in Singapore. It is a specialised treatment programme initiated and implemented by PSU, in collaboration with the Prisons Department psychologists. The programme is intended for selected sex offenders from the Probation Service Branch (PSB) and the Singapore Boys' Home. The primary objective of the programme is to provide comprehensive and specialised treatment to reduce the frequency and extent of re-offending by convicted youth sex offenders. Specifically, the programme aims to develop the essential skills, knowledge, and awareness needed to change the youth's sexual offending behaviour.

The programme consists of 11 modules that are delivered over 15 weekly sessions and utilises a "cognitive-behavioural/relapse prevention" model of treatment. This means teaching participants how to monitor their own thoughts and feelings in different situations, how to recognise when they are in a high-risk situation, or have "high-risk" thoughts and feelings, and how to proactively plan to prevent such high-risk situations from occurring or escalating. Research has consistently shown this approach, relative to other treatment models, to be the most effective for reducing recidivism in sex offenders.[35] A combination of lectures, interactive group discussions, therapeutic games/activities (for example, participants may be asked to build a "wall of trust" to symbolise their return to the community and what they can do to restore their parents' and others' trust in them), and role plays (where participants practise their newly learned skills in simulated high-risk situations) are used during the programme. Thorough assessments are conducted on the participants before and after they complete the group programme. Intellectually disabled sex offenders are not included in the group programme. Instead, PSU provides individual psychological therapy that can better address their specific needs.[36]

Special Needs Adolescent Programme (SNAP)

Individuals with an intellectual disability are likely to face significant functional limitations in at least three of the seven areas of major life activity: self-care, receptive and expressive language, learning, mobility, self-direction, capacity for independent living, and economic self-sufficiency (Diagnostic and Statistical Manual-IV).[37] These limitations present special challenges when juveniles with intellectual disabilities are placed in correctional settings (such as the Singapore Boys' Home). Consequently, programmes will have to be specially designed to cater to their special needs and limitations.[38] Research has shown that successful rehabilitation of intellectually disabled offenders is and will continue to be guided extensively by the principles of behavioural psychology.[39] One of the key principles of behavioural psychology is that if a person is engaging in positive activity/behaviour, he or she will not behave negatively. Thus, the strategy in treating individuals who have been engaging in negative behaviour is to engage them in positive activities and events.

With the above principles in mind, SNAP was jointly developed and conducted by PSU and the case workers for the intellectually disabled residents in the Singapore Boys' Home. The programme consciously integrates three main treatment approaches that have been adopted worldwide: the behavioural, the didactic, and the advocacy models.[40] The behavioural model suggests that behaviour can be changed by arranging contingencies that either reward desired behaviour or punish undesired behaviour. The didactic model suggests that the key to rehabilitation is to teach a person to acquire important skills that will assist him in adapting to life in the community. The advocacy model concentrates on helping a person to achieve a sense of self-competence and consequently, to achieve self-determination.

SNAP is targeted to equip intellectually disabled Singapore Boys' Home residents with adaptive problem-solving and coping skills in dealing with potentially challenging social situations within the residential facility as well as in the community, and eventually to reduce recidivism in relation to sexual offences.[41] Case workers were asked to identify focus areas that would most benefit the residents. The four identified broad areas were then covered in SNAP: problem-solving skills, anger management, resisting peer pressure, as well as personal rights (for example, the right that each human being has to his personal space and privacy). SNAP comprises 16 sessions and is conducted through a series of activities such as discussion groups, drawings and role-play. Positive behaviour is socially reinforced through praise from facilitators and peers.

Responsible Adolescent Group (RAG)

Depressed moods and feelings of hopelessness in adolescents place them at increased risk of depressive disorders, suicide, anti-social behaviour and substance abuse.[42] RAG is a group therapy programme developed for residents at the Toa Payoh Girls' Home which is designed to tackle this problem. RAG aims to teach these residents effective emotional management skills, thereby enabling them to combat depression and anxiety. Participants are selected based on their scores in established psychological questionnaires measuring depression and anxiety. This programme is designed to teach participants to build resilience, to promote positive coping abilities, and to maintain a sense of self in the face of stressful and difficult circumstances, by focusing on each individual's strengths. The programme consists of 11 sessions and covers areas such as identifying personal strengths, identifying, challenging and replacing unhelpful thinking patterns, and enhancing interpersonal problem-solving skills. Therapeutic change is measured by comparing pre- and post-programme scores of the participants on established psychometric scales.

Anger Management

The anger management programme is called the Emotional Intelligence Programme. It consists of four modules, and ten sessions. It covers issues such as:

- understanding the feeling of anger;
- control and responsibility;
- empathy; and
- conflict resolution skills

The Emotional Intelligence Programme is conducted by a psychologist from the PSU together with a rehabilitation officer. The programme is intended for boys assessed to be at a moderate to high risk of violence, who are easily provoked and have previously been involved in fights. The programme is not meant for chronic bullies, who believe in using force to instil fear in others to get what they want. Such residents, who are considered to have very violent mindsets, and very violent traits, are counselled individually or referred for specialised therapy with the PSU.

Sports and Arts Collide

Sports and art have become a tool in the rehabilitation process. The Homes and the Hostel set aside some time each day for the residents to be engaged in sports activities such as sepak takraw, basketball, netball, table tennis and soccer. Annually, the Singapore Boys' Home organises a soccer tournament to allow the residents to compete with residents of other voluntary welfare organisations for the coveted Lim Hsiu Mei Cup.

In the Homes, the residents also pick up guitar and keyboard skills and dance steps through music and dance classes. With these skills, the residents have put up performance items at various functions.

Involving the Family in Programmes

The family is the basic building unit of society. Hence, it is important that the resident's family is involved in the rehabilitation process. Programmes have been tailored to involve the residents' parents, to enhance their understanding of how they can contribute to their children's development. The Pre-Day Release Scheme programme assists in preparing residents for work or school, and includes a module involving the parents in a series of activities with their children to help them get an idea on how they can contribute to the progress of the child at school or at work. The activities include group interaction in the form of games, and also sharing sessions by ex-residents. Talks are held at the Homes for parents to educate them on various issues in relation to the crucial period of adolescent development.

Aftercare Service

The MCDS Aftercare Service works closely with schools and employers in gathering feedback on the progress of clients after they leave the Homes or the Hostel. This allows officers to make assessments on whether the resident is ready to be returned to the community to continue his or her rehabilitation under the Aftercare Service. Even after the resident is released from the Home or the Hostel, he will undergo supervision until the discharge date indicated in the court order. Aftercare Officers play an instrumental role in the successful re-integration of the residents of the Homes and the Hostel in schools, employment and society.

REFERENCES

Correctional Services of Canada. (1995). *Sex Offenders and Programmes in CSC.* Ottawa.

Diagnostic and Statistical Manual of Mental Disorders.(DSM-IV). (1994). 4th edition. Washington, DC : American Psychiatric Association.

Denkowski, G. K., Denkowski, K.& Mabli, J. (1983). A 50-state Survey of Current Status of Residential Treatment Programmes for Mentally Retarded Offenders. *Mental Retardation*, 21.

Ellis, J. W. & Luckasson, R. A. (1985). Mentally Retarded Criminal Defendants. *George Washington Law Review*, *53*, 414-93.

Endicott, O.R. (1991). *Persons with Intellectual Disability who are Incarcerated for Criminal Offences : a Literature Review*. A report prepared for The Research Branch, Communications and Corporate Development, Correctional Services of Canada.

Forman, S. G. (1993). *Coping Skills Intervention for Children and Adolescents*. San Francisco: Jossey-Bass Inc.

Freeman-Longo, R. E. & Knopp, H. F. (1992). State-of-the-art Sex Offender Treatment: Outcome and Issues. *Annals of Sex Research*, *5 (3)*, 141-60.

Lewinsohn, P. M., Clarke, G. N., Hops, H. & Andrews, J. (1990). Cognitive-behavioural Treatment for Depressed Adolescents. *Behaviour Therapy, 21*, 385-401.

Marshall, W. L. & Barbaree, H. E. (1990). Outcome of Comprehensive Cognitive-behavioural Treatment Programmes. In William L. Marshall, D. R. Lawa, & H. E. Barbaree (eds.), *Handbook of Sexual Assault: Issues, Theories, and Treatment of the Offender* (pp. 363-85). New York: Plenum Press.

Mufson, L., Moreau, D., Weissman, M. M. & Klerman, G. L. (1993). *Interpersonal Psychotherapy for Depressed Adolescents*. New York: Guilford Press.

Peterson, A. C., Compas, B. E., Brooks-Gunn, J., Stemmler, M., Ey, S. & Grant, K. E. (1993). Depression in Adolescence. *American Psychologist, 48*, 155-68.

Stermac, L. E. & Sheridan, P. (1993). The Developmentally Disabled Adolescent Sex Offender. In H. E. Barbaree, W. L. Marshall & S. M. Hudson (eds.), *The Juvenile Sex Offender* (pp. 235-242). New York: Guilford.

ENDNOTES

1 Source: The Report of the Inter-Ministry Committee on Dysfunctional Families, Juvenile Delinquency and Drug Abuse (October 1995), Chapter 3, p.31.

2 Details on how to obtain copies of these reports, and also further details on other research studies funded by the IMYC are available on the IMYC website at **http://www.imyc.org.sg**

3 For more information on the StreetWise programme, see pages 181-82.

4 For more information on the Peer Mediation programme, see pages 59-60.

5 For more details on the Guidance Programme, see pages 216-19.

6 For more details on the IMYC, see pages 165-71.

7 For the full names of these organisations, see Annex A to this chapter at page 231.

8 For more details on the Guidance Programme, see endnote 5, supra.

9 Juveniles are defined as persons aged 7 years or above and below 16 years of age.

10 These studies include:

- (a) Strategic Analysis Section, Police Intelligence Department. (1994). *A Report on Criminal Behaviour of Juveniles in Singapore.*
- (b) Strategic Analysis Section, Police Intelligence Department. (1994). *A Report on Juvenile Recidivism.*
- (c) Secret Societies Branch, Criminal Investigation Department. (1995). *A Report of the Secret Society Situation in Singapore (1993) for the Subcommittee on Juvenile Delinquency.*
- (d) Alfred Choi and Chan Cheng. (1995). *Report of a Study on Problem Youths in Singapore*, funded by National Crime Prevention Council and conducted for the Singapore Police Force.

11 The IMYC was formerly known as the Inter-Ministry Committee on Juvenile Delinquency (IMJD). The IMJD was reconstituted as IMYC in 1998 as it expanded its terms of reference to include persons between the ages of 16 and 19 years to keep track of crimes committed by this age group.

12 The statistics for juveniles arrested between 1990 and 2000 are based on the Annual Statistical Reports on Crime in Singapore published by the Statistics Branch, Police Intelligence Department. The figures for 2001are provisional.

13 The latest figures in 2001 as at preparation of this article.

14 For more information on the IMYC, see endnote 6, supra.

15 For more information on the Guidance Programme, see endnote 5, supra.

16 Statistics from the Secret Society Branch, Criminal Investigation Department. There were four recidivists out of a total of 325 youths who were enrolled in the SWP between Nov 1997 and Dec 2001. (A participant is considered to be a recidivist if he re-offends during the period of one year after he has completed the programme.)

17 "Home Team" agencies that are actively involved in CSSP include the Singapore Police Force, Singapore Prison Service, Central Narcotics Bureau and Singapore Civil Defence Force.

18 The case example cited here is based on an actual case. However, the name of the juvenile has been changed to protect her identity.

19 U.S. Department of Health and Human Services. (1997). Risk Factors Surrounding Children, *Drug Abuse Prevention: What Works*.

20 The Henderson Survey published in the *Straits Times*, 9 January 2002.

21 The Henderson Survey, supra.

22 "Effectiveness" is defined as nurturing children who develop into well-adjusted, responsible, competent, adaptable, co-operative and confident adults.

23 Huxley, R. (1998). *Love & Limits: Achieving a Balance in Parenting*. US: Singular Publishing Group.

24 Gaustad, Joan. (1992). School Discipline. ERIC Clearinghouse on Educational Management, Eugene, Oregan. ED350727.

25 See pages 59-60 for more details on these programmes.

26 See page 58 for more details on this programme.

27 See page 32 for more information on the role of an Operations Manager.

28 The pupils surveyed consisted of mediators, disputants as well as pupils of the school who were neither mediators nor disputants. Three of the four pilot schools took part in the survey. The survey results for Bedok North Secondary School are attached as Annex B to this chapter, at page 234.

29 For more information on the different grades of probation, see endnote 5 at page 146.

30 The Court will usually call for a Probation Report on the offender before making any orders in respect of him, in order to help it assess what would be the most suitable orders to make for his rehabilitation. The probation report will be prepared by a Probation Officer from the Probation Services Branch. The Probation Officer may give the offender the "curfew compliance test" by asking him to stay at home at certain times, for example, from 8 p.m. to 6 a.m. the following morning. The offender's compliance with the curfew imposed will be set out in the Probation Report.

31 Report of the Inter-Ministry Committee on Dysfunctional Families, Juvenile Delinquency and Drug Abuse, October 1995.

32 Copies of the said studies may be obtained by submitting a written request for the same to the Ministry of Community Development and Sports.

33 See Section 76 of the Children and Young Persons Act (Cap. 38).

34 BEST classes give students a basic grounding in English and Mathematics. WISE classes are more advanced classes in English and Mathematics.

35 Correctional Services of Canada, 1995; Freeman-Longo & Knopp, 1992; Marshall & Barbaree, 1990.

36 Stermac & Sheridan, 1993.

37 The DSM-IV is a publication of the American Pyschiatric Association. It is a reference book which lists down all the possible mental disorders and psychological conditions that can be suffered by an individual, classifies them, and provides details of each disorder and condition.

38 Ellis & Luckasson, 1985.

39 Denkowski, Denkowski & Mabli, 1983.

40 Endicott, 1991.

41 Forman, 1993.

42 Peterson, Compas, Brooks-Gunn, Stemmler, Ey, & Grant, 1993.

ANNEX A
LIST OF MALAY/MUSLIM ORGANISATIONS PROVIDING SERVICES

No.	Names of Organisations	Add 1	Add 2	Postal Code	Tel	Fax	Email
Statutory Board							
1	MUIS - Islamic Religious Council of Singapore - Family Development	Islamic Centre, 273 Braddell Road	–	579702	6256 8188	6253 7572	info@muis.gov.sg
Self-Help Group							
1	Yayasan Mendaki - Council for Development of Singapore Muslim Community	51 Kee Sun Avenue	–	457056	6245 5710	6245 5751	mendaki@mendaki.org.sg
Social Service Agencies							
1	AMP - Association of Muslim Professionals	1 Pasir Ris Drive 4	#05-11	519457	6416 3966	6583 8028	corporate@amp.org.sg
2	Darul Arqam - The Muslim Converts' Association of Singapore	32 Onan Road, The Galaxy	–	424484	6440 6924	6440 6724	info@darul-arqam.org.sg
3	JAMIYAH - Muslim Missionary Society Singapore	31 Lorong 12 Geylang	–	399006	6743 1211	6745 0610	info@jamiyah.org.sg
4	LBKM - Prophet Muhammad's Birthday Memorial Scholarship Fund Board	9 Stadium Link, Blk I , PA HQ	Kallang Road	397750	6447 4770	6447 4469	admin@biasiswa.org.sg
5	Muhammadiyah Association	14 Jalan Selamat	–	418534	6242 7388	6449 2781	secretariat@muhammadiyah.org.sg
6	4PM - Malay Youth Literary Association	Blk 606 Bedok Reservoir Road	#01-736	470606	6242 6288	6242 0610	4pm@qala.com.sg
7	PPIS - Young Women Muslim Association	Blk 1 Eunos Crescent	#01-2509	400001	6744 0258	6748 1417	enquiry@ppis_ywma.com.sg
8	PERTAPIS - Islamic Theological Association of Singapore	1 Lorong 23 Geylang Road	–	388352	6745 3969	6747 0845	admin@pertapis.org.sg
9	PERDAUS - Adult Religious Students' Association	Blk 364 Bukit Batok St 31	#01-259	650364	6566 5795	6566 4852	saff@perdaus.org.sg
10	SANA - Muslim Counselling Service	2 Orchard Boulevard	–	248643	6732 1122	6732 4564	mcs@sana.org.sg
11	Singapore Tenkasi Muslim Welfare Society	Blk 334 Kreta Ayer Road	#02-02	080334	6327 1296	6743 7087	–

ANNEX A (Cont'd)

No.	Names of Organisations	Add 1	Add 2	Postal Code	Tel	Fax	Email
12	SKML - Singapore Kadayanallur Muslim League	Blk 125 Bukit Merah Lane 1	#04-156	150125	6775 6296	6775 9678	–
13	Taman Bacaan - Singapore Malay Youth Organisation	Blk 672 Jalan Damai	#01-25	410672	6741 7977	6749 0300	taman_bacaan@pacific.net.sg
14	Darul Ihsan Lilbanin - Boys' Orphanage	5 Mattar Road	–	387713	6747 7556	6744 1770	–
15	Darul Ihsan Lilbanat - Girls' Orphanage	23 Wan Tho Avenue	–	347552	6285 2973	6283 4712	–
16	Jamiyah Children's Home - Darul Ma'wa	No. 1 Chin Cheng Avenue	–	429404	6344 9533	6344 3202	info@jamiyah.org.sg
17	Muhammadiyah Welfare Home	716/718 Mounbatten Road	–	437736	6344 7551	6348 2661	mwhome@singnet.com.sg
18	Pertapis Centre for Women and Girls	91 Kovan Road	–	540000	6745 3969	6747 0845	–
19	Pertapis Children's Home	993B Kovan Road	–	545676	6383 0914	6383 0913	–
20	Majlis Pusat - Central Council of Malay Cultural Organisations	9 Stadium Link, Blk K, PA HQ	Kallang Road	397750	6348 0541	6440 2162	–
21	FIM - Federation of Indian Muslims	531A Upper Cross Street	#04-95	051531	6533 7115	6392 3981	–
22	UIMA - United Indian Muslim Association	228B South Bridge Road		058777	6224 0405	–	–
Family Service Centres							
1	YWMA - Mendaki Family Service Centre	Blk 520 Jurong West Street 52	#01-195	640520	6561 3462	6560 5852	ywmamendakifsc@pacific.net.sg
2	4PM - Mendaki Family Service Centre	Blk 534 Bedok North Street 3	#01-814	460534	6449 1440	6242 2040	4pmfsc@mendaki.org.sg
3	Muhammadiyah - Mendaki Family Service Centre	Blk 139 Petir Road	#01-448	670139	6767 1740	6767 2771	mmfsc@singnet.com.sg
4	Taman Bacaan-North East CDC Family Service Centre	Blk 672 Jalan Damai	#01-25	470672	6741 7977	6748 0300	taman_bacaan@pacific.net.sg
5	As-Salaam YWMA Family Support Centre	Blk 322 Ubi Ave 1	#01-591	400322	6745 5862	67432749	nc00441f@starhub.net.sg

ANNEX A (Cont'd)

No.	Names of Organisations	Add 1	Add 2	Postal Code	Tel	Fax	Email
MUIS - Mosque Family Development Centres							
1	Al-Ansar	155 Bedok North Ave 1	–	469751	6449 2420	6445 4702	alansar@mosque.org.sg
2	Al-Khair	1 Teck Whye Crescent	–	688847	6760 1139	6763 6023	alkhair@mosque.org.sg
3	Almukminin	271 Jurong East St 21	–	609603	6567 7777	6567 3441	mukminin@mosque.org.sg
4	Al-Muttaqin	5140 Ang Mo Kio Ave 6	–	569844	6454 7472	6451 0781	muttaqin@mosque.org.sg
5	An-Nur	6 Admiralty Road	–	739983	6363 1383	6365 4449	annur@mosque.org.sg
6	Darul-Ghufran	503 Tampines Ave 5	–	529651	6786 5545	6786 5485	darulghufran@mosque.org.sg
7	Mujahidin	590 Stirling Road	–	148952	6473 7400	6473 6241	mujahidin@mosque.org.sg

ANNEX B:
SURVEY ON THE IMPACT OF THE PEER MEDIATION PROGRAMME ON PUPILS (NOVEMBER 1998) CONDUCTED BY THE MINISTRY OF EDUCATION (PSYCHOLOGICAL AND GUIDANCE SERVICES)*

Results for Bedok North Secondary School

A. Target group : Mediators
Number of respondents : 18

No.	Statement Being a mediator has helped me to:	No.	%
1.	be more confident in resolving future problems	18	100.0
2.	improve my listening skills	17	94.4
3.	improve the way I talk to other people	13	72.2
4.	get along with others better	17	94.4
5.	be aware that conflicts with others are very often caused by differing points of view	17	94.4
6.	be aware that other people's point of view may be just as valid	18	100.0
7.	be more confident	18	100.0
8.	feel a greater sense of belonging to the school	15	83.3

	Statement		
9.	Having the peer mediation programme shows that the school believes pupils can resolve their own conflicts.	18	100.0
10.	The peer mediation programme teaches us that conflicts can be resolved peacefully.	18	100.0
11.	I would recommend mediation to my schoolmates if they should have conflicts with each other.	17	94.4
12.	I'm willing to refer myself for mediation should I have conflict with a schoolmate.	14	77.8
13.	The peer mediation programme is a good programme for pupils.	17	94.4
14.	I feel proud that my school has the peer mediation programme.	18	100.0

ANNEX B (Cont'd)

B. Target group : Disputants
Number of respondents : 37

No.	Statement My experience with the mediation process has helped me to:	No.	%
1.	have a better idea how to resolve future conflicts on my own	27	73.0
2.	be more aware of the importance of listening to other people	34	91.9
3.	improve the way I talk to other people	31	83.8
4.	get along with others better	30	81.1
5.	be aware that conflicts are very often caused by differing points of view	26	70.3
6.	be aware that other people's point of view may be just as valid	26	70.3
7.	be more confident	28	75.7
8.	feel a greater sense of belonging to the school	22	59.5

	Statement		
9.	The peer mediators listened to both sides of the problem.	33	89.2
10.	The peer mediators were skilled in mediation.	19	51.4
11.	Having the peer mediation programme shows that the school believes pupils can resolve their own conflicts.	30	81.1
12.	The peer mediation programme teaches us that conflicts can be resolved peacefully.	31	83.8
13.	I would recommend mediation to my schoolmates if they should have conflicts with each other.	25	67.6
14.	I'm willing to refer myself for mediation again should I have a conflict with a schoolmate.	21	56.8
15.	I would like to learn the skills of mediation.	17	45.9
16.	The peer mediation programme is a good programme for pupils.	32	86.5
17.	I feel proud that my school has the peer mediation programme.	31	83.8

ANNEX B (Cont'd)

C. Target group : Pupils
Number of respondents : 168

No.	Statement	No.	%
1.	I am aware that the school has peer mediators who can help me resolve conflicts with my schoolmates.	153	91.1
2.	I have some idea of the process of mediation.	94	56.0
3.	There is enough publicity about the role of peer mediators.	98	58.3
4.	I have high regard for the peer mediators in my school.	86	51.2
5.	Having the peer mediation programme shows that the school believes pupils can resolve their own conflicts.	129	76.8
6.	The peer mediation programme teaches us that conflicts can be resolved peacefully.	141	83.9
7.	I would recommend mediation to my schoolmates if they should have conflicts with each other.	127	75.6
8.	I am willing to refer myself for mediation should I have a conflict with a schoolmate.	101	60.1
9.	I would like to learn the skills of mediation.	79	47.0
10.	I would like to be a peer mediator.	49	29.2
11.	The peer mediation programme has increased my sense of belonging to the school.	95	56.5
12.	The peer mediation programme is a good programme for pupils.	138	82.1
13.	I feel proud that my school has the peer mediation programme.	141	83.9

*** Previously named the Pastoral Care and Career Guidance branch.**

CHAPTER 6

Stories from the Community

6.1 Grown-ups Speaking

The grown-ups speaking in this section are all dedicated to helping and educating children and their families.

We hear from a teacher who buys shoes for his juvenile delinquent student who has no money of his own to buy them. We hear from Probation Officers and Aftercare Officers — who watch over their charges with vigilance, and counsel them with understanding. We hear from the Singapore Children's Society counsellors who try to prevent disobedient and unruly children from slipping into a path of destruction. Finally, we hear the testimonies of the Child Protection Officers whose task is to protect children from abuse, and to teach their parents how to treat these children with the patience and the gentleness that all children deserve.

The stories[1] of these teachers, counsellors and social workers illustrate their extraordinary sensitivity to personalities and relationships, enabling them to build those invisible bonds of respect and affection which serve to gladden and strengthen the hearts and minds of the children they care for. Their management of delicate family dynamics, their patience, and their faith, have all combined in each of these cases to change the life of a child for the better.

6.1.1 Making a Difference — A Teacher's Perspective

MR TEO HEOK KHIANG

Discipline Master, Damai Secondary School

I believe that at-risk adolescents will respond positively if they perceive that the teacher is genuine, caring and fair. Getting to the root of the adolescent's problems and understanding his or her struggles will help to build a trusting relationship with that adolescent, based on mutual respect. Misbehaviour is often a symptom of larger issues that may have their genesis in dysfunctional family relationships. Corporal punishment should be judiciously employed for it may treat the symptoms temporarily — it will not solve the root problems. Before meting out punishment, the reasons must be explained clearly to the adolescent to avoid misunderstanding and resentment. It is too easy to label the adolescent as a "problem kid", instead of a kid with problems who needs help. A basic tenet to bear in mind for all educators is that the child is in a process of growth. After all, education is about changing lives for the better and making a difference in the lives of the young. In the following story, I share my personal encounter with *MF*, a Normal stream student.

MF came from a disturbed family background. His parents were divorced and he shuttled between their homes, which created much instability in his turbulent adolescent years. Without a supportive home structure and supervision, and the security of family bonding, he was left adrift and floundering. Added to his family woes was his high level of anxiety concerning his father who had committed drug-related offences and had been arrested for alleged drug-trafficking.

Bereft of clear directions and goals in life, and burdened by anxiety and a sense of social isolation, *MF* could not adjust to the discipline and order of the classroom. He rebelled by being disruptive and rude to the teachers. He also engaged in anti-social activities like shoplifting and it was not long before the law caught up with him. The Juvenile Court sentenced him to serve a term in the Boys' Hostel.

The school intervened by introducing some structure to his school life. He had to report to me every day to get his attendance notebook signed. *MF* preferred to volunteer for school activities held during after-school hours to spending time at the Boys' Hostel. He approached me for help to liaise with the Hostel for permission to perform voluntary services after school hours. When I helped *MF* with this request, I sensed his resistance breaking down and a gradual growth in his respect and trust for me. His behaviour changed. From a belligerent and aggressive student, he became polite and tried to curb his impulses and observe classroom protocol. As he became more involved in voluntary services at school, I observed that his behaviour was more subdued and restrained.

The turning point in *MF*'s relationship with me ironically centred round a violation of a school rule. He wore the wrong type of shoes to school and did nothing about it despite promises to do otherwise. After some counselling, he revealed that he did not have the financial means to purchase a new pair. I gave him $20 and allowed him time off to make the purchase before returning to the Hostel. The neglected adolescent was touched by my concern. He saw in me not only a firm disciplinarian but also a caring adult with a heart. The kind gesture was reciprocated with a visit from his mother who expressed her deep appreciation for the care and concern I showed for her son.

As his trust in me grew, *MF* began confiding his personal struggles to me. He disclosed to me that the haunting spectre of a possible conviction and death penalty for his father, who was alleged to be involved in drug-trafficking, had caused him many sleepless nights. I counselled him and helped him to deal with the issue.

I was his Technical Studies teacher. Recognising the major obstacles he faced in adjusting to school life, I tried to be patient and understanding, but firm. I always gave him the impression that I expected the best from him. His workshop instructors and I gave *MF* extra attention and help in working on an artefact for the "N" level exam. We tried to motivate him by making the project interesting and also sought permission from the Hostel for extra time at school for him to complete the project. *MF* eventually secured a pass grade in Technical Studies and completed the "N" level course. *MF* has now enrolled for the Precision Engineering programme at ITE. Upon graduation from school, he proudly assured me that he was trying to keep out of mischief by not gallivanting at night. I take pride and cherish this special experience of making a difference in the life of this young man. Hopefully, this story will inspire my fellow teachers to continue to find meaning and hope in their vocation.

6.1.2 Rehabilitation through Probation — The Work of a Probation Officer

BERNADETTE ALEXANDER
Assistant Director (Operations/Youth),
Ministry of Community Development and Sports

Susan's mother, Mdm Ong was a single parent. Susan had never known her father. Mdm Ong had a serious psychiatric condition and was frequently warded for treatment. With her ill health, she was never really able to provide adequate care for Susan since her birth. Mdm Ong was also considered the "black sheep" of the family and received little support from her relatives. Susan's childhood was one where she passed through a succession of transient caregivers.

At the age of 12, even as she was attending school, Susan was already doing part-time jobs as a kitchen helper to support herself and her mother. She was only 13 when she witnessed her mother jump from the family's flat. After her mother's suicide, Susan was placed in the care of her maternal relatives, with her eldest uncle as her legal guardian. But she could not get along with them. She did not feel close to any of them and could not accept the strict discipline that they imposed on her. Just three months after her mother's death, Susan's relatives placed her at the Marymount Teenage Centre as they could not manage her. Being placed in a hostel instead of being taken in by a relative so soon after her mother's sudden death was perceived as complete rejection to Susan.

Staying at the hostel meant other difficulties. Susan could not adjust to the daily structured routine and often broke the rules, such as stealing food and returning late to hostel. Her behavioural problems in school also escalated. She often played truant or skipped school, engaged in late night activities and experimented with smoking and drugs. The hostel, school, Child Guidance Clinic, and Susan's uncle, often met to discuss how to manage her, but Susan just could not sustain good behaviour inside or outside the hostel or school. Nevertheless, the agencies involved believed that there was still hope in working with Susan and that through time, her issues could be resolved.

When Susan was 15 years old, she was caught and handed over to the police for shoplifting. She was charged in the Juvenile Court. Susan admitted to the charge and expressed remorse. The Court called for a Probation Report.

At school, Susan was an average Express stream student who was scheduled to sit for the GCE "O" level examinations at the end of the year. The Probation Officer, Miss Lim, considered Susan's expressed and apparent remorse as well as the support from the hostel and the school. Susan was assessed to be suitable for probation and amenable to rehabilitation. She was placed on 24 months' probation by the Juvenile Court, with the condition that she continued to voluntarily reside in the hostel. Miss Lim developed a plan of action for Susan. Firstly, Susan had to develop the discipline and coping skills to meet the school's and hostel's requirements. Secondly, Susan needed to deal with her mother's demise. Hence the need to provide grief counselling for Susan. Thirdly, Miss Lim intended to guide Susan in setting achievable short- and long-term goals. This would boost Susan's self-esteem and confidence. Finally, Miss Lim hoped to create opportunities for the relatives to witness Susan's growth and efforts and start to trust and believe in her again. This would be the first step towards re-integrating Susan with her family.

Miss Lim encouraged Susan in her studies and also explored her educational and career options. Miss Lim's work with Susan focused on building her independence and self-reliance. The process of gaining the trust and confidence of her relatives was very trying especially when Susan's uncle and older relatives were sceptical of her potential for positive change. Miss Lim was concerned that her relatives were quite distant and rarely gave her positive encouragement.

Fortunately, the hostel was able to provide Susan with positive socialisation. An older cousin served as a positive role model for Susan. Since Susan was not able to return home during her home-leave, the female maternal cousin took her out for meals or movies. She encouraged Susan to take her studies seriously; advised her not to be discouraged by the relatives' rejection of her but rather to work hard to prove herself to them. She advised Susan to work hard to obtain what she wanted; that things to be reaped have to be earned.

Susan wanted to get a computer when she finally returned to live with her family. When the cousin was sure that Susan was taking her life seriously and sincerely trying to make positive changes in her life, the cousin helped Susan with half of the cost of the computer and Susan paid the rest from her scholarship allowance. Positive reinforcement for good behaviour worked well for Susan. Whenever she displayed manipulative behaviour, Miss Lim or the guardians would directly address the issue and confront the manipulative behaviour.

Susan's progress on supervision was not always smooth. Working as a sales assistant while waiting for her GCE "O" level results, she succumbed to temptation and took money from the cash register to pay for her meals. This occurred after her employer had cut her working hours. Correspondingly her salary had also been reduced. Susan felt justified in taking the money.

Miss Lim noticed that Susan's underlying concerns and insecurity were of very basic needs. She hoarded money or food for "rainy days" because she had had so many of these days in her life. Since Susan had also shown positive changes in many aspects of her life since she was first put on probation, Miss Lim recommended that Susan's probation be extended for a period of six months and made a note to tackle her insecurity issues.

Susan passed her GCE "O" level examinations with an aggregate of 16 for six subjects and her conduct in school was rated excellent. With the good results, she considered several career options such as food nutritionist, social worker and nursing. She decided on a career in nursing and obtained a scholarship from a medical facility for a Diploma in Nursing at a polytechnic. The scholarship gave her a monthly allowance of $850 for the three-year course.

With the scholarship, Susan gained some financial security and independence. She managed her monthly allowance to pay for school fees, miscellaneous expenses and her room and board at the hostel. She saw that she had much to gain if she continued to work hard and make the right decisions, and much to lose if she decided to take illegal "short-cuts". Another offence would cost her dearly. She could lose her scholarship, her nursing career and her independence.

In the polytechnic, Susan had opportunities to involve herself in community service projects. She also took on the role of mentor for the new students. She joined a youth group and a theatre group in the polytechnic. All these activities gave her the opportunity to demonstrate her leadership qualities.

However, Susan was making little progress in getting her relatives to accept her. Although her cousins were supportive, the older relatives still saw her as the troublesome girl that she once used to be. They refused to take her home during her home leave. Susan's cousin was her strongest advocate. She tried to coax the older maternal relatives to accept Susan, but found it very frustrating.

It took more than a year for Susan to demonstrate her maturity and independence to her relatives, before her uncle softened towards her. He was quietly impressed that she received her scholarship. He could see, and was persuaded by Susan's cousin, that Susan had shown that she knew what she wanted in life. It was only then that the other relatives accepted her.

With the combined effort of all involved in her rehabilitation, Susan completed her probation successfully in 1999, and received her Nursing Diploma two years later. Today, Susan is a cheerful and positive young lady and a registered nurse in an established hospital. She takes pride in her work and presents herself with confidence. There is no more bitterness in her and she now sees her relatives as her family. They are proud of her accomplishments. As Susan reflects on her experiences during probation, she values the many chances that she was given and the people who continued to have faith in her in spite of all her failings. Susan continues her journey through life with confidence and strength.

6.1.3 Rehabilitation through Reformative Training — The Work of an Aftercare Officer

DAHLIA ARIS and GOH SOK HOON

Aftercare Supervision Officers,

Prisons Department

Life before Reformative Training

Ashwin is 22 years old and is currently serving his National Service at the Singapore Civil Defence Force (SCDF) Headquarters. Looking back upon his past one day when talking to his counsellor, he lamented that he had hurt his family.

He lost interest in his studies half way through Secondary 4. He played truant, disrupted lessons, smoked and took part in fights when he was in school. He was rude and openly defiant towards his teachers during lessons. He also threatened his fellow schoolmates. Ashwin received public caning for his misbehaviour. His parents also received numerous complaints from the school about his poor conduct and advised him to change but it was to no avail. He refused to listen to them. He preferred to keep company with his friends. He would go to his mother only when he ran out of money. He was not close to his brothers (he is the youngest in a family of five sons) and he did not tell them about his troubles. He eventually dropped out of school, which deeply disappointed his parents.

Ashwin joined the secret society Sio Kun Tong for protection and fun when he was 15 years old. He enjoyed the company of his gang friends and gang activities such as taking part in settlement talks and making trouble with rival gangs. He also abused alcohol and experimented with cannabis with his gang friends. He left the gang when he was 18 years old as he got tired of the lifestyle as a gang member.

Reformative Training

Ashwin was sentenced to undergo Reformative Training in 1997 for the theft of a motorcycle when he was 18 years old. He claimed that he committed the offence as he wanted to go on a joy ride with his friend, who was also his accomplice. He had committed similar offences on other occasions without being caught and he thought that he could continue to get away with it. He was astonished that he was apprehended for the offence and sentenced to a term in the Reformative Training Centre (RTC). It was the most shocking and painful incident in his life. His parents were devastated too.

Ashwin underwent 21 months of reformative training followed by 12 months of Aftercare Supervision with electronic monitoring. During his incarceration at RTC, his conduct was good and he did not commit any prison offences. It was noted that he was a friendly and obedient lad in RTC. While in RTC, he came to realise the importance of education and he managed to achieve a full "N" level certificate.

Progress while on Supervision

During the period of aftercare supervision, Ashwin was found to be a responsible supervisee who took his supervision seriously. He was assigned to work as a production worker earning $750 salary per month at a fish tank manufacturing company and stayed on the same job throughout his supervision period. The employer reported that they were happy with his work performance. He maintained an excellent violation-free curfew record and he reported punctually and regularly to his Aftercare Officer (ACO).

During the early reintegration phase, Ashwin was reserved and had difficulty opening up to the ACO. Through intensive rapport building coupled with patience and persistence, the ACO managed to gain Ashwin's trust. He became more and more forthcoming during reporting sessions. He shared his feelings, experiences and aspirations freely with his ACO. Ashwin was also receptive to the ACO's counsel. He formulated future plans and concretised his plans with the ACO's guidance.

Ashwin's parents co-operated with the ACO by giving the ACO regular feedback on his behaviour at home. They were pleased that Ashwin contributed $300 to the family's household income every month. They also observed positive changes in him. His parents noted that Ashwin showed more respect and concern towards them. They were glad that he was amenable to their advice. They were particularly pleased that Ashwin made it a point to steer clear from his old peers and that he would introduce his new friends to them. His parents hoped that he would continue to maintain his good progress even after his supervision.

A Year after Supervision

One year after the supervision, Ashwin's mother feels that Ashwin is a changed person. She attributes his changes to several factors that happened during and after the supervision period.

Ashwin's mother is of the opinion that the Electronic Monitoring Scheme[2] helped Ashwin to acquire effective time management skills. During supervision he would call his mother and inform her of his whereabouts, and he continued to do so even after the supervision period was over. This changed behaviour has restored trust between Ashwin and his parents, and has brought great comfort to them.

Even after supervision, Ashwin continued working for the same employer till he was enlisted in the Singapore Civil Defence Force. Currently, he is holding the vocation of a clerk and seems well adjusted in his new working environment.

Ashwin's mother observed that Ashwin had good rapport with his ACO. She added that the ACO had frequent contact with the family to discuss Ashwin's progress with her. The synergy between the two parties helped Ashwin to realise that there are people who are concerned about him. As she recalls, Ashwin often spoke to her about the issues explored with the ACO during counselling sessions. She felt that the counselling sessions forced Ashwin to think about, and reframe his worldview.

Eventually, Ashwin unlearned some of his old negative behaviours and began adopting new positive behaviours, especially with family interaction at home. The relationship between son and mother became stronger as they often made time to talk about what was happening in their lives. She feels that Ashwin has made an effort to initiate and improve communication with the family, thus lessening possible misunderstandings with the family.

In retrospect, Ashwin's mother feels that apart from her son's own desire and willpower to improve himself, he would not have achieved such results had it not been for the collaborative efforts of the family, the ACO, his employer, positive peer support and being on the EMS. Despite having trouble with Ashwin earlier, his mother was satisfied with the outcome. She felt that the experience also improved her parenting skills.

Ashwin's Perspective

Ashwin confessed that the supervision period was one of the toughest times in his life. The initial phase of supervision was tough. He remembered the days when he had to go for counselling sessions. He was facing peer pressure, and felt the need to restructure his life. He was also faced with the challenge of strengthening family bonds, but felt overwhelmed by everything. He often wondered if he had the ability to complete supervision. He admits that his mother was his main support. She was there when he needed someone to talk to and helped him to achieve his goals.

Ashwin related that he often felt challenged by his ACO as they progressed through the sessions. However, after a year of supervision, he gained a better understanding of his family interaction patterns, which helped him to understand that his behaviour had repercussions not only for himself but for his family as well. As a result, he is less impulsive now.

As time went by, Ashwin was able to identify his strengths and weaknesses. Currently, he is happy with his life and glad that he is no longer the person he was before. Presently, he is going out with a long-time girlfriend and is taking up motorcycle-riding lessons.

Reflections

Ashwin's case is a success story because he had managed to lead a crime-free lifestyle after his release from RTC. Despite the disappointment and hurt inflicted by Ashwin on his family, they did not lose hope. They rose to the occasion and were the pillars for Ashwin in his rehabilitation. Credit must also be given to Ashwin, who was fervent in his desire to change, and harnessed all his energy and willpower to overcome his weaknesses.

6.1.4 Bringing Parents and Their Children Together — The Work of a Guidance Programme Counsellor

CAROL BALHATCHET
Director, Youth Development Centre,
Singapore Children's Society[3]

The five case studies set out below feature children who were beyond parental control, but who had not been charged with any offence in the Juvenile Court. In the first two cases, the children have been placed on the Guidance Programme. These children never attended the Juvenile Court. In the next case, the child was referred by the Juvenile Court for pre-Complaint counselling.[4] In the last two cases, the Juvenile Court had placed the children on Statutory Supervision, under the Beyond Parental Control Statutory Supervision regime.[5] The supervision of the children in all five cases was done by counsellors from the Singapore Children's Society. The counsellors not only supervised the lifestyle and activities of the children, but helped to strengthen their bonds with their families.

Liza (aged 15, student)

Fifteen-year-old Liza, caught for shoplifting two rings, was shocked to be hauled to the police station. She never imagined that she would be arrested. It was after all a small amount, just $7.80. Surely the police had more important crimes to solve than a petty theft?

The police, of course, take all crimes seriously. However, they also saw that Liza had no previous record and that the offence concerned a rather small amount. So they recommended to the prosecutor that she be offered the chance to participate in the Guidance Programme run by the Singapore Children's Society. If she progressed well and completed the programme, the police would let her off with just a warning.

Initially, Liza was reluctant to work with Anne, her counsellor. She was unwilling to discuss issues brought up during their sessions and she would resort to lying to avoid confrontations. Anne knew that she needed to build up trust and rapport with Liza. She arranged for more frequent sessions to get Liza used to the idea that Anne was now in her life and could be trusted. With time, Liza became more open, friendly, and willing to co-operate in organised activities and counselling sessions.

Through their sessions together, Anne found out that Liza was trying to cope with her parents' separation. Without a home of their own and limited financial resources, Liza and her mother had to reside with her maternal aunt. Liza also shared that her mother often embarrassed her in public and in front of her friends. Her mother had been known to pick up the telephone extension to shout at her, while she was on the telephone with her friends. On other occasions, her mother would scold and nag at her loudly in public.

Through role-play and practice, Anne helped Liza to communicate with her mother and express her feelings about the embarrassment she felt as a result of her mother's behaviour towards her. Gradually, the relationship between mother and daughter improved.

Liza started making long-term plans and goals, such as completing her studies and wanting to go to University. She was even pro-active in enrolling herself in a tuition programme held by the Singapore Children's Society so as to improve her academic work.

Liza completed the Guidance Programme and a satisfactory report was sent to the police. She was let off with a warning. A lesson had been learnt, her relationship with her mother had improved, and she now had new goals to work towards.

Luke (aged 13, student)

Luke was 13 years old when he was referred to the Guidance Programme for the petty offence of "stealing Pokemon cards". Luke had an over-demanding mother, an absent father, and a sister who was doing very well in school. It was almost inevitable that his mother would compare him to his academically successful sister, and constantly nag him to study, even though Luke was already doing quite well in his schoolwork. The father had left the supervision and discipline of the children to the mother. He was absent most of the time and therefore had little to do with the children.

Since childhood, Luke had been suffering from asthma attacks. In the months preceding Luke's arrest, his asthma attacks had become more frequent and seemed to be triggered off by almost anything. Consequently, his mother tended to be over-protective of Luke. The over-protectiveness, unrelenting pressure to study, and constant checks on Luke had become unbearable for him.

In the sessions with the mother and son, Luke's mother explained that she wanted her son to do better because she did not want him to make the same mistakes she had made. She had not tried very hard and had failed to complete her education. It became clear that her own past had coloured her perception and understanding of her son.

When his mother's fears and regrets were brought to the surface, Luke was better able to understand her motives and her fears. At the same time, Luke's mother also came to realise that her behaviour towards her son would only make matters worse. She learnt to moderate her expectations of her son to more realistic levels, and realised that comparing Luke's achievements to his sister's was not fruitful.

The petty theft of the Pokemon cards was just the symptom. The issues, as are often the case, lay with the parent-child relationship. As Luke and his mother learnt to communicate with each other effectively, they were better able to negotiate their expectations of each other more realistically, and their relationship improved. Luke completed his term under the Guidance Programme successfully, and he was eventually let off with a warning.

Norena (aged 15, student)

Norena, at the age of 15, was behaving so uncontrollably that her mother felt that she was powerless to restrict any of her activities. Sometimes, Norena would take it upon herself to stay away from home for days. Once, she even stayed at a friend's home for about two months without informing her mother where she was. When Mrs Mohammad came to Court to seek assistance for her daughter's behaviour, she was referred to the Singapore Children's Society under the Pre-complaint regime because the counsellor felt that the issues highlighted by Mrs Mohammad about her daughter were ones that could be helped with some counselling.

The counsellor found out that Norena would only inform her father about her whereabouts and discuss her personal issues with him, but she would not communicate at all with her mother. A family counselling session was convened for both mother and daughter at the Singapore Children's Society Youth Development Centre. The first impression the counsellor had when she saw Noreena's mother, very conservatively dressed, as a staunch Muslim woman would be, with long sleeves and head-scarf, was that she was probably the parent who had higher expectations of Norena. Norena dressed completely opposite to her mother, in terms of style and colours. She was the image of total rebelliousness, not only in her attitude of "silence" (i.e. refusing to talk to her mother), but in her dressing. She wore a skimpy top, skin tight pants, earrings pierced from the top of her ear loops to the bottom, a nose ring, ginger coloured hair and had thinly arched, plucked and shaped eye-brows. The contrast and potential for conflict between mother and daughter was obvious.

However, during the session, the counsellor was surprised to find that Norena was the one with a higher expectation of her mother than her mother had of her. She wanted her mother to treat her like her father did. Norena's father was lax in his parenting because he left it to his wife. Therefore, he had nothing to lose when he agreed to everything that Norena wanted. Norena's expectations of her mother were so high that when her mother fell short of them (by wanting Norena to live up to some of her own expectations), she refused to communicate or acknowledge her mother's presence. This hurt Mrs Mohammad so much that she pursued her quest to get closer to Norena by constant nagging. Thus the vicious cycle started, and the relationship between mother and daughter went on a path to destruction.

During the family conferences which were held, the counsellor managed to get both mother and daughter to understand what their expectations of each other really were. Norena's high expectations of her mother were put to a "reality check" and Mrs Mohammad was made to understand that her present behaviour of nagging would not resolve her need to get closer to her daughter. At the end of five sessions, it was heartening to receive word that Mrs Mohammad was pleased that her daughter had changed. The turning point was when, in one session, Norena, not having touched or spoken to her mother for a very long time, took her mother's hand and kissed it in a "*salam*" (a Malay form of showing respect to an elder). Both mother and daughter acknowledged their mistakes and unrealistic views of each other.

The last time when the counsellor met Norena and Mrs Mohammad in Court, the counsellor was pleased to see that the duo were happily discussing things together, holding hands and were even able to hug each other. Norena confessed that work at her new job as a cashier in a supermarket was hard, but she was determined to see it through, at least for a while, until something better turned up. It seemed that the good communication she had with all the older women or "aunties" in her work place was partly due to her improved understanding of and relationship with her own mother. A sense of contentment could be seen reflected on Mrs Mohammad's face as she listened to her daughter talking to the counsellor about her job.

Ali (aged 15, student)

Ali's mother did not know what to do with him anymore. He had been such a good boy when he was younger, but these days he just would not listen. She could not understand why. He had started to stay out later, and had begun to return home only in the early hours of the morning. He was 15 years old, and no one could tell him what to do.

He hung out with the local gang, started to smoke and to skip school. In 1999, the principal called Ali's mother to the school. Ali had stolen a guitar from the school. That was the final straw for Ali's mother.

The principal suggested that she seek help from the authorities and she took up the suggestion. She went to the Juvenile Court

Magistrate to report Ali to be beyond her control[6] and asked for the Court to help her. The Juvenile Court agreed that Ali was beyond his parents' control, and ordered him to be supervised by the Singapore Children's Society.

As far as Ali was concerned, the social worker Andrea was just an extension of his parents and another figure of authority. He was 15 years old and among his friends his views were heard, his opinions were considered, and he had respect, but not when he was with his family.

Ali felt that the adults did not have much respect for his views and only wanted to tell him what to do. Andrea was sensitive to this and, quite quickly, built a strong rapport with him. The method she found useful in working with Ali was in providing him with opportunities to analyse each issue relating to his own actions and formulating alternative plans to approaches that did not work. The technique of conducting "reality checks" whilst supporting him when he made his own decisions provided Ali with the respect he so desperately craved.

Then, Ali's father was diagnosed with tuberculosis. Ali found himself in a new role with new responsibilities. As the eldest child with two younger siblings, he had to start taking on responsibilities and be a role model to his younger siblings. Even as he was just beginning to grapple with his new responsibilities, Ali read in the local newspapers that a close friend of his was killed in a gang fight.

The two events had a profound effect on Ali's perspective. He realised his past behaviour was immature, irresponsible, and even harmful. As a result of this, Ali broke off his ties with the gang, and started to play an active role in his family. Furthermore, the school commented about his good behaviour and celebrated with him when he successfully completed his "N" level exams.

Ali did not forget the people who helped him. He volunteered to share his experience as a testimony to the success of the supervision programme for children beyond parental control and on one occasion, he even sang a song he had composed specially for the social workers at the Singapore Children's Society.

From the irresponsible, rebellious teen he had been, Ali had become a brother his siblings could look up to and a son his parents could be proud of.

Stella (aged 17, cashier)

When Stella was just 15 years old, her parents realised that she was already beyond their control. She was skipping school, running away from home, staying with her boyfriend, and smoking. When her parents tried to guide her, she would abuse them with vulgarities. Not knowing how to deal with her, Stella's parents filed a complaint with the Juvenile Court citing Stella to be beyond parental control.

Karen, the social worker for Stella, decided to get Stella to reflect on her behaviour and how it affected people around her. Stella was also allowed to make her own decisions and to choose the strategies she would use to resolve some of her problems or issues.

At the same time, both of Stella's parents were provided with information on parenting styles, on how to communicate with their teenage daughter, how to understand her needs and her level of maturity, and how to manage their expectations of their child, as well as the child's own expectations of them. They realised that they needed to change their expectations if they want to see a change in their daughter's behaviour. So they began to work actively with Karen. Stella's parents started communicating more openly about their feelings with their daughter, and became more actively involved in their daughter's life.

Stella's mother started to spend more time with her daughter, such as going shopping or jogging with her. The effect of the changed relationship also extended to Stella's younger brother who had been behaving badly. He started to model Stella's changed behaviour. Both parents were glad to see the change in their son's behaviour too.

Stella did not go back to the school system. Instead she enrolled herself in night classes to catch up with her academic studies. At the same time, she got a day-job as a cashier in a fast-food restaurant. Both parents are very happy with her. Her mother said that Stella seems more sensible now, does not argue with them and is more respectful. Stella still goes out at night, but will call home if she stays out too late. Now, at 17 years, Stella has a boyfriend, whom both parents have met and approved. She has also quit smoking and seems to have a better control of her life.

6.1.5 Protecting Children from Abuse — The Work of a Child Protection Officer

NGO LEE YIAN
Senior Assistant Director (Child Protection)
Child Protection and Welfare Service,
Ministry of Community Development and Sports

Andrew, aged 3

Looking at Andrew, aged three years old, chuckling away at his mother's antics, you would never have guessed that he was once removed from his mother's care — for his own safety. He adores his mother, Mrs Lim, and looks forward to her return from work each day at the childcare centre, running to the door excitedly each time he hears the familiar footsteps of his mother and that cheery greeting, "Hello, Andrew darling — Mommy's here to pick you up!" It is hard to imagine that Mrs Lim, a mild-mannered, soft-spoken and attractive lady, is the reason why Andrew was admitted to a children's home previously.

Prior to Andrew's arrival, the relationship between his parents was already strained. Mr Lim was consistently out of a job, and seldom brought money home to help pay for the household expenses. He would resort to borrowing, and he did it so often that friends and relatives shunned him. Mrs Lim accused her husband of being indifferent, good-for-nothing, a lousy father and husband. In turn, Mr Lim accused his wife of being over-suspicious, petty, over-protective, and prone to violent and destructive behaviour.

When Andrew came along, the relationship worsened, as Mrs Lim grew increasingly frustrated with the burden of being a full-time mother, with no physical and emotional support from her husband or family members. In a bid to escape the frequent arguments between them, Mr Lim stayed out late often, only to give his wife the mistaken notion that he was having an affair. One day, whilst suffering from post-natal depression, Mrs Lim attempted suicide after a heated argument with her husband. She was found with her wrists slashed and lying in a pool of blood by her neighbour, who was alerted to baby Andrew's cries. Mrs Lim was referred to the Institute of Mental Health (IMH), and the Ministry of Community Development and Sports was roped in to assess the well-being of baby Andrew.

However, Mrs Lim was unco-operative and refused to attend counselling sessions at IMH. She was emotionally unstable, and started abusing Andrew whenever she was frustrated with his demands. Andrew became a withdrawn toddler, and his development was stunted for his age. He was described as unkempt by the neighbours, and was often found in tattered clothes. Once, the Child Protection Officer found, to her horror, Andrew being chained to the dining table by a bicycle lock. Mrs Lim was sitting nearby with a vacant look in her eyes. When the lock was finally removed, his skin was found to be badly grazed and bleeding. The family had also run into financial troubles as the little savings they had were quickly depleted and Mr Lim continued to be unemployed. In a bid to galvanise his parents into action, the Child Protection Officer decided to bring the case to the attention of the Juvenile Court. The Juvenile Court made a Care and Protection Order[7] in respect of Andrew. Andrew was then placed under a Fit Person's Order[8] for a year, and was admitted to a children's home.

The experience with the Juvenile Court and an admonishment from the Magistrate brought Andrew's parents to their senses. It was an embarrassment for them to know that the law had to intervene in their family matters. Mrs Lim started attending sessions at IMH. To be adequately armed in parenting skills, Andrew's parents started attending counselling sessions at a family service centre. They also learned how to relate to each other as husband and wife. Andrew progressed well under the care of the children's home, and his developmental growth rate caught up with those children in his age group. He learned to interact with other children in the children's home, and looked forward to his parents' visits. More than a year later, the Juvenile Court decided that Andrew was ready for discharge from the children's home and placed him on Statutory Supervision.[9] By then, Andrew's parents were both gainfully employed, and the marriage was on the mend.

Today, Mrs Lim continues to receive counselling and therapy at IMH. She is a lot happier and is now emotionally stable. She no longer uses violence to manage Andrew, and finds in her husband a supportive partner in child rearing. Indeed, the situation is a far cry from the days of frequent fights and financial anxiety. Mr and Mrs Lim shudder at the thought of losing Andrew again, and have pledged to be good parents in every way possible.

Diana, aged 10 years

Diana used to think that she was the happiest child in the world. Her parents both worked full-time and she stayed with her paternal grandparents since birth. Her grandparents doted on her and would buy her favourite food and toys for her. Her paternal aunts understood her well and she enjoyed sharing her feelings with them. She also enjoyed going to school as she had close friends and teachers whom she could communicate well with. She did well in her studies and was a good student. She had a lot of dreams and ambitions about her future.

Diana's world changed when she was about ten years old. Her mother, Mdm Lee, had some disputes with her paternal family members and insisted that Diana return home to stay with the family. Mdm Lee, being paranoid, suspected that the paternal family members schemed to separate Diana from the family. She refused to let Diana maintain contact with her paternal relatives and would get upset whenever her paternal grandparents tried to contact Diana. She started to monitor Diana's movements closely and would not allow Diana to go to school by herself. She would get Diana to perform household chores and help her younger siblings in their schoolwork. She also beat Diana up when she was not satisfied with the latter's performance. Whenever Diana's father tried to intervene, he would be shouted at by his wife. A mousy chap by nature, he could only tell Diana to bear with her mother's behaviour.

Diana had difficulties adjusting to the changes in her lifestyle and meeting her mother's expectations of her. She also missed her paternal grandparents badly and would try to contact them secretly.

This worried Mdm Lee and her checks on Diana became tighter. She would check with the teachers and classmates on Diana's behaviour in school. This embarrassed Diana badly and she developed a phobia about going to school. Her grades started falling, and she soon lagged behind in class. One day, after returning home from school late because of remedial classes, Diana was beaten up by her mother again. Mdm Lee refused to believe that Diana was in school, and suspected that she had gone to visit her grandparents. Infuriated at the denial, Mdm Lee beat the daylight out of Diana, and forbade her to contact her grandparents. Diana felt helpless in the face of her mother's treatment of her, but she could only cry her heart out in a corner.

Diana's plight was brought to MCDS' attention when the school reported on the injuries that a teacher found on Diana's body. A child protection officer tried working with Mdm Lee on her management of Diana. The child protection officer explained to Mdm Lee the need to temporarily separate Diana from her parents so as to allow them to work on the parent-child relationship before reintegrating the family. However, Mdm Lee refused to arrange for alternative care for Diana. She continued beating Diana whenever the household chores were not completed to her satisfaction. Diana's case was subsequently brought to the attention of the Juvenile Court, who ordered that Diana be placed under the care and protection of a Fit Person, namely, a MCDS' registered foster mother, for a period of one year. Although Mdm Lee was reluctant and had created a scene during the Court hearing, she realised the importance of working closely with the child protection officer and the psychologist on her relationship with Diana.

Diana progressed well under the care of the foster parents who provided her with support and care. The foster parents were made aware of Diana's background and helped Diana to regain her self-esteem and confidence. The foster mother also helped her to understand her mother better. Diana realised that her mother's insecurities stemmed from an unhappy childhood of abuse and violence. She forgave her mother for what she had done, and resolved to be a filial daughter to make up for her mother's past hurts.

With guidance and constant encouragement, Diana's grades in school started to improve. She learned to overcome her nightmarish past and to work on reconciliation with her family. During her stay at the foster home, Diana went for an outing and subsequently, home-leave, with her parents. At the same time, she and her parents received regular counselling from the Child Protection Officer and the psychologist to improve the parent-child relationship. Mdm Lee also attended counselling sessions on anger management and parenting skills.

At the Court review a year later, Diana was returned to the care of her parents. The Court was satisfied that Mdm Lee was determined to be a good mother and nurturer. Diana is no longer afraid of Mdm Lee who now treats her well. The reunion between mother and child was a tearful one. Diana missed her parents although her foster family was wonderful. Mdm Lee's relationship with her in-laws had also improved and she would bring Diana to visit them regularly.

Thus, Diana and her family were given a new lease of life.

6.2 Voices of the Children

In the following pages, you will hear the children[10] speak. We have the voices of children who have learned the ways of soothing anger, and bringing calm, turning quarrels into opportunities for friendship, and dissipating disputes with words. These are the Peer Mediators. They share with us their insights and experiences on Peer Mediation, and the satisfaction that comes from being a Peer Mediator.

We also have the voices of children who were once angry, but have now achieved a measure of calm, children who were defiant, but have been tamed by kindness, children who were unhappy, but who now write proudly of their achievements. These are children who have committed offences, and been sent to stay in Approved Homes and Approved Schools, and who, ultimately, have left these places and gone on to build new lives for themselves. In their essays, they give thanks to the community who embraced them and supported them. From what these children say, it is clear that it was alienation from their families, ignorance, a general lack of structure and purpose in their lives which made them commit crimes and engage in anti-social activities. It is equally clear that it was the people in their lives that brought them back onto the right path: their parents, their teachers, their aftercare officers, and their hostel wardens. The voices of these children carry a message to all of society: that restorative justice is not possible without love, and that the future of any child lies in the strength of his family and the support of his community.

6.2.1 Hard Lessons, Good Teachers

AHMAD

Aged 15, student[11]

I have always felt alienated from my parents and could not communicate with them. A major quarrel in April 2001 proved to be the last straw. I made the fateful decision to run away from home. My older sister's home was my first refuge, but I left after a week for fear of being tracked down by my parents. There seemed to be no option but to seek the support of my neighbourhood friends. Together, we made the void deck in an HDB estate our home. It was all too easy to stop attending school as I had the solace and support of peers who shared and understood my struggles. Two months went by with us indulging ourselves, talking, playing the guitar and smoking through the nights.

The lure of freedom soon lost its attraction. Living in the void deck was miserable as I had no financial means to acquire basic necessities. During this period, I heard that my form teacher, Mr Yee, was trying to find me. He and the Operations Manager,[12] Mr Lee, had made a home visit and enlisted my classmates to look for me. It touched me deeply to know that my form teacher cared for me and had not given up on me. In desperation, I turned to him and confided my family problems in him. I indicated that I wanted to go to a home. He referred me to the Discipline Mistress, Mrs Tan, who arranged for me to be placed at the Muhammadiyah Welfare Home. In the course of waiting to be placed, the school provided me with food and also sought the consent of my family for me to be placed in the Home.

The regimen of institutional living proved to be punishing and restrictive for me. Once again, I ran away and joined the community of homeless teens at the void deck of an HDB estate. Reality hit us when we ran out of money, and as a last resort, I colluded with the group to rob a coffeeshop. We stole cigarettes but were caught red-handed by the police. We were charged at the Juvenile Court and then remanded at the Singapore Boys' Home for two months. It was a humbling downfall and it led me to reflect on the direction of my life. I was determined to redeem myself by obtaining a good education and advancing myself in my future career. Supported by favourable references from my primary and secondary schools, my probation officer at the Home consented to help me return to school.

The Juvenile Court officer organised a Family Conference that involved my parents, older brother and the Discipline Mistress, to explore our family issues. It was then that I became aware that my parents did care for me after all. Guilt and regret replaced the anger and resentment I had felt towards my parents. We had a communication breakdown and many misunderstandings. But knowing that they cared meant so much to me.

The school was very supportive in giving me a second chance. Despite my lapse in conduct, the school did not label me, but recognised that I was an interested student who had the potential to perform well in the "N" level exam. The school also initiated counselling sessions for me to help me cope with my family issues and to resolve the conflicts I faced. I was eventually sentenced to one year in the Boys' Hostel and another year of close supervision.

Returning to school after an absence of a few months was difficult, as I struggled with guilt and shame. The school was sensitive to my needs, however, and helped to structure a support network for me. A teacher-pupil conference was arranged, during which my form teacher assured me of confidentiality. He was encouraging and affirmative, and offered advice on coping with family problems. The school counsellor, Mr Sim, also attended to me regularly. Initially, it was difficult to share such sensitive issues, but his fatherly acceptance, concern and empathy soon helped me to share my innermost thoughts. I learnt to take responsibility for my past actions instead of blaming others. He also helped me to grapple with my family issues. I continued to receive encouragement from the Discipline Mistress and the Operations Manager. The school has a strong culture of care and respect for its students, which filters down from the administration to the teachers. I feel that I am the lost son who has learnt some hard lessons about life and returned to my family and school, both of which have given me a chance to start on a clean slate. I am now committed to doing the best in my studies and mending my relationship with my parents.

6.2.2 Finding a Home in Gracehaven[13]

LINDA

Aged 20, assistant administrator in a pre-school

Three years ago, my life was in a total mess. My family did not accept me. I did not have pocket money so I had to study and work at the same time. It was not long before I started mixing with the wrong group of friends and became a juvenile delinquent.

Life as a kid was never fun for me. My parents divorced when I was merely two years old. My father remarried soon after and a stepmother came into my life. The communication between my father and me broke down and life became very miserable for me. My father was very cold towards me and was indifferent to what was happening in my life. He also refused to stay at home whenever I was home. In times when I needed pocket money, I would need to ask for it from my stepmother. As years passed, I felt even more unloved, despised, lost and lonely. I started running away from home just to get away from my family. Soon after, I was placed in Gracehaven.

Initially, I dreaded the place. I felt lost and afraid. I was also very lonely. I cried every day, and fell into a depression. My depressive behaviour was so bad, I was placed on medication.

However, I was lifted out of my unhappiness very quickly. The special touch of love and concern by the staff at Gracehaven worked wonders. In my moments of ups and downs, I would always have someone to share my joy or sadness. The staff became friends and maternal figures to me. Together with the social workers, they helped to pull me together. After knocking on the doors of many schools, they managed to enrol me into a school, giving me a chance to complete my studies. I did not do well in my studies eventually, but the staff at Gracehaven encouraged me to carry on striving and not give up in life.

Like many others in Gracehaven, I was given a second chance, an opportunity to change, to discover the real me and to find my goals in life. Gracehaven has played a huge role in moulding me into a better, stronger person. Why? Because the love they gave so freely motivated me to change. Although relations with my family were still shaky when I was ready to come home, I was encouraged to continue building the bond that I had lost with my parents. To my complete surprise, Gracehaven continued to support me. They went the extra mile for me even after I was discharged from the Home.

Later on, I found a job that interested me — as an administrator in a pre-school. It was the start of a career that I wanted for myself. The staff at Gracehaven continued to motivate me to further my studies. After half a year, I mustered all my courage and decided to move back with my family. And it worked! Now, one year after my discharge, I am living in harmony with my parents. I have a stable job and I am leading a happy life. Looking back, I do not blame the judge who sentenced me to Gracehaven. I am who I am today because of the wonderful people at Gracehaven. They showed me what true giving is by devoting themselves in their work.

Today, I have learnt to think positively, and set goals for my own future. I hope that I can be of use to society, giving back what I have received so generously, and reaching out to those in need.

6.2.3 Learning to Study at the Singapore Boys' Hostel[14]

WAI SENG

Aged 14[15], student

" You'll be sent to the Singapore Boys' Hostel for a period of one year... ," said the judge.

Anger, not sadness, was what I felt when I received the order. I could not believe that I was sent to the Hostel just for smoking!

Life in the Hostel was a lesson that will be hard to forget.

I felt thousands of eyes on me when I first stepped into the Hostel. Anger seeped away and fear gradually conquered me. I thought I was prepared for life in the Hostel as I had been "briefed" by friends who had been there. But I found that the actual experience of being there was so different. Everything in my life seemed to have been taken away from me from the moment I stepped into the Hostel. Freedom, family, friends, self-identity were replaced by rules, discipline, and more rules and discipline.

The first week in the Hostel was the worst of my life. The comfort and privacy of my former life were replaced by having to share a room with people I barely knew and with no air-conditioning. Life in the Hostel meant no privacy, bad food, and too many other people. I realised then that my mother's cooking was many times better. How could I have complained so much about her cooking! Sigh!

The first night in the Hostel was unbearable. The hot and stuffy room and the fear of being "sabotaged" by the rest kept me from dozing off for even a second. For the first time, I missed my home, my room, my bed, and my family.

My case worker was a soft-spoken and fair man. He made a great effort and was very patient in getting me to accept my stay in the Hostel. He helped me face the fact that the decision made by the Court was not based on only my smoking but also on my previous misbehaviours. He was like a father to me, giving me encouragement, care and concern. He listened readily to my problems and never let go of me when I was down. When I needed a scolding, he would not hold back my punishment either.

Drills and exercise were conducted daily, rain or shine. Though most of us hated it, slowly I came to see the beauty of it. I also learnt how to live with others in a group, not only with boys of my own ethnic group, but also with boys of different ethnic groups. I also learnt the importance of tolerance, responsibility, and consideration. I began to realise that I had a future waiting for me.

My family visited me weekly in the Hostel when I was not eligible for home leave yet. I was really touched and moved by their subtle expression of love and concern for me. Before admission to the Hostel, I could stay away from home for a few months, and my parents would seem oblivious to my absence. I always thought that my presence in the family did not make any difference in their life. I was especially taken back when my sister came along for the parents' visit. We were not on good terms with one another since young, and I always thought that she hated me as I had always bullied her in the past. Though she was her usual self during the visits, not speaking to me or addressing me, I felt that she actually had a lot to say to me. She wrote me a letter, and I recall this line in it which said: "...though I have not addressed you as my brother since young, deep in my heart, you are my good brother..." I still keep this letter with me.

Through the letter, it dawned on me that my family cared about me. My mother cried very hard on the day that I was sent to the Hostel, and even after that, she cried at times. My dad, though he did not attend the hearing, was also controlling himself so that he did not break down. I realised that my parents were the ones always supporting me and who would be there for me. I felt touched and at the same time, guilty. I felt that I had taken their love and concern for granted, and had abused the freedom they gave me.

I went back to school after a month in the Hostel. The NUS and NTU Volunteers[16] came down to the Hostel twice every week to give tuition to those who were studying. They helped me to see the importance of education and spurred me on to study hard. My tutors were very patient and persistent. In the past, studying to me meant using my intelligence or rather my common sense. I had never revised my work, nor even paid attention in class. The books were never touched and opened. I spent my days in school at the back of the classroom dozing off. Through the NUS and NTU volunteer tutors, I learnt how to study. It may sound ridiculous to some, but I started to realise that to study meant to open the book, and read through it page by page. On top of that, I would have to spend hours reading and understanding the idea and to seek help when I do not understand something.

I came in fourth in class that year, and I was really very impressed with myself. I had never thought I could make it to the top four in my class given the fact that I had always been the last in class. I did my "O" level revision in the Hostel. With the encouragement from my volunteer tutors and my case workers and staff, I passed my "O" levels, and made it to the Polytechnic. Getting to the Polytechnic is not something that most people would be proud of. But to me, it was a recognition of my self-worth and pride, and a way of showing appreciation and gratitude to the people who were, and still are, supporting me. My achievements were not mine alone.

My case worker and Probation Officer helped me to appeal for early discharge. The judge granted me an early discharge based on my performance and growth in the Hostel. I continued my life outside the Hostel. Even now, without the guidance of my tutors and case worker, I am still going on to fight for my life.

I have no regrets spending almost one year in the Hostel. If not for all these experiences, I would never experience the beauty of studying, and the beauty of my life. I would never learn how to appreciate people, and would still be taking things for granted. If not for the judge's foresight, I guess I would have wasted my youth in idleness and crime. Most important of all, I would never understand the love of my family. To me, it was a second chance given. Even up to today, though my sister has not addressed me as her brother,[17] it is no longer important to me anymore. I know that deep inside her, she respects me as her brother and it will be for life.

6.2.4 Life in the Singapore Boys' Home[18] — And Life After[19]

KHAIRUL

Aged 16, student

There was no furniture at all in the large room, except for a small box for each boy to keep his things. There was a straw mat for each of us to sleep on. The floor was cold and hard. I could not sleep that first night.

Instead, I thought about all the things I had lost, and I thought of all the chances I had. I stared at the ceiling and it was blurry from the tears in my eyes. I had not cried for a long time. Even when I was in remand, I did not feel afraid because I did not believe that it would be for a long time.

I remember asking the man in the Court what the judge had said. He told me "three years". I have to stay in this big empty room for three years. Three years is a long time.

Before all this happened, my life was simpler and happier. My friends were all very "happening" — they knew the best places to hang out late at night, like bowling alleys, arcades, midnight shows, and funeral wakes. The police do not check on you when you hang out at funerals, and you can talk all night with free drinks and snacks.

I knew my friends were gang members, but they were good to me and we had fun. At that time I felt that they were better for me than my own family. I quarrelled with my brothers a lot, and there was one time when I even threatened my father when he tried to control me. I did not care about them. My teachers also could not handle me. I would talk back at them, and skip classes when I felt like it.

I still have a very bad temper even today, but at that time I would lose my temper over the smallest things. Usually it was because I thought people like my parents or the school were against me and were trying to take away my freedom.

And then I really lost my freedom.

At the Home, I had to attend many courses. I remember one course very well. It was called "Stop-Think-Do", and it was about thinking about the results of my action. I realised at that time that I often act without thinking about what will happen after that. I realised that every time I lost my temper, I lost control and I stopped thinking, and the results were not good.

I also remember another speaker who even addressed us as "sir". It felt good to be respected, and I remembered how it felt to be respected by my friends. Then I realised how it was much better to be respected by people who knew what respect was and what was respectable.

I understood then that what I had wanted was not freedom to do what I wanted, but respect for what I did. The speaker really motivated me to change, and I started to take my WISE (Work Improvement through Secondary Education) classes seriously. I also attended religious classes, and those classes also helped me to understand that my actions can come back to affect me.

My decision to change helped me to get the chance to study in a real school again. I was almost too old to go back to school, but my Aftercare Officer (ACO) strongly encouraged me as she felt that I could do it. I was not too confident. When I thought of going back to my old school, I felt very nervous, and also very ashamed. So when the principal of my old school refused to take me back, although I was very hurt, I was also quite relieved that I would not have to face my former teachers and old schoolmates.

Although the principal would not take me back, he did agree to help me get into another school. He called another school and got the other principal to take me in. For that I was grateful.

The new school gave me a fresh start. My form teacher knew of my past but did not condemn me. She would spend time talking to me to find out more about me. She also encouraged me to advise other students who were going down the wrong path. At first, I had no friends at the new school, but she made me work with my classmates on projects so that my circle of friends would grow. As I got to know some of them better, I began to trust some of them enough to tell them of my past. I was very glad that they still accepted me, and that I did not lose their friendship.

My family became very important to me when I was in the Home. On the first parents' visit day, it rained very heavily. Many boys' parents did not turn up because of the rain. The boys had to go back to the dormitory. I remembered thinking that my parents probably would not come, but at the same time, I hoped and wished that they would.

I was very happy when I heard the staff calling me to go to the visitors' room.

My father cried that day as he advised me to change and not to fight. I did not know what to say. I had never seen my father cry before. When I think of him crying for me that day, I realise how much he cares for me. My mother was recovering from chicken pox, but she also made the long trip that day. She was still very weak, and I felt very bad that she had come all that way just to visit me. I realised how badly I had let them both down, and I wanted to make them proud of me again.

After a few months of going to school on Day Release, the Home decided that I could be Released on Licence.

I could go home.

The ACO would still supervise me and I had to report to her regularly. During the school holidays, the ACO and her colleagues would organise camps, trekking and other outdoor activities for us.

Another time, we were involved in a concert. It was a "Thank You" function for the employers of some of the boys from the Home who were not studying. I even wrote a song and sang it at the concert. The employers were people who gave a second chance to the working boys, just like the principals gave the schooling boys (like me) a second chance.

It felt good to express our thanks to people who were willing to give us a second chance.

I still have a bad temper. Some things cannot change. I remember one incident. It was after I had completed my aftercare supervision. A schoolmate said something about my girlfriend and I lost my temper. I told him to meet me after school. I was going to beat him up. The vice-principal found out about it and gave me a warning. I remember saying something about how he had no right to control me, and that only my ACO could tell me what to do.

So he called my ACO. She scolded me. She also reminded me of what was important to me. She made me think about what I would lose if I went back to my old ways. She calmed me down and I controlled my temper. When I think about that day, I am ashamed that I lost control, but I also realised how highly I regarded my ACO.

I had done very well in the last three years of school. I was the top student in the first two years, and was quite disappointed when I dropped to second place in the third year.

I realised that my thinking had changed in the last three years. Three years ago, I would be happy and surprised just to have passed. Now I was actually disappointed for being only second best!

I think today I expect more from myself, and I believe in myself. I am now waiting for my "O" level results, and hope to go onto "A" levels or a Polytechnic diploma. Because of the help I received from my ACO, case worker, the Home, my school, the teachers and the principal, I think I would like to help others who may be like me.

6.2.5 Life at the Toa Payoh Girls' Home[20] — and Life After[21]

CHARMAINE

Aged 20, make-up artist

My first sight of Toa Payoh Girls' Home through the wire-meshed windows of the police van was of the high, stark, unfriendly walls and barb wire fences that seemed to say, "Keep out! You don't want to know what's inside." Except that I was going inside. My heart beat faster as the gates rolled shut behind the van. The final "clang" of the gate meeting the frame seemed to signal the end of my freedom, and the fading echoes reflected my rapidly draining spirit.

I did not feel that it was real at all. It seemed like the events leading to my banishment to the Home happened too fast, like waking from a dream feeling scared but even as I tried to remember the reasons why I was afraid, the details and the memories of the dreams begin to fade. But unlike a dream, my fear remained and grew even stronger.

That first night, I was in a dormitory with more girls in it than I had family members. Yet, I never felt lonelier. I remembered thinking "this is hell." I half expected to see the Hell Guardians with their horse and bull heads dragging a lost spirit in chains. I was sad not because I regretted what I had done, but because I did not want to be there. It did not seem fair that I was placed in this "prison" when my friends could have their fun outside. It was not until later that I realised that I was not there to be punished, but was there because I needed to know how to live.

The first few days went by in a sort of blur. The days started early and were filled with exercising, marching, and cleaning. By dinner I was so tired I fell asleep immediately at bedtime.

Living in the Home meant living with others. The girls in my dormitory each had a different character. At first, I kept to myself. I felt that I did not belong there with the others. Perhaps if I showed them that I did not belong, I could leave. It did not happen, of course. And I needed to talk to someone, anyone. It took me awhile, but soon I was talking to some of the girls in the block. Sharing a dormitory required everyone to understand one another and to tolerate others. Yes, there were the quarrels, but the staff would step in and soon, we all learnt that raised voices and fists would not be tolerated.

There were three staff that had a great impact on our lives in the Home. The two housemothers had the most to do with us in terms of the day-to-day activities in the Home. The first time I tried to defy them I found myself suddenly without friends. I came to realise that they might be strict, but they were fair. If they found out that we had tried to play one against the other, they would find some ways to make our lives quite miserable. For a while, anyway. The girls who had been there for some time seemed afraid of them. It took me a while to realise that it was not fear, but respect. I realised that when I became less afraid of them myself, and started respecting them for their fairness, and their wisdom.

The other staff member that had a great impact on me was my case worker. Mdm Lee was a kind yet firm lady who had been working there for a long time. I could see it in the way she took no nonsense from any of us. She'd seen all the tricks before, and she knew how to catch every one of them. I had thought that I was smarter than she was. I was wrong. I had spent many afternoons cleaning the drains of the compound as punishment for my misdeeds.

Mdm Lee was the one who explained to me what was expected of me, and what I could expect. She explained how I would be given opportunities to study, or learn a trade or skill, but I had to earn the right to them. I had to show that I was willing to put in the time and effort to persevere and succeed in either. As I proved myself, I would be given more opportunities, including going back to school or even being released earlier. At the time, all these goals seemed far in the future and hardly attainable. But Mdm Lee did not seem to doubt that it was possible, so I borrowed some of her confidence until I had some of my own.

In time I realised that I started to look forward to our discussions. I still thought that she might just be doing her job, and that she cared for me only because she was paid to. But she remembered things that we talked about, little things that were not jotted down in a file somewhere or in her notebook. These were things that had nothing to do with being in the Home, or studying, or discipline, yet things that had meaning for me.

I began to believe that she cared for me as a person, and not just as another girl she had to handle or deal with. What made up my mind for me was the time when I was trying to remember a song, but I did not have the words. The song was in my head, but not knowing the words was driving me crazy. Two days later, she handed me a sheet of paper with the lyrics.

My parents visited me regularly and I started to look forward to their visits. The visits were a welcome break from the routine and dreariness of Home life. I was still very selfish then, and honestly, I looked forward more to the food and other goodies they brought and to the break in routine than to seeing them.

But I did see some of the other girls trying to pretend that it did not matter that their parents never bothered to visit them anymore. But I could tell that it did. At least one of my parents would always be there on visiting day. My father used to travel often in his work, but he started to arrange his travels around visiting day as much as possible. I understood that my parents could also stop caring, stop making the effort, but they never stopped. They had realised that they had to spend time with me. I realised how much effort they were making, and in time I came to appreciate it all.

When I was promoted to the higher grade, I was allowed to go for classes. I took WISE (Work Improvement through Secondary Education) classes in the Home, not for any noble reasons, but simply because I was allowed to. It was a privilege, and I had come to realise that too. But at the same time, the Home provided me with an environment to think about where I was going with my life. Everyone said that education would get me a better future. I did not quite believe it, but I had no reason not to believe either. And it was something to do. With no distractions, I found myself doing quite well for my studies. The teacher encouraged me to aim for the "N" level certificate. I started to believe that I could do it.

There were also other programmes such as personal grooming, cooking and Basic Life Skills to either give me a skill or to prepare me to be more independent and responsible. We learnt handicrafts as a matter of interest. There was also group work on anger management and one-to-one counselling with Mdm Lee.

Some of the best times I had were the sporting events. Sports were major events in the Home. Dormitories would compete in netball and volleyball tournaments. Because of my height, I was naturally selected to play the games. These activities taught us dorm-mates how to communicate, and build a closer and stronger bond amongst ourselves. We learnt to take care of one another. After all, we were already staying together.

When I was ready to return to school on the Day Release Scheme, my Aftercare Officer contacted my former school to arrange for an interview. With the report on my progress in the Home, my principal agreed to take me back. My teachers, who were all too familiar with my past, accepted me without much comment. In a way, I was touched by their willingness to let me put my past behind me and start afresh. I was neither treated differently from the others nor put down in front of my classmates. In fact, the staff made a conscious effort not to let others know that I was spending time in the Home.

Going back to school was not easy, though. I had almost forgotten about the stress and the frustrations. There were instances when I lost my cool, but my teachers were quick to remind me that it was my anger that sent me to the Home. They understood my frustrations, and were willing to make allowances for it, but I had to do my part and learn to cope. It was then that my aftercare officer reminded me of the anger management skills I had learnt. It was time to practise.

I spent a year at school and managed to pass my "N" levels. I was very glad I made it through, and though I was still in the Home, I felt that I had more freedom, more choices. I chose to train to be a make-up artist.

When I was released on licence from the Home, my aftercare officer took over my supervision from the Home. Mdm Koh had helped me with my re-enrolment in school, and now was preparing me for my "life". The first few days of freedom brought me mixed feelings. On the one hand, I was home, but after more than a year in the Home, I missed the friends, the shared responsibilities, and the closeness. After a while I learnt to enjoy my freedom again, but within limits. Mdm Koh provided a guide for my life. She helped me with my choices and with my relationship with my parents. I thought I had grown closer to my parents, while I was in the Home, but going back home and staying with them re-opened old issues, and re-awakened old petty arguments.

Mdm Koh helped with the adjustments. In some sense, I found that being on licence was a lot harder than being in the Home. But I guess that's what progress means. As I learn to handle easy things, I will get more difficult ones to handle in order to grow. Real life means having to deal with all the little irritating things so that you can enjoy the important things.

6.2.6 A New Beginning — The Care Centre in School

IRENE

Aged 16, student[22]

I had learnt to smoke by the time I was 12, under the influence of some of my peers in school. Caught in the act by my form teacher, I had to face my tearful mother who found it difficult to believe that her normally well-behaved child was involved in smoking at such a tender age. Overcome by regret for hurting her, I gave up the habit. However, in secondary school, I renewed ties again with the same anti-social peer group. I was taunted into joining them to smoke, fight and extort money. I succumbed to them as I dreaded being shunned and labelled a coward.

Things started to fall apart when we extorted money and beat up a victim in a shopping area, leaving her injured and terrified. We were soon arrested and subsequently sentenced to the Toa Payoh Girls' Home for two years. I regretted my actions as the consequences hit me hard. After one year, my aftercare officer informed me that I would be offered the opportunity to resume my education. I grabbed at this new lease of life which my principal, Mr Goh, offered to me.

The school had — and still has — a Pupil Activity Centre, known as the *Care Centre*. A programme is organised for pupils under probation, to ease the transition from juvenile home to school, and help them stay away from negative peer groups. The programme is run by a teacher-in-charge and a school counsellor. The school counsellor and teachers helped me to let go of the past and overcome my shame and fear of rejection by fellow students. They made me feel accepted and validated as a person despite my past mistakes. The programme offered a wide repertoire of activities, which were meaningful, interesting and fun. I learnt adaptive skills such as managing my emotions, goal-setting and study skills. Fun activities like ice-skating, games and camps, provided good outlets for my energy. As I became more integrated into the school environment, my self-confidence and self-esteem grew.

The teachers and counsellor believed in me and motivated me to excel in my studies. My hard work and commitment paid off when I emerged the top performer in the final exams of the Secondary 1 Normal Technical stream, which I had repeated. I was promoted to the Secondary 2 Normal Academic stream. This increased my self-confidence tremendously. I continued with the programme at the *Care Centre*, where I developed friendships with peer leaders and other students, who were good role models for me. The involvement in the *Care Centre's* programmes buffered me from negative peer influences during after-school hours. I continued to excel in my studies, securing the 16th position in the examination rankings of the Secondary 2 Normal Academic stream classes. The school had so much faith in my ability that I was offered a place in the Secondary 3 Express stream. I turned it down as I felt that the Normal Academic stream would be more suitable for my learning pace. I was consistent in maintaining my good performance in my Secondary 3 year.

I am now in Secondary 4 and feel a sense of pride and achievement that I have turned my life around. I have come to terms with my past and matured emotionally and socially. I have developed my sense of identity and no longer feel the need to belong to a group for recognition and acceptance at the expense of compromising my principles. I am proud to be involved in the school's Girls Touch Rugby Team — which would have been unthinkable in my early years as a wayward adolescent! This is a fun Co-Curricular Activity that gives me an opportunity to make friends and learn about teamwork and sportsmanship. I guess the ball is in my court now. I have been given a new beginning by the school, and have come a long way, thanks to my counsellors, teachers, family and friends.

6.2.7 My Experience as a Peer Mediator[23]

POON YAN TONG

Secondary 5A, St Hilda's Secondary School, aged 17

"Finally, we are done," I whispered into Deepa's ears. She smiled in agreement. It was a really tough case. We spent over an hour at that mediation session. The dispute was between two girls over a boyfriend. It was the first time we had to deal with pupils speaking in dialect, and who were so aggressive.

Mary was angry that her best friend, Jane, flirted with her boyfriend. Upset by it, she decided to confront Jane but Jane denied everything. Mary started an argument with Jane, creating a commotion in the classroom. A teacher witnessed the incident and sent them to the general office. They were referred for mediation. At the mediation session, we began by asking for their agreement to the five golden rules of mediation.[24] Mary was sullen and reserved until we assured her that this session would be kept private and confidential. When it was Jane's turn, she got so emotional that she began calling Mary names. I stopped her immediately and reminded her of the rules. After both of them had their turns, we told them that we were not there to solve their problem but to work together with them to come up with possible solutions. Mary was unwilling to co-operate at first, and spoke of settling the matter outside — meaning, to fight. Deepa and I were rather nervous on hearing that. However, we put up a brave front and announced that they had the choice to either continue the peer mediation session or be referred back for disciplinary action. Both parties decided that the mediation session was a preferred choice for them. Thereafter, discussion resumed in a more cordial atmosphere and a solution was finally reached. Talking in an atmosphere of calm and neutrality provided by the mediators gave them the opportunity to articulate their feelings and to hear each other's point of view. Mary accepted Jane's explanation that she was not trying to steal her boyfriend. They apologised to each other and made up.

This case left a deep impression on me. It was the first time I had to deal with conflicts involving boy-girl relationships. I had to be sensitive to the disputants' feelings and try to understand their points of view. I also had to be an interpreter, as Deepa, my partner, was Indian, and the girls spoke mainly Hokkien. It was challenging and confusing at times, as I tried to make sense of what they were saying and to translate it for my partner, and ended up misinterpreting some information. A touch of humour helped us to laugh at our misinterpretations and lightened up an otherwise charged atmosphere.

I enjoy being a peer mediator, as I find fulfilment in playing the role of a peacemaker who is trusted by my peers to help them deal with conflicts. The role also helps me improve my communication skills. Some of us are given opportunities to give assembly talks about our role and experiences. Two years ago, I participated in a video conference with peer mediators from Ohio, USA, in an event organised by the Subordinate Courts. This kind of exposure was awesome! It boosted my self-confidence. Peer mediation has made my school life much more interesting, fun and exciting.

6.2.8 Learning to do Peer Mediation

CHIANG LEE SIA and CHEN REN HAO

Aged 13, peer mediators from Yishun Secondary School

We belong to a group of peer mediators in Yishun Secondary School. In October 2001, all of us attended a one-day Peer Mediation workshop organised by Sembawang-Hong Kah CDC. Pupils from three other secondary schools also participated. The workshop was conducted mainly by Professor Lim Lan Yuan from the National University of Singapore. Guidance specialists from the Ministry of Education and teachers from the four schools helped to conduct some sessions and facilitate the discussions. In addition, we had speakers from the Subordinate Courts, Sembawang-Hong Kah CDC and the Community Mediation Centre.

There was a general consensus that the workshop had been an enjoyable and enriching experience. The speakers were effective communicators who generated interest and a lively response from the audience. The sessions were interspersed with humour, and there was a light-hearted atmosphere to the whole workshop, which was much appreciated.

The speakers spoke about the benefits of mediation to the school and its impact on society at large. We learnt about the Community Mediation Centre and its role in helping to resolve neighbourly disputes, and how mediation is used in the judicial process. We became clearer about the roles and responsibilities of a peer mediator in school. Mediation skills were taught and the realistic role-play scenarios provided a non-threatening environment for the students to practise the skills they had just learnt. The role plays enhanced both our self-understanding and understanding of others. We found that learning to listen well needs effort, and realised that we have to practise hard at paraphrasing what the mediating parties say, in order to reflect their feelings. These communication skills are of primary importance to let the mediating parties know that we are attentive and interested in finding out about their problems and in helping them. We also learned from the workshop sessions that patience and perseverance are of vital importance in the process of resolving a conflict. Some students talked about the need to stay unbiased as a peer mediator and always to be able and willing to listen to both sides of the story. We realised how important and helpful our role as peer mediators in school can be, as we help to resolve peer conflicts without the involvement of teachers in the mediation process.

The workshop helped us to appreciate the professional nature of the job and also enhanced our self-confidence. We were able to voice our views publicly and with conviction, and this boosted our self-esteem.

On the whole, the workshop was very well received by the students. Many commented that they would not hesitate to recommend the workshop to others. One student even mentioned that the workshop was equally appropriate for adults and that they should similarly be encouraged to participate.

ENDNOTES

1 Names of the children and their parents in these stories have been changed to protect their privacy.

2 This is a scheme set up and run by the Prisons Department. After an offender has spent at least 18 months in RTC, he may be considered for release on licence and placed under the Electronic Monitoring Scheme. This means that the offender can stay at home, and during the day he can go to school or go out to work. However, he has to be at home during certain times, usually from the evening all the way until the next morning. An electronic tag is placed on the offender's ankle or wrist. An electronic monitoring device is placed in the offender's residence. If the offender does not come home when he is supposed to, or leaves the home when he is supposed to remain there, the monitoring device will be triggered off. A signal will be sent to the relevant authorities, who will take action on the matter. Such action can include sending the offender back to RTC to serve out the remaining period that the Court had ordered him to spend in RTC.

3 Stories based on actual cases related to Carol Balhatchet by counsellors from the Singapore Children's Society, or on actual cases handled by Carol Balhatchet herself. The names of all parties in these stories have been changed to protect their privacy.

4 See page 24 for more information on the pre-Complaint counselling regime.

5 See pages 216-19 and 23-26 for more information on the Guidance Programme and the Beyond Parental Control Statutory Supervision regimes respectively.

6 For more information on the Beyond Parental Control regime, see endnote 5, supra.

7 A Care and Protection Order is made by the Court when it is satisfied that the child is in need of care and protection, for example, if the child has been neglected or abused. (See Section 4 of the Children and Young Persons Act (Cap. 38) for the definition of a child who is in need of care and protection.) After making the Care and Protection Order, the Court will then go on to make other orders for the child's living arrangements, such as the Fit Person order. (See Section 49(1) of the Children and Young Persons Act for details of all the other orders that the Court can make.)

8 The Court can order a child who has been abused to be placed under the care of a Fit Person, who may be anyone from the superintendent of a welfare home to a relative or foster mother who is registered under the Ministry of Community Development and Sports' Fostering Scheme. (See Section 49(1)(b) of the Children and Young Persons Act (Cap. 38.)

9 Statutory Supervision in the context of a Care and Protection Order means that the child is allowed to return to live with his parents, but he is placed under the supervision of a Protector who is an approved welfare officer or any person appointed by the Court. (See Section 49(1)(d) of the Children and Young Persons Act (Cap. 38.)

10 Unless otherwise indicated, the names of the children and their families, their social workers and teachers in these true stories have been changed to protect their privacy. Also unless otherwise indicated, the stories have been written by the children themselves. The stories have been edited to

preserve the language and style consistent with the rest of the book. However, the facts of each story have not been altered in the editing.

11 Author's name has been changed, and the full names of all his teachers have been omitted, to protect his privacy.

12 For more information on the role of the Operations Manager in the school, see page 32.

13 The Salvation Army Gracehaven (which is a residential home caring for non-Muslim boys and girls) is gazetted as an Approved School, and Approved Home and a Place of Safety under the Children and Young Persons Act (Cap. 38).

14 The Singapore Boys' Hostel is gazetted as an Approved Institution under the Probation of Offenders Act (Cap. 252), and provides residential care and rehabilitation for those children and young persons who have committed offences.

15 Wai Seng was 14 years old at the time when he first appeared in the Juvenile Court.

16 Volunteers are from the National University of Singapore (NUS) and Nanyang Technology University (NTU).

17 In certain Asian cultures, particularly for the more conservative families, members of a family will address each other by the titles of their family relationships, rather than by their names, as a mark of respect. Thus, for example, a girl with three older brothers named John, Alex and Jim, would address the eldest as "Big brother", the next oldest brother, "Second brother", and the youngest brother "Third brother", rather than calling them by their names, John, Alex and Jim.

18 The Singapore Boys' Home is gazetted as an Approved School, Approved Home and Place of Detention under the Children and Young Persons Act (Cap. 38), and provides residential care and rehabilitation for those male children and young persons who have committed offences or are beyond parental control. It provides a stricter regime for its residents than the Singapore Boys' Hostel.

19 Story narrated by Khairul to Andy Lee, Community Liaison Officer, Residential Rehabilitation Branch, Ministry of Community Development and Sports.

20 The Toa Payoh Girls' Home is gazetted as an Approved School, Approved Home and Place of Detention under the Children and Young Persons Act (Cap. 38), and provides residential care and rehabilitation for those female children and young persons who have committed offences or are beyond parental control.

21 Personal story narrated by Charmaine (not her real name, in order to protect her privacy) to Andy Lee, Community Liaison Officer, Residential Rehabilitation Branch, Ministry of Community Development and Sports.

22 Author's surname and the full name of the principal of her school has been omitted to protect her privacy.

23 This account is based on a true story, but the names of the disputants have been changed to protect their privacy.

24 The five golden rules of mediation are: no interrupting, no name calling or putting down the other person, to tell the truth, not to get into a physical fight, and to keep all matters discussed confidential.

PART **III**

BUILDING BRIDGES

The International Perspective – Dealing with Troubled Youths in the Global Village

The International Perspective

In this section, we see the Singapore juvenile justice system through foreign eyes, and also learn about foreign juvenile justice systems.

In the first chapter of this section, the Chief District Judge of New Zealand compares the Singapore and New Zealand juvenile justice systems, and explores how the theme of restorative justice is played out in each system, but in different ways. The second chapter, by renowned juvenile justice academic Dr Willie McCarney, contains an in-depth discussion of the concept of restorative justice, its processes and procedures, and examines its practice in different countries around the world, including such countries as Australia, Northern Ireland, France, England and Wales, the Netherlands, Singapore and New Zealand. The final chapter by Dr David M. Altschuler, focuses on the American experience with various juvenile justice programmes involving community intervention — that is, the direct involvement in the correctional effort of both a juvenile offender's social network and the relevant community institutions.

CHAPTER 7

Restorative Justice and Juvenile Justice – A Comparison of the Singapore and New Zealand Experience

CHIEF DISTRICT JUDGE DJ CARRUTHERS[1]

I. Introduction

> "It does not matter which part of the world we come from, there are strong parallels and commonalities in the problems that we face in the administration of juvenile justice."[2]

Punishing young offenders by inducing fear of prison and harsher treatment with little or no emphasis on teaching new skills or reducing risk factors seems to serve no constructive purpose. Increasingly, statistics confirm that a system embracing a wide range of human emotions, including healing, forgiveness, mercy and reconciliation, (as well as sanction, where appropriate), has much to offer.[3]

This realisation is manifested in the trend toward the use of restorative justice approaches in juvenile justice systems in many jurisdictions. It is also reflected in the torrent of international agreements promoting use of diversionary and restorative measures, and advocating a focus on rights and safeguards. These include the UN Guidelines for the Prevention of Juvenile Delinquency, the UN Rules for the Protection of Juveniles

Deprived of their Liberty, the UN Standard Minimum Rules for the Administration of Juvenile Justice, and the International Convention on the Rights of the Child.

Restorative Justice is not a grand system imposed by "experts" but has deep roots in the needs and experiences of ordinary people.[4] It responds to the reality that criminals are made, not born; that is, that criminality is often a symptom of much deeper problems within the offender, his family and the community.[5] Thus the Restorative Justice approach, metaphorically, views crime as a point in the middle of a motion picture, with action both before and after the criminal event, rather than a singular snapshot without the context of the past or a vision for the future.[6] In doing so, it recognises that a successful criminal sanction must be both retrospective (denouncing the offence (not the offender) and investigating its causes), and prospective (rectifying damage done to the victim/s and the general community while actively facilitating the young offender's moral and social development).

At the heart of the Restorative Justice model, is a philosophy in which I firmly believe: that crime is a community[7] problem. In response to that proposition, many jurisdictions have created juvenile justice systems that enable communities to become involved in fixing the problem. This approach to crime involves all who have an interest in a particular offence in the process of group decision-making with the purpose of determining how to handle the effects of the crime and its consequences for the future.

Many jurisdictions around the world are now utilising Family Group Conferences (FGCs) as a means of encouraging and facilitating the participation of the "community", and they are consequently playing a key role in the restorative disposition process in those jurisdictions.

Restorative Justice means different things to different societies. Often the application of "restorative" principles differs between jurisdictions. This article will examine the conceptions of the restorative justice model adopted by Singapore and New Zealand in their respective juvenile justice systems, with particular reference to the FGC processes in place in each jurisdiction.

II. Juvenile Justice: The Singapore Experience

> "We realise that we can never rely alone on laws and punishment to meet the challenge of juvenile crime. Effective family support and control can help to keep our juveniles out of crimes in the first place and equip them to lead a law-abiding life."[8]

While retaining the fundamentals of previous legislation,[9] Singapore has established a new juvenile justice system which implements a paradigm shift toward the restorative approach.

1. Underlying Principles

The system reflects the classic "broken window" ideology, which envisages that a broken window in the community may start in mischief, but if not repaired will escalate into acceptance of unlawfulness by young persons and a breakdown in social order.

A primary goal of the system is to prevent the juvenile justice system from becoming the "farm system" for adult criminal offenders. It therefore aims to reform young offenders and re-integrate them into society at the point of first contact with the Juvenile Court when, developmentally, there is greater potential for rehabilitation.[10] This aim is enshrined in the Children and Young Persons Act 1993.

Singapore's current juvenile justice system deals with the underlying causes of offending and integrates offenders and their families into society. It involves the offender, the parents of the offender and the victim, their school and religious teachers, their extended families and even their peers as essential to the process of seeking a solution and support system for the offenders and their families. It brings within its remit all available community resources and relevant juvenile justice constituents or stakeholders including faith-based organisations.[11]

In short, it advocates and implements immediate and therapeutic intervention by appropriate agencies, and shifts responsibility for the rehabilitation of the offender to the offender's family. It involves the victim and the community of the victim. The new system is therefore restorative by nature.

However, the Singapore model retains the Court as the central and primary caretaker of the juvenile justice system, "for the purpose of lending authority and legal credibility to it."[12] Further, it extends the role of the Court beyond the traditional role of adjudicator providing for its control of the entire justice process. This approach differs from other restorative-based juvenile justice models, such as New Zealand's, which decentralises the process away from the Court, restricting rather than extending the Court's role.[13]

2. Implementing the System

In adopting a communitarian approach to the treatment of juvenile offenders and enlisting the assistance of the community, Singapore is reforming and rehabilitating juvenile offenders through the use of innovative programmes together with court determinations.[14]

Several restorative and diversionary programmes have been developed in Singapore during the last decade. These programmes have been implemented, not as a model of diversion from the Juvenile Court but as an integrated juvenile justice system, essential to the judicial disposition process.[15] They include peer mediation, youth family care, family care conferencing, the streetwise programme, educational talks and visits to prisons, community service orders and family conferencing.

Family Group Conferencing

Nature of Family Conferencing

The Juvenile Court introduced family conferences on a pilot basis in July 1994 for young offenders. They were premised on the theory of re-integrative shaming: that obedience to the law is not founded on a fear of official punishment but on the fear of social disapproval associated with the offending, and acts on the offender's pangs of conscience.[16] After the success of the pilot, they were retained as a process for selected cases to enhance the effectiveness of the sentences.

Family conferences aim to hold the offender accountable for the offending behaviour and make the offender take responsibility for the offending act. The latter aim is achieved by allowing the offender to make appropriate reparations in the form of community work, restitution, compensation or an apology to the victim. The process is also tailored for parents to take responsibility for their youth's behaviour, empowering and enabling them to play a greater role in their youth's rehabilitation.

Family conferences are considered valuable because they facilitate constructive consideration of both static variables (e.g. the nature of offence, prior convictions, age of offender, etc.) and dynamic variables (e.g. the level of remorse, rehabilitative potential and attitudes of family, etc.). This leads to individualised sentencing and placement decisions.[17]

In Singapore the family conference embodies a four-step methodology involving confrontation, reconciliation, assessment, and an evaluation that culminates in the formulation of recommendations.[18]

During the first step, conference members confront the offender regarding issues such as honesty and denial, taking responsibility and being held accountable, and the impact of the crime on the victim and others (especially family). This step may involve reprimands, cautions, compensation and re-integrative shaming elements.

During the second step, the offender is guided towards apologising to the victim of the offence, family and others involved, and is encouraged to reconcile with others as remorse is expressed.

During the third step, the Court considers issues relevant to resolving any familial relationship problems involving the young offender; rehabilitating or assisting in the rehabilitation of the young offender; and enabling parents or guardians to continue the rehabilitation of the young offender.

At this stage, utilisation of the Juvenile Offender Behaviour (JOB) criteria, a particular Singapore invention worthy of adoption elsewhere, enables the conference members to develop and implement individualised rehabilitation of the whole person. This is achieved by evaluating the offender differentially, taking into account the offender's life history in order to more effectively map out future pathways.[19]

At the final stage, members of the conference explore issues (if the Magistrate deems them appropriate) which would otherwise be inappropriate for court consideration (due to large numbers involved, time constraints etc.). Examples might include determination of appropriate custody (care etc.) arrangements, investigation of additional offences etc.

Use of Family Conferences

Family conferences are not utilised in every case. In deciding whether to refer the case to a family conference, the Court examines, amongst other factors, the nature of offences committed, the extent of the juvenile delinquency and the degree of family support available.[20]

Further, given their nature as described, family conferences have a variety of uses that are individually determined by the Juvenile Court Magistrate. In general, family conferences are being utilised in Singapore in pre-sentencing situations and in post-order situations or case reviews. Surveys evaluating the effectiveness of family conferences have confirmed that both the youths and their family members have benefited from the programme; indicating both improved familial relationships and a decrease in re-offending.

Other Restorative-inspired Programmes

As already mentioned, family conferences are but one aspect of Singapore's multi-systemic approach to juvenile justice. Other programmes, inspired by restorative ideals, have been implemented and operate alongside Family Group Conferencing. These include another form of conferencing termed Family Care Conferencing which has subsequently been renamed "Family Conferencing."

Family Conferencing is similar to the Family Group Conference system already described, but is targeted at juveniles who are beyond parental control. It is not invoked as a result of police charges, though a youth may have committed a criminal offence.

The Youth Family Care Programme,[21] implemented in 1996, is a mentoring programme which uses volunteer families as models who monitor the youth offender and family throughout a period of probation or statutory supervision ranging from between one to three years. Community Service Orders, also first effected in 1996, are court orders requiring the offender to perform unpaid work for a specified number of hours as a condition of probation.

The Peer Advisers Programme,[22] implemented in 1996, involves selected secondary school students sitting in appropriate court proceedings with the aim of giving the Juvenile Court a contemporary peer group perspective of the offending criminal act.

The Streetwise programme,[23] commenced in 1997, is utilised by the Juvenile Court as a condition of probation for offenders involved in gang-related offences. It is an intensive six-month programme which incorporates elements of counselling, family conferencing, peer support, recreation and academic activities. In 1999, this programme was awarded the Commonwealth Regional Youth Service Award in recognition of the sustained and meaningful impact of the programme on society, especially the youth sector.

Peer Mediation,[24] also introduced in 1997, aims to undercut disciplinary problems in schools before they start by imparting practical skills to manage and resolve conflicts before it escalates into behaviour that requires intervention by the police or courts.

Also, more generally, probation standards have been reviewed and refined to ensure more effective individualised assessment prior to the imposition of orders.

Together with family conferencing, these programmes and the restorative principles guiding them have earned Singapore the joint acclaim of being an "early-mover in embracing the Restorative Justice movement against the grain of their traditional commitment to state punitiveness".[25]

III. Juvenile Justice: The New Zealand Experience

> Traditional theories of punishment seem unable to provide solutions to increasing crime rates. ... Restorative Justice seeks

to repair the damage caused to people and to relationships by criminal offending and, in particular, to restore harmony in the lives of victims and offenders. Under such a system, the Courts take a much less prominent role in sentencing, relying instead on "community group conferences" to provide negotiated, community-based responses to offending.[26]

1. Underlying Principles

Prior to the enactment of the Children, Young Persons and Their Families Act 1989, a "welfare" approach was the favoured response to youth offending in New Zealand. Under this approach, offending was considered to be caused by remediable family or individual dysfunction. Young people in these situations were considered to be a symptom of such dysfunction. Further, discretionary decisions concerning young people's future were made by professionals who usually had no previous relationship with the young person.

New Zealand has since implemented a system with objectives which are all predominantly restorative in their approach. They include:

1) Emphasising the need for young offenders to pay for their wrongdoing in an appropriate way;
2) Facilitating the involvement of families, offenders and victims in decision-making arising from the offending; and
3) Ensuring that decision-making is consensual.

The New Zealand juvenile justice system now reflects an understanding that contact with the criminal justice system is often itself harmful; that youth offending is often opportunist behaviour which will be outgrown; and that young people should be confronted, held accountable for their offending behaviour and given opportunities to take responsibility for their actions by making amends to their offence victim(s). Our system addresses this understanding by facilitating face-to-face meetings with the victim, compelling the young offender to confront the effects of their conduct in human terms.[27]

2. Implementing the System

There is both an informal system and a formal system. In the informal system, having established an intention to charge, police are able to divert a youth to a Youth Justice Co-ordinator without reference to the Court. The formal youth justice system operates if a young offender is arrested, unless the youth is diverted by informal police action. The restorative aspects of the system then take effect if the young offender indicates formally to the Court that the charge is "not denied".

New Zealand's juvenile justice system is a manifestation of the restorative view that victims, offenders and their corresponding communities are in a better place than judges and other professionals to negotiate and support appropriate outcomes and to identify what might prevent future crime. It recognises that because communities are where criminal offenders, victims and their families live, it is from within our communities that our lives may be shaped for the future.

As such, "community" is fundamental to New Zealand's juvenile justice system. "Community", in that context, is a collection of people who are concerned in some way about the offence. It involves people concerned for the well-being of either the victim or the offender, those who have concerns about the offence and its consequences, and those who may be able to contribute towards a solution to the problem presented by the offence.

Family Group Conferencing

Nature of Family Group Conferences

Family Group Conferences (FGCs) are the manifestation of the above community concept as they encourage and facilitate the participation of the "community" in resolving the factors giving rise to the offending. Consequently, they are central to New Zealand's diversionary process.

While FGCs are restorative by nature, Restorative Justice per se did not feature in the debates surrounding their introduction. They originated in New Zealand in 1989, and were the result of a number of different concerns. One was the previous focus on young offenders as individuals. This focus conflicted with the Maori view of youth as persons who had obligations to wider family and whose wider family had obligations to them. Other concerns included increasing international recognition that victims' interests had been wrongly overlooked previously and that institutions were in fact part of the problem and not part of the solution.[28]

Thus, the New Zealand model of conferencing was the culmination of a combination of ideas flowing from Maori critics of conventional justice processes and from victim's advocates, together with a deep dissatisfaction of current youth justice processes.[29] The resulting process, existing today, shares both Maori and restorative ideologies.

In pre-colonial New Zealand, Maori had a fully integrated system of Restorative Justice that used Maori legal processes.[30] Collectivity is an integral concept in that process.

Maori do not view themselves as individuals. Rather, they are individuals who are part of a collective — tangible and intangible. Tangible aspects of collectivity include *whanau* (family), *hapu* (sub-tribe) and *iwi* (tribe), and every person coming in contact with Maori. Intangible aspects include *hinengaro* (desire, heart, conscience, mind), *wairua* (spirit), and the *tinana* (body). Maori believe that anything presenting as "disease" in the *hinegaro* or *wairua* eventually manifests itself as disease in the *tinana*, and offending behaviour is such a manifestation. Restorative conferencing is the means of discovering the source of the disease. *Marae* justice is about healing both the victim and offender. The offender cannot effectively heal while the energy from the disease, the offence and the victim is not addressed.[31] Therefore in FGCs, as in the traditional Maori model, young offenders, their families, and victims join together to restore social balance by reintegrating young offenders in their family and community and by determining appropriate means of redress for victims.

The governing legislation envisages considerable variation in practice at FGCs with the family of the offender and victims applying the procedures which suit them. However, there are two mandatory ingredients to the successful completion of a conference: the juvenile must not deny responsibility for the offence, and all parties must consent to the FGC plan. If either of these conditions are not met, the juvenile's case will typically be referred to the Youth Court.

Professionals play a low-key role in an FGC. The Youth Justice Co-ordinator is merely a facilitator, ensuring the process is managed constructively. The role of the police is usually limited to describing the offence, and possibly the impact of it on the victim, if the latter is not present. They may also voice concerns if family proposals seem inadequate or excessive. A youth advocate's main role is to advise on legal issues and to protect the young person's rights, though they may also express an opinion about the proposed penalties if they seem excessive. A social worker, if present, will normally only provide background information on the young person and participate in supporting the plans of the family and the young person for the future.

The New Zealand legislation expressly allows FGC members to recommend that proceedings continue or discontinue, that a formal police caution should be given, and/or that reparation be paid to the victim of the offence.[32] In fact, of course, there are no limitations to the imagination and ideas which might flow from a group of people who wish to produce constructive solutions to the problems of a young person's behaviour. Further, the legislation requires that FGC plans reflect the principles laid down in the Act, for example, that any measures for dealing with offending should be designed to strengthen family, *whanau*, *hapu*, *iwi* and family group and to foster the ability of those groups to develop their own means of dealing with offending by their children and young persons.[33]

In practice, there is no legislative or other formal or informal prescription for FGC plans. The established processes merely provide the platform from which creative and individualised resolutions are formulated. This is, in many ways, the strength of the system. The plan, designed by the offender, victim and community of each, is very likely to be realistic, reflecting the resources and support available to those same parties. FGC plans commonly include an apology and/or reparation to the victim (the amount of which is often far in excess of what is available to the Court to order), community service plans, counselling and rehabilitation programmes, and education requirements.

Use of Family Group Conferences

In New Zealand, of all offending referred to specialist police officers (Youth Aid officers), approximately 75% are dealt with by police diversion schemes devised and operated by these specialist officers. Of the balance, approximately 8% are referred by police to FGCs and outcomes are agreed and implemented without referral to a Court. In the other 17%, the youth is arrested and is referred to the Youth Court, which must refer all cases within its jurisdiction to an FGC for a recommendation.[34]

However, the Youth Court has the right to review the cases and to make a different disposition from that recommended if there are grounds for this and, for the most serious offences, the Youth Court may, if it considers appropriate, refer the matter to the adults' courts for sentence. The Youth Court will also decide outcomes when participants at an FGC fail to agree. Cases of murder and manslaughter are dealt with in the High Court for public policy reasons.

The FGC process has also been successfully utilised to conference the community and government agencies to establish programmes and projects aimed at prevention which have been identified as necessary to help young persons to move away from criminal offending. One of the essential elements has been the use of family group conference processes to determine and identify patterns of offending. A number of these community-based initiatives have been successful in lowering the rate of youth offending in specific regions.

Restorative processes have also been promoted to, and have been introduced by, schools as a fresh way of thinking about school discipline. This recognises that schools, as communities, have a strong influence on children and young people, and not only play an important role in the prevention of problem behaviour, but can be influential in its production.[35] Elements of the juvenile justice system (including, group conferencing and mediation) are used in some schools instead of automatically suspending college students. The aim is of course to strengthen family and community involvement and enhance each student's chance of completing a college education.

Schools are also helped to access community resources providing drug rehabilitation and anger management courses for at-risk students. Obviously, school faculty (including Principal, Deputy Principal, Form Dean and School Counsellor) are usually involved in such conference processes, together with student representatives and sometimes parent groups.

The statistics are positive. It is just over a decade since inception and there is real hope. Recidivism rates have decreased, parties involved in the system are positive, and there is enormous strength and great goodwill in our various communities to do better in this difficult area. The system is one of hope and optimism limited only by the imagination and energy of those who are invited to contribute.

IV. Juvenile Justice: A Comparison

> "There is a risk that Restorative Justice programmes will be promoted on utopian grounds. The value of restorative processes must, in the end, be demonstrated by their ability to deliver a better quality of justice, and to do so efficiently."[36]

A number of arguments have been made in favour of restorative approaches. I believe the most exciting and promising aspect of restorative processes is the resulting reparation of harm caused by the offending. This is in contrast to the compounding of harm which may be caused by the application of purely punitive processes.

Singapore and New Zealand are world leaders in their incorporation of family conferencing processes in the legislation governing their respective juvenile justice systems. This step illustrates the commitment of both countries to restorative processes and provides an example to other countries that restorative processes need not be marginally applied or "added on". Rather, they can be formally integrated into a comprehensive criminal justice response by replacing other mechanisms, including, in New Zealand's case, court hearings.

New Zealand's Youth Justice system remains quite unique. Others have copied it but have never gone as far.[37] What is distinctive about the New Zealand approach to conflict resolution is its use of the group conferencing process in almost all juvenile justice cases and its relegation of the Court and other professionals in favour of offender, victim and community.

1. Utilisation and Focus of Restorative Processes

There is a tendency in many parts of the world to restrict the scope of Restorative Justice initiatives to minor offenders as opposed to more serious (or persistent) ones, and to corresponding minor offences. This is a contributing factor to the marginalisation of restorative processes.

In New Zealand, all Court-based juvenile justice cases, except murder and manslaughter cases, are referred to an FGC after guilt is established. In contrast, Singapore's group conferencing initiatives were first piloted in 1994 for less serious cases. Over time, group conferencing has been expanded to include more serious offences where appropriate. However, in cases involving dangerous and potentially incorrigible juvenile offenders, a retributive and deterrent approach is adopted to ensure that the larger community is protected from the destructive acts of juvenile offenders. As implied above, this approach is in line with other jurisdictions. However after time, positive statistics proving the value of family conferences in the Singapore Juvenile Justice system may encourage the utilisation of such processes to address more serious cases. This possibility is illustrated by recent amendments to relevant legislation (effective October 2001) which have extended the nature of cases dealt with by FCs (to include some arrest cases) and making wider outcomes available to the Juvenile Court facilitator.

The role of restorative processes is different in each juvenile justice system. Singapore predominantly utilises restorative ideologies in preventative programmes. This directly reflects the factors leading to Singapore's re-invention of their juvenile justice system, as already discussed.[38] While not strictly restorative (because they are not repairing harm) they implement the spirit of restorative justice processes and principles. Singapore's public education programmes,

TeenQuest[39] and Peer Mediation[40] programmes exemplify the possible scope of such preventative programmes.

New Zealand is following Singapore's lead, as should others, and is currently working closely with schools and communities to develop effective programmes aimed at preventing offending.

2. Decentralisation of the Legal Disposition Process

Probably the most obvious difference between the approaches taken in Singapore and New Zealand is Singapore's retention of the Court as the controller of the juvenile justice system, the suggested purpose being to lend credibility to the system. It could also be a response to the argument that restorative processes, which give priority to the needs of individual victims and offenders, may fail to meet wider public expectations of the criminal justice system.[41] If so, this approach may change in the future, particularly in the light of Singapore's focus on educating the community about the system. However, for now, Singapore's restorative justice programmes are "not a model of diversion" but rather part of the court controlled system.

The aim of family conferences differs between the two jurisdictions as a result of the different role played by the Court in each. The goal of family conferences in New Zealand is for the family or community group to develop and implement a plan that resolves the issues surrounding offending. In Singapore, the goal is to create a forum whereby information is exchanged and recorded to facilitate a Court determination. New Zealand statistics show that plans are more likely to be completed if they are imposed by the conference rather than by a Court. However, non-completion of court imposed sanctions may not be the issue in Singapore that it currently is in New Zealand.

Singapore is certainly moving towards a fully restorative system. This is illustrated by its general aim to facilitate offenders' re-integration into society. As statistics begin to illustrate the benefit of a community focus, the Juvenile Court may relinquish the reins and transfer more responsibility to those community agencies best able to help the offender and repair the damage caused by the victim and the community.

New Zealand's decentralised approach is very much a manifestation of the collective decision-making process traditionally employed by indigenous Maori, as explained above.[42] New Zealand's unique history in large part explains the extent and nature of our embrace of the restorative model, as it, in many ways, mirrors the Maori model of justice. The nature of the systems implemented in Australia and Canada reinforce this view. Building on similar indigenous traditions, they have embraced restorative processes and implemented them in a way that reflects their unique cultural inheritance. Singapore, of course, does not have the same indigenous foundation. They have therefore retained many fundamentals of their existing, centralised system while adding restorative programmes and processes to renovate that system ahead of international trends.

Singapore has shown bold leadership in forging restorative processes to new ends. Other countries like Japan, Maldives and Philippines have indicated their desire to adopt such measures for dealing with juvenile offenders.[43] In this context, Singapore is progressive and courageous in the steps they have already taken and will no doubt continue to be leaders in the juvenile justice arena as their programmes naturally expand.

Conclusion

Despite differences in structure, both models implement the fundamental objective of restorative processes, and group conferencing in particular, within a criminal justice system. That is, they both force offenders to re-engage their conscience and face up to the effects of their crime on the victim;[44] they force victims to re-examine their own "derogating view of the criminal as a moral monster,"[45] and they require parents of offenders to take responsibility for their child's behaviour and empower them to play a greater role in the rehabilitation of the offender.

The value of *any* process must, in the end, be demonstrated by its ability to deliver a better quality of justice, and to do so efficiently. The reality is that conventional, punitive criminal justice systems often do not work. They fail because offenders and their victims do not engage and stimulate a sense of respect for themselves and each other. Instead, they give predominance to the needs of professionals who represent the state. This is not helpful to the victim or the offender, and fails to provide either with meaningful justice.

Both Singapore and New Zealand have developed systems that hold offenders accountable in ways that repair the harm caused by offending, rather than creating harm by the processes implemented to deal with the offender. Both have developed elements that were already present or had been previously utilised in their respective jurisdictions. Statistics are positive for both systems. The future looks good, particularly if both countries continue to co-operate in testing new ideas, and implementing progressive programmes to reduce youth crime and to encourage and assist our young people to contribute productively to the advancement of our communities.

ENDNOTES

1 Judge Carruthers was appointed Principal Youth Court Judge of New Zealand in 1995 and Chief District Judge on 1 June 2001. Married with five children, ranging in age from 20 to 30, Judge Carruthers is a keen family man and a strong advocate of youth and family issues.

2 Senior District Judge Richard Magnus, Magistrate May Mesenas & Ms Chan Wai Yin. "Balancing Opposing Paradigms between Retributive and Restorative Youth Justice, the Singapore Experience: Factorial Approach Towards Juvenile Justice Management in Singapore" (Youth Justice Conference 2000) 1.

3 Jim Consedine. (1999). *Restorative Justice: Healing the Effects of Crime*. (p.10). Lyttleton: Ploughshares Publications.

4 Dr Willie McCarney, JP (Lay Magistrate, Belfast Youth Court and Belfast Family Proceedings Court). "Restorative Justice International Approaches". Address at 64th Annual Conference of National Council of Juvenile and Family Court Judges, 15-18 July 2001, Monteray, California, p. 3.

5 Erik Luna. "Reason and Emotion in Restorative Justice". 5 July 2000. Lecture transcript, New Zealand Institute for Dispute Resolution, Victoria University of Wellington Faculty of Law. <<**http://www.scoop. co.nz/archive/scoop/stories/51/19/200007051755.74daa57b.html**>> (last accessed 8 Jan 2002).

6 Luna, above.

7 As I discuss below in the context of the New Zealand juvenile justice system, "Community" is a collection of people who are concerned in some way about the offence. It involves people concerned for the well-being of either the victim or the offender, those who have concerns about the offence and its consequences, and those who may be able to contribute towards a solution to the problem presented by the offence.

8 Yong Pung How, The Honourable Chief Justice of Singapore, (Subordinate Workplan 1997/8) cited in Mark Tay (District Judge, Juvenile Court, Singapore). "The Juvenile Justice System in Singapore" (14 Oct 1998) <**http://www.ejustice.org.sg/archives/whitepapers.html#singapore**> (last accessed 18 Jan 2002).

9 Including the founding principles of the Juvenile Court, the guiding principle of youth justice (being the welfare of the juvenile), the age of criminal culpability, the legislative principles for care orders, fit person orders, social work and supervised treatment, approved school and young offender incarceration and the already established balance between parental authority and State intervention — The Honourable the Chief Justice of Singapore, above, 4.

10 The Honourable, The Chief Justice of Singapore, above, 7.

11 The Honourable, The Chief Justice of Singapore, above, 6.

12 The Honourable, The Chief Justice of Singapore, above, 6.

13 See further, Part III of this article.

14 Mark Tay, above, 10.

15 The Honourable, The Chief Justice of Singapore, above, 6.

16 Magnus and others, above, 9.

17 *Judicare* (September 2001) a publication of the Subordinate Courts of Singapore.

18 All information regarding the nature of the family conferencing process in Singapore is taken from *Judicare* (September 2001) a publication of the Subordinate Courts of Singapore.

19 Joseph Paul Ozawa. "Juvenile Offender Behaviour (JOB) Criteria: Assessing Risk of Recidivism in Juvenile Court" <**http://www.lawgazette.co.sg/2001-7/July01-focus3.htm**> (last accessed 18 Jan 2002) 1.

20 Mark Tay (District Judge, Juvenile Court, Singapore). "The Juvenile Justice System in Singapore" (14 Oct 1998) <<**http://www.ejustice.org.sg/archives/whitepapers.html#singapore**>> (last accessed 18 Jan 2002) 4. See also "Family Conferences" on pages 20, 52 and Chapter on the "Family and Juvenile Justice Centre" on page 46.

21 See page 57 for more details.

22 See page 59 for more details.

23 See page 181 for more details.

24 See article on "Working with Students on the Peer Mediation Programme" on pages 209-12.

25 John Braithwaite. "Restorative Justice and a Better Future". 17 October 1996. Lecture transcript, Dalhousie University. 9. <**http://www.realjustice.org/Pages/braithwaite.html**> (last accessed 17 Jan 2002).

26 His Honour Judge F W M McElrea (Auckland District Court, New Zealand). (1994). "Restorative Justice – The New Zealand Youth Court – A Model for Development in Other Courts?" *Journal of Judicial Administration, 4(1)*, 33.

27 Anne Hayden. (2001). *Restorative Conferencing Manual of Aotearoa New Zealand.* (pp. 61-62). Wellington: Department for Courts.

28 Dr Willie McCarney, JP (Lay Magistrate, Belfast Youth Court and Belfast Family Proceedings Court). "Restorative Justice International Approaches". Address at 64th Annual Conference for National Council of Juvenile and Family Court Judges, 15-18 Jul 2001, Monteray, California, pp.6-7.

29 Allison Morris and Gabrielle Maxwell. "Restorative Justice in New Zealand: Family Group Conferences as a Case Study" (1998) 1. Western Criminology Review 1. <<**http://wcr.sonoma.edu/ v1n1/morris.html**>> (last accessed 8 Jan 2002).

30 Consedine, above, 11.

31 Anne Hayden. (2001). *Restorative Conferencing Manual of Aotearoa New Zealand.* (pp. 2-3). Welligton: Department for Courts.

32 Children, Young Persons and Their Families Act (NZ), s260.

33 Children, Young Persons and Their Families Act (NZ), s208(c).

34 Gabrielle Maxwell, Jeremy Robertson & Tracy Anderson. (2002). "Police Youth Diversion: Final Report". Prepared for New Zealand Police and Ministry of Justice by the Crime and Justice Research Centre, Victoria University. p. 42.

35 Hayden, above, 82.

36 Ministry of Justice (New Zealand). (1996). "Restorative Justice: A Discussion Paper". para 5.10. <<**http://www.justice.govt.nz/pubs/reports/1996/restorative/chapter5.html**>> (last accessed 25 Jan 2002).

37 Anne Hayden. (2001). *Restorative Conferencing Manual of Aotearoa New Zealand.* (p.10), quoting Judge McElrea. "A Youth Court Judge's Perspective". Wellington: Department for Courts.

38 See Part II, Section 2 on "Other Restorative-Inspired Programmes" above for details on pages 290-91.

39 A yearly event organised by the Family and Juvenile Justice Centre (FJJC) in collaboration with external agencies like the Community Development Councils (CDCs) as an outreach programme targeted at juveniles below 16 years old. The objective of the programme, which is usually held during the school holidays, is to make them aware of juvenile justice issues through games and fun activities. See also Chapter on the "Family and Juvenile Justice Centre" on page 46.

40 See pages 60-61 for more details.

41 Suggestion regarding restorative justice systems in general, in Ministry of Justice of New Zealand Discussion Paper.

42 Refer to Part II, Section 2 of "Family Group Conferencing" above for more details at pages 288-90.

43 Correspondence from Magistrate May Lucia Mesenas, Juvenile Justice Division, Subordinate Courts of Singapore (22 January 2002).

44 Dr Charles Barton. (2000). "Theories of Restorative Justice". (p. 5).

45 Barton, above, 6.

CHAPTER 8

Restorative Justice: International Approaches

DR WILLIE McCARNEY

Introduction

In this paper, I look at Restorative Justice from an international perspective. Perhaps I should begin by explaining what I mean by this term. A definition is not as straightforward as it might at first appear! Restorative Justice is not a unitary concept and is therefore difficult to define.[1] In some ways, it is an "Alice-in-Wonderland" term because it means whatever the speaker wants it to mean. While most commonly used to describe a response to offending behaviour, it is also used to describe a range of complementary and broadly related developments that lie outside the sphere of criminal justice responses to conventional crime. The term "Restorative Justice" has been used to describe everything from micro approaches, e.g. stand-alone victim support projects, to the macro e.g. South Africa's Truth and Reconciliation Commission or the gacaca system of justice in Rwanda dealing with those accused of genocide.

I will concentrate on "Restorative Justice" as a response to offending behaviour as well as focus on a variety of practices, which seek to respond to crime in a more constructive way than is conventionally achieved through the use of punishment.

An Idea Whose Time Has Come

His Honour Judge F W M McElrea, a senior District Court and Youth Court Judge in New Zealand summarises the current situation succinctly:[2]

> While there is a variety of views about the theory of punishment, the one thing about our criminal justice system today that seems to be agreed by all is that in practise it is not working. Crime rates keep climbing and prison populations keep growing, at considerable expense in human and financial terms. The needs of neither offenders nor victims are satisfied. The existing theoretical bases of punishment seem bankrupt. The deterrent aspect of imprisonment is questioned by the failure of longer prison sentences to reduce serious crime; ...

It seems fair to say that our justice system is in crisis. However, I would like to draw an analogy from the Chinese language where the same character is used for two meanings "crisis" and "opportunity". Today's crisis in the justice system represents an opportunity for changing the system. Restorative Justice is an idea whose time has come.

A Truly Revolutionary Movement

"A revolution is occurring in criminal justice. A quiet, grassroots, seemingly unobtrusive, but truly revolutionary movement is changing the nature, the very fabric of our work."

This is how the US Government's National Institute of Corrections introduces a recent set of articles dealing with restorative and community justice. Paradoxically, Restorative Justice is moving from a peripheral grassroots movement to centrestage, its ideas migrating from the margins to the mainstream, at a time when society has reached unprecedented levels of punitiveness.

Punishment in response to crime and other wrongdoing is the prevailing practice in most modern societies. Those who fail to punish naughty children and offending youths and adults are generally labelled as permissive. Over the past 100 years or so, the pendulum has swung from punitive to permissive and back again. The problem has been that neither approach appeared to work. The Punitive-Permissive continuum provides a narrow perspective and limited options. The choice is either to punish or not to punish. The only variable is the severity of the punishment.

FIGURE 8.1: PUNITIVE-PERMISSIVE CONTINUUM

According to Ted Wachtel, Executive Director of the International Institute for Restorative Practices, Bethlehem, Pennsylvania, we can construct a more useful view of social discipline by looking at the interplay of two more comprehensive variables — control and support.

"Control" is defined as discipline or limit setting and "support" as encouragement or nurturing. Adding these two variables means we can combine a high or low level of control with a high or low level of support to identify four general approaches to social discipline: neglectful, permissive, punitive (or retributive) and restorative.

FIGURE 8.2: SOCIAL DISCIPLINE WINDOW
(Wachtel, 1999)

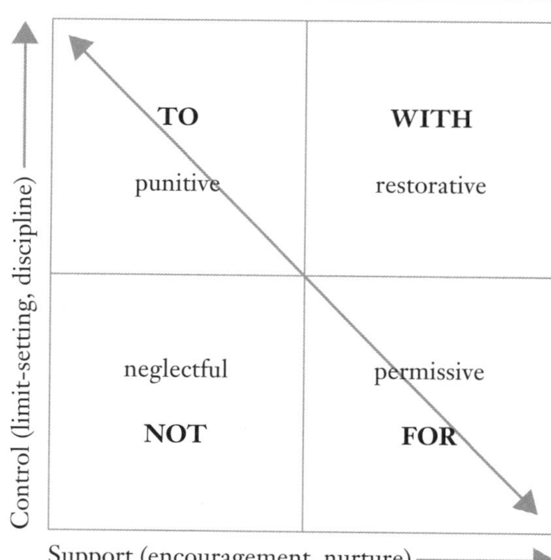

In this way the traditional punitive-permissive continuum is subsumed within a more inclusive framework. The permissive approach is comprised of low control and high support, a scarcity of limit setting and an abundance of nurturing. Opposite to permissive is the punitive (or retributive) approach, high control and low support. The third approach, with an absence of both limit setting and nurturing, is neglectful. The fourth possibility is restorative. This approach has high control and high support. It confronts and disapproves of wrongdoing while supporting and valuing the intrinsic worth of the wrongdoer. Control in this context means control of wrongdoing and not control of the individual.

Wachtel explains the use of the four key words "TO, WITH, NOT and FOR" in his social discipline window. If we are neglectful towards troubled youths, we do NOT do anything in response to their inappropriate behaviour. If we are permissive, we do everything FOR them and ask little in return. If we are punitive, we respond by doing things TO them. If we respond in a restorative manner, we do things WITH them and involve them directly in the process. A critical element of the restorative approach is that, whenever possible, WITH also includes victims, family, friends and community — those who have been affected by the offender's behaviour.

So this is where Restorative Justice fits into the picture. But, will this new revolutionary movement really change the nature and very fabric of our work or is it just another passing fad?

The first thing to say is that Restorative Justice is not new. In fact it is as old as most people's histories. In my own country, Ireland, the Brehon law system which operated from pre-history up to the 17th century contained many of the elements of Restorative Justice. The victim and offender were seen in the context of their community. The emphasis of judgement was on restoring the *status quo* rather than simply retaliation and retribution. The same is true of the other countries we will look at.

Restorative Justice

Restorative Justice is not a grand system imposed by "experts" but has deep roots in ordinary people's needs and experiences. Restorative

Justice begins with value statements about the primary goal of intervention and the process itself. Specifically, because crime is viewed first as harm to victims and victimised communities, the justice intervention must focus on repairing this harm, or healing the wound crime causes. The process necessarily elevates the role of the victim and focuses on victim needs, while allowing for victim, offender, and community input and involvement in a process that seeks to find common ground and attend to the mutual needs of each co-participant.

Repairing harm

Currently, when a crime is committed, two primary questions are asked: Who did it? and What should be done to the offender? The latter question is generally followed with another question about the most appropriate punishment and, when the crime is committed by a child or young person, about the most appropriate treatment or service. Viewed through the restorative "lens," however, crime is understood in a broader context than that suggested by the questions of guilt and what should be done to the offender. In Restorative Justice, three very different questions receive primary emphasis. What is the nature of the harm resulting from the crime? What needs to be done to make it right or repair the harm? Who is responsible for making it right or repairing the harm?

The "Centrality of the Victim"

Howard Zehr says that the "centrality of the victim" is a distinguishing feature of Restorative Justice. The moment the system forgets about the victim as the central person, it moves to an offender-based system and then we get the excusing, condoning, explaining conduct, which is in fact self-defeating and finally hopeless.

The difficulty with our present system, particularly in dealing with adults, is that it is an offender-based system where we regard the offender's position always — did the offender do this or did he not do it — if he did do it, what is a just deserts appropriate, measured and consistent response? The problem with this approach is that it does not take into account victims' interests. Similarity of outcome for offenders, on which we place so much emphasis, particularly with adults, means widely dissimilar outcomes for victims.

Three Unique Dimensions

Restorative Justice has three unique dimensions: the central and elevated role of the victim, the general focus on repair and the emphasis on a process that seeks mutual involvement and support for three co-participants and is explicitly attuned to the role of each in producing justice outcomes.

For the victim, Restorative Justice offers the hope of restitution or other forms of reparation, information about the case, the opportunity to be heard, and input in the case, as well as expanded opportunities for involvement and influence.

For the community, there is the promise of reduced fear and safer neighbourhoods, a more accessible justice process, and accountability, as well as the obligation for involvement in sanctioning crime, restoring victims' sense of well-being, re-integrating offenders, and crime prevention and control.

For the offender, Restorative Justice requires accountability in the form of obligations to repair the harm to individual victims and victimised communities and the opportunity to develop new competencies and social skills and the capacity to avoid future crime.

"Balance of Interests"

The conventional criminal justice system focuses on the "public interest" as the principal consideration to be taken into account when deciding whether or not to prosecute an offender. Restorative Justice seeks to address and balance the rights and responsibilities of victims, offenders, communities and the government.

Related Processes

The following processes and practices are related to Restorative Justice initiatives. Victim support services, victim impact statements or "victim allocution" rights are not restorative as defined here because they focus only on the victim. Likewise, reparative court-based sanctions such as compensation or reparation orders for victims or community service orders are not truly "restorative". These are coercive measures and one of the key attributes of Restorative Justice is that it is non-coercive.

Parallel Developments

Conflict resolution, based on a process of mediation, is an important parallel development. "Alternative dispute resolution" is widely used in a variety of sectors including disputes within families and schools, commercial disputes, and those involving environmental conflicts or complaints relating to health care and medical matters. Clearly, these are relevant because civil disputes could escalate to the criminal level if not resolved.

In Northern Ireland, England, New Zealand and Australia and, I am sure, in many other countries, schools are increasingly using Restorative Justice approaches to problems of discipline with a view to preventing suspensions, expulsions and exclusions. This reflects the fact that here is a community which has been affected by "crime", and the community needs to be fully involved in restoring the balance if something goes wrong. Margaret Thorsbon's research in Australia, which focused on 73 schools in Queensland, showed markedly improved outcomes for everybody from a Restorative Justice approach to disciplinary problems.

Similarly, Restorative Justice approaches are now being used widely in prisons for the same reasons — to look at a communitarian response to breaches of the community's rules, rather than an offender-based one.

Restorative Justice Processes

In this paper, I will focus on what I consider to be the two main Restorative Justice approaches — Family Group Conferencing and Victim Offender Mediation. Under Family Group Conferencing,

I will mention the New Zealand Model, the Wagga Wagga Model, a range of Neighbourhood Sanctioning Boards and Circle Sentencing. Each is built on the philosophy of what Dignan[3] called the "three R's" of Responsibility, Restoration and Re-integration. I would like to add a fourth "R" for "Respect".

- **Responsibility:** One of the primary aims of most Restorative Justice approaches is to engage with offenders to try to bring home the consequences of their actions and an appreciation of the impact they have had on the victim(s) of their offences.
- **Restoration:** A second aim is to encourage and facilitate the provision of appropriate forms of reparation by offenders, towards either their direct victims (provided they are agreeable) or the wider community.
- **Re-integration:** A third aim is to seek reconciliation between victim and offender where this can be achieved and, even in cases where this is not possible, to strive to re-integrate both victims and offenders within the community as a whole following the commission of an offence.
- **Respect:** The victim often feels a sense of shame for being victimised. The offender and his/her family may also feel ashamed. People need to feel that they are being treated with respect and consideration.

Erik Luna stresses the importance of respect in restorative sanctioning:

"Successful restorative sanctioning begins with a single principle that structures the entire process: respect. As used here, respect is a sense of dignity, worth and recognition accorded oneself, another individual, a physical object or an abstract concept. Crime and a criminal lifestyle are driven, to a large extent, by the pursuit of respect by the offender and a lack of respect for those affected by the offence. From the viewpoint of the victim, crime is the ultimate statement of disrespect for her privacy, autonomy, property, security and general well-being. For the community and its members, offending is a sign of disrespect — of law and authority, the concept of civility, the benefits of organised society, and so on. The human tendency is towards reciprocity, to meet disrespect with disrespect, leaving victims and communities to reject the offender of being worthy of dignity."[4]

It is easier to respect the victim than the offender. But respect is essential if there is to be any hope of breaking the spiral of offending behaviour. Respect holds the best hope of dissolving alienation.

Respect implies a belief that the individual has within himself/herself the capacity to grow and to change. It implies an understanding that, out of defensiveness and inner fear, individuals can and do behave in ways which are incredibly cruel, horribly destructive, immature, regressive, anti-social, hurtful. Respect implies that, for all his or her failings, the individual is still part of the community. It implies an acceptance that the offender exists as a separate valued person with an identity.

If a person finds himself/herself positively understood, he/she will develop a set of growth-promoting or therapeutic attitudes towards self which is the first step in the change process. This is not letting the offender off the hook! Most find the thought of taking responsibility for self a frightening prospect and would rather leave it to the Court. It is easier to shirk responsibility than to shoulder it. The restorative process will support the offender in facing up to his/her responsibilities. Respect is the key which will unlock the door and allow the rehabilitation process to begin.

Family Group (or Community) Conferencing

The "Family Group Conferencing" approach originated in New Zealand in 1989. It was the result of a number of different movements.[5]

One of them was the anger felt by Maori and Pacific Island communities in New Zealand that the previous youth justice system regarded young people as individuals in their own right and not as people who had obligations to wider family and whose wider family had obligations to them. That was a major initiator of change leading to an attempt to include ancient Maori traditions of resolving disputes within its process.

The second major factor leading to change was the international recognition of victims' interests and the way in which they had been overlooked in the past.

The third major factor was the recognition, which was again an international movement, that institutions were in fact part of the problem and not part of the solution. The vision of New Zealand's changed legislation looked towards harnessing community strengths and community wisdom and connecting victims and offenders as individual people, in a way which had previously been excluded by the processes. This resulted in the enactment of a radical new set of practices for dealing with young offenders under the Children, Young Persons and Their Families Act 1989.

Quite apart from the issues pressing the need for change in the way young offenders were dealt with, there was also a concern on the "care" side that professionals were failing to keep children safe through professional case management and that the community needed to be involved in the same way to bring its collective wisdom and strengths to the problems of child abuse and neglect. There were a number of pilot schemes involving family decision-making to help resolve neglect and abuse cases and child protection. Now in New Zealand the welfare system also uses conferencing as the central diversionary device.

"Conferencing" encourages the participation of a wide collection of people who are "concerned" in some way about the offence.[6] They include those who are concerned for the well-being of either the victim or the offender, those who have concerns about the offence and its consequences, and those who may be able to contribute towards a solution to the problem presented by the offence. This collection of people — which might also include those who are indirectly affected by the offence — have been described as making up a "community of interest"[7] and the whole approach is sometimes referred to as a "communitarian" model.[8] However, the community in question is not a geographical entity as such, nor does it comprise "representatives" (whether elected, appointed or self-appointed).

The New Zealand conferencing approach has a number of distinctive features, as set out by McElrea.[9]

1. It is integrated and fully incorporated into the youth justice system as a whole (which deals with those over the age of 14 but not older than 17).
2. There is an effective "gate-keeping" procedure whereby both the traditional means of obtaining a suspect's appearance in Court — arrest and summons — are carefully restricted. The aim of this is to ensure that young persons are diverted from the Court wherever possible. Thus, no arrest can be effected unless it is necessary to prevent further offending, absconding of the young person or interference with witnesses or evidence.
3. Further, no summons can be issued without first referring the matter to a youth justice co-ordinator, who will then convene a Family Group Conference (FGC), which recommends for or against prosecution, with a presumption in favour of diversion. All members of the FGC (including the young person) must agree to the proposed diversionary programme, and its implementation is essentially consensual.
4. Where the young person has been arrested, the Court must refer all matters (charges) that are not denied to a FGC, which recommends a disposition to the Court. This usually consists of a plan of action incorporating a "restorative outcome" (e.g. apology, financial reparation, work for the victim or for the community, curfew and/or an undertaking relating to future behaviour). The plan normally nominates persons to supervise its implementation, and the Court is asked to adjourn proceedings for a suitable duration to allow for this to happen. Occasionally, an FGC recommends a sanction for imposition by the Court.
5. Apart from murder and manslaughter, which for public policy reasons are excluded from the Youth Court, every offence (including indictable only and including all the other very serious charges) must be dealt with by means of a Family Group Conference. In the case of purely indictable charges (the really serious) the young person may be dealt with in an Adult Court. The young person who wishes to admit the charge may be given the right to remain in the Youth Court and be dealt with there

rather than be transferred to the Adult Court. In practice the emphasis is on such cases remaining in the Youth Court unless all the options and strengths of the family and community-based Youth Court have been exhausted and no further options remain.

6. All FGCs are facilitated and convened by a youth justice co-ordinator, who is an employee of the Department of Social Welfare. Those in attendance will be the young person, members of the (extended) family, the victim, a youth advocate (if requested by the young person), a police officer (usually from the specialist Youth Aid division), a social worker (in certain cases only), and anyone else the family wishes. The latter category could include a representative from a relevant community organisation (for example, an addiction treatment agency or a community work sponsor).
7. FGC plans are nearly always accepted by the Youth Court. Outstanding successes, in respect of very serious offending, which have not required any formal Court sanctions, have been achieved.

   A wide range of sanctions is available to the Court for both serious and non-serious cases where there has not been effective family or community intervention and the young person fails to be sentenced by the Court. However, such cases are quite rare. If there is a referral to the District Court, the sanctions include imprisonment for up to five years.
8. If the plan is carried out as agreed, the proceedings are usually withdrawn. However, if the plan is not implemented satisfactorily, the Court can impose its own sanctions. The Court thus acts both as a "quality control" mechanism, which is capable of coming into play in the event of patently unsatisfactory recommendations, and as a "default" procedure in cases where plans break down.

The New Zealand style FGC model is now well-established in New Zealand, and has been exported to a number of other jurisdictions. We will see in the next section that Australia has developed its own unique model. However, FGC was introduced to

South Australia in early 1994,[10] and later to Victoria[11] and Queensland.[12] New South Wales has Family Group Conferencing as its central device. It is widespread across most states of the United States of America. There are pilot schemes operating in Belgium. In the United Kingdom, all of the Youth Offending Panels are operating Family Group Conferencing as part of their options for dealing with young people. It has been introduced in South Africa. A range of schemes are running in Northern Ireland, some operated by the police, some by the Probation Service and some by voluntary groups.

The Australian Model

An Australian model of "conferencing" evolved from John Braithwaite's theory of re-integrative shaming. It originated within a police district in Wagga Wagga, in New South Wales, in 1989, and is generally known as the Wagga Wagga model. It differs in a number of key respects from both the New Zealand Model and also from the Victim Offender Mediation Model, which we will discuss below.

1. The Australian variant is police-led, in the sense that the police not only decide which cases might be appropriate for conferencing but are expected and encouraged to convene and facilitate the conferences. This represents a clear break from the values and practice-base associated with victim offender mediation, which emphasises the need for a scrupulously independent mediator, who should be capable of eliciting the trust of both main parties. As a result of the criticism surrounding this lack of independence, conferencing in New South Wales has recently shifted from a police base to the Office of Juvenile Justice.
2. The conference itself is carefully scripted, partly to ensure consistency, but also to ensure that the "restorative" nature of the process is maintained,[13] even though those delivering it may be unfamiliar with it, and relatively untrained (in comparison with conventional mediators).

3. The approach has been consciously developed as a distinctive model of policing in its own right, with a view to crime prevention. It is sometimes referred to as "restorative policing"[14] or "restorative community policing",[15] and is seen by many of its instigators as an effective method of transforming police attitudes, role perceptions and organisational culture.

Following the developmental work in Wagga Wagga, police-based restorative conferencing techniques have been introduced in a number of other Australian jurisdictions — notably Canberra and Sydney. They have also been "exported" to a number of other countries. They include the United States,[16] Canada,[17] the United Kingdom[18] and Northern Ireland.

In Thames Valley, England, the Wagga Wagga model is evolving along lines which brings it closer to FGC. All those personally affected by an offence are invited to attend and take part in the cautioning session. This includes any victims and their supporters, those in caring relationships with the offender, such as parents, partners or siblings and sometimes members of the wider community. The name changes according to who is in attendance: a Restorative Caution (if the victim is not present), a Restorative Conference (if the victim is present) or a Community Conference (if members of the wider community attend).

Restorative Justice in Singapore

Singapore introduced Restorative Justice programmes in 1995, "not as a model of diversion from the Juvenile Court but as an integrated juvenile justice system, essential to the judicial disposition process" (Chief Justice Yong Pung How, 2000).

Restorative Justice seeks to deal with the underlying causes of offending and to integrate offenders and their families into society. It involves the offender, the parents of the offender and the victim, their school and religious teachers, their extended families and even their peers as essential to the process of seeking a solution and support system for the offenders and their families. It brings within its remit all available community resources and relevant juvenile justice constituents or stakeholders including faith-based organisations. As a critical juvenile justice programme, Restorative Justice is rightfully driven by the juvenile court judge lending authority and legal credibility to the process (*op cit.*).

Family Conferencing is premised on notions of "re-integrative shaming". The Conference brings together the offender and his family, the victim and his family, the offender's school teacher or employer, the Prosecutor, the Probation Officer and any other significant person. The facilitator, through skilled interview techniques, facilitates the session to have the offender realise the impact of his offending behaviour on those near and dear to him. The facilitator will also formulate concrete steps, through the inputs of the participants, which the offender can take to make good his offending act to those affected by it.

Rather than focus merely on increasing the culpability and shame of the offender, the idea behind family conferences is to enhance the judicial process itself, in an adjunctive manner, providing input which will facilitate sentencing. After the Conference, the offender and his parents appear in Court for the judge to make an order on the case. The "sword of Damocles" effect in which the imminent sentencing is to be passed has a strong effect of enhancing increased interaction and candid responses where avoidance would otherwise be used.

While New Zealand focuses on the family group conference as a key element of the justice process, Singapore sees the family conference as one option in a wide range of programmes.

The Honourable Chief Justice Yong Pung How outlined the approach to be taken in his keynote address at the Subordinate Workplan 1997/8 when he said:

"The complexity of juvenile crime requires a multi-prong approach. It has to incorporate elements of deterrence, incapacitation and rehabilitation. A balance will have to be struck between the need for rehabilitation and accountability for the offending behaviour. Restorative Justice seeks to achieve this. We realise that we can never rely alone on laws and punishment to meet the challenge of juvenile crime. Effective family support and control can help to keep our juveniles out of crimes in the first place and equip them to lead a law-abiding life. Already this is being done by the Government through the Inter-Ministry Committee on Dysfunctional families, Juvenile delinquency and Drug abuse. Similarly, on the Court's part, there is a communitarian approach to the treatment of juvenile offender. Through family conferencing, boot camps, peer group advisers, family care conferencing, we enlist the support and assistance of the community in reforming and rehabilitating the juvenile offender. We build on this approach through a blend of measures focusing not just on the offender but the victims as well."

There has been a steady decrease in offending in Singapore over the five-year period of 1994 to 1999.[19]

Circle Sentencing

"Circle Sentencing" is a recently updated version of ancient and settlement practices adapted from the traditions of Canadian aboriginals, as well as those of indigenous people in the South-Western United States. It is based, not only on the concept of mutual forgiveness but on the *responsibility* placed on every member of the community to forgive.

There is a strong belief that, when the state takes ownership of the process of crime and punishment, it draws away from the community and loses touch with the wishes and needs of the people. As with other Restorative Justice approaches, supporters argue that it is not possible to design a programme which is applicable to every community in the country, or, indeed, in the state. Every community has the right to decide how offenders should be dealt with. The offence arises within the community and that is where the solution must be found.

The modern version of Circle Sentencing involves a partnership between traditional circle rituals and criminal justice procedures in which victims and their supporters, offenders and their supporters, judge and court personnel, prosecutor, defence lawyers, police and all community members who have an interest come together. The process is presided over by the judge but the judge sits amongst the participants and is just another member of the circle, contributing like everyone else. The aim is to work consensually to devise an appropriate sentencing plan to meet the needs of all interested parties. The plan does not just deal with the needs of the offender or with the needs of the victim and the offender. It will have all kinds of cross commitments and covenants about what various people have agreed to do. At the end of the day, it is the judge's responsibility to incorporate the plan into a formal court sentence. Judge Barry Stuart of the Territorial Court of the Yukon has presided over more than 300 Sentencing Circles. He recalls[20] only three occasions on which the Circle failed to reach a consensus and he was forced to make the decision. The judge does have the authority to impose a prison sentence if appropriate and this could be the decision of the Circle. However, prison sentences are rare.

In Saskatchewan, Judge Bria Huculak and her colleagues began using sentencing circles in 1992, building on the experience of Judge Stuart in the Yukon. "In the first year," Huculak says,[21] "we made it up as we went along, learning from our mistakes." What they now have is a process that is a mixture of aspects of victim/offender mediation, ancient aboriginal traditional peace-making circles and democratic discussion. The aim is to identify the harm done and to work out appropriate ways of responding to it, and, if possible, repairing it.

The key ingredient is a safe atmosphere in which people can discover the real issues and needs. Anyone from the public can observe. The judge relays the bare facts, and asks the offender to respond. Then, one after another, everyone in the circle has an equal opportunity to say what they wish.

"My role is broadly like that of a facilitator," says Huculak. "I'm in control, but I say very little. I strive for consensus — not total agreement."

At any stage, people can choose not to comment, but at a later point they are always given an opportunity to speak. Sometimes, a "talking piece" is handed round — an object held by the person talking, until they are ready to hand it to their neighbour. "It's not a linear process," Huculak says. "It's more like a spiral — or like peeling the layers of an onion. What happens is very demanding on the accused. The idea that they're getting off easy is not realistic. They have to account for their behaviour in a very direct way."

But what about the vulnerability of the victim — particularly in more serious cases such as rape or other violence? Sensitivity is crucial, says Huculak. "The victim often feels a sense of shame for being victimised. The offender and their family may also feel ashamed. People need to feel that they are being treated with respect and consideration. But they also often want to ask questions of the offender — to ask, for instance, 'Why me'?"

Deep feelings often emerge, and Huculak does not see her role as reining people in. "I tell participants that no one is required to cry, but if they feel they want to, that's OK."

The process may take six or seven hours. Sometimes, sentencing circles recommend to the judge novel forms of sentence. Prison sentencing is much reduced. One offender, whose drunk and dangerous driving had caused the death of his father, had to spend the next year or so explaining his crime and waywardness to public meetings of young people as part of his punishment. A variety of penalties may be imposed, including close community support and accountability. The judge can overrule the proposed action plan, but rarely does.

Even in cases where offenders may not have seen their family for years, family members do turn up. The process helps make better connections. The family realises they could have a role.

Today in Saskatchewan, only a small percentage of cases are dealt with by sentencing circles, but a new courtroom in Saskatoon has been designed specially to adapt for them. Several other Canadian provinces are now using similar approaches.

Huculak says, "At the end of a day in a traditional courtroom, judges may leave disappointed. In circles, I usually leave feeling hope for the offender, hope for their rehabilitation, hope for the victims, and hope for a safer community."

One difficulty facing Circle Sentencing is that such practices are only likely to be relevant to communities with a strong sense of identity and a relevant set of traditions, and even this is unlikely to be sufficient if the offenders themselves have become alienated from these traditions.[22] However, this is not unique to Circle Sentencing.

The British Lord Chief Justice (Lord Woolf) appeared greatly impressed by Judge Huculak's presentation at the Winchester Conference in March and by the Circle Sentencing role play presented by her team. It seems likely that Circle Sentencing will find a place in the British system in the not-too-distant future.

Neighbourhood Sanctioning Boards

Neighbourhood Sanctioning Boards, or Community Panels, have a long history in the United States and the rest of North America. These are closer to the Victim Offender Mediation model than to Family Group Conferencing. This model, variously called Neighbourhood Sanctioning Boards, Community Panels or Neighbourhood Justice Centres, has become established in North America, Australia and Norway (where they are known as Municipal Mediation Boards). They deal with cases involving disputes that are referred by either the police or the Courts, and attempt to mediate by using trained independent mediators or those selected from a community panel. If successful, the prosecution is dropped.

A somewhat different variant on the same theme is illustrated by the adoption of *Community Reparative Boards* in the State of Vermont in the United States.[23] These have been used in the main for offenders who are convicted of non-violent and minor offences after they have been convicted and sentenced by the Court to participate in the process. The Community Reparation Board itself is composed of a small group of citizens who have been intensively trained for the purpose. Their role is to conduct public, face-to-face meetings with offenders, during which they discuss the nature of the offence and its negative consequences.

The members of the board then develop a set of proposed sanctions, which they discuss with the offender until they agree on a set of reparative measures which the offender is to undertake within a given time period. The primary emphasis is placed on encouraging offenders to learn ways of avoiding re-offending. The offender's progress in discharging these undertakings is monitored, and after the period (90 days) has elapsed, the board submits a report to the

Court indicating the extent to which the offender has complied with the sanctions.

Children's Hearing Panels in Scotland share with mediation and conferencing processes a procedure founded on informal and inclusive discussion involving the child and the family. However, attendance is compulsory and the victim is not included. There is no obligation on the panel to facilitate or encourage the production of restorative outcomes. Although the procedure does have some restorative "potential", it would require major modification of the process for this to be realised, which in turn would necessitate legislative reform.

Staying in the UK, a Home Office White Paper in 1997 spoke of the need "*to reshape the criminal justice system in England and Wales to produce more constructive outcomes with young offenders*".[24] It proposed the setting up of a "*Youth Panel Scheme*", which would build on the three key Restorative Justice principles: restoration, re-integration and responsibility. First-time and less-serious offenders who plead guilty will be referred to a new, non-criminal, "Youth Panel" for a specified period (not less than three months or more than 12 months[25]) by way of disposal. This panel would seek to involve the offender and others (including the offender's family, the victim, provided they consent, and youth justice workers) in drawing up an agreed "contract". This would seek to achieve reparation for either the victim or community and also rehabilitation and support for the offender (which should assist with the aim of re-integration). Moreover, once the contract had been successfully completed and "signed off" by the Youth Court, the original conviction would be regarded as spent for the purposes of the Rehabilitation of Offenders Act.[26]

The Youth Justice and Criminal Evidence Bill, which was introduced in the House of Lords on 3 December 1998, seeks to implement these proposals. Under Clause 6 of the Bill, the responsibility for establishing a Youth Offender Panel (and also for supervising the offender's compliance with any agreement reached) would rest with the Youth Offending Teams introduced under the Crime and Disorder Act, 1998.

Although the primary purpose of any agreement reached with the offender is said[27] to be the "prevention of re-offending by the offender", restorative outcomes feature prominently (though not exclusively) in the terms of the programmes specified in the Bill. They include financial or other reparation to a (direct or indirect) victim, attendance at a mediation session and unpaid work for the community. The Bill rules out the imposition of physical restrictions on the offender's movements,[28] including monitoring (whether electronically or otherwise) their whereabouts. The Bill also specifically prohibits the imposition of any other sanctions.[29] As such, these latest proposals represent a much more radical set of reforms to the English criminal justice system than those contained in the Crime and Disorder Act, 1998. Indeed, they could encourage the development of a New Zealand style conferencing procedure, but do not require it. Alternatively, they could come to function more along the lines of the Scottish Children's Hearing system, but with a restorative focus.

Victim Offender Mediation

Mediation has a long tradition in many countries around the world. However, Victim Offender Mediation (VOM) as most widely used today originated in Elmira, Ontario, in 1974, under the influence of the Christian Mennonite movement.[30] The primary emphasis is on the quest for "reconciliation" between victims and offenders. Thus the disputants themselves are central to the process.

Victim Offender Mediation involves a process of dialogue between victims and offenders relating to the offence. It provides a safe and structured setting for any meeting between the parties, in the presence of a trained mediator. It offers victims the chance to tell offenders about the physical, emotional and financial impact that their offence may have caused, and gives them an opportunity to put unanswered questions to the offender. It also enables them to participate in discussions about what may be required of the offender in order to make amends, and may help victims psychologically to bring about a "closure" of the incident, enabling them to put the matter behind them. It requires offenders to face up to the reality of what they have done, but also offers them the opportunity to begin to restore their own reputations and sense of self-worth.

Mediation may be direct ("face-to-face") or indirect (where the mediator acts as a "go-between"). The direct approach is more common in North America while the indirect approach is more common in Britain where it is frequently included in "cautioning plus" schemes (mostly aimed at juveniles). Pre-court schemes generally involve police cautioning. Court-based schemes operate either by way of adjournment or deferment. Some schemes operate post-sentence, including the period prior to an offender being released from custody.

Victim/offender mediation services are not operated formally in New Zealand. It is an inherent part of Family Group Conference processes, and a good number of police diversion schemes use a type of victim/offender mediation as part of police diversion from Court and from FGC. In New Zealand, FGC is held back as a high level intervention and every effort is made to try to use police diversion across a number of headings as a lower level option to avoid flooding the FGC process.

In the adult system, in New Zealand, a number of groups are popping up all around the country as adult restorative justice movements grow stronger and these groups are offering themselves as possibilities for diversion from the adult criminal court. Often, too, after admission of guilt, the judges in Adult Courts are now beginning to seek a restorative justice community conference and take the recommendations into account as part of sentencing.

In 1998, Umbreit[31] estimated that Victim Offender Mediation services operated in more than 290 communities in the United States, with a similar number operating in Germany, 130 in Finland, 54 in Norway, 40 in France and 26 in Canada. There were 20 in England, 8 in Belgium, 5 in Australia, 2 in Scotland and 1 in South Africa. The first youth-targeted victim-offender mediation took place in Russia in October 1998 and VOM has recently been introduced into China.

Clearly, the use of VOM has continued to expand since Umbreit's survey three years ago.

Integrating Restorative Justice into the System

When we come to consider the extent to which Restorative Justice has been integrated into the system we find, once again, that there are a range of models.

Subsidiary Model

Programmes can operate in a subsidiary role to "plug the gaps" in the current system. One of the main shortcomings of the retributive criminal justice system is its failure to adequately acknowledge the personal harm experienced by victims. Court-ordered compensation by the offender to the victim attempts to redress that failing, while Community Service Orders attempt to redress the debt to the community. However, there is no attempt, in either case, to repair any relationships that might have been damaged as a result of an offence. In addition, neither victims nor offenders are greatly empowered by the award of compensation, since they are not involved in the decision-making process. We have already noted that these are coercive measures and one of the key attributes of Restorative Justice is that it is non-coercive.

Stand-Alone Model

Restorative Justice programmes can operate outside the existing criminal justice system in a supplementary capacity, rather than as an alternative to it. The defining characteristic of this "stand-alone" model is simply the absence of any statutory authorisation for the programme. On the whole, these tend to be experimental, pilot-type, projects hence there is a considerable degree of diversity. It is possible to find examples of all four of the Restorative Justice models outlined above operating as stand-alone programmes, including the majority of Victim Offender Mediation schemes, some Family Group Conferencing initiatives, Vermont-style Community Reparative Boards and also Sentencing Circles.

The criminal justice contexts within which they operate are also highly variable. Some are pre-trial initiatives, which might be either police-based or accessed by a prosecutor. Stand-alone police-based schemes include those which combine a traditional caution with the possibility of mediation and possibly reparation, which are often referred to as "caution plus". In some parts of Scotland, stand-alone mediation and reparation schemes receive referrals direct from the independent prosecutor, or Procurator Fiscal, provided both parties consent.[32] Most of the court-based victim offender mediation schemes also operate as stand-alone schemes, and some also accept referrals at the post-sentence stage.

Stand-alone Restorative Justice initiatives offer a number of benefits. This is particularly true during the experimental and developmental phases of a particular process or programme, when there may be an acute need to explore different forms of practice, and to test and refine those that have been developed within different criminal justice and institutional contexts. They can be used to extend boundaries beyond existing practice limits, particularly in relation to older, or more serious, offenders.

Partially Integrated Models

In some instances, programmes are partially integrated into the system.

In the Netherlands, the HALT programme (from the Dutch: **H**et **ALT**ernatief — the alternative) was originally developed in the 1980s for young offenders who committed acts of vandalism against the public transport undertaking in Rotterdam. The programme was designed to provide speedier, more effective action at a time when petty crime was rising, and the regular criminal justice system was felt to take too long, and to deliver ineffectual sanctions.[33] Police can refer offenders under the age of 18 to HALT programmes provided they admit guilt and consent to the referral, the offence is minor and they have not been dealt with in this way on two previous occasions. After consultation with both parties, the HALT co-ordinator tables a proposal, which entails work by the offender that is relevant to the offence and, if possible, benefits the victim, payment of damages and/or an educational component. Offenders are required to wear distinctive clothing while performing reparative tasks, which would appear to put the emphasis on stigmatic shaming which sits uneasily alongside claims to be a "restorative" approach.

Since its introduction, the HALT scheme has received official backing from both the Ministry of Justice, which now provides 50% of the cost, and local authorities, which fund the remaining expense. This has fuelled an expansion in the number of HALT schemes to 70, which are now available to half of the local authorities in the Netherlands. In the Hague, one-third of all young offenders — around 700 per year — are referred to the scheme. About 95% of HALT programmes are successfully completed; unsuccessful cases are referred back to the police for prosecution. 40% of HALT participants are said to re-offend, compared with 80% of those who are prosecuted.[34]

Despite these apparent successes, the scope of the HALT programme is still relatively restricted — both in terms of the offence types, and offender categories for which it caters, and also in the sense that its coverage is by no means universal. Moreover, critics have suggested[35] that reactive measures such as HALT may be an inferior substitute for primary crime preventive measures (such as teaching children how to deal with conflict resolution in schools).

The STEP Programme: Northern Ireland

The aim of the RUC's STEP programme is crime prevention — providing socially disadvantaged young people, at the beginning of an offending career, with a pathway from criminality to that of being responsible members of the community. While the police service is the lead agency, a key strength of STEP is its multi-agency approach. A strong partnership has been formed with local Colleges of Education, The Probation Board, the Training and Employment Agency and the Youth Service.

STEP's target group is young people who are unemployed, socially disadvantaged and at the beginning of an offending career. The programme consists of ten weeks of challenging interventions designed to tackle issues of offending behaviour and equip the individual with skills which will move them towards employment.

Initially this project was aimed at young people over 16. However it soon became apparent that more success might be achieved with 14-16 year old offenders. In running this project, the RUC in Northern Ireland entered into a Transnational Partnership with Stockholm (Sweden), Rotterdam (Holland — the HALT project) and Fucecchio (Italy), all of whom were running similar projects. The partnership allowed the exchange of information and facilitated research and the development of new methods of intervention. Initial indications are that the scheme has been an outstanding success.

Penal Mediation: France

In common with a number of other European countries, France has introduced a system of "Penal Mediation" in recent years.[36] Under the Law of 4 January 1993, the State Prosecutor now has the discretion to refer offenders who are under the age of 18 to mediation, as an alternative to prosecution. The practice of penal mediation is encouraged by the Ministry of Justice and by associations for the assistance of victims. As a result, recourse to the measure is increasing steadily, though mainly in respect of minor offences, committed by first-time offenders.

Victims' interests appear to be reasonably adequately safeguarded since they not only have to consent, in order for mediation to proceed, but may also seek reparation from the offender before a judge if dissatisfied with the outcome of the mediation process. However, concerns have been expressed[37] about the extent to which the offender's interests are safeguarded under the penal mediation procedure. Offenders do have a formal choice whether to take part in mediation or not, but since they are likely to be informed that the alternative is prosecution, most of them do agree. If the mediation is successfully concluded, the prosecutor terminates the prosecution. If the mediation is unsuccessful and the prosecutor refers the matter to court, however, the offender's position is seriously disadvantaged since guilt is now assumed. Moreover, the offender may be more likely to be convicted for a relatively minor offence that possibly might not have been prosecuted before penal mediation was introduced in 1993.

Thus, even where Victim Offender Mediation is given legislative backing, care still needs to be taken to ensure, firstly, that the practice is not marginalised by excessively restricting its application; and secondly, that an appropriate balance is achieved between the various sets of interests that are in play.

Reparation: New Zealand

The New Zealand Criminal Justice Act, 1985, enabled Reparation as a victim-focused sentencing option in its own right.[38] Initially it applied only to property offences. This was extended in 1987 to cover cases in which victims had suffered emotional harm, and again in 1993 to enable Courts to take account of any offer of reparation made by an offender, when imposing any sentence. The measure was intended to provide opportunities for victims and offenders to negotiate the amount of reparation payable and it has been used by some probation officers to construct victim/offender mediation. It was also intended to make offenders more accountable for what they had done. Reparation orders for payment for both property loss and for emotional harm are widely used as formal orders in the adult system and it is increasingly common to see adult restorative justice conferences held. The challenge that awaits the adult court is to see those more particularly embedded in the mainstream of the adult criminal system.

In the Youth Court, FGCs operate as a matter of course. One of the formal orders which the Youth Court can make is a reparation order requiring the formal pay back of money following a Family Group Conference.

Reparation Order: England and Wales

In England and Wales, the Crime and Disorder Act of 1998 introduced the Reparation Order as part of its youth justice reform package, though the measure is only due to be implemented nationally after it has been piloted in four sets of geographical locations. There are a number of differences between the English legislation and that in New Zealand.

First, the Reparation Order is restricted to offenders between the ages of 10 and 18. Second, the English legislation introduces a presumption in favour of such orders, and reasons will need to be given for not imposing one in cases where the Court has power to do so. However, a Reparation Order cannot be combined with a custodial sentence, a Community Service (or Combination) Order, a Supervision Order with requirements or the new Action Plan Order, which is also introduced as part of the same Act. Third, the English legislation enables courts to impose reparation "in kind" rather than financial. Fourth, the Courts will be able to order offenders to make reparation either to the victim or the community, though the victim's consent will need to be obtained before reparation can be awarded in favour of an individual. Victim Offender Mediation is encouraged but is not compulsory.

The English legislation assigns responsibility to the new local multi-agency "Youth Offending Teams" which local authorities will be obliged to establish once the Act comes fully into force. Each team will consist of police and probation officers, together with staff from social services (juvenile justice staff), health and education services. In New Zealand responsibility is given to the probation service.

Concerns have been expressed[39] that the UK Act may not have done enough to prioritise support for a Restorative Justice approach in the face of continuing support — even within the Act itself — for more traditional retributive responses. Efforts to introduce restorative programmes continually run into opposition from a powerfully entrenched retributive criminal justice system.

Fully Integrated Model

The most effective way of securing Restorative Justice's undoubted potential is to adopt a fully integrated approach. By establishing Restorative Justice as a mainstream response that operates at the heart of the criminal justice system, it is much more likely that the problems of marginalisation and subordination, which are associated with stand-alone programmes or a partially integrated compromise approach, will be avoided. Even under a more fully integrated system of implementation, some implementational difficulties are likely to be experienced, but these are less likely to be "systemic" in nature than the problems that are associated with the other more restrictive implementational options.

No jurisdiction has, as yet, sought to fully integrate a Restorative Justice approach into its criminal justice system. New Zealand has come closest, by incorporating Family Group Conferencing at the heart of its youth justice system. Paradoxically, it was never intended to be a restorative justice system. It was intended to deal with the concerns of Maori and Pacific Islanders and with their exclusion from matters affecting their young people; it was intended to deal with victims' interests in a more effective way; and it was intended to call on the strengths of the community to replace institutions which were not meeting young people's needs. The new system was in fact planned and put into place before restorative justice was properly understood to be such a powerful driving force in these matters. It was New Zealand's good fortune that they had a legal system in place which supported Restorative Justice so beautifully. Chief Judge David Carruthers[40] points out that practice has in fact led the law in that regard in New Zealand, because the most successful models have been able to use the law and enhance Restorative Justice practices and processes without ever that being the full intention of the original legislation.

Several jurisdictions in Australia have also introduced legislation which seeks to incorporate such an approach into the justice system. They include South Australia, New South Wales and Queensland.

Scope of Restorative Justice Initiatives

There has been a tendency in many parts of the world to restrict the scope of Restorative Justice initiatives to minor offenders as opposed to more serious (or persistent) ones, and to juveniles rather than adult offenders. This tendency is one reason for their marginalisation.

The New Zealand experience argues strongly in favour of accepting the principle that Restorative Justice should not be confined to cases below a given level of seriousness, or to particular categories of offenders, whether on grounds of age or prior criminal experience. In

New Zealand, only the more serious cases are referred for conferencing. Indeed, all cases, even the most serious ones (with the exception of murder and manslaughter) are referred automatically.[41] Consequently, the top 20-30% of offences result in conferences. Chief Judge David Carruthers and Allen McRae, Youth Justice Co-ordinator in Wellington, believe that the most serious cases are the best cases for Restorative Justice conferencing. There is evidence also from North America and from Britain, which demonstrates that victim offender mediation can be used very successfully in respect of very serious offences.

"Points of Entry" for Restorative Justice Interventions

The New Zealand experience supports a "multiple entry level" model in which Restorative Justice interventions might, in principle, be available at all stages of the process from arrest to post-sentence.

Of 100% of offences caused by young people in New Zealand, between 80 and 85% will be diverted by Police Youth Aid using a variety of techniques ranging from simple warnings to formal cautions to visits to parents, to mini conferences, to meetings with victims and so forth. Dr Gabrielle Maxwell and Professor Alison Morris are currently researching police diversion, with a view to finding out what works and what does not. Their research should provide us with some very useful information.

Of the last 15 to 20%, half will go to Family Group Conferences by way of non-Court ordered FGCs — simple referral by police, accepted by the co-ordinator and the conferences held and finalised without Court involvement. This often involves extremely serious offending — aggravated robbery, rape, sexual violence and so forth, but if there is complete agreement and a fully accepted plan, which is monitored and concluded, the Court is not involved at all.

The 7 to 10% remaining will go to the Youth Court. They usually spring from arrests or from non-agreed conferences. Even now the Court must direct that a conference be held before it can exercise jurisdiction. Sometimes the Court is required to make decisions about custody in the meantime or bail terms etc.

Where the system works well there is a high police diversion rate, a high non-Court FGC rate (because that shows the agencies trust each other to work together and ensure successful outcomes) and a low number of children coming to Court. Before the legislation was introduced, approximately 12,000 young offenders were appearing before the Court each year. This dropped to 2,500 offenders in the year after the legislation was introduced.

How Effective is Restorative Justice?

Research to date shows a high level of participation amongst victims and offenders and a consensus that they are being dealt with fairly. Evaluations consistently report that a high proportion of cases result in an agreement being reached, in respect of the main Restorative Justice approaches. We noted above Judge Barry Stuart's experience in the Yukon where agreement is reached in 99% of cases. High levels of compliance — ranging between 70 to 100%[42] — are reported for agreements that involve the payment of compensation or performance of other types of reparation. There is evidence[43] that the compliance rate is higher for restitution obligations that are reached in the course of mediated agreements, than for those that are imposed by the Courts (81% and 58% respectively).

Restorative Justice evaluations also demonstrate that, for many victims, material reparation is less important than symbolic forms of reparation.[44] These include the tendering of an apology, a desire for information or the right to express feelings and even an opportunity to display civic responsibility (including a desire to "help" the offender, or reduce the likelihood of someone else being victimised in the same way).[45] Initial findings from the RISE Experiment[46] in Canberra show that victims whose cases were randomly assigned to police-led conferences were much more likely to receive an apology from their offenders than those whose cases were assigned to Court.[47]

Impact on Re-Offending

The research findings, with regard to the impact of Restorative Justice on offending, are inconclusive. But, before we dismiss this approach as ineffective, it is important to remember that, whichever model is used, it will have relatively limited impact when set against the kinds of factors that are known to be associated with offending behaviour.[48] Consequently, provided the recidivism rate for offenders is no worse, the high levels of satisfaction recorded by victims and others provide ample justification for continuing to promote Restorative Justice approaches.

Some studies suggest cautious grounds for optimism that, under the right conditions, Restorative Justice approaches could have preventive effects. Young people who participate in a Victim Offender Reconciliation Programme are significantly less likely to re-offend, and their reconvictions are less serious than those assigned to the normal criminal justice process.[49]

Family Group Conferences are more likely to be successful in reducing subsequent re-offending where they are memorable events, evoke remorse and lead young people to attempt to make amends for what they have done.[50]

Recent reports from New Zealand suggest that Family Group Conferencing can be very effective in reducing offending behaviour.[51] On 27 November 2000, Chief Judge David Carruthers reported:[52]

"We have recently celebrated outstanding successes in working this system in a highly professional way in the Wellington area. Youth offending has reduced by about two thirds over the last three years. One of the key factors in that reduction has been the use of the Family Group Conference processes to determine and identify patterns of offending and then using the same process to conference the community and government agencies to establish programmes and projects aimed at the preventions necessary which have been identified".

Careful Preparation and Training are Essential

Restorative Justice is resource intensive and is not going to be successful unless the resources are made available. It makes little sense to invest scarce resources in dealing with minor offences, which can be dealt with by way of police caution or the like. Family Group

Conferencing should be reserved for more serious offences, as is the case in New Zealand.

In Canada, Danny Graham[53] expresses concern that the capacity to do Restorative Justice programming has often been absent in Canadian communities because programmes have been under-funded and under-supported, particularly by governments. Many organisations have received funding to provide diversion programmes or alternative measures that have restorative components, but are not Restorative Justice in the full context of what is meant by the term. Some leading experts have expressed concern at the proliferation of programmes and projects organised by people who have little understanding of the philosophy and concepts underpinning Restorative Justice.

Chief Judge David Carruthers, New Zealand, says:

> "One of the concerns that I have is that the skills in running a Family Group Conference process properly have never been dissected, identified, and valued. There is a very great skill in all this. Part of this, of course, is in dealing with people so that the process itself at the meeting runs smoothly and well and is respectful of everybody who is there. The other part of the process which is equally important is the connections which the co-ordinator or facilitator makes with the community so that key people from the community are also invited and are able to support the family decisions by action, resources, and intervention. Getting the right people present seems to be a crucial matter and empowering the community to be involved in conferencing and to support a family decision-making also seems to be crucial".[54]

Procedural Safeguards

On the positive side, the models discussed above represent some of the most promising approaches for changing the nature of the sanctioning function in youth justice. On the negative side, the movement to devolve justice to the neighbourhood level is fraught with dangers ranging from concerns about "net-widening" (broadening the reach of the system to take in more offenders), to power imbalances for young offenders and adults in conferencing settings, to insensitivity to victims, to the "tyranny of community" in cases where community dynamics have resulted in a variety of abuses.

Clearly there is a need for procedural safeguards to protect the legitimate interests of both victims and offenders, and in order to secure the "balance" between their respective interests.

From the victim's point of view, one of the paramount requirements is the avoidance of further harm in the course of dealing with their offence (often referred to as "secondary victimisation"). Consequently, victims should be offered the chance to take part in whatever Restorative Justice processes might be made available, and they should be provided with sufficient unbiased information and guidance to enable them to reach an informed decision. However, they should on no account be coerced into taking part in the process.

The same principle also applies with respect to the decision-making process itself, particularly in relation to the more serious cases. Victims are entitled to make their views known if they wish to. They should not be made responsible in any way for the decision that is reached. The responsibility for the final decision, at least in serious cases, must ultimately rest with criminal justice personnel, not with victims. Indeed, the retention of an effective mechanism for providing judicial oversight of the process in such cases offers a valuable safeguard for victims, offenders and the wider community alike. It is unlikely that the cost of ensuring judicial oversight can be justified for less serious cases (those that are not initiated by the Courts themselves). Here, other forms of safeguards (which apply equally to offenders) may be more appropriate. They include the promulgation of good practice standards, appropriate and accredited training procedures and effective complaints procedures in case of grievances.

From the offender's point of view, there is a need for effective safeguards to guard against wrongful conviction and also excessive punishment. Consequently, offenders should always have recourse to a judicial hearing if they do not admit the charges brought against them. In principle, it is highly desirable that offenders' participation in any Restorative Justice processes should be based on *their* informed consent. However, it is also reasonable to expect them to accept responsibility for acts which they admit to, and for making reasonable amends to those who have been harmed by them. Ultimately, if they are unwilling to do this voluntarily, the victim's right to justice demands that the normal judicial process will take effect and so, to that extent, an offender's freedom of choice will inevitably be subject to constraint. Because of the element of indirect coercion that may be involved, and also the risk that offenders may agree to assume undertakings that are excessive in relation to the harm caused, other safeguards may also be advisable. One possibility is for legal advice to be made available for offenders before they agree to take part in a conference. Another possibility is for a legal adviser to be on hand to offer advice in relation to the final outcome. However, there are genuine concerns over the part that lawyers might play if given unrestricted "rights of audience" within conferences, particularly if these were used to convert them into a more adversarial (and thus less appropriate) form of procedure.

The issue of standards and safeguards is important, whatever mechanisms and procedures are adopted for the delivery of Restorative Justice interventions. This is particularly important where these interventions are intended to operate as alternatives to existing criminal justice procedures since, whatever their other imperfections might be, these do normally incorporate judicial safeguards to protect individual rights. In order to ensure adequate protection for the legitimate interests of all the parties, therefore, and also to maintain public confidence in Restorative Justice programmes, it is strongly advisable to devise, promote and enforce a comprehensive set of practice standards that will seek to secure the integrity of all such programmes.

Who should Draft Such a Set of Practice Standards?

Shortly after the 9th UN Crime Congress in 1995, the NGO Alliance on Crime Prevention and Criminal Justice (NY) created a Working Party on Restorative Justice. The Working Party was made up of interested NGOs in consultative status with the UN as well as other NGOs and individuals who had practical, research or academic expertise in the subject.

The Working Party prepared a draft document entitled "Preliminary Draft Elements of a Declaration of Basic Principles" for consideration by the 10th Crime Congress in April 2000.[55]

Why "Basic Principles" and not "Standard Minimum Rules"?

The UN has issued a number of standards and norms related to many aspects of criminal justice. Sometimes these are done in the form of basic principles, sometimes as standards and norms, and sometimes in the form of conventions or treaties.

One of the administrative and practical concerns for the UN in adopting any standards is that they can lead to requests for UN technical support to implement the standards. This is a logical concern: how can the UN propose standards it expects countries to follow without providing the resources to do so, particularly in relation to developing countries? The UN has limited funds, and if it is to establish standards and expect countries to meet those standards, it should have sufficient funds to help them do so. If it does not, it should not adopt the standards in the first place. This is one reason why the Basic Principles were written as *principles* and not as *standard minimum rules*. They are designed to give guidance, not to impose rules or standards on countries.Perhaps more importantly, unlike other topics the UN has addressed before, no country is required to use Restorative Justice programmes. Consequently the UN would not be imposing a burden on countries, since they are not obliged to implement Restorative Justice. Every country has prisoners, victims, law enforcement officials, juveniles, courts, and so forth. The UN standards that have been adopted on those topics automatically apply to every country. But not every country will choose to use restorative processes, so the development of guidelines for those countries that do will not impose a burden on those who do not. What the Basic Principles do is permit countries that are considering implementing Restorative Justice to draw from the experience and wisdom of other countries, so that they can establish them in ways that are most likely to be effective. In other words, they do what Basic Principles ought to do — give guidance.

UN Acts to Advance Restorative Justice

Representatives from nearly 200 governments assembled in Vienna from 10-17 April 2000 for a Congress on Crime Prevention and Treatment of Offenders. At the conclusion of the Congress, the delegates approved a summary resolution, known as the *Vienna Declaration*. This resolution included recognition of the growth of Restorative Justice programmes, and called on governments to increase their use of Restorative Justice interventions.

The Canadian and Italian governments called on the UN to distribute the draft set of Basic Principles prepared by the Working Party on Restorative Justice, to solicit comments from governments and others, and to convene a meeting of experts to review those comments and suggestions and propose modifications or alternatives to the UN's Commission on Crime Prevention and Criminal Justice.

The Commission met immediately after the Crime Congress, and on its first morning, 20 countries signed as co-sponsors to the Canadian-Italian resolution. After lengthy discussion on the wording, the Commission adopted the resolution and provided that the Secretary-General should report back at the 2002 Commission meeting on the progress. It referred the resolution to the Economic and Social Council (ECOSOC). The resolution was adopted by ECOSOC on 27 July 2000.

In September, the Centre for International Crime Prevention sent a letter to member states, intergovernmental organisations, NGOs in consultative status with the UN, and institutes of the UN asking for comments on the "desirability and means of establishing common principles on the use of Restorative Justice programmes in criminal matters" and on the contents of the draft elements of Basic Principles attached to the resolution. The deadline for replies was set at 1 March 2001.

It was agreed that, if the Centre received replies from fewer than 30 nations, that this would be taken as an indication of insufficient interest and no further action on Basic Principles would take place. If the Secretariat received 30 or more replies, it would convene a meeting of experts to review the comments received, and to examine proposals for further action including development of Basic Principles on the Use of Restorative Justice. The experts meeting, hosted by Canada, was held in Ottawa in October 2001.

Overview of the Basic Principles

The draft declaration consists of two parts: a preliminary resolution and the Basic Principles themselves, contained in the annex. The resolution refers to previous UN documents on the topic, showing that the annexed Basic Principles are consistent with a long progression of previous UN actions. The first section provides definitions of several terms used in the Basic Principles: Restorative Justice programme, restorative process, restorative outcome, parties and facilitator.

The second section covers the use of programmes and provides that:

1) they be generally available and voluntary;
2) they typically be used when facts are not contested;
3) the fact of participation by the offender should not be used as evidence of guilt if the matter goes to trial;
4) the process should be fair for both victims and offenders;
5) all the parties should be protected against threats and intimidation; and, finally,
6) when the restorative process cannot be used, the offender should still be encouraged to assume responsibility for reparations, and both victim and offender should be aided in their re-integration into the community.

Section three covers the operation of these programmes, providing:

1) for the development of guidelines and standards;
2) for the protection of fundamental due process rights;
3) that the discussions in proceedings be kept confidential;

4) when a case has been discharged after an agreement is reached, there should be no new prosecution, but that when no agreement is reached, the matter should be returned to the referring authority (police, prosecutor or judge) for a decision about how to proceed;
5) the same approach should be used when the agreement is not kept.

Section four deals with facilitators. They should be:

1) drawn from the community as a whole;
2) familiar with local cultures and traditions;
3) impartial and fair in regard to the parties, affording them dignity and respect.
4) The facilitator is responsible to create an environment that is safe for each of the parties and the Basic Principles note that this is particularly important if any of the parties is particularly vulnerable.
5) facilitators should receive initial and on-going training.

The final section provides:

1) there should be regular consultation between those responsible for restorative programmes and officials in the criminal justice system;
2) that research into both the processes and the outcome of these programmes should be carried out; and
3) for continuing the development of new programmes.

Restorative Justice Has Come of Age

In this paper, I have outlined the phenomenal growth of Restorative Justice and demonstrated the need to establish common principles on its use. The philosophy and practice of Restorative Justice are now being discussed at the highest levels and worldwide. The UN has established the year 2002 as a date for states to review their practices in support of crime victims, "including mechanisms for mediation and Restorative Justice". Clearly, Restorative Justice has moved from the periphery to centrestage.

At the same time, it is clear that, in many countries, support in the justice community for moving toward more Restorative Justice, while strong, is qualified. The qualification relates to whether the theory and principle can be anchored in consistently sound working practice.

We can only hope that the drafting of Basic Principles by the UN will ensure that theory is anchored in consistently sound practice and that this will guarantee support within the justice community. If this happens, the quiet revolution which I mentioned at the beginning of this paper will indeed change the nature and very fabric of our work.

I would like to end with the words of Chief District Court Judge David Carruthers of New Zealand, which I think could be applied to Restorative Justice projects in general.

"At the present time we are full of hope and optimism, but it seems to me to be an important message from our experience to say that Family Group Conferences simply on their own, whilst useful, important, reconciling, and possessed of their own strength and dynamics, also need an enormous amount of preparation, work, and linking to the community to be fully effective."

REFERENCES

Allott, A. N. (1977). The People as Law Makers: Custom, Practice and Public Opinion as Sources of Law in Africa and England. 1 *Journal of African Law*, 21.

Audit Commission. (1996). *Misspent Youth: Young People and Crime.* Abingdon, Oxon: Audit Commission.

Auld, J., Gormally, B., McEvoy, K. & Ritchie, M. (1997). *Designing a System of Restorative Community Justice in Northern Ireland: A Discussion Document.* Published by the authors.

Bazemore, G. & Umbreit, M. (1998). *Conferences, Circles, Boards and Mediations: Restorative Justice and Citizen Involvement in the Response to Youth Crime.* University of Minnesota and Florida Atlantic University.

Braithwaite, J. (1989). *Crime, Shame and Reintegration.* Cambridge: Cambridge University Press.

Branken, N. & Batley, M. (1998). *Family Group Conferences: Putting the Wrong Right.* Pretoria: Inter-Ministerial Committee on Young People at Risk.

Cario, R. (1998) quoted in Dignan, J. (2000). *Restorative Justice Options for Northern Ireland: A Comparative Review.* London: HMSO.

Carruthers, D. (2000). Contribution to E-Corridor discussion on Restorative Justice, 27 November 2000.

Carruthers, D. (2001). Restorative Justice: Justice of the Future : A View from the Bench, keynote address to the International Conference on Restorative and Community Justice: Inspiring the Future, March 2001, Winchester, England.

Carruthers, D. (2001). Personal correspondence, May 2001.

Centre for Legal and Judicial Reform. (2000). Legal Principles of Reconciliation Programmes (Russian Context), Paper issued by the Centre for Legal and Judicial Reform, Moscow.

Dignan, J. (1999a). The Crime and Disorder Act and the Prospects for Restorative. *Justice Criminal Law Review*, 48-60.

Dignan, J. (2000). *Restorative Justice Options for Northern Ireland: A Comparative Review.* London: HMSO.

Dignan, J. & Cavadino, M. (1996). Towards a Framework for Conceptualising and Evaluating Models of Criminal Justice from a Victim's Perspective. *International Review of Victimology, 4*:153-82.

Dlamini, C. (1988). *The Role of Chiefs in the Administration of Justice.* Unpublished LLM thesis University of Pretoria.

Dooley, M. J. (1995). *Reparative Probation Programme.* Waterbury, Vermont: Vermont Department of Corrections.

Dooley, M. J. (1996). *Restoring Hope through Community Partnerships: The Real Deal in Crime Control.* Monograph. American Probation and Parole Association.

Goodes, T. (1995). *Victims and Family Conferences: Juvenile Justice in South Australia.* Adelaide: Family Conferencing Team.

Hayes, H. & Prenzler, T. with Wortley, R. (1998). *Making Amends: Final Evaluation of the Queensland Community Conferencing Pilot.* Brisbane: Centre for Crime Policy and Public Safety, School of Justice Administration, Griffith University.

Huculak, B. (2001). Oral presentation to the Restorative and Community Justice: Inspiring the Future International Conference, March 2001, Winchester, England.

Jervis, B. (1996). Developing Reparation Plans through Victim Offender Mediation by New Zealand Probation Officers. In B. Galaway and J. Hudson (eds.), *Restorative Justice: International Perspectives* (pp. 417 - 30). Monsey, New York: Criminal Justice Press.

Law Commission of Canada. Communities and the Challenge of Conflict: Perspective on Restorative Justice Video **www.lcc.gc.ca** <http://www.lcc.gc.ca>; Email: **info@lcc.gc.ca** <mailto:info@lcc.gc.ca>

Luna, E. (2000). *Reason and Emotion in Restorative Justice* (p. 3). Wellington: New Zealand Centre for Conflict Resolution.

Maksudov, R. (2000). Restorative Justice Programs in Russia: Challenges and Our Responses. A presentation to the Community Service and Restorative Justice Section of the 10th UN Congress on Crime Prevention and Working with Offenders.

Markiewicz, A. (1997). *Juvenile Justice Group Conferencing in Victoria: An Evaluation of a Pilot Programme*. Melbourne: Children, Young People and Families Research Unit, University of Melbourne.

Marsh, P. & Crow, G. (1998). *Family Group Conferences in Child Welfare*. Oxford: Blackwell.

Marshall, T. F. (1999). *Restorative Justice: An Overview*. London: HMSO.

Marshall, T. F. & Merry, S. (1990). *Crime and Accountability: Victim/Offender Mediation in Practice*. London: HMSO.

Maxwell, G. (1998b). Crossing Cultural Boundaries: The Experience of Family Group Conferences. Paper presented to conference session on Implementing Restorative Justice in the International Context, November 1998, Florida.

Maxwell, G. (1998c). Researching Offending. Paper presented at the International Youth Justice Conference on Youth Justice in Focus, October 1998, Wellington, New Zealand.

Maxwell, G. & Morris, A. (1996). Research on Family Group Conferences with Young Offenders in New Zealand. In J. Hudson *et al.*(eds.), *Family Group Conferences: Perspectives on Policy and Practice* (pp. 88 -110). Monsey, New York: Criminal Justice Press.

Mayhew, J. (1998). Mediation in Northern Ireland: An Overivew. *Mediation, 14(1)*, 1.

McDonald, J., Moore, D. B., O'Connell, T. & Thorsborne, M. (1995). *REAL JUSTICE Training Manual: Co-ordinating Family Group Conferences*. Pipersville, PA: Piper's Press.

McElrea, F. W. M. (1994). Restorative Justice — The New Zealand Youth Court: A Model for Development in Other Courts?, *Journal of Judicial Administration, 4(1)*, 34.

McElrea, F. W. M. (1996). The New Zealand Youth Court: A Model for Development in Other Courts? Paper for the National Conference of District Court Judges, 6-9 Apr 1994.

McElrea, F. W. M. (1996). The New Zealand Youth Court: A Model for Use with Adults? in B. Galaway and J. Hudson (eds.), *Restorative Justice: International Perspectives*. Monsey, New York: Criminal Justice Press.

McGold, P. (1998). Police-facilitated Restorative Conferencing: What the Data Show, Paper presented to the Second Annual Conference on Restorative Justice for Juveniles, November 1998, Fort Lauderdale, Florida.

McGold, P. & Wachtel, B. (1998). *Restorative Policing Experiment: The Bethlehem Pennsylvania Police Family Group Conferencing Project*. Pipersville, PA: Community Service Foundation.

Mesenas, M. (2001). Contribution to the e-Justice debate on Restorative Justice.

Mika, H. (1992). Mediation Interventions and Restorative Justice: Responding to the Astructural Bias. In H. Messmer and H.-U. Otto (eds.), *Restorative Justice on Trial: Pitfalls and Potentials of Victim-Offender Mediation — International Research Perspectives* (Chap. 40) Dordrecht: Kluwer.

Nugent, W. & Paddock, J. (1995). The Effect of Victim-Offender Mediation on Severity of Re-Offence. *Mediation Quarterly, 12(4)*, 353-67.

Pinnock, D., Skelton, A. & Shapiro, R. (1994). New Juvenile Justice Legislation for South Africa — Giving Children a Chance. 3 *SACJ* 338.

Shapland, J. (1992). Reparative Justice: Complexity and Apple Pie, Paper presented to the 3rd European Colloquium on Crime and Public Policy in Europe, Noordwijkerhout, The Netherlands.

Sherman, L. W. & Strang, H. (1997). The Right Kind of Shame for Crime Preventioin, Paper 1, RISE Working Paper, Law Program, RSSS, ANU, Canberra.

Sherman, L. W., Strang, H., Barnes, G., Braithwaite, J. & Inkpen, N. (1998). *Experiments in Restorative Policing: a Progress Report to the National Policy Research Unit on the Canberra Reintegrative Shaming Experiments (RISE)*. Canberra: Australian Federal Police and Australian National University.

Skelton, A. (1996). Developing a Juvenile Justice System for South Africa: International Instruments and Restorative Justice. In *Acta Juridica*. Juta, Cape Town.

Skelton, A. (1998). International Trends in the Re-emergence of Traditional Systems. In C. Petty and M. Brown (eds.), *Justice for Children: Challenges for Policy and Practice in Sub-Saharan Africa*. London.

Skelton, A. (1999). Juvenile Justice Reform: Children's Rights and Responsibilities Versus Crime Control. In C.J. Davel (ed.), *Children's Rights in a Transitional Society*. Pretoria: Protea House.

Skelton, A. (2000). *A Restorative Framework for Juvenile Justice Reform: Lessons from South Africa*. Paper delivered to the Conference on International Perspectives on Restorative Justice, 26-27 Oct 2000, Belfast.

South African Law Commission. (1999). *Discussion Paper: Community Dispute Resolution on Community Courts*. Pretoria.

Umbreit, M. (1998). Restorative Justice through Victim-Offender Mediation: A Multi-site Assessment, *Western Criminology Review*, 1(1). [Online]. Available: http://wcr.sonoma.edu/v1n1/umbreit.html

Umbreit, M. & Coates, R. (1993). Cross-site Analysis of Victim Offender Mediation in Four States. *Crime and Delinquency*, *39(4)*, 565-85.

Wundersitz, J. (1996). *The South Australian Juvenile Justice System: A Review of its Operation*. Adelaide: South Australian Juvenile Justice Advisory Committee, South Australia Attorney-General's Department.

Yong, P. H. (2000). Keynote address to the Youth Justice Conference 2000: Managing a New World in Transit, 13-15 Sep 2000, Singapore.

Young, P. (1997). *Crime and Criminal Justice in Scotland*. Edinburgh: The Stationary Office.

Young, W. & Morris, A. (1998). Reforming Criminal Justice: Reflecting on the Present and Imagining the Future. Inaugural lecture presented at the International Youth Conference, October 1998, New Zealand.

Zehr, H. (1985). *Retributive Justice: Restorative Justice*. Elkhart, Ind.: Mennonite Central Committee US, Office of Criminal Justice.

Zehr, H. (1990). *Changing Lenses: A New Focus for Criminal Justice*. Scottdale, Pa.: Herald Press.

ENDNOTES

1 Shapland, 1992: 2; Dignan and Cavadino, 1996.

2 McElrea, 1994.

3 1999a: 48.

4 Luna, Erik, 2000.

5 Private correspondence from His Honour Judge David Carruthers, Chief District Court Judge, New Zealand.

6 Young and Morris, 1998: 10.

7 Young and Morris, *op. cit.*

8 Dignan and Cavadino, 1996: 169.

9 1996.

10 Wundersitz, 1996.

11 Markiewicz, 1997.

12 Hayes and Prenzler, 1998.

13 McDonald *et al.*, 1995; McGold, 1998.

14 McGold, 1998.

15 Sherman *et al.*, 1998.

16 Five separate police departments, the best known of which is Bethlehem, Pennsylvania (McGold and Wachtel, 1998) (McGold, 1998: 2).

17 Involving the Royal Canadian Mounted police based in Regina.

18 At least three police forces including Thames Valley, Humberside and North Nottinghamshire.

19 National Agenda to Combat Juvenile Delinquency and Youth Crime, by Associate Professor Ho Peng Kee, Minister of State for Law and Home Affairs, Chairman, Inter-Ministry Committee on Youth Crime, a paper delivered at the conference Youth Justice 2000: Managing a New World in Transit, September 2000.

20 Law Commission of Canada Video.

21 Huculak, 2001.

22 Marshall, 1999: 15.

23 Dooley, 1995; 1996; Bazemore and Umbreit, 1998: 3.

24 At para. 9.21.

25 Clause 3(1)c.

26 paragraph 9.33.

27 Clause 8.

28 although a home curfew may be imposed.

29 Clause 4.

30 Howard Zehr, 1985; 1990.

31 1998: 9.

32 Young, 1997: 66.

33 Audit Commission, 1996: 47.

34 Audit Commission, 1996: 47.

35 Hauber, 1991.

36 Cario, 1998.

37 Cario, 1998.

38 Jervis, 1996: 417.

39 Dignan, 1999a: 53.

40 Private correspondence from His Honour Judge David Carruthers, Chief District Court Judge, New Zealand.

41 Maxwell, 1998b: 2.

42 Marshall, 1999: 18.

43 Umbreit and Coates, 1993.

44 Marshall and Merry, 1990; Cario, 1998.

45 Goodes, 1995.

46 Reintegrative Shaming Experiments (RISE) is described as the largest criminological experiment ever conducted in Australia and one of the largest in the world. For further information check **http://www.courts.sa.gov.au/courts/youth/index.html**

47 Sherman and Strang, 1997.

48 Wundersitz, 1996: 198; see also Hayes and Prenzler, 1998: 10.

49 Nugent and Paddock, 1995;Hayes and Prenzler, 1998: 10.

50 Maxwell, 1998c:7.

51 Carruthers, 2001.

52 Contribution to e-Corridor discussion on Restorative Justice, 27 Nov 2000.

53 Contribution to e-Corridor discussion on Restorative Justice.

54 Those of you who wish to get an idea of just how much preparation is required for a successful conference should watch the video "Facing the Demon" in which Sergeant Terry OConnell demonstrates that endless patience and perseverance are essential.

55 Crime Congresses are held once every five years.

DR McCARNEY has been a Lay Magistrate (a part-time, voluntary role) in Northern Ireland for the past 26 years. He sits in the Youth Court dealing with young offenders aged 10 to 17 years and in the Family Proceedings Court dealing with children in need of care and protection aged 0 to 17 years. He is a Justice of the Peace for the City of Belfast. He is also the President of the International Association of Youth and Family Judges and Magistrates.

CHAPTER 9

Community Intervention and Intermediate Sanctions with Juvenile Offenders: Perspectives and Practices in America

DAVID M. ALTSCHULER,[1] PH.D.

Introduction

This chapter discusses recent developments in American juvenile corrections with a particular focus on community intervention practices and their relationship to so-called intermediate sanctions. It should be noted that the term "community intervention" as used here is not synonymous with the term "community justice," at least as it is ordinarily used. *Community intervention* in a juvenile corrections context refers to what occurs 1) in neighbourhoods, 2) with families, friends, acquaintances, and various socialising institutions (e.g., schools, religious organisations, recreational programmes and clubs, employers), and 3) in connection with community-based groups, service providers and resources. The emphasis is on the direct involvement in the correctional effort of both a juvenile offender's social network and the applicable socialising institutions in the community (Altschuler, 1984). According to this definition, merely locating a correctional programme in a community setting is clearly not a community intervention. Similarly, it is possible to begin pursuing a community intervention strategy even when the correctional programme is not located directly in the specific community in which the juvenile resides or to which the juvenile will eventually return.

By contrast, the *community justice* movement of the last decade commonly refers to citizen involvement in crime control efforts and bringing informal justice processes into neighbourhoods (Barajas, 1995; Bazemore and Griffiths, 1997; Bazemore and Schiff, 1996; Griffiths and Hamilton, 1996). Depending on the commentator, community justice programmes can include victim-offender mediation and reconciliation, conflict resolution, family group conferencing, circle sentencing, reparative probation, restitution, community service, and victims services. Some commentators include community policing, neighbourhood courts, and community revitalisation (Barajas, 1995; NIJ, 1996a). Others include any effort in which justice decisions are handled by local communities or indigenous groups (NIJ, 1996b; Griffiths and Hamilton, 1996). Some of these community justice programmes would undoubtedly fit the definition of community intervention noted above, but it is arguably also evident that some of the identified community justice programmes do not conform to the definition.

Intermediate sanctions, in one form or another, have been around in America for quite some time. Included are sanctions such as electronic monitoring, house arrest, home detention, drug and alcohol testing, community tracking, intensive supervision, boot camps, split sentences, day treatment/reporting centres, community service and restitution. While some of the sanctions such as electronic monitoring (Baumer and Mendelsohn, 1992; Vaughn, 1991) and boot camps — also known as shock incarceration — (MacKenzie and Parent, 1992) came on board in the mid-80s and are of relatively recent vintage, intensive supervision programmes for adult offenders actually go back to the 1960s (Armstrong, 1991; Clear and Hardyman, 1990; Lurigio and Petersilia, 1992; Morris and Tonry, 1990). Intensive probation supervision (IPS) programmes for adult and juvenile offenders have been around the longest and are one of the most popular intermediate sanctions. The interest in correctional boot camps, that for a time was fever-pitch in America, has waned in both the juvenile and adult corrections systems (MacKenzie and Hebert, 1996; Cowles and Castellano, 1995; Thomas *et al.*, 1996). It should also be recognised that various intermediate sanctions are often combined in practice.

For example, intensive supervision may utilise some electronic monitoring and community service; community tracking programmes may incorporate drug and alcohol testing. Moreover, individual programmes can include both institution-bound juvenile offenders and those who are candidates for routine probation.

Intermediate sanctions, as well as community interventions that incorporate intermediate sanctions, are being used in America with juvenile offenders as alternatives to 1) institutionalisation, 2) routine probation, and 3) routine parole or aftercare.

Used as an alternative to institutionalisation, such intermediate sanctions are typically (though not exclusively) intended for non-violent, as well as chronic but still relatively less serious, delinquents who are considered "incarceration-bound." For the institution-bound class of offenders, the intent is generally to reserve limited and expensive bed space for others deemed more appropriate. Thus the strategy is one largely designed to address institutional crowding and save money — this is the classic intermediate sanctions as an institutional population control mechanism.

By contrast, intermediate sanctions in juvenile corrections are also used as an alternative to routine probation, where they are conceived as the means to provide greater accountability (punishment if you like), control (through more monitoring) and public safety (through deterrence, treatment, or both). For the probation-bound class of offenders, the fundamental intent of intermediate sanctions is to get at least serious, if not tougher, with juvenile probationers than would ordinarily be possible through routine probation.

In a similar vein, the very same intermediate sanctions are increasingly being used as an alternative to traditional juvenile parole and aftercare (the terms "parole" and "aftercare" are used interchangeably), when it is believed to be necessary to offer more accountability, control and public safety than that routinely available through standard parole.

Juvenile repeat offenders who have committed serious and even violent offences, as well as those at risk of committing such offences, are in fact, represented to various degrees among those who receive intermediate-type sanctions. Juveniles on probation, incarcerated and on parole display wide variation in terms of the extent and nature of both their criminal record and their risk of recidivism. This chapter is intended to clarify how and in what ways the goals of intermediate sanction and community intervention programmes relate to one another, what types of juvenile offenders are potentially best suited for the different sanctions, and what are some of the major issues that must be addressed from the standpoint of programme design, management, practice and evaluation.

Goals and Programme Purposes

Indications are that intermediate sanction programmes in America that meet the definition of community intervention as described above, are in the minority. Byrne and Pattavina (1992) reviewed the basic findings about recidivism, cost effectiveness and diversionary impact from 18 evaluations of intermediate sanction programmes for adult offenders as of 1989. They found that the majority of the evaluations did not show intensive supervision significantly reducing the risk of offender recidivism. Speculating on why, Byrne and Pattavina suggested that the day-to-day emphasis of the programmes was more on offender surveillance and control (e.g., drug and alcohol testing, electronic monitoring, curfew checks, strict revocation policies) and less on treatment, services and community interventions related to substance abuse, employment, and family problems. That intensive supervision did not generally reduce recidivism in their review of 18 studies as well as most other studies (see, for example, Neithercutt and Gottfredson, 1973; Banks *et al.*, 1977; Byrne, Lurigio and Baird, 1989; Petersilia, 1987; Petersilia and Turner, 1990; Petersilia, Turner and Deschenes, 1992; Byrne and Kelly, 1989) prompted Byrne and Pattavina to suggest that perhaps surveillance and control *accompanied* by treatment and community intervention might make the difference.

The call for community intervention to accompany intensive supervision has many proponents, but it remains abundantly clear that in practice, most intermediate sanction programmes — even those for juveniles — are first and foremost, surveillance and control oriented. Even juvenile intensive probation programmes, which at least in theory, emerged from a model in which counselling and rehabilitation are at least on an equal footing with control and punishment, succumb to surveillance-oriented intermediate sanctions (Armstrong, 1991). In a 1986 survey of 157 juvenile probation departments throughout the United States, more than one-third reported providing a juvenile intensive probation supervision (JIPS) component, and of those with JIPS, 78% stated their primary goal was intensifying the level of surveillance (Armstrong, 1988). This is hardly surprising and is consistent with Byrne, Lurigio and Baird's (1989) observation that "IPS is quite compatible with broad changes in correctional policies that emphasise community protection over offender rehabilitation" (p. 8). Lurigio and Petersilia (1992: 9,10) summed it up by acknowledging that most IPS models advocate control and that "in essence, IPS has become a way for probation administration to combat long-standing negative perceptions, to restore public and judicial confidence in probation as a meaningful and 'tough' sentence, and to 'revitalise' probation, establishing it again as a powerful cog in the machinery of justice." (Clear and Hardyman, 1990: 47)

Reductions in Risk to Public Safety

One might reasonably wonder how compatible goals associated with intermediate sanctions and community intervention are, as defined above? After all, punishment and treatment goals have been traditionally pitted against each other and viewed as inconsistent. The paradox is that high-risk offenders in particular tend to exhibit a high level of need that requires treatment and community intervention in order to reduce risk of re-offending. Stated simply, punishment or surveillance, in the absence of treatment and community intervention, is unlikely to reduce risk. For example, Lipsey and Derzon (1998), as well as Hawkins *et al.* (1998), have shown that risk and protective factors associated with serious and violent juvenile (SVJ) offenders include much more than criminal history characteristics (e.g., early age of onset, number of prior referrals to juvenile services, number of prior commitments to juvenile facilities) alone. Rather, it is the combination of justice system contact factors and particular problem/need factors — so-called criminogenic (Andrews and Bonta, 1994) or instability factors (Krisberg *et al.*, 1989) — that cumulatively place a juvenile into a "high risk" category. *It is not the presence of one factor but the potent combination of several that seems to make the difference.* Among the several risk/need factors that are commonly included in the potent combination are those involving family functioning, participation in school and/or work, nature of peer group, and drugs. It is precisely these factors that those community interventions are explicitly designed to address.

To the extent that intermediate sanctions are principally punishment and surveillance-oriented and do not incorporate community treatment, it is obvious that such sanctions are not intended to address, at least directly, the risk/need factors. Rather, the aim is "...that IPS — its case monitoring, coupled with threats of detection and subsequent incarceration — will influence the crime-related choices by individuals participating in the programme" (Lurigio and Petersilia, 1992: 9). But, the research to date on intermediate supervision strongly suggests that the predominantly surveillance-oriented intermediate sanctions that have been employed are, on the whole, not producing lower recidivism. This finding is certainly consistent with the view that when intermediate sanctions reflect the classic deterrence strategy, they are largely not succeeding. To be sure, as Lurigio and Petersilia (1992) remind us, the close supervision, increased probability of detection and swift revocation are regarded by some as an incentive for participants to be employed, go to school, attend counselling and perhaps be rehabilitated, but IPS is not counting on rehabilitation and treatment to ensure public safety and as already suggested, the surveillance orientation has generally edged out concerns over community treatment and rehabilitation.

Byrne and Pattavina (1992) have speculated that it is the combination of treatment, surveillance and control that can produce lower recidivism. As evidence for this, they point to the evaluation of the Massachusetts Intensive Probation Supervision programme (Byrne and Kelly, 1989), where surveillance (i.e., contacts) and more intensive treatment provision (i.e., changes in employment, substance abuse and marital/family problems) best predicted success. But the questions remain: Is it possible, in practice, to combine punishment with treatment and how might this be accomplished? On a practical basis, is it even possible to differentiate clearly between intermediate sanctions that serve punishment purposes and those that are predominantly treatment oriented? Clear (1991) proposes an interesting test to differentiate intermediate sanctions on the basis of their punishment and treatment orientation:

> ...even if we knew beforehand that restitution (or community service, for that matter) would not change a particular juvenile's attitude, we would still impose the intervention. The reasoning would be something like this: "Just because the kid's attitude is bad doesn't mean that he can avoid paying back the victim or the community. He has to pay that price because his actions deserve it." The underlying rationale is clearly punitive, although we are pleased that in many instances the imposition of such punishment seems to have a remarkably ameliorative effect on juvenile attitudes. *Yet even without the ameliorative effect, we would feel justified in imposing these sanctions because they demonstrate the unacceptableness of the behaviour* (p. 39, emphasis added).

In contrast, it is hard to imagine that community intervention and various rehabilitation components, such as family therapy, job placement, educational remediation, drug counselling, anger management, conflict resolution and social skills training, would be imposed only because some delinquent action warranted them; rather, a positive rehabilitative outcome is quite explicitly being sought.

The point is that punitive interventions and intermediate sanctions *need not* demonstrate an ameliorative effect in order to justify their use, but treatment and rehabilitation *are expected* to demonstrate success in order to justify their use. The result is that it is common for punishment to be accepted for punishment's sake and it requires neither further justification nor an independent demonstration of success while community treatment is held to an entirely different standard. Intermediate sanctions are viewed by some as appropriate "justice" precisely because the sanction is regarded as tough and demanding; any other purpose such as rehabilitation and community treatment only serves to dilute and undermine the intent of intermediate sanctions. Is it therefore realistic to expect that intermediate sanctions can in practice be combined with community interventions? Is it reasonable to think that intermediate sanctions can incorporate community interventions without the former dominating and thereby undercutting the value of the latter?

Promising Types of Interventions

Research suggests that the answer is a very *qualified* yes. As already noted, Lipsey and Derzon (1998), as well as Hawkins *et al.* (1998), found that SVJ offenders, as a group, tend to exhibit a variety of risk factors that when accumulated over time, produced an increased likelihood for anti-social and offending behaviour. The four domains that seem to consistently emerge include family, peers, school and community, which collectively constitute the focal point of community intervention. While it is obviously critical to know the domains that require attention and intervention, more specific information is still required in order to understand what kind of strategy and programmes are most likely to reduce individual offending and protect the public.

Meta-analysis conducted by Lipsey and Wilson (1998) is instructive in this regard because it points to certain types of treatment that show promise in lowering recidivism *when compared* to customary or more traditional and routine forms of sanctioning. Most notable among those types of interventions for *non-institutionalised* juveniles that produced the greatest reduction in recidivism was the grouping of evaluated programmes that included interpersonal skill training (Chandler, 1973; Delinquency Research Group, 1986), behavioural contracting (Barton *et al.*, 1985; Gordon *et al.*, 1987; Jesness *et al.*, 1975; Kantrowitz, 1980; Schwitzgebel and Kolb, 1964), and individualised counselling that is cognitive-behavioural oriented (Bean, 1988; Borduin *et al.*, 1990; Kemp and Lee, 1975; Lee and Haynes, 1978; Lee and Haynes, 1978a; Lee and Olejnik, 1981; Moore, 1987; Moore and Levine, 1974; Piercy and Lee, 1976). It is the non-institutional community treatment settings where enhanced probation, intensive aftercare and institution diversion cases are likely to be found and thus it is Lipsey and Wilson's non-institutional category that initially seems most relevant for providing guidance on an appropriate intermediate sanctioning strategy. These three types of treatment can be regarded as intermediate sanctions in that they clearly are more demanding than routine probation and standard aftercare.

Common to the types of treatment that displayed the most positive results was their highly structured and focused emphasis around the development of basic social skills, behaviour-specific management through contingency contracting, and individual counselling in which conduct, attitudes and perceptions are confronted and addressed in an ongoing way. The treatments mostly involved highly trained staff (including some volunteers) who largely maintained a sharp focus on skills, conduct and attitudes relating to a variety of settings and influences, such as family, peers, school, work and community.

Regarding cautions and caveats, it should be emphasised that the evaluated programmes included in the Lipsey and Wilson meta-analysis represent only those programmatic efforts that meet certain methodological standards and consequently the programmes have likely been developed and implemented under relatively optimal circumstances with better than average treatment integrity. In fact, among the non-institutional programmes, the more successful programmes were those that involved the researcher in the design, planning and delivery of the treatment. These more successful programmes can thus be contrasted with many operational programmes in which the researcher is only involved in the evaluation. Thus, an important qualification is that the *quality and integrity of programme implementation, as well as the competence and quality of the staff, are necessary ingredients in effective programming*. This should serve as a caution in thinking that *any* programme claiming to provide the identified treatments can expect success.

Lipsey and Wilson (1998) also subjected to meta-analysis a variety of institutional programmes, but of course, these would not be directly applicable to intermediate sanctions related to enhanced probation and institutional diversion. Enhanced and intensive parole/aftercare is a distinct case, however, because the transition from the institution, as well as the connection of institutional services and culture to aftercare services and supervision, are all potentially important aspects of institutional life that may impact success in the community (Altschuler and Armstrong, 2001). Several of the more successful programmes included in Lipsey and Wilson's institutional meta-analysis focused to varying degrees on community re-entry. Moreover, and quite interesting, was the fact that among those types of treatments in institutional settings that produced the greatest reduction in recidivism was the grouping of evaluated programmes that included interpersonal skill training (Glick and Goldstein, 1987; Shivrattan, 1988; Spence and Marzillier, 1981), teaching family homes (Kirigin *et al.*, 1982; Wolf *et al.*, 1974), and cognitive behavioural approaches (Guerra and Slaby, 1990; Schlicter and Horan, 1981). As already noted, two of these types of treatment were also among those included in the most successful non-institutional programmes. Also included among the most successful type of institutional programmes were multimodal approaches (Grunhut, 1955; Kawaguchi, 1975; Moore, 1978; Seckel and Turner, 1985; Thambidurai, 1980), which were among the treatments offered by the second most effective group of non-institutional programmes.

The overlap of effective treatment types between the institutional and non-institutional programmes would suggest the *potential for stronger and more lasting recidivism reduction if effective institutional programmes were followed up with quality (non-institutional) aftercare programmes* (Altschuler, Armstrong and MacKenzie, 1999). The overlap of treatment types also suggests that from a treatment modality and programmatic standpoint, aftercare programmes and their staff have a sound basis for their being integrated into the institutional setting. The goal would be to establish direct continuity and reinforcement across the institutional and non-institutional settings. The outstanding research question that must be asked, however, is whether the types of treatment among those found most effective in either institutional or non-institutional programmes could be even *more effective and enduring* when linked to a full-fledged reintegrative-oriented intervention. It is research that answers this question that will directly address the value of transition and aftercare over and above what has been gained during confinement.

In short, at least some intermediate sanctions that also incorporate the types of community intervention efforts noted above, appear to hold promise. In order to satisfy the punishment, accountability and control objectives demanded by at least some segments of the American public, law enforcement, judiciary and legislators, certain intermediate sanctions will clearly not be jettisoned, and thus, a sensible direction to take is to explicitly (i.e., by programme design) incorporate highly promising community intervention efforts into intermediate sanction programmes. At the same time, intermediate sanctions in the absence of community interventions should be approached with great caution. One good example of why caution must be exercised is illustrated by what has been found through research in America on one of the intermediate sanctions — boot camps.

In an eight-state evaluation of adult shock incarceration programmes, MacKenzie and Souryal (1994: 30) concluded that "if success is measured in terms of recidivism alone, there is little evidence that the in-prison phase of boot camp programmes have been successful. Unfortunately, however, since individual level data were not available on supervision intensity in several of the sites and the comparison groups were not intensively supervised, it was not possible for the study to disentangle the effects of intensive community supervision from the in-prison boot camp phase. Still, the researchers point out, if the boot camp phase alone had an impact on participants, one would anticipate that they would have lower recidivism rates than their comparison groups, but this did not occur. In fact, in several of the sites the boot camp graduates did worse (i.e., had more technical revocations) than prison parolees.

MacKenzie and Souryal speculate that devoting a considerable amount of time to rehabilitation and treatment-oriented programming (e.g., education, employment, substance abuse, problem-solving/decision-making skills) followed up by intensive supervision and continued educational, employment and treatment opportunities, may explain why participants in particular programmes did better than comparison cases on at least some measures of recidivism. This lends further support to the notion that community intervention issues may be key. Boot camps without such community intervention may prove detrimental. This same lesson was learned in another evaluation that bears mention.

In an Office of Juvenile Justice and Delinquency Prevention-funded demonstration initiative, three juvenile boot camps were developed, implemented and evaluated using an experimental design (Thomas *et al.*, 1996; Peters *et al.*, 1996; Peters *et al.*, 1996a; Peterson, 1996). The boot camps were located in Cleveland, Ohio, Denver, Colorado and Mobile, Alabama and focused on adjudicated, non-violent offenders under the age of 18. The programmes were designed as highly structured, three-month residential programmes followed by six to nine months of community aftercare. All three programmes experienced considerable difficulty in their aftercare component, both in terms of the transition into aftercare from the boot camp and the linkage between aftercare operations and the local community. In none of the boot camps did graduates exhibit less recidivism than the control group and in one site, boot camp graduates did worse. The evaluation points to a number of implications for future boot camp projects, notable among them that more attention be paid *at the outset* to developing the aftercare and transition strategy and to anticipating likely problems and challenges related to procuring critically needed, high quality support services involving education, employment and counselling. Once again, attention is drawn to the critical role that community interventions can potentially play.

What type of offenders are included in these kinds of programmes? Intermediate sanction programmes designed principally as an institutional population reduction mechanism are intended for the *likely* institution-bound offenders, not customary probation cases. This is because of the intent of intermediate sanctions to alleviate institutional crowding while still providing a meaningful sanction. By contrast, intermediate sanction programmes designed principally as enhancements to probation generally want to target those customary probation cases for whom a tougher form of probation is desired. The problem is that while diverting facility-bound offenders can reduce overcrowding, this has been offset in many facilities by the revocation and incarceration of probationers who had not originally been candidates for incarceration but have amassed technical violations while on IPS. Many of the intermediate sanction programmes are being used for the "easier, less risky, or safe" type offenders (Austin and Krisberg, 1982; Clear and Byrne, 1992; Erwin, 1987; Pearson, 1988) and it is some of these very offenders that are having their probation revoked and being incarcerated strictly on the basis of committing technical violations, not new crimes.

Research has shown, however, that low-risk offenders subjected to intermediate sanctions such as intensive supervision tend to do worse than if supervised less intensively (Andrews, 1978; Baird, 1983; Clear 1988; Erwin and Bennett, 1987; Markley and Eisenberg, 1986), much of this is attributable to detected technical violations. This is especially alarming given the lack of evidence indicating that technical violations are predictive of future offending (Lurigio and Petersilia, 1992; Petersilia and Turner, 1991). As a result, intermediate sanctions emphasising electronic monitoring, drug testing and intensive supervision — some of the staples of surveillance-oriented intermediate sanctions — potentially constitute a terrible waste of resources when applied to lower-risk offenders who are unlikely to commit new crimes. It is particularly ironic that intensive supervision is contributing to facility overcrowding, since some of these very intermediate sanctions programmes were supposed to reduce overcrowding by diverting offenders from the facilities.

Part of the solution is to have 1) graduated sanctions as an alternative to revocation for technical violators and 2) graduated incentives to discourage involvement in technical violation behaviour before it starts (i.e., encourage compliance). Another part of the solution is to restrict the most intensive intermediate sanctions only to those offenders who are identified through an objective assessment process as being at the highest risk to public safety (Altschuler, 1999).

Intensive Aftercare

In many respects, intermediate sanctions pose similar challenges and opportunities for juvenile aftercare as they do for probation. In fact, innovation and experimentation in intensive aftercare — though still in its infancy — was substantially drawn from the earlier experiences and lessons of intermediate sanctions used with adults and juvenile probationers (Altschuler and Armstrong, 1991; Armstrong, 1991.) A number of recent studies specifically on intensive aftercare are instructive.

Rand conducted a four-year evaluation of two experimental intensive aftercare programmes, one in Michigan and the other in Pennsylvania (Greenwood *et al.*, 1993). In one of the programmes, the average age at first arrest was 14.4 and the participants averaged 2.5 prior arrests. Over half of the participants were known to be drug dealers, nearly half had a drug use problem and the current offence of just over half was a crime against persons. In the other programme, the average age of first arrest was 14 and the participants averaged 4.6 prior arrests and 3.7 adjudications. Their current offence was most frequently a property crime. The study found no difference between experimental and control groups in the proportion of youth arrested, self-reporting offences or drug use during a 12-month follow-up period. Equally important, compared to the controls, youth in the experimental programmes did not participate any more frequently in educational or work activities. Also, most of the families viewed delinquency as the youth's problem to deal with and were not interested in making major changes, and in neither of the two sites did the aftercare programme have a significant effect on the youth's associations with delinquent peers. In the one programme that did not use early release, there were no apparent cost savings in residential placement costs and the aftercare programme resulted in an overall increase in cost per placement. In the other programme, the reduced time in residential placement produced a slight reduction in total placement costs.

It could well be argued that not having impacted participation in school and work, family involvement, and delinquent peer associations, there is in fact very little reason to expect lowered recidivism. Stated differently, the community intervention was found lacking and inadequate. Specifically, Greenwood *et al.* (1993) concluded that a number of factors could explain what happened. These include: 1) aftercare workers provided only general support and assistance, rather than targeting specific problems that were contributing to risk, 2) aftercare workers devoted less attention to programming that addressed risk factors more directly related to delinquent behaviour, such as substance abuse treatment and anger management, 3) inappropriateness of a surveillance/casework model, particularly when faced with the kind of problems and temptations encountered by the youth in their home communities, and 4) the need for more formal methods of ongoing needs and progress assessments, including drug testing, reports by third parties, or tests of specific skills.

In another experimental design study, Sontheimer and Goodstein (1993) found that compared to traditional aftercare in Philadelphia, intensive aftercare reduced the average number of re-arrests, but not the percentage of subjects re-arrested. They concluded that although the programme did not turn youths away from their propensity to commit crime, it appears to have prevented youths in the community *from incurring multiple arrests.* The mean number of annualised re-arrests was less for the experimental group (1.65 versus 2.79), as was the mean number of felony arrests (0.41 versus 0.76). To be eligible for the programme, the incarcerated juveniles had to have at least one prior adjudication for aggravated assault, rape, involuntary deviate sexual intercourse, arson, robbery, or a felony-level narcotics offence, or at least two prior adjudications for burglary.

Sontheimer and Goodstein (1993) propose two models or mechanisms through which recidivistic behaviour might be reduced by intensive aftercare. There is the "aftercare effect" model, whereby close surveillance deters crime commission and rehabilitation prompts behavioural change. Collectively, according to Sontheimer and Goodstein, specific deterrence and rehabilitation would produce an actual change in the propensity to commit crime and this aftercare effect would be apparent in a lower percentage of subjects re-arrested. In contrast, the "system response" effect model does not assume reduced propensity to criminality, but rather an officer's quick response (e.g., house arrest, court review) to a violation or relapse would serve to reduce the number of offences a juvenile would have the opportunity to commit.

Though study data support a system response effect using the researchers' own decision rules, Sontheimer and Goodstein (1993) reject the idea that intensive aftercare officers merely revoke all intensive aftercare offenders after the first arrest subsequent to release and do away with service delivery. They believe that the reduced number of offences committed by the experimental group can be attributed to both the increased knowledge of each case gained by the supervising officer and the officers' ability to devote considerable attention to each case. The question remains, however, why the programme — much like the two programmes studied by Rand — did not reduce the propensity to re-offend?

One possibility can be gleaned from the finding that the average number of reported *contacts completed* fell substantially short of the minimum number mandated, leading the researchers to comment that this situation raised serious questions about programme implementation. In fact, the reason for the low contact rates was that during a two-month period the six-person intensive aftercare team experienced complete turnover, and as a result, many of the participants had no supervising officers for extended periods. Moreover, this astounding turnover problem and the difficulties likely to have both preceded and followed it, must have created enormous programmatic turmoil and confusion, including questionable commitment from staff, and at best, uneven staff training and accountability. In fact, aftercare staff reportedly received few guidelines about the philosophy or mission of the programme (Sontheimer and Goodstein, 1993: 204):

> The programme was not defined, for example, as emphasising a social control or rehabilitative perspective. No effort was made to articulate whether the emphasis of the programme would be on enhancing family ties and prosocial relationships, on facilitating educational or vocational growth, on increasing probationers' perceptions of accountability through surveillance, or on some other combination of principles assumed to reduce criminality.

Supervising officers were simply given the contact requirements and they followed a fairly traditional casework approach. Indeed, it is hard to imagine how the programme could not have faltered under such circumstances.

The experience in Philadelphia draws particular attention to the philosophical and programmatic thrust of the programme, the type of services provided, and the allegiance, commitment and orientation of staff. It is no wonder that recidivism has been so difficult to impact. Part of the problem is the tendency for intermediate sanction programmes to function much more as surveillance-enhancement than treatment-enhancement. It has also been shown that the traditional probation/parole casework model is not oriented toward the direct immersion into the community; that is, focusing on family, peer group, daily routine, and neighbourhood.

It has unfortunately not been uncommon for programmes that have attempted to transition juvenile offenders from various forms of residential placement into the community phase of aftercare to encounter difficulties in providing the very community interventions that are deemed so critical in breaking the cycle of recidivism. It is this fact that is often cited to explain why gains made in various residential programmes tend to dissipate. For example, a Rand study (Deschenes, Greenwood and Marshall, 1996) of a Michigan programme designed to test the impact of three months of wilderness challenge followed by nine months of intensive community-based aftercare, found that alternative programme participants only received formal substance abuse treatment during the residential phase and that compared to juveniles in traditional residential placements, apparently less family counselling took place in the alternative programme. Over time, moreover, families of youths in both the experimental and comparison groups showed a general decline in family functioning.

There also was a substantial problem encountered by the alternative programme in successfully retaining participants during the first 12 months (including residential and community phases). A staggering 60% of youths in the alternative programme were either transferred or placed in another custodial programme during the first year and an additional 10% were re-arrested during the second 12 months of the total 24-month study period. By contrast, the traditional residential programme participants that comprised the comparison group exhibited a 16% unsuccessful completion rate (where length of stay averaged 15.5 months) and a 14% re-arrest rate during the remaining months in the 24-month study period. The Rand analysis suggests that the main weakness in the alternative programme was related to the community phase, which of course, is the ultimate test of any sanction or disposition. During that phase, the traditional residential programme participants were re-arrested at about the same rate. The researchers concluded that regardless of the intervention, youths who were released back into the same environment faced the same difficulties with re-adjusting to the community setting without relapse. They recommend strengthening the community intervention phase, particularly with reference to substance abuse treatment, family functioning, and targeting younger juveniles.

Conclusion

As has been shown, issues regarding the inadequacy of the service model and orientation of the programme along with the quality and fidelity of the implementation are never far removed from evaluations attempting to explain the "no difference on recidivism" finding. The research response has taken several distinct directions. More and more research are looking at the extent, nature and quality of the implementation, as well as the conceptual logic linking a programme's orientation with the desired outcome (Fagan, 1990). Some research is sorting out which type of offender is succeeding and under what circumstances in individual programmes (Palmer, 1992). Other researchers are using meta-analysis to see if patterns may be detected from looking at groups of studies that meet certain criteria and standards (see, for example, Lipsey and Wilson, 1998). Still others are employing cost-benefit analysis to understand more fully how one approach or method compares to another on a variety of possible impacts including multiple measures of recidivism; behavioural, psychological and cognitive changes; institutional population projections and crowding; and the public's perceptions about crime, safety and justice (Greenwood *et al.*, 1996).

It would be easy and a misreading of the evidence discussed in the chapter to conclude that it is not possible to craft an implementable intermediate sanction programme that 1) incorporates community intervention, 2) addresses directly the risk and protective factors, and 3) maintains surveillance and control over SVJ offenders who are high risk. It does require, however, heeding the lessons learned and insights gained from existing research, analysis and evaluation. Truly intervening with families, maintaining active participation in education and employment, keeping focus on the peer group, providing drug treatment (not just testing), incorporating various cognitive-behavioural and skill-oriented techniques, and handling all the transitions from facilities to community so as to facilitate information flow, consistency and transferability are crucial.

Also critical is having ready access to information on the extent and quality of day-to-day implementation as well as outcome. Some very basic questions concerning implementation, impact and costs associated with intermediate sanctions and community intervention remain unanswered. Future research needs to carefully examine these questions, which means that the research should be designed and initiated at the same time that the intervention programme is designed and initiated. As noted, existing research on intermediate sanctions strongly suggests that treatment availability *and* participation are associated with lower recidivism, but three problems in particular have compelled researchers to present a less than definitive response.

First, the lack of existing treatment and appropriate services in the community, the frequency with which offenders did not receive the prescribed treatment and services, the paucity of resources allocated specifically for community intervention, and the generally subordinate role treatment has played in intermediate sanctions have led to programmes exhibiting much less treatment than surveillance. The lack of treatment intensity has extended both to the percentage of offenders left untreated (Petersilia and Turner, 1993) and the generally low level of treatment provided to those who receive it (Petersilia, Turner and Deschenes, 1992). Future intermediate sanction programmes and research on them would benefit from having risk-based community intervention services playing a prominent role in philosophy, design and implementation. Such risk-based community intervention services need to be directed toward family, peers, school and/or work, and neighbourhood-based socialising institutions.

Second, the research on intermediate sanction programmes has generally suffered from too few participants, so that it becomes exceedingly difficult to generate any statistically significant differences in the analysis. Stated differently, in order to conclude that one group of offenders has performed better than another, differences are required in small-sample studies that exceed those one might reasonably expect to find. The solution is to launch a large enough effort so that a sufficient number of participants will be assured.

Finally, disentangling the effect of particular programme components can be crucial to determining the relative importance of different aspects of intermediate sanctions. The reviewed research was mostly designed to evaluate the effect, for example, of intermediate sanctions *to the extent* that they combined surveillance and community treatment, or boot camps *to the extent* they may have included transition and intensive aftercare. It would be useful for future efforts, for example, to test specifically and systematically the impact of differential levels of treatment and surveillance and the effect of boot camps with and without intensive aftercare. Random assignment to surveillance-oriented and community treatment-oriented intermediate sanctions or very different kinds of boot camps would represent a move in this direction. It would also be advisable to directly incorporate into future research and programme efforts those offenders who are first screened on the basis of risk and then placed randomly into either an experimental community intervention or a regular correctional programme. In addition, focusing specifically on strategies designed to prevent and respond to technical violations is another aspect that would benefit from research and programming.

On the matter of applicability of the American experience to Singapore and other countries, it must be emphasised that the lessons learned in the United States can best be used as a framework for considering options. These options relate to programme design and structure, management and staffing, implementation policies and procedures, and evaluation. Applicable to all cultures and nations is the fact that for offenders who re-enter communities, it is how well they function in the community that indicates the real impact and value of correctional sanctioning. It is community intervention, tailored appropriately to different settings, contexts and cultures, that addresses directly how well offenders function in the community, and thus it is community intervention that holds great promise in establishing a high level of public safety.

REFERENCES

Andrews, D.A. & Bonta, J. (1994). *The Psychology of Criminal Conduct*. Cincinnati, OH: Anderson Publishing Co.

Altschuler, D.M. (1984). Community Reintegration in Juvenile Offender Programming. In R. Mathias, P. DeMuro & R. Allinson (eds.), *Violent Juvenile Offenders: An Anthology* (pp. 365-76). San Francisco: National Council on Crime and Delinquency.

Altschuler, D.M. (1999). Issues and Challenges in the Community Supervision of Juvenile Offenders. *Southern Illinois University Law Journal*, *23*, 469-83.

Altschuler, D.M. & Armstrong, T.L. (2001). Reintegrating High-risk Juvenile Offenders into Communities: Experiences and prospects. *Corrections Management Quarterly*, *5(2)*, 72-88.

Altschuler, D.M. & Armstrong, T.L. (1991). Intensive Aftercare for the High-risk Juvenile Parolee: Issues and Approaches in Reintegration and Community Supervision. In T.L. Armstrong (ed.), *Intensive Interventions with High-risk Youths: Promising Approaches in Juvenile Probation and Parole* (pp. 45-84). Monsey, NY: Criminal Justice Press.

Altschuler, D.M., Armstrong, T.L. & MacKenzie, D.L. (1999). Reintegration, Supervised Release, and Intensive Aftercare. *Juvenile Justice Bulletin*. Washington, DC: Office of Juvenile Justice and Delinquency Prevention, US Department of Justice.

Andrews, D.A. (1978). Implications of Classification for Treatment of Juveniles. Paper presented at American Probation and Parole Association Meeting in Salt Lake City.

Armstrong, T.L. (1988). National Survey of Juvenile Intensive Probation Supervision, Part I. *Criminal Justice Abstracts*, *20(2)*, 342-48.

Armstrong, T.L. (1991). Introduction. In T.L. Armstrong (ed.), *Intensive Interventions with High-risk Youths: Promising Approaches in Juvenile Probation and Parole* (pp. 1-26). Monsey, NY: Criminal Justice Press.

Austin, J. & Krisberg, B. (1982). The Unmet Promise of Alternatives to Incarceration. *Crime & Delinquency*, *28(3)*, 274-409.

Baird, S.C. (1983). *Report on Intensive Supervision Programs in Probation and Parole*. Washington, DC: National Institute of Justice, US Department of Justice.

Banks, J., Porter, A.L., Rardin, R.L., Silver, T.R. & Unger, V.E. (1977). *Phase I Evaluation of Intensive Special Probation Projects*. Washington, DC: US Department of Justice.

Barajas, E., Jr. (1995). Moving toward Community Justice. *Topics in Community Corrections*. Washington, DC: National Institute of Corrections.

Barton, C., Alexander, J.F., Waldron, M., Turner, C.W. & Warburton, J. (1985). Generalizing Treatment Effects of Functional Family Therapy: Three Replications. *American Journal of Family Therapy, 13(3)*, 16-26.

Baumer, T.L. & Mendelsohn, R.I. (1992). Electronically Monitored Home Confinement: Does it Work? In J.M. Byrne, A.J. Lurigio & J. Petersilia (eds.), *Smart Sentencing: The Emergence of Intermediate Sanctions* (pp. 54-67). Newbury Park, CA: Sage Publications.

Bazemore, G. & Griffiths, C.T. (1997). Conferences, Circles, Boards, and Mediations: The "New Wave" of Community Justice Decision-making. *Federal Probation, 61(2)*, 25-37.

Bazemore, G. & Schiff, M. (1996). Community Justice/Restorative Justice: Prospects for a New Social Ecology for Community Corrections. *International Journal of Comparative and Applied Criminal Justice, 20(2)*, 311-34.

Bean, J.S. (1988). The Effect of Individualized Reality Therapy on the Recidivism Rates and Locus of Control Orientation of Male Juvenile Offenders (Doctoral dissertation, University of Mississippi, 1988). *Dissertation Abstracts International, 49(06)*, 2370B. University Microfilms No. 88-18138.

Borduin, C.M., Henggeler, S.W., Blaske, D.M. & Stein, R.J. (1990). Multisystemic Treatment of Adolescent Sexual Offenders. *International Journal of Offender Therapy and Comparative Criminology, 34*, 105-13.

Byrne, J.M. & Kelly, L. (1989). *Restructuring Probation as an Intermediate Sanction: An Evaluation of the Massachusetts Intensive Probation Supervision Program*. Unpublished final report to US National Institute of Justice.

Byrne, J.M., Lurigio, A.J. & Baird, S.C. (1989). *The Effectiveness of the New Intensive Supervision Programs* (Research in Corrections, No. 5). Washington, DC: US National Institute of Corrections.

Byrne, J.M. & Pattavina, A. (1992). The Effectiveness Issue: Assessing what Works in the Adult Community Corrections System. In J.M. Byrne, A.J. Lurigio & J. Petersilia (eds.), *Smart Sentencing: The Emergence of Intermediate Sanctions* (pp. 281-303). Newbury Park, CA: Sage Publications.

Chandler, M.J. (1973). Egocentrism and Antisocial Behavior: The Assessment and Training of Social Perspective-taking Skills. *Developmental Psychology, 9*, 326-33.

Clear, T. (March 1988). Statistical Prediction in Corrections. *Research in Corrections*. Washington, DC: National Institute of Corrections, US Department of Justice.

Clear, T.R. (1991). Juvenile Intensive Probation Supervision: Theory and Rationale. In T.L. Armstrong (ed.), *Intensive Interventions with High-risk Youths: Promising Approaches in Juvenile Probation and Parole* (pp. 29-44). Monsey, NY: Criminal Justice Press.

Clear, T.R. & Byrne, J.M. (1992). The Future of Intermediate Sanctions: Questions to Answer. In J.M. Byrne, A.J. Lurigio & J. Petersilia (eds.), *Smart*

Sentencing: The Emergence of Intermediate Sanctions (pp. 319-31). Newbury Park, CA: Sage Publications.

Clear, T.R. & Hardyman, P.L. (1990). The New Intensive Supervision Movement. *Crime & Delinquency*, *36(1)*, 42-60.

Cowles, E.L. & Castellano, T.C. (1995). *Boot Camp Drug Treatment and Aftercare Intervention: An Evaluation Review*. Washington, DC: US National Institute of Justice.

Delinquency Research Group. (1986). *An Evaluation of the Delinquency of Participants in the Youth at Risk Program*. Claremont, CA: Claremont Graduate School, Center for Applied Social Research.

Deschenes, E.P., Greenwood, P.W. & Marshall, G. (1996). *The Nokomis Challenge Program Evaluation*. Santa Monica, CA: Rand Corporation.

Erwin, B.S. (1987). New Dimensions in Probation: Georgia's Experience with Intensive Probation Supervision. *Research in Brief*. Washington, DC: US National Institute of Justice.

Erwin, B.S. & Bennett, L. (1987). New Dimensions in Probation: Georgia's Experience with Intensive Probation Supervision. *Research in Brief*. Washington, DC: National Institute of Justice, US Department of Justice.

Fagan, J.A. (1990). Treatment and Re-integration of Violent Juvenile Offenders: Experimental Results. *Justice Quarterly*, *7(2)*, 233-63.

Glick, B. & Goldstein, A.P. (1987). Aggression Replacement Training. *Journal of Counseling and Development*, *65*, 356-62.

Gordon, D.A., Graves, K. & Arbuthnot, J. (1987). *Prevention of Adult Criminal Behavior using Family Therapy for Disadvantaged Juvenile Delinquents*. Unpublished manuscript, Ohio University, Athens.

Greenwood, P.W., Deschenes, E.P. & Adams, J. (1993). *Chronic Juvenile Offenders: Final Results from the Skillman Aftercare Experiment*. Santa Monica, CA: Rand Corporation.

Greenwood, P.W., Model, K.E., Rydell, C.P. & Chiesa, J. (1996). *Diverting Children from a Life of Crime: Measuring Costs and Benefits*. Santa Monica, CA: Rand Corporation.

Griffiths, C.T. & Hamilton, R. (1996). Spiritual Renewal, Community Revitalization and Healing: Experience in Traditional Aboriginal Justice in Canada. *International Journal of Comparative and Applied Criminal Justice*, *20(2)*, 289-311.

Grunhut, M. (1955). Juvenile Delinquents under Punitive Detention: A Study of the First Hundred Campsfield House Boys. *British Journal of Delinquency*, *5*, 191-209.

Guerra, N.G. & Slaby, R.G. (1990). Cognitive Mediators of Aggression in Adolescent Offenders: 2. Intervention. *Developmental Psychology*, *26(2)*, 269-77.

Hawkins, J.D., Herrenkohl, T., Farrington, D.P., Brewer, D., Catalano, R.r. & Harachi, T.W. (1998). A Review of Predictors of Youth Violence. In R. Loeber & D.P. Farrington (eds.), *Serious and Violent Juvenile Offenders: Risk Factors and Successful Interventions* (pp. 106-46). Thousand Oaks, CA: Sage Publications, Inc.

Jesness, C.F., Allison, F.S., McCormic, P.M., Wedge, R.F. & Young, M.L. (1975). *Evaluation of the Effectiveness of Contigency Contracting with Delinquents*. Sacramento, CA: California Youth Authority.

Kantrowitz, R.E. (1980). Training Non-professionals to Work with Delinquents: Differential Impacts of Varying Training/supervisions/intervention Strategies (Doctoral dissertation, Michigan State University, 1980). *Dissertation Abstracts International*, *40(10)*, 5007B. University Microfilms No. 80-06139.

Kawaguchi, R.M. (1975). *Camp Fenner Canyon Evaluation: Final Report.* Los Angeles County Probation Department. (NCJRS Document Reproduction Service No. NCJ036121).

Kemp, M. & Lee, R. (1975). *Project Crest: A Third Year Experimental Study.* Gainesville, FL: Project Crest.

Kirigin, K.A., Braukmann, C.J., Atwater, J.D. & Worl, M.M. (1982). An Evaluation of Teaching Family (Achievement Place) Group Homes for Juvenile Offenders. *Journal of Applied Behavior Analysis*, *15(1)*, 1-16.

Krisberg, B., Rodriguez, O., Bakke, A., Neuenfeldt, D, & Steele, P. (1989). *Demonstration of Post-adjudication Non-residential Intensive Supervision Programs: Assessment Report.* San Francisco: National Council on Crime and Delinquency.

Lee, R. & Haynes, N.M. (1978). Counseling Delinquents: Dual Treatment Revisited. *Rehabilitation Counseling Bulletin*, *22*, 130-33.

Lee, R. & Haynes, N.M. (1978a). Counseling Juvenile Offenders: An Experimental Evaluation of Project Crest. *Community Mental Health Journal*, *14(4)*, 267-71.

Lee, R. & Olejnik, S. (1981). Professional Outreach Counseling can Help the Juvenile Probationer: A Two-year Follow-up Study. *Personnel and Guidance Journal*, *59*, 445-49.

Lincoln, S.B. (1976). Juvenile Referral and Recidivism. In R.M. Carter & M.W. Klein (eds.), *Evaluation and Empirical Data* (pp. 321-28). Englewood Cliffs, NJ: 61, 823-830.

Lipsey, M.W. & Derzon, J.H. (1998). Predictors of Violence or Serious Delinquency in Adolescence and Early Adulthood: A Synthesis of Longitudinal Research. In R. Loeber & D.P. Farrington (eds.), *Serious and Violent Juvenile Offenders: Risk Factors and Successful Interventions* (pp. 86-105). Thousand Oaks, CA: Sage Publications, Inc.

Lipsey, M.W. & Wilson, D.B. (1998). Effective Intervention for Serious Juvenile Offenders: A Synthesis of Research. In R. Loeber & D.P. Farrington (eds.), *Serious and Violent Juvenile Offenders: Risk Factors and Successful Interventions* (pp. 313-45). Thousand Oaks, CA: Sage Publications, Inc.

Lurigio, A.J. & Petersilia, J. (1992). The Emergence of Intensive Probation Supervision Programs in the United States. In J.M. Byrne, A.J. Lurigio & J. Petersilia (eds.), *Smart Sentencing: The Emergence of Intermediate Sanctions* (pp. 3-17). Newbury Park, CA: Sage Publications.

MacKenzie, D.L. & Hebert, E.E. (eds.). (1996). *Correctional Boot Camps: A Tough Intermediate Sanction.* Washington, DC: US National Institute of Justice.

MacKenzie, D.L. & Parent, D. (1992). Boot Camp Prisons for Young Offenders. In J.M. Byrne, A.J. Lurigio & J. Petersilia (eds.), *Smart Sentencing: The Emergence of Intermediate Sanctions* (pp. 103-19). Newbury Park, CA: Sage Publications.

MacKenzie, D.L. & Souryal, C. (1994). *Multisite Evaluation of Shock Incarceration.* Washington, DC: US National Institute of Justice.

Markley, G. & Eisenberg, M. (1986). *The Texas Board of Pardons and Parole Case Management System*. Austin, TX: Texas Board of Pardons and Paroles.

Moore, C.B. (1978). Ego Strength and Behavior: A Study of a Residential Treatment Program for Delinquent Girls (Doctoral dissertation, The California School of Professional Psychology, 1977). *Dissertation Abstracts International, 38(10)*, 5033B. (University Microfilms No. 78-02837).

Moore, R.H. (1987). Effectiveness of Citizen Volunteers Functioning as Counselors for High-risk Young Male Offenders. *Psychological Reports, 61*, 823-30.

Moore, R.H. & Levine, D. (1974). *Evaluation Research of a Community-based Probation Program*. Lincoln, NE: University of Nebraska at Lincoln, Department of Psychology.

Morris, N. & Tonry, M. (1990). *Between Prison and Probation: Intermediate Punishments in a Rational Sentencing System*. New York: Oxford University Press.

National Institute of Justice. (1996a). *National Symposium on Restorative Justice Proceedings*. Washington, DC: National Institute of Justice, US Department of Justice.

National Institute of Justice. (1996b). *Communities Mobilizing against Crime: Making Partnerships Work*. Washington, DC: National Institute of Justice, US Department of Justice.

Neithercutt, M.G. & Gottfredson, D.M. (1973). *Caseload Size Variation and Difference in Probation/parole Performance*. Pittsburgh, PA: National Center for Juvenile Justice.

Palmer, T. (1992). *The Re-emergence of Correctional Intervention*. Newbury Park, CA: Sage Publications.

Pearson, F.S. (1988). Evaluation of New Jersey's Intensive Supervision Program. *Crime and Delinquency, 34(4)*, 437-48.

Peters, M., Bullman, S., Gimbel, C., Thomas, D., Laxton, G., Opanga, M., Afflerbach, M. & Croan, G. (1996). *Evaluation of the Impact of Boot Camps for Juvenile Offenders: Mobile Interim Report*. Fairfax, Virginia: Caliber Associates.

Peters, M., Albright, K., Gimbel, C., Thomas, D., Laxton, G., Opanga, M. & Afflerbach, M. (1996a). *Evaluation of the Impact of Boot Camps for Juvenile Offenders: Denver Interim Report*. Fairfax, Virginia: Caliber Associates.

Petersilia, J. (1987). *Expanding Options for Criminal Sentencing*. Santa Monica, CA: Rand Corporation.

Petersilia, J. & Turner, S. (1990). Comparing Intensive and Regular Supervision for High-risk Probationers: Early Results from an Experiment in California. *Crime & Delinquency, 36(1)*, 87-111.

Petersilia, J. & Turner, S. (1991). An Evaluation of Intensive Probation in California. *The Journal of Criminal Law and Criminology, 82(3)*, 610-58.

Petersilia, J. & Turner, S. (1993). Evaluating Intensive Supervision Probation/parole: Results of a Nationwide Experiment. *Research in Brief*. Washington, DC: US National Institute of Justice.

Petersilia, J., Turner, S. & Deschenes, E.P. (1992). The Costs and Effects of Intensive Supervision for Drug Offenders. *Federal Probation, 56(4)*, 12-17.

Peterson, E. (1996). *Juvenile Boot Camps: Lessons Learned* (Fact Sheet #36). Washington, DC: US Office of Juvenile Justice and Delinquency Prevention.

Piercy, F. & Lee, R. (1976). Effects of a Dual Treatment Approach on the Rehabilitation of Habitual Juvenile Delinquents. *Rehabilitation Counseling Bulletin, 19*, 482-92.

Schlicter, K.J. & Horan, J.J. (1981). Effects of Stress Inoculation on the Anger and Aggression Management Skills of Institutionalized Juvenile Delinquents. *Cognitive Therapy and Research, 5(4)*, 359-65.

Schwitzgebel, R. & Kolb, D.A. (1964). Inducing Behaviour Change in Adolescent Delinquents. *Behavior Research and Therapy, 1*, 297-304.

Seckel, J.P. & Turner, J.K. (1985). *Assessment of Planned Re-entry Programs (PREP)*. Sacramento, CA: California Youth Authority.

Shivrattan, J.L. (1988). Social Interactional Training and Incarcerated Juvenile Delinquents. *Canadian Journal of Criminology, 30*, 145-63.

Sontheimer, H. & Goodstein, L. (1993). An Evaluation of Juvenile Intensive Aftercare Probation: Aftercare Versus System Response Effects. *Justice Quarterly, 10(2)*, 197-227.

Spence, S.H. & Marzillier, J.S. (1981). Social Skills Training with Adolescent Male Offenders — II: Short-term, Long-term and Generalized Effects. *Behavior Research & Therapy, 19*, 349-68.

Thambidurai, G.A. (1980). A Comparative Outcome Study of a Contract Parole Program for Individuals Committed to the Youth Correctional Complex in the State of New Jersey (Doctoral dissertation, Rutgers University, The State University of New Jersey, 1980). *Dissertation Abstracts International, 41(01)*, 371B. (University Microfilms No. 80-16503).

Thomas, D., Peters, M., Gimbel, C., Laxton, G., Opanga, M., Afflerbach, M. & Croan, G. (1996). *Evaluation of the Impact of Boot Camps for Juvenile Offenders: Cleveland Interim Report*. Fairfax, Virginia: Caliber Associates.

Turner, S. & Petersilia, J. (1992). Focusing on High-risk Parolees: An Experiment to Reduce Commitments to the Texas Department of Corrections. *The Journal of Research in Crime and Delinquency, 29(1)*, 34-61.

Vaughn, J.B. (1991). Use of Electronic Monitoring with Juvenile Intensive Supervision Programs. In T.L. Armstrong (ed.), *Intensive Interventions with High-risk Youths: Promising Approaches in Juvenile Probation and Parole* (pp. 189-210). Monsey, NY: Criminal Justice Press.

Wolf, M.M., Phillips, E.L. & Fixson, D.L. (1974). *Achievement Place: Phase II* (Vol. I). Rockville, MD: Center for Studies of Crime and Delinquency, National Institute of Mental Health.

ENDNOTES

1 David M. Altschuler is a Principal Research Scientist at the Institute for Policy Studies at the Johns Hopkins University in Baltimore, Maryland. He is also Adjunct Associate Professor in both the Johns Hopkins School of Public Health and the Sociology Department. Dr. Altschuler is the director of a national project on intensive juvenile aftercare for serious juvenile offenders which is run by the US Department of Justice, and he co-directs the Juvenile Reintegration and Aftercare Center.

APPENDIX **A**

List of Child and Family Services

I. Approved Homes/Approved Schools/Approved Institutions/Places of Safety/Other Institutions

The following is a list of institutions which provide residential and rehabilitative services for children and youths. The institutions are categorised into Approved Homes, Approved Schools, Approved Institutions, and Other Institutions. An institution may be gazetted as both an Approved School or an Approved Home under the Children and Young Persons Act (Cap. 38) (CYPA). Approved Schools take in Juvenile Arrest Cases (i.e. those juveniles who have been charged in Court with committing an offence, and found guilty). A juvenile may be sent to an Approved School for a minimum period of two years, and a maximum period of three years.[1] Approved Homes take in Beyond Parental Control cases and Care and Protection Order cases.[2] For Beyond Parental Control cases, the juvenile must reside in the Home for a minimum of two years. The maximum period of residence is three years. For a Care and Protection Order case, there is no minimum or maximum period. Approved Institutions are gazetted as such under the Probation of Offenders Act (Cap. 252). A juvenile may only be sent to an Approved Institution for a maximum of 12 months.[3] There are also a number of private institutions which provide residential facilities for children who have no homes of their own to go to, which are run by voluntary welfare organisations (Other Institutions).

Several institutions have also been designated as Places of Safety. These institutions are exclusively for Care and Protection Order cases. The Court can also order a child who is the subject of a Care and

Protection Order to be committed to a Place of Safety for such period as may be specified by the Court.

Two Homes have been designated as *Places of Detention* under the CYPA — the Singapore Boys' Home and the Toa Payoh Girls' Home. They are also gazetted as remand homes for boys and girls respectively. A juvenile would be put there if he is charged for an offence, and the Court decides not to release him on bail. The Court may also order that juveniles in Beyond Parental Control cases be placed in a remand home pending the Social Report to be furnished by Ministry of Community Development and Sports on him or her. The Court may also order that a juvenile who is found guilty of an offence be placed in a Place of Detention for up to six months under Section 44(1)(g) of the CYPA. (This is unlike an Approved School order where the minimum period of residence is two years.)

1. Approved Homes

Andrew & Grace Home
116 Lorong J, Telok Kurau
Singapore 425946
Email: andrew@pcs.org.sg
Home: 63485674
Fax: 63485081

Canossaville Children's Home
1 Sallim Road
Singapore 387621
Email: canossa@pacific.net.sg
Tel: 67485777 / 67440307
Fax: 67480381

Chen Su Lan Methodist Children's Home
202-210/A
Serangoon Garden Way
Singapore 556057
Email: nc0066@starhub.net.sg
Tel: 62854941
Fax: 62854942

Children's Aid Society
(Melrose)
503 Clementi Road
Singapore 599488
Tel: 64665758 / 64673095
Fax: 64620729

Convalescent Home
420 Keramat Road
off Admiralty Road
Singapore 758859
Email: mywong@childrensociety.org.sg
Tel: 62573172
Fax: 67597907

Gracehaven
3 Lorong Napiri — Tel: 64881510
Singapore 547528 — Fax: 62841479
Email: social_services@SMM.salvationarmy.org

Muhammadiyah Welfare Home
716/718 Mountbatten Road — Tel: 63447551
Singapore 437736 — Fax: 63482661
Email: mwhome@singnet.com.sg

Pertapis Centre for Women and Girls
91 Kovan Road — Tel: 62844707
Singapore 540000 — Fax: 62894508
Email: drsaba@pertapis.org.sg

Pertapis Children's Home
993B Kovan Road — Tel: 63830914
off Yio Chu Kang Road — Fax: 63830913
Singapore 545676
Email: firuz@pertapis.org.sg

Singapore Boys' Home
30 Jurong West Street 24 — Tel: 67923534
Singapore 649696 — Fax: 67924096
Website: www.mcds.gov.sg

The Haven
350 Pasir Panjang Road — Tel: 67749588
Singapore 118692 — Fax: 67793225
Email:peter_khoo@SMM.salvationarmy.org

Toa Payoh Girls' Home
506 Lorong 1 Toa Payoh — Tel: 62505644
Singapore 319760 — Fax: 62560812
Website:www.mcds.gov.sg

2. Approved Schools

Gracehaven
3 Lorong Napiri — Tel: 64881510
Singapore 547528 — Fax: 62841479
Email: social_services@SMM.salvationarmy.org

Jamiyah Children's Home
1 Chin Cheng Ave (off Still Road) — Tel: 63449533
Singapore 429400 — Fax: 63443202
Email: ysjch@yahoo.com.sg

Muhammadiyah Welfare Home
716/718 Mountbatten Road — Tel: 63447551
Singapore 437736 — Fax: 63482661
Email: mwhome@singnet.com.sg

Pertapis Centre for Women and Girls
91 Kovan Road — Tel: 62844707
Singapore 540000 — Fax: 62894508
Email: drsaba@pertapis.org.sg

Singapore Boys' Home
30 Jurong West Street 24 — Tel: 67923534
Singapore 649696 — Fax: 67924096
Website:www.mcds.gov.sg

Toa Payoh Girls' Home
506 Lorong 1 Toa Payoh — Tel: 62505644
Singapore 319760 — Fax: 62560812
Website: www.mcds.gov.sg

3. Approved Institutions

Bukit Batok Hostel
10 De Souza Ave — Tel: 64650457 / 64650458
Singapore 599499 — Fax: 64623019

Muhammadiyah Welfare Home
716/718 Mountbatten Road — Tel: 63447551
Singapore 437736 — Fax: 63482661
Email: mwhome@singnet.com.sg

Pertapis Centre for Women and Girls
91 Kovan Road — Tel: 62844707
Singapore 540000 — Fax: 62894508
Email: drsaba@pertapis.org.sg

Singapore Boys' Hostel
32 Jurong West Street 24 — Tel: 67926380
Singapore 649697 — Fax: 67924498
Website:www.mcds.gov.sg

4. Places of Safety

Alexander Hospital
378 Alexandra Road — Tel: 64722000
Singapore 159964 — Fax: 63793880
Email: hwee_ping_tan@alexhosp.com.sg
Website: http://www.alexshosp.com.sg

Ang Mo Kio Community Hospital
17 Ang Mo Kio Avenue 9 Tel: 64538033
Singapore 569766 Fax: 64541729
Email: enquiry@com.sg
Website: http://www.amkh.com.sg

Changi General Hospital
2 Simei Street 3 Tel: 67888833
Singapore 529889 Fax: 67880933
Email: chgenquiry@com.sg
Website: http://www.chg.com.sg

Communicable Disease Centre
Moulmein Road Tel: 63577900
Singapore 308433 Fax: 62524056
Website: http://www.ttsh.com.sg/cdc

Convalescent Home
420 Keramat Road Tel: 62573172
off Admiralty Road Fax: 67597907
Singapore 758859
Email: mywong@childrensociety.org.sg

Good Shepherd Centre
Blk 250 Yishun Avenue 9, #01-213 Tel: 67556496
Singapore 760250 Fax: 67520670
Email gscentre_sg@yahoo.com

KK Women's and Children's Hospital
100 Bukit Timah Road Tel: 62934044
Singapore 229899 Fax: 62937933
Email: info@kkh.com.sg
Website: http://www.kkh.com.sg

Muhammadiyah Welfare Home
716/718 Mountbatten Road Tel: 63447551
Singapore 437736 Fax: 63482661
Email: mwhome@singnet.com.sg

National University Hospital
5 Lower Kent Ridge Road Tel: 67795555
Singapore 119074 Fax: 67795678
Email: enquiries@nuh.com.sg
Website: http://www.nuh.com.sg

Pertapis Centre for Women and Girls
91 Kovan Road Tel: 62844707
Singapore 540000 Fax: 62894508
Email: drsaba@pertapis.org.sg

Pertapis Children's Home
993B Kovan Road — Tel: 63830914
off Yio Chu Kang Road — Fax: 63830913
Singapore 545676
Email: firuz@pertapis.org.sg

Singapore General Hospital
Outram Road — Tel: 62223322
Singapore 169608 — Fax: 62249221
Email: sghfeedback@sgh.com.sg
Website: http://www.sgh.com.sg

Tan Tock Seng Hospital
11 Jalan Tan Tock Seng — Tel: 62566011
Singapore 308433 — Fax: 62527282
Website: http://www.ttsh.com.sg

The Haven
350 Pasir Panjang Road — Tel: 67749588
Singapore 118692 — Fax: 67793225
Email: peter_khoo@SMM.salvationarmy.org

The TENT
11 Hillside Drive — Tel: 62837696/5
Singapore 548926 — Fax: 62843988
Email: toy_leng_wan@hotmail.com

Toa Payoh Girls' Home
506 Lorong 1 Toa Payoh — Tel: 62505644
Singapore 319760 — Fax: 62560812
Website: www.mcds@mcds.gov.sg

Woodbridge Hospital
10 Buangkok View — Tel: 63892000
Singapore 539747 — Fax: 63851050
Email: enquiry@imh.com.sg
Website: http://www.imh.com.sg

5. Other Institutions

Darul Ihsan Lilbanat
23 Wan Tho Avenue — Tel: 62852973
Singapore 347552 — Fax: 62834712
Email: ihsan4@singnet.com.sg

Darul Ihsan
5 Mattar Road — Tel: 67477556
Singapore 387713 — Fax: 67441770
Email: ihsan1@singnet.com.sg / zainahush@hotmail.com

Infant Jesus Home & Children's Centres
Block 442 Clementi Avenue 3 — Tel: 67773893
#03-99 — Fax: 67773893
Singapore 120442
Email: ijhcc1@singnet.com.sg

Singapore Boys' Town
622 Upper Bukit Timah Rd — Tel: 67691618
Singapore 678117 — Fax: 67627846
Email: ang@boystown.org.sg

Ramakrishna Mission Boys' Home
179 Bartley Road — Tel: 62887324/ 63835760 (DID)
Singapore 539784 — Fax: 62885798
Email: nc0007a@starhub.net.sg

Teen Challenge Youth Centre
119 Lorong K Telok Kurau — Tel: 63469334/ 63462136 (DID)
Singapore 425760 — Fax: 64401374
Email: ej@teenchallenge.org.sg

The Hiding Place
3 Jalan Kayu, — Tel: 64835348/ 64830036
Singapore 799434 — Fax: 64834071
Email: hidplace@singnet.com.sg
Website: www.hidingplace.com.sg

II. General

The following is a list of community organisations providing counselling, welfare, educational and other services for children and their families. They have been categorised as follows:

1. Assistance and Family Support Services
2. Counselling and Family Life Education
3. Drug Counselling and Rehabilitative Services
4. Family Violence/Shelters
5. Youth Outreach and Child Services
6. Special Needs

The list is not intended to be exhaustive, but is rather to give the reader an idea of all the different services available in the community, and to give him a starting point when sourcing for services which best meet his requirements. The various organisations have been categorised according to their key functions, for ease of reference. However, it should be noted that a significant number of these organisations actually provide a wider range of services than their categorisation would indicate.

1. Assistance and Family Support Services

Association of Muslim Professionals

Provides counselling, a helpline service, befrienders' scheme and marriage guidance courses for young couples. Runs childcare and preschool centres and assists low-income families. Runs IT and computer skills classes for children.

AMP Centre
25 Jalan Tembusu
(Off Haig Road)
Singapore 438234
Tel: 63460911
Fax: 63460922
Hotline: 63452911
Email: amprimma@pacific.net.sg
Website: http://www.amp.org.sg

Asian Women's Welfare Association

Pioneers and develops a range of services, from infancy to old age, for the disadvantaged. Services include counselling, financial assistance and food rations to poor and needy individuals and families.

10, Kwong Avenue
Singapore 348884
Tel: 62859515
Fax: 62855982
Email: awwahq@cyberway.com.sg
Website: http://www.cyberway.com.sg/~awwahq

Bukit Ho Swee Social Service Centre

Serves the disadvantaged and troubled, especially those from the low-income community. Runs services for children, youth, families and the elderly.

Blk 26 Jalan Klinik
#01-42/52
Singapore 160026
Tel: 62742646
Fax: 62721923

TOUCH Community Services

Provides counselling, financial assistance and welfare services to individuals and families in need. Provides services for children, youth and the elderly as well as free legal counselling services and advice to needy and low-income families.

3rd Floor
Touch Community Theatre
3615 Jalan Bukit Merah
Singapore 159461
Tel: 63770122
Fax: 63770121
Email: tcs@touch.org.sg
Website: http://www.touchnet.org.sg

Majlis Ugama Islam Singapura
(Islamic Religious Council of Singapore)
Provides financial relief to poor and needy Muslims, study grants and bursaries to Muslim students, conducts the Skills Assistance Programme, religious guidance and counselling in prisons, drug rehabilitation centres and welfare homes.
273 Braddell Road — Tel: 62568188
Singapore 579702 — Fax: 62537572

Salvation Army, The
Provides residential services for children and adolescents, family support services, childcare services, social work and counselling services.
20 Bishan St 22 — Tel: 65550255
Singapore 579768 — Fax: 65528541
Website: http://www.salvationarmy.org.sg

Singapore Indian Development Association (SINDA)
Provides education and family development programmes to families facing educational and socio-economic problems.
No 1 Beatty Road — Tel: 1800-2954554
Singapore 209943 — Fax: 62947293
Email: bimel@sinda.org.sg
Website: www.sinda.org.sg

Singapore Malay Youth Organisation (Taman Bacaan)
Administers a financial aid programme for needy students and low-income families and provides services to parents who have problems with their children.
672 Jalan Damai — Tel: 67417977
#01- 25 — Fax: 67490300
Singapore 470672
Email: taman_bacaan@pacific.net.sg

2. Counselling and Family Life Education

Adventist Better Living Centre
Provides the Children-At-Risk Empowerment programme, public lifestyle and wellness programmes and assistance for the needy regardless of race, religion or status.
90 Jurong East St 13 — Tel: 62831455
Singapore 609648 — Fax: 62870745
Email: teob4wsa@singnet.com.sg

Agape Counselling and Training Centre
Provides counselling to ex-drug addicts, youth-at-risk, disadvantaged children and their families.
10, Lorong 11, Geylang — Tel: 68422922
Singapore 388702 — Fax: 68422322
Email: agapectr@pacific.net.sg

Family Life Society
Provides youth, family and marital counselling, pregnancy crisis service, sex education and seminars.
51 Goldhill Plaza — Tel: 63559345/ 46
#16-12 — Fax: 63559345
Singapore 308900
Email: lifectre@singnet.com.sg

Samaritans of Singapore
Provides counselling, a toll-free hotline, and an emergency service for suicides. Also provides community education in such matters.
10 Cantonment Close — Tel: 1800-2214444
#01-01 — Fax: 62207758
Singapore 080010
Email: samlink@singnet.com.sg
Website: http://www.samaritans.org.sg

Shan You Counselling Centre
Provides professional counselling and social work to individuals, couples or families, based on Buddhist principles, to those seeking assistance, regardless of race, religion or ability to pay. Also distributes food rations to the needy.
9 Upper Boon Keng Road — Tel: 67419293
#01-960 — Fax: 67419352
Singapore 380009
Email: shanyou@shanyou.org.sg
Website: http://www.shanyou.org.sg

Young Women Muslim Association
Provides counselling for individuals and families with emotional, child-management and divorce-related concerns. Provides information and referral services as well as short-term financial relief to needy families, along with casework.
Blk 322, Ubi Ave 1 — Tel: 67455862
#01-591 — Fax: 67432749
Singapore 400322

3. Drug Counselling and Rehabilitative Services

Singapore Anti-Narcotics Association (SANA)
Educates the public in general and, in particular, the juvenile population, on the perils of drug abuse and provides counselling and both in-care and after-care services to drug consumers, abusers of drugs, solvents and other substances.
No 2 Orchard Boulevard — Tel: 67321122
Singapore 248643 — Fax: 67324564
Email: sana@pacific.net.sg
Website: http://www.sana.org.sg

Teen Challenge (Singapore)
Runs a residential programme for ex-drug addicts and alcoholics, inhalant abusers, juvenile delinquents and troubled teenagers, as well as a Crisis Hotline.
735 Choa Chu Kang Road — Tel: 67938816
Singapore 699798 — Fax: 67928192
Email: Davec@teenchallenge.org.sg
Website: http://www.teenchallenge.org.sg

4. Family Violence/Shelters

Society Against Family Violence
Develops and implements programmes that support frontline professionals working with families in crisis. Assists in the setting up of support groups and rehabilitation services for the victims and perpetrators of family violence.
545 Orchard Road — Tel: 62353341
Far East Shopping Centre, #16-04 — Fax: 62357176
c/o Family Works Pte Ltd
Singapore 238882

5. Youth Outreach and Child Services

Bethesda Community Service Society
Provides before and after school services, youth and counselling services, mentor and tuition programmes.
209 New Upper Changi Road — Tel: 62428040
#04-639 — Fax: 62428050
Singapore 460209
Email: bethesco@singnet.com.sg

CARE Community Services Society
Provides before and after school care service, school-based counselling, students' aides programmes and community projects for youths and children.
103 Lavender Street — Tel: 62987337
Carepoint — Fax: 64671477
Singapore 338725
Email: ccss@carecom.org.sg
Website: http://www.carecom.org.sg

Fei Yue Counselling Centre
Provides school social work, counselling and group work for youths and children.
371 Bukit Batok St 31, #02-332 — Tel: 65631106
Singapore 650371 — Fax: 65695868
Email: fyfsc@singnet.com.sg
Website: http://www.feiyuebb.org.sg

Methodist Welfare Services (Bukit Batok)
Provides before and after school care, counselling services, family life education programmes, learning support programmes and nursery/kindergarten programmes.
Blk 106 Bukit Batok Central, #01-217 Tel: 65622211
Singapore 650106 Fax: 65698038
Email: admin@mws.org.sg

Ramakrishna Mission
Runs a Boy's Home, a kindergarten, free public library, counselling services, moral education classes for children and youth, and provides free counselling for children and youth.
179 Bartley Road Tel: 62885288
Singapore 539784 Fax: 62811305
Email: office@ramakrishna.org.sg
Website: http://www.ramakrishna.org.sg

Singapore Children's Society
Provides a range of preventive services, community services and rehabilitation services for children, as well as a helpline for children, called Tinkle Friend. Also provides services relating to child abuse and child neglect.
6 Jalan Klapa Tel: 62969909
Singapore 199318 Fax: 62975755
Email: info@childrensociety.org.sg
Website: http://www.childrensociety.org.sg

Student Care Centre
Provides casework/ family counselling, social and educational programmes for youth and children, talks and training workshops.
Blk 202 Yishun St 21, #01-89 Tel: 67596821
Singapore 760202 Fax: 67596829
Email: scs_h01@students.org.sg
Website: http://www.students.org.sg

Trans Centre
Provides counselling, information and referrals, family life education, runs children, youth drop-in centres, holds tuition classes and Learning Aid Programmes.
411 Bedok North Ave 2, #01- 106 Tel: 64490762
Singapore 460411 Fax: 64498135
Email: transbd@starhub.net.sg
Website: http://www.transcentre.org.sg

Young Men's Christian Association of Singapore (YMCA)
Runs developmental camps for the disabled, children and youths, before and after school care services, children and youth outreach activities.
1 Orchard Road Tel: 64302200
Singapore 238824 Fax: 63368003
Email: valerie@ymca.org.sg
Website: http://www.ymca.org.sg

Young Women's Christian Association
Provides before and after school care services, a hostel, vacation camps for children between 4-14 years of age, educational forums and seminars on social issues.
6 Fort Canning Road — Tel: 63384222
Singapore 179494 — Fax: 63374222
Email: ywcasin@singnet.com.sg
Website: http://www.ywcafclodge.org.sg

Youth Guidance Outreach Services
Works with children-at-risk and youth-at-risk and their families, through tuition, reading and foundational programmes for children from low-income families, also conducts befriending and outreach activities in housing estates and schools.
Blk 125 Ang Mo Kio Ave 6, #01-4077 — Tel: 65526477
Website: http://www.syfc.org.sg/ministry/yg/yg.htm

6. Special Needs

Association for Persons with Special Needs
Provides counselling for parents of educationally sub-normal children and home visits by social workers. Provides diagnostic psycho-educational services in relation to the needs and abilities of children, conducts music and speech therapy, remedial and therapeutic physical education and training.
4 Anthony Road — Tel: 68353367
Singapore 229945 — Fax: 68353368
Email: apsnhq@singnet.com.sg

Autism Association (Singapore)
Provides parent support network and the Starkid programme for children with autism. Runs a diagnostic centre, an information and advice bureau and an outreach programme.
381 Clementi Ave 5 — Tel: 67746649
#01-398 — Fax: 67746957
Singapore 120381
Email: autism@singnet.com.sg
Website: http://www.autismlinks.org.sg

Dyslexia Association of Singapore (DAS)
Offers programmes for children with dyslexia and also provides public education in this area.
DAS Learning Centre (Redhill) — Tel: 64759535
New Town Primary School — Fax: 64762597
402 Commonwealth Drive
Blk A #03-01
Singapore 149599
Email: enquiry@das.org.sg
Website: http://www.das.org.sg

Handicaps Welfare Association
Provides befriending, food rations, transportation, rehabilitation services and other services for the disabled, including children and youth.
16 Whampoa Drive — Tel: 62543006
Singapore 327725 — Fax: 62537375
Email: hwa@hwa.org.sg
Website: http://www.hwa.org.sg

Movement for the Intellectually Disabled of Singapore (MINDS)
Seeks to maximise the potential and ability of intellectually disabled children through a day activities centre, employment development, special school and residential services.
800 Margaret Drive — Tel: 64731148
Singapore 149310 — Fax: 64733885
Email: MINDS@minds.org.sg
Website: http://www.minds.org.sg

Rainbow Centre
Provides special education schools for children below four years old with intellectual and multiple physical disabilities, and/or autism, as well as training for parents and a parent support group.
501 Margaret Drive — Tel: 64727077
Singapore 149306 — Fax: 64739739
Email: Rcmdss@pacific.net.sg

III. Family Service Centres

Family service centres offer counselling and casework services for individuals, families and groups of all ages. They provide information, referrals and public education on family life enrichment.

Central

Asian Women's Welfare Association Family Service Centre
Blk 107 Towner Rd — Tel: 62911712
#01-356 — Fax: 62916639
Singapore 321107

Bukit Ho Swee Family Service Centre
Blk 5 Delta Ave #01-09 — Tel: 62742646
Singapore 160005 — Fax: 62721923

Care Corner Family Service Centre (Queenstown)
Blk 107 Commonwealth Crescent — Tel: 64761481
#01-230 — Fax: 64761483
Singapore 140107

Care Corner Family Service Centre (Toa Payoh)
Blk 158 Toa Payoh Lor 1 Tel: 63561622
#01-1522 Fax: 63561623
Singapore 310158

Kampong Kapor Family Service Centre
Blk 2 Kitchener Road Tel: 62997662
#03-89 Fax: 62942116
Singapore 200002

MacPherson Moral Family Service Centre
Blk 91 Paya Lebar Way Tel: 67414255
#01-3023 Fax: 67416989
Singapore 370091

Reach Family Service Centre
Blk 187 Bishan St 13 Tel: 62522566
#01-475 Fax: 62522445
Singapore 570187

SINDA Family Service Centre
1 Beatty Road Tel: 63937260 / 62954554
Singapore 209943 Fax: 62947293

Tanjong Pagar Family Service Centre
Blk 18 Jln Membina #04-01 Tel: 62706711
Singapore 164018 Fax: 62709663

TRANS Centre (Bukit Timah)
Blk 1 Toh Yi Drive Tel: 64662287
#01-143 Fax: 64692790
Singapore 591501

North

Care Corner (Admiralty)
Blk 718/9 Woodlands Ave 6 Tel: 63658751
#01-628 Fax: 63656267
Singapore 730718

Care Corner Family Service Centre (Woodlands)
Blk 345 Woodlands St 32 Tel: 63622481
#01-198 Fax: 63624824
Singapore 730345

Daybreak FSC (Yishun)
Blk 855 Yishun Ring Rd Tel: 67564995
#01-3539 Fax: 67524709
Singapore 760855

Sembawang FSC
Blk 326 Sembawang Crescent
#01-52
Singapore 750326
Tel: 67547050 / 67542890
Fax: 67540112

Singapore Children's Society — Yishun Family Service Centre
Blk 107 Yishun Ring Road
#01-233
Singapore 760107
Tel: 67537331
Fax: 67532697

Northeast

The Ang Mo Kio Family Service Centre (Ang Mo Kio)
Blk 230 Ang Mo Kio Ave 3
#01-1264
Singapore 560230
Tel: 64535349
Fax: 64556183

The Ang Mo Kio Family Service Centre (Cheng San)
Blk 445 Ang Mo Kio Ave 10
#01-1647
Singapore 560445
Tel: 64546678
Fax: 64547995

Covenant Family Service Centre
Blk 613 Hougang Ave 8
#01-432
Singapore 530613
Tel: 62828558
Fax: 62836361

Hougang Sheng Hong FSC
Blk 237 Hougang St 21
#01-406
Singapore 530237
Tel: 62895022
Fax: 62898242

Serangoon Moral Family Service Centre
Blk 238 Serangoon Ave 2
#01-47
Singapore 550238
Tel: 62847123
Fax: 62845221

The Ang Mo Kio FSC (Sengkang)
Blk 223D Compassvale Road
#01-673
Singapore 544223
Tel: 63128100
Fax: 63125631

East

4PM-MENDAKI Family Service Centre
Blk 534 Bedok North St 3
#01-814
Singapore 460534
Tel: 64499054 / 64491440
Fax: 62422040

Marine Parade FSC
Blk 53 Marine Terrace, #01-227 Tel: 64450100
Singapore 440053 Fax: 64460100

Muhammadiyah-MENDAKI FSC
Blk 139 Petir Road Tel: 67671740
#01-448 Fax: 67672771
Singapore 670139

Pasir Ris Family Service Centre
Blk 534 Pasir Ris Drive 1 Tel: 65812159
#01-266 Fax: 65843580
Singapore 510534

SBL Vision FSC
Blk 946 Tampines Ave 4 Tel: 65442263
#01-338 Fax: 65442253
Singapore 520946

TRANS Centre (Bedok)
Blk 411 Bedok North Ave 2 Tel: 64490762
#01-106 Fax: 64498135
Singapore 460411

Tampines Family Service Centre
Blk 470 Tampines St 44 Tel: 67872001
#01-194 Fax: 67874459
Singapore 520470

West

Fei Yue Family Service Centre (Bukit Batok)
Blk 185 Bukit Batok West Ave 6 Tel: 65690381
#01-187 Fax: 65695868
Singapore 650185

Fei Yue Family Service Centre (Choa Chu Kang)
Blk 280 Choa Chu Kang Ave 3 Tel: 67625215
#01-360/362 Fax: 67628120
Singapore 680280

Lakeside Family Centre (Jurong West)
Blk 516 Jurong West St 52 Tel: 65671908
#01-73 Fax: 65656435
Singapore 640516

Lakeside Family Centre (Jurong East)
Blk 302 Jurong East St 32 Tel: 65649722
#01-22 Fax: 65649422
Singapore 600302

Rotary Family Service Centre
Blk 346 Clementi Ave 5 — Tel: 67799477
#01-10 — Fax: 67762673
Singapore 120346

Whispering Heart FSC
Blk 646 Jurong West St 61 — Tel: 67951008
#01-142 — Fax: 67958970
Singapore 640646

YWMA-MENDAKI Family Service Centre
Blk 520 Jurong West St 52 — Tel: 65613462
#01-195 — Fax: 65605852
Singapore 640520

IV. Student Care Centres

The Student Care Centre (SCC) programme is targeted at school-going children aged between 7-14 years old, who do not have alternative forms of care before or after school. The SCCs aim to ensure that these children are constructively occupied while their parents are at work.

4PM-Mendaki Student Care Centre
Blk 534 Bedok North St 3 — Tel: 64491415
#01-806
Singapore 460534

Agape Student Care Centre (Bedok)
Blk 13 Bedok South Rd — Tel: 62444193
#01-605
Singapore 460013

Aljunied Tung Ling Student Care Centre
Blk 138 Lor Ah Soo — Tel: 63822276
#01-115
Singapore 530138

AMP-East Coast Primary-Student Care Centre
8 Chai Chee Lane — Tel: 64419539
East Coast Primary School
Singapore 469031

Ananias Centre Student Care Centre
220 Clementi Ave 4 — Tel: 67783829
Clementi Community Centre
Singapore 129880

Ananias Centre (Bishan)
20 Bishan St 22 Tel: 65521129
Salvation Army Bldg
#B1-00
Singapore 579768

Ananias Centre
(Choa Chu Kang Centre)
Blk 210 Choa Chu Kang Central Tel: 67634535
#B1-162
Singapore 680210

Ananias Centre (Choa Chu Kang Ave 3)
Blk 288 Choa Chu Kang Ave 3 Tel: 67629195
#B1-288
Singapore 680288

Ananias Centre (Head Office)
5A Parry Ave Tel: 63831959
Singapore 547227

Ang Mo Kio Family Service Centre
(Cheng San)
Blk 445 Ang Mo Kio Ave 10 Tel: 64546678
#01-1647
Singapore 560445

Ang Mo Kio Family Service Centre (Sengkang)
Blk 223A Compassvale Walk Tel: 63125632
#01-633
Singapore 541223

Aspiration Student Care Centre
Blk 871 Tampines St 84 Tel: 67836869
#01-55
Singapore 520871

AWWA FSC-BASC1
Blk 107 Towner Rd, #01-356 Tel: 62911712
Singapore 321107

Baptist Student Care Centre
Blk 714/715 Jurong West St 71 Tel: 67926026
#B1-147
Singapore 640714

Baptist Community Care Centre (Bishan Branch)
Blk 213 Bishan St 23 Tel: 64514624/ 93190974
#B1-235
Singapore 570213

Baptist Community Care Centre (Serangoon Garden Branch)
89 Serangoon Garden Way — Tel: 64514624/ 93190974
Singapore 555985

Baptist Student Care Centre
Blk 714/715 Jurong West St 71 — Tel: 67926026
#B1-147
Singapore 640714

BCS Centre — Fengshan
Blk 125 Bedok North Rd — Tel: 64422302
#01-125/127
Singapore 460125

BCS — Xinghua Centre
30 Parry Ave — Tel: 62866256
Xinghua Primary School
Singapore 547258

Bendemeer Thinkers Club
1062 Serangoon Rd — Tel: 62968587
Bendemeer Primary School
Singapore 328174

Beng Wan BASC[4]
1060 Serangoon Rd — Tel: 63920193/ 67414255
Beng Wan Primary School
Singapore 328173

Bethesda Chapel Student Care Centre
27 Lor Melayu — Tel: 67493219
Singapore 416913

Bethesda Community Services Society (Bedok)
Blk 525 Bedok North St 3 — Tel: 64441304
#01-410
Singapore 460525

Bethesda Community Services Society
Blk 253 Tampines St 21 — Tel: 67838925
#01-406
Singapore 520253

Bethesda Student Care Centre
112 Serangoon Ave 3 — Tel: 62834419
Singapore 556109

Bishan East 3-in-1 Student Care Centre
Blk 186 Bishan St 13 — Tel: 62551993
#01-345
Singapore 570186

Bukit Ho Swee Community Centre Student Care Centre
300 Jalan Bukit Ho Swee — Tel: 62738598/ 62731463
Singapore 169566

Cana-BP-Church BASC
Blk 102 Simei St 1, #01-914 — Tel: 67883397
Singapore 520102

Canossaville Children's Home
1 Salim Rd — Tel: 67485777
Singapore 387621

Care Corner BASC (Woodlands)
Blk 321 Woodlands St 32 — Tel: 62695784
#01-227
Singapore 730321

Care Corner Student Care Centre (Admiralty)
Blk 719 Woodlands Ave 6 — Tel: 63651075
#01-628
Singapore 730719

Care Corner Student Care Centre (Toa Payoh)
381 Toa Payoh Lor 1 — Tel: 62585170
Joint Social Service Centre
#02-03
Singapore 319758

Chao Yang Before & After School Care
4 Anthony Rd — Tel: 67374427
Chao Yang Special School
Singapore 229945

Charis Student Care Centre
Blk 122 Geylang East Central — Tel: 67444296
#01-74
Singapore 380122

Chen Su Lan Methodist Children's Home
202 Serangoon Garden Way — Tel: 62854941/ 62891070
Singapore 556057

Ci You Student Care Centre
Blk 75 Whampoa Dr, #01-378 — Tel: 62569455
Singapore 320075

Compassion Student Care Centre
Blk 252 Compassvale Street — Tel: 63841944
#01-01
Singapore 541252

COS (Woodlands) BASC
268 Woodlands Centre Rd Tel: 63672120
Woodlands Point
#03-08/09/10
Singapore 738931

Daybreak Family Service Centre (Student Care Centre)
Blk 855 Yishun Ring Rd Tel: 67572907
#01-3539
Singapore 760855

D'Joy Children Centre
Blk 1 Maude Rd Tel: 62949960
#03-30
Singapore 200001

East Coast Care Centre
511 East Coast Rd Tel: 63464939
Singapore 429064

Emmanuel Student Care Services
165 Upper East Coast Rd Tel: 64459747
Singapore 455266

Evangel Student Care Centre
1 Woodlands St 83 Tel: 63653071
Singapore 738488

Fei Yue Student Care Centre (Bukit Batok)
Blk 186 Bukit Batok West Ave 6 Tel: 65691447
#01-181
Singapore 650186

Fei Yue Student Care Centre (Choa Chu Kang)
Blk 6 Teck Whye Ave Tel: 67627321
#01-110
Singapore 680006

Fuchun Jolly Kidz Student Care Centre
29 Woodlands Centre Rd Tel: 63674980
Fuchun Primary School
Singapore 738926

Glory Centre BASC
Blk 540 Hougang Ave 8 Tel: 63860213
#01-1231
Singapore 530540

Golden-Link Education Centre
Blk 249 Jurong East St 24 Tel: 65674560
#01-84
Singapore 600249

Good News Community Services Centre
Blk 37B Commonwealth Drive Tel: 64749209
#01-01, #02-01
Singapore 142037

Heartfriends BASC
Blk 3 Dover Rd Tel: 67764906
#01-354
Singapore 130003

Hearty Care Centre
Blk 72 Geylang Bahru Tel: 62954622
#01-3018
Singapore 330072

Henderson Student Care Centre
Blk 129 Bukit Merah View Tel: 62718411
#01-174
Singapore 150129

Hougang Sheng Hong Student Care Centre
Blk 238 Hougang Ave 1 Tel: 62852726
#01-292
Singapore 530238

Huamin BASC
21 Yishun Ave 11 Tel: 67570318
Huamin Primary School
Singapore 768857

Hui Ann Student Care Centre
7 Geylang Lor 29, #03-00 Tel: 67426703
Singapore 388063

Hwa Chong Student Care Centre
673 Bukit Timah Rd Tel: 64662146
Singapore 269735

IConnect Student Care @ FTPPS
7 Toa Payoh Lor 8 Tel: 63525996
Singapore 319252

Infant Jesus Centre Clementi
Blk 442 Clementi Ave 3, #03-99 Tel: 67773893
Singapore 120442

Iyad Perdaus Student Care
Blk 244 Jurong East St 24 — Tel: 65677781
#01-593
Singapore 600244

Jia Ying Student Care Centre
1 Valley Rd — Tel: 62881331
Singapore 534449

Jiemin Primary School BASC
2 Yishun St 71, Yishun Ring Rd — Tel: 67548819
Jiemin Primary School
Singapore 768515

Kebun Baru Student Care
216 Ang Mo Kio Ave 4 — Tel: 65526139
Singapore 569897

Lakeside (Jurong East) BASC
Blk 302 Jurong East St 32 — Tel: 65649876
#01-22
Singapore 600302

Lakeside BASC
Blk 514 Jurong West St 52 — Tel: 65677270
#01-18
Singapore 640514

Life Spring Before & After School Care
88 St Francis Rd — Tel: 62993421/ 63913026
Singapore 328070

Life Student Care Centre
144 Prinsep St — Tel: 63360373
Singapore Life Church
Singapore 188657

Life Student Care Centre (Hougang)
Blk 665 Hougang Ave 4 — Tel: 64898720
#01-365
Singapore 530665

Life Student Care Centre (Sengkang)
Blk 306C Anchorvale Link — Tel: 64898718/ 64898719
#01-77
Singapore 543306

Living Spring Student Care Centre
30 Lorong 27 — Tel: 67459778
Citi Raya Centre, #03-01
Singapore 388164

Macedonia BP Student Care Centre
Blk 227 Simei St 4 Tel: 67868687
#01-50
Singapore 520227

Marian Centre
790 Thomson Rd Tel: 62500877
Singapore 298142

Marine Parade — Charis Student Care Centre
Blk 125 Geylang East Ave 1, #01-05 Tel: 68482472
Singapore 381125

Marine Parade — Maha Bodhi Student Care
Blk 316 Ubi Ave 1 Tel: 67450181
#01-371
Singapore 400316

Marine Parade Student Care Centre
Blk 53 Marine Terrace Tel: 64450400
#01-215
Singapore 440053

Marine Parade — Red Swastika Student Centre
Blk 91 Bedok North St 4 Tel: 64486710
#01-1527
Singapore 460091

Marine Parade — Yu Neng Metta Student Care Centre
Blk 508 Bedok North Ave 3 Tel: 64465324
#01-369
Singapore 460508

Merah Saga 10 Student Care Centre
10 Jln Bukit Merah Tel: 62709242
Zhangde Primary School
Singapore 169544

Moral BASC Centre
Blk 28 Telok Blangah Rise Tel: 62736171
#01-219
Singapore 090028

Moral Student Care Centre (MacPherson)
Blk 37 Circuit Rd Tel: 67415266
#02-455
Singapore 370037

Mountbatten Student Care Centre
35 Jln Satu Tel: 63447387/ 63484037
Singapore 399479

New Life Family Care Centre
10 Marsiling Lane Tel: 63689567
Singapore 739147

Northeast CDC — Metta Student Care Centre
Blk 415 Pasir Ris Dr 6, #01-215 Tel: 65853373
Singapore 510415

Northeast — Kampung Senang Student Care Centre
Blk 840 Tampines St 82 Tel: 67852569
#01-111
Singapore 520840

NTUC Income Student Care Centre (AMK)
Blk 336 Ang Mo Kio Ave 1 Tel: 64514834
#01-2079
Singapore 560336

NTUC Income Student Care Centre (Sin Ming Court)
Blk 443 Sin Ming Ave, #01-443 Tel: 64526796
Singapore 570443

Pasir Panjang BASC
Blk 363 Clementi Ave 2 Tel: 67749300/ 2
#01-441
Singapore 120363

Pasir Ris 21 BASC
Blk 229 Pasir Ris St 21 Tel: 65852396
#01-28
Singapore 510229

Pasir Ris 51 Student Care Centre
Blk 561, 562 Pasir Ris St 51 Tel: 65813437
#01-265
Singapore 510561

Pasir Ris Family Service Centre
Blk 534 Pasir Ris Dr 1, #01-266 Tel: 65812156/ 65813467
Singapore 510534

PCF Telok Blangah Student Care Centre
450 Telok Blangah St 31 Tel: 62701828
Telok Blangah Community Club
Singapore 108943

PCF Toa Payoh East Student Care Centre
Blk 43 Toa Payoh Lor 5 Tel: 62501642
#01-131
Singapore 310043

PCF Potong Pasir Student Care Centre
6 Potong Pasir Ave 2 Tel: 62881720/ 62836986
Potong Pasir Community Club
Singapore 358361

PCF Marine Parade —
Siglap Student Care Centre
Blk 70 Bedok South Rd Tel: 68760561
#01-280
Singapore 460070

PCF Tampines East 3-in-1 Family Centre: Student Care
Blk 203 Tampines St 21 Tel: 62606364/ 67863133
#01-1271/1273
Singapore 520203

PCF Tampines Changkat Student Care Centre
Blk 285 Tampines St 22 Tel: 62605561
#01-217
Singapore 520285

PCF Tampines North Student Care Centre
Blk 424 Tampines St 41, #01-188 Tel: 67852686
Singapore 520424

PCF Aljunied Student Care Centre
Blk 110 Hougang Ave 1 Tel: 62890690
#01-1048
Singapore 530110

PCF Hougang Student Care Centre
35 Hougang Ave 3 Tel: 62805326
Hougang Community Club
Singapore 538840

PCF Cheng San Student Care Centre
6 Ang Mo Kio St 53 Tel: 64588222
Cheng San Community Club
Singapore 569205

PCF Thomson Student Care Centre
194 Upper Thomson Rd Tel: 63557121
Thomson CC
Singapore 574339

PCF Yuhua Student Care Centre
Blk 214 Jurong East St 21 Tel: 65602772
#01-421
Singapore 600214

PCF Yuhua — Happy Days Student Care Centre
Blk 319 Jurong East St 31, #01-58 Tel: 65661968
Singapore 600319

PCF Jurong Central Student Care Centre
Blk 552/553 Jurong West St 42 Tel: 65636020/ 65665534
#01-311
Singapore 640553

PCF Nanyang Student Care Centre
Blk 933 Jurong West St 91 Tel: 67921220
#01-375
Singapore 640933

PCF Hong Kah North Student Care Centre
Blk 315 Bukit Batok St 32 Tel: 65699168
#01-111
Singapore 650315

PCF Student Care Centre
(Bukit Batok)
21 Bukit Batok Central Tel: 65620409
Bukit Batok Community Club
Singapore 659959

PCF Yew Tee Student Care Centre
20, Choa Chu Kang St 52 Tel: 63143758
Yew Tee Community Building
#04-08
Singapore 689286

PCF Nee Soon South Student Care Centre
Blk 812 Yishun Ring Rd Tel: 67562875
#01-4153
Singapore 760812

Pei Tong Care Hut
15 Clementi Ave 5 Tel: 67767339
Pei Tong Primary School
Singapore 129857

PPIS Student Care Centre
Blk 136 Bedok Reservoir Rd Tel: 67450613
#01-1425
Singapore 470136

PPIS-MENDAKI Family Service Centre
Blk 520 Jurong West St 52 Tel: 6561346
#01-195
Singapore 640520

Red Swastika Student Centre
Blk 110 Bedok North Ave 3 Tel: 62451809
#01-2282
Singapore 460110

Rotary — Ayer Rajah Students' Care Centre
300 Teban Gardens Rd Tel: 65674528
Singapore 608877

Saint Andrew's House
1 Francis Thomas Dr Tel: 62888664
Singapore 359340

Sembawang FSC Student Care Centre
Blk 326 Sembawang Crescent Tel: 67542890
#01-44
Singapore 750326

Sembawang Tamils Association BASC
Blk 660, Yishun Avenue 4 Tel: 67543621
#01-305
Singapore 760660

Serangoon Moral Student Care Centre
Blk 239 Serangoon Ave 2 Tel: 62844511
#01-37
Singapore 550239

Star of the Sea — BASC
Blk 265 Yishun St 22 Tel: 67559535
#01-226
Singapore 760265

Star View Student Care Centre (Yishun)
Blk 407 Yishun Ring Rd Tel: 67557714
#01-1284
Singapore 760407

Study and Care Centre
Blk 107 Bukit Batok West Ave 6 Tel: 65631641
#01-65
Singapore 650107

Sunshine Club Student Care Centre
300 Bedok North Ave 3 Tel: 64452975/ 62423791
Singapore 469717

Sunshine Club Student Care Centre
50 Bedok Reservoir Road Tel: 62441600
Telok Kurau Primary School
Singapore 479239

Tampines Family Service Centre
Blk 470 Tampines St 44 Tel: 67872001
#01-194
Singapore 520470

The Salvation Army Bukit Panjang Family Service Centre
Blk 404 Fajar Rd Tel: 67630837
#01-267
Singapore 670404

The SBL MacPherson Vision Student Care Centre
6A Mattar Rd Tel: 67438538
MacPherson Primary School
Singapore 387715

The SBL Vision Student Care Centre
Blk 945 Tampines Ave 4 Tel: 65442264
#01-328
Singapore 520945

The Stepping Stones Student Care
50 East Coast Rd Tel: 63443200
Roxy Square #B1-01
Singapore 428769

The Students' Place
Blk 112 Pasir Ris St 11 Tel: 65819157
#01-657
Singapore 510112

The Students' Place (Ghim Moh)
170 Ghim Moh Rd Tel: 64683725
Ulu Pandan Community Bldg
#06-01
Singapore 279621

The Students' Place (Toa Payoh)
Blk 192 Toa Payoh Lorong 4 Tel: 63550641
#02-672
Singapore 310192

Thong Kheng Before and After School Care Centre
Blk 842C Tampines St 82 Tel: 65873446
#01-46
Singapore 523842

Thye Hua Kwan M. S. Student Care Centre (Yung An Pri)
101 Yuan Ching Rd Tel: 62663677
Yung An Primary School
Singapore 618653

Thye Hua Kwan M. S. Student Care Centre (Merlimau Pri)
105 Yuan Ching Rd Tel: 62616315
Merlimau Primary School
Singapore 618655

TLC Student Care Centre
Blk 621 Ang Mo Kio Ave 9 Tel: 64546686
#01-68
Singapore 560621

Topmarks Student Care Centre
Blk 143 Mei Ling St, #01-153 Tel: 64792500
Singapore 150143

Trans Students' Care
Blk 3 Toh Yi Dr, #01-189 Tel: 64678191
Singapore 591503

Tung Ling Student Care Centre
145 Marine Parade Rd Tel: 63455316
Singapore 449274

Wat Patthar Student Care Centre
Blk 223 Choa Chu Kang Central Tel: 67640986
#01-237
Singapore 680223

Wat Patthar Student Care Centre (Woodlands)
Blk 664 Woodlands Ring Road Tel: 63669561
#01-206
Singapore 730664

Waterfalls Student Care Centre
Blk 51 Lengkok Bahru Tel: 64723901/ 92144112
#01-281
Singapore 150051

Whispering Hearts Student Care Centre
Blk 617 Jurong West St 65 Tel: 67958967
#01-488
Singapore 640617

Yishun Ring BASC
10 Yishun St 11 Tel: 67557990
Ahmad Ibrahim Primary School
Singapore 769063

YMCA Student Care Centre — St Margaret's Primary School
99 Wilkie Rd Tel: 63335084/ 90031365
St Margaret's Primary School
Singapore 228391

YMCA Jurong West Student Care Centre
Blk 666A Jurong West St 65 Tel: 67947759
#01-191
Singapore 641666

YMCA Student Care Centre — Bukit Batok
Blk 212 Bukit Batok St 21 Tel: 6650324
#01-225
Singapore 650212

YMCA Woodlands Circle Student Care Centre
Blk 742 Woodlands Circle Tel: 63655358
#01-443
Singapore 730742

YWCA Student Care Centre
254 Outram Rd Tel: 62231227
Singapore 169051

ENDNOTES

1 See Section 44(1)(i) of the CYPA.

2 See Sections 49(1)(c) and 50(1)(ii) of the CYPA. (As stated in the text above, the Court can also order a child who is the subject of a Care and Protection Order to be committed to a Place of Safety for such period as may be specified by the Court.)

3 See Section 5(3)(b) of the Probation of Offenders Act (Cap. 252).

4 BASC stands for "Before and After School Care"

APPENDIX **B**

Reading List on Issues Related to Juvenile Justice[1]

1. Juvenile Delinquency

(a) Choi, A. & Lo, T.W. (2002). *Fighting Youth Crime: Success and Failure of 2 Little Dragons*. Singapore: Times Academic Press.
(b) Chua, T. S. & Tan, A. (1990). *Lost Innocence*. Singapore: EPB Publishers.
(c) Koh, E. H. C. & Wong, P. Y. (2000). *A Study on the Juvenile Shoplifting Phenomenon*. Singapore: Students Care Service.
(d) Lim, K. T. & Balotta, L. (eds). (2002). *Hedges and Edges: A Compendium for Social Workers. Counsellors and Family Therapists*. Singapore: Care Corner.
(e) Ministry of Community Development and Sports. (1995). *Report of the Inter-Ministry Committee on Dysfunctional Families, Juvenile Delinquency and Drug Abuse*.

2. Parenting

(a) Tan, N. T., Tan, V. & Yeo, A. (1992). *Parenting Today*. Singapore: Ministry of Community Development and Sports.
(b) Supka, N. (1997). *Singapore for Kids: A Parent's Guide*. Singapore: Times Publications.
(c) Tan, E. (1997). *Winning Ways with Teens*. Singapore: Federal Publications.
(d) Ministry of Community Development and Sports. (1995). *Essential Parenting Tips*. Singapore: Ministry of Community Development and Sports.
(e) Cai, Y.-M. & Fung, D. (1998). *Help Your Child to Cope — Understanding Childhood Stress*. Singapore: Times Publications.

3. Child Abuse and Child Protection

(a) Chan, J. S., Chow, Y. & Elliott, J. M. (2000). *Professional and Public Perceptions of Physical Child Abuse and Neglect in Singapore*. Research Monograph No.3. Singapore: Singapore Children's Society.

(b) Cherian, M. & Tan, S. P. (1999). *Resilient Periwinkles: Working with Young Children at Risk*. Singapore: National Council of Social Services.
(c) Elliott, J. M., *et al.* (2002). *Emotional Maltreatment of Children in Singapore: Professional and Public Perceptions*. Research Monograph No.4. Singapore: Singapore Children's Society.
(d) John, M. E. (2000). *Professional and Public Perceptions of Physical Child Abuse and Neglect in Singapore: An Overview*. Research Monograph No.2. Singapore: Singapore Children's Society.
(e) Ministry of Community Development and Sports. (2002). *Singapore's Initial Report to the UN Committee on the Rights of the Child*. Singapore: Ministry of Community Development and Sports.
(f) Tong, C. K., Elliot, J. M. & Tan, M.E.H. (1996). *Public Perceptions of Child Abuse and Neglect in Singapore*. Research Monograph No.1. Singapore: Singapore Children's Society.

4. Marriage and Family Life

(a) Quah, S. (1999). *Study on the Singapore Family*. Singapore: Ministry of Community Development and Sports.
(b) Yeo, A. (1995). *Partners in Life*. Singapore: Blues Bookshop.
(c) Yeo, A. (1994). *Making Your Marriage Glow*. Singapore: Catalyst Books.
(d) Ministry of Community Development and Sports. *Families Today: a Quarterly Newsletter of the Ministry of Community Development and Sports (1994 -)*.
(e) Chew, S. B., Leu, G. J. M. & Tan, K. L. (1998). *Values and Lifestyles of Young Singaporeans*. Singapore: Simon & Schuster.

For more information on juvenile and family justice matters, please visit our websites at:

www.juvenilecourtofsingaopre.gov.sg
www.familycourtofsingapore.gov.sg

ENDNOTE

1 This reading list consists of local literature on issues related to juvenile justice. It is not intended to be exhaustive, but is meant to give the reader an idea of the materials available on the topics covered, and act as a springboard for further reading and research on these matters.

Index